D1521902

Ivan Sergeevich Gagarin

Ivan Sergeevich Gagarin,
courtesy of the Archives de la Bibliothèque Slave, Paris.

Ivan Sergeevich Gagarin

The Search for Orthodox and Catholic Union

JEFFREY BRUCE BESHONER

UNIVERSITY OF NOTRE DAME PRESS
Notre Dame, Indiana

Notre Dame, IN 46556

http://www.undpress.nd.edu

Manufactured in the United States of America

A record of the Library of Congress Cataloging-in-Publication Data is available upon request from the Library of Congress.

∞ *This book is printed on acid-free paper.*

Contents

Preface

Tensions between East and West remain an ever present part of world affairs. Despite the end of the Cold War, the struggles between traditionalism and progressivism, between democracy and authoritarianism, between Catholicism and Orthodoxy, continue to influence Russia's national and ecclesiastical identity. This monograph examines the issues of Russian national identity and the Roman Catholic church's relationship with the churches of the East as presented in the life and work of the nineteenth-century Russian Jesuit Ivan Sergeevich Gagarin.[1] His activity throws much-needed light on the "Russian question" as well as the "Catholic question," each of which remains problematic today.[2]

Beginning with a brief summary of the historical relationship between Russia and Rome, this work will discuss Gagarin's life before his conversion from Orthodoxy to Catholicism, his work in the Russian foreign ministry, his association with major Russian writers such as Aleksandr Sergeevich Pushkin, Fydor Ivanovich Tiutchev, Iuri Fyodorovich Samarin, and Petr Iakovlevich Chaadaev, and the intellectual and religious influences which affected him. The focus will then shift to Gagarin's growing belief in Roman Catholicism as the source of Western progress, his connections with Roman Catholics in Paris, his conversion and decision to enter the Jesuits and the reaction that these actions generated in Russia, and his initial decision to work for the conversion of the Orthodox Slavs.[3] The third and fourth chapters will discuss Gagarin's early attempts to promote union between Russian Orthodoxy and Roman Catholicism. A discussion of Polish and Russian reactions to Gagarin's initiatives follows. Chapter 6 will analyze issues of Russian national identity, church community (*sobornost'*), Catholicism, and Gagarin's relation to the Slavophiles. Chapter 7 will analyze his activities in the Middle East, among the Bulgarians and Byzantine Catholics, and his interests in linguistic nationalism. Chapter 8 will discuss his suggested reforms for the Russian clergy. Chapter 9 will treat Gagarin's final vision of church union and his lasting influence.

This examination of Gagarin's life and work will demonstrate how Russian Orthodoxy's tendency to conflate nationality and religion combined with Catholic religious and cultural arrogance to obstruct Christian unity in the nineteenth century. The receptiveness of such Russian elites as Gagarin to Catholic ideas will also demonstrate the need for greater religious inclusiveness in Russian conceptions of national identity.

Gagarin's unionist activity occurred within a particular religio-historical context that encouraged his conversion from Orthodoxy to Catholicism yet hindered his attempts to promote union between the Orthodox and Catholic churches. In order to understand this, some historical observations need to be made. First, the state of religious animosity between the East and West which had existed since the schism of 1054 severely limited the possibility for peaceful reunion of churches in the nineteenth century. Furthermore, ever since Saints Cyril (Constantine) (827–869) and Methodius (825–884) brought Christianity from Constantinople to the Slavs in 863, Russia's cultural heritage was linked to that of Byzantium. Thus, after Constantinople's break with Rome, Moscow too ended its ecclesiastical relations with the papacy. This rupture between Rome and Russia which arose from theological disagreements intensified as a result of Polish Catholic military aggression and forced conversion of the Russian Orthodox in the seventeenth century.

Attempts to end this animosity and reunify the churches demonstrated both the problems of seeking union through agreement among the religious elites as well as the continuing existence of important theological ties which could encourage union. Conclusions of church councils at Lyons in 1274 and Ferrara-Florence in 1438, though favorably received by the ecclesiastical hierarchies of East and West, were rejected by the Orthodox masses. Roman attempts to establish Byzantine Catholic churches among certain groups of Orthodox, as at the Union of Brest (1596), proved problematic as well. Byzantine Catholic churches were not fully accepted as equals by the Latin West. Orthodox churches perceived them as part of a Catholic attempt to create new schisms within Orthodoxy.

The influence of such Jesuits as Petr Skarga (1536–1612) and Antonio Possevino (1534–1611) among the Russian Orthodox demonstrated the receptiveness of certain Russian Orthodox elites to Jesuit polemics, but the Jesuits' very successes reinforced their image as tools of Roman Catholic aggression against Russia. Jesuit successes also demonstrated the poor status of theological education in the East. As Father George Florovsky has noted, "With sorrow and anguish contemporaries tell of 'the great rudeness and ignorance' of the common people and the local clergy. The [Orthodox] hierarchy was little better equipped to do battle [against Jesuit theologians]. The Orthodox themselves deplored and exposed their low moral standards and worldliness. It was commonly complained that the bishops were more interested in politics, personal prestige, and privilege than in matters of faith or the spiritual needs of the people."[4] In sum, the seventeenth-century Orthodox clergy were theologically unprepared to oppose sophisticated Catholic apologetics. Some Orthodox divines who opposed the Jesuits turned to Protestant theological texts for ammunition against Roman Catholicism. Thus, Orthodox theologians adopted both Protestant and Catholic insights in their struggle to arrive at a defensible Russian Orthodox worldview.

Jesuit schools at Nemetskaia Sloboda in the late seventeenth century and under Catherine II, Paul, and Alexander I in the late eighteenth and early nineteenth centuries also demonstrated the attractiveness of Roman Catholicism to influential Russian families such as the Golitsyns, Tolstois, Gagarins, Rostopchins, Shuvalovs, Kutuzovs, Viazemskiis, Odoevskiis, Kamenskiis, Glinkas, Pushkins, Stroganovs, Novosil'tsovs, and Kochubeis. Eighteenth-century Russian nobles saw in the Jesuits a means of obtaining Western scientific and technical knowledge. Even after the Jesuits' expulsion from Russia in 1820, Russian nobility traveling abroad maintained their ties to the Society of Jesus. Furthermore, the Jesuits were able to obtain broad access to Russian society as a result of the perception that the Jesuits would prove useful in preventing the spread of revolutionary ideas, particularly in the Polish territories. It was for this reason that Catherine II refused to promulgate Pope Clement XIV's brief *Dominus ac Redemptor*, which would have suppressed the Jesuits in Russia in 1773. Perceptions of Jesuit usefulness against revolution continued under Paul and Alexander I.

Opposing the pro-Western, pro-Catholic current in Russian thought, Slavophiles instead gloried in the perceived superiority of Russia over the West. Whereas the West had sacrificed the spiritual for gross materialism, strong communities for unchecked individualism, and an ordered state for chaotic democracy, Russia had avoided these sins. Official nationalists, for their part, put forward Russia's divine obligation to protect Orthodoxy from Roman contamination, especially after Constantinople's perceived apostasy at Ferrara-Florence and its capture by the Turks in 1453. As Nicholas I's doctrine of Official Nationality stated on 2 April 1833:

> A Russian, devoted to his fatherland, will agree as little to the loss of a single dogma of our *Orthodoxy* as to the theft of a single pearl from the tsar's crown. *Autocracy* constitutes the main foundation of the political arrangement of Russia. The Russian giant stands on it as on the cornerstone of his greatness. . . . The saving condition that Russia lives and is protected by the spirit of a strong humane and enlightened autocracy must permeate popular education and must develop with it. Together with these two national principles there is a third, no less powerful: *Nationality.*[5]

Support for this exclusive national conception, which was articulated by Nicholas I but actually predated his reign, sometimes led to the persecution of Russia's religious minorities, including Roman and Byzantine Catholics. Particularly egregious examples of such persecution were the massacres of Byzantine and Roman Catholics by the Orthodox Cossacks in 1623, the closing of 251 Roman Catholic monasteries between 1804 and 1847, and the elimination of the Byzantine Catholic church in Russia in 1839.

Meanwhile, Russian hostility to and persecution of Roman Catholics created obvious problems for the Vatican. The Vatican wanted to support the legitimacy of Russian secular authority in Catholic Poland; the papal bull *Ecclesia Iesu Christo* in 1821 and the encyclical *Cum Primum* in 1832 condemned Polish revolutionary activity. However, by supporting the Russian political authority, the Vatican seriously alienated Polish Catholics. Furthermore, while the Vatican sought religious accommodation with the Russian government and defended the religious freedoms of its Catholic faithful, for example through the concordat of 3 August 1847, Russian Catholics continued to be perceived as disloyal to the Orthodox state.[6]

Gagarin's conversion and church unionist activity arose from a particular Russian historical context. Russian hatred of Roman Catholicism existed against the background of a significant history of Roman Catholic, particularly Jesuit, influence among Russian nobility. Gagarin's desire to immerse himself in the problematic question of Russia's relationship to the West provides an opportunity to explore many of the deepest roots of Russia's conflicted religious and national identity. Unwilling to deny the benefits of the West and equally unwilling to deny the greatness of his homeland, Gagarin found himself caught between antireligious Westernizers such as Aleksandr Ivanovich Herzen and Orthodox Slavophiles such as Alexei Stepanovich Khomiakov.

Gagarin also found himself within the Catholic church as it moved its ecclesiastical relations with the East from unionism to ecumenism.[7] Gagarin sought the union of the Orthodox church with the Roman Catholic church en masse, with the Russian church leading the way; however he also sought to ensure that the Orthodox church in union would not sacrifice its traditions or beliefs. He believed that by recognizing the authority of the papacy the Orthodox would be returning to the pre-schism church, free from secular control. Seeds of the future ecumenical movement may be found in Gagarin's desire for peaceful, prayerful church union rather than a union obtained through force. This pacific approach toward ecumenism would influence later Roman Catholics in their own desires for church union.

In this book, I shall not use the term "Uniate" to describe members of formerly Orthodox churches which united with Roman Catholicism; instead I will employ the term "Byzantine Catholic," because "Uniate" is considered by many Eastern-rite Catholics as derogatory (however, the term "Uniate" does sometimes appear in direct quotations). The terms "Latinize" and "Latinization" refer to the process or desire of some Roman Catholics to make Byzantine Catholics leave their traditional rite and adopt the rite of Rome.

I would especially like to thank Professor G. M. Hamburg for his support during my graduate career and for his assistance in seeing this book to publication. I would also like to thank Drs. Laura Crago, Thomas Kselman, and Andrzej Walicki for their many kindnesses and intellectual advice. I owe a debt of gratitude to all those who assisted my archival research, especially Father François Rouleau, S. J., and Sister Natalie Lajarte of the Bibliothèque Slave in Meudon and the staff of the Russian State Historical Archive. The University of Notre Dame supported this archival work with a Zahm Travel Grant and a fellowship from the Helen Kellogg Institute for International Studies. I am also deeply indebted to Chris Fox and the Institute for Scholarship in the Liberal Arts at the University of Notre Dame for their financial support for the publication of this work. Finally, I wish to thank my family, especially my parents, Jerry and Alice, and my Franciscan brothers for their faith and support. Of course, any errors in this work are my own.

CHAPTER ONE

Moscow, Munich, and Petersburg

> Between the oppressors and the oppressed there existed a small cultivated class, largely French speaking, aware of the enormous gap between the way which life could be lived—or was lived—in the West and the way in which it was lived by the Russian masses. They were, for the most part, men acutely conscious of the difference between justice and injustice, civilization and barbarism, but aware also that the conditions were too difficult to alter, that they had too great a stake in the regime themselves, and that reform might bring the whole structure toppling down. Many among them were reduced either to an easy-going quasi-Voltarian cynicism, at once subscribing to liberal principles and whipping their serf; or to noble, eloquent and futile despair.[1]

Ivan Sergeevich Gagarin was born in Moscow on 20 July 1814. Descendants of Rurik and the Great Prince Vladimir Sviatoslavich, the Christianizer of Russia, via the princes of Starodub, the Gagarins belonged to one of Russia's most ancient and politically powerful families.[2] In 1612, Roman Ivanovich Gagarin served as an army commander in the battle to free Muscovy from the Poles. In 1615, Afanassii Fedorovich Gagarin helped defend Pskov against the army of Swedish king Gustavus-Adolphus. Under Peter the Great, Prince Matvei Gagarin served as governor of Moscow and later of Siberia. Under Alexander I, Prince Gavril Gagarin was minister of commerce. Prince Grigorii Ivanovich Gagarin (1782–1837) served as an ambassador to Rome and Munich. The tsars granted many of the Gagarin princes fiefdoms, Orders, and other signs of autocratic favor for their state service. The Gagarin family bloodline was linked to that of the Pushkins, Volkonskiis, Saltykovs, Samarins, and Dolgorukovs.[3]

Ivan Gagarin's father, Sergei Ivanovich Gagarin (23 June 1777–16 December 1862), was grand master of the court, a member of the council of the empire, and a knight of St. Aleksandr Nevski and St. Vladimir, first class. Ivan's mother, Vavara Mikhailovna (neé Pushkina) (1776–21 August 1854), was described as "a woman of great sense, of admirable devotion and perfectly good faith in the practice of the Orthodox religion."[4]

Gagarin's father possessed 30,000 *desiatina* of land and 5,000 serfs. In addition to a house in Moscow on Povarskaia street[5] and the estate of Dankovo near Moscow, Sergei Gagarin also owned land in Riazan' province, Vladimir province, and Simbirsk province. In the village of Spasskii in Riazan', Sergei established a sugar beet factory. The Gagarins also owned a profitable paper factory. Sergei Gagarin was famous for the innovative agricultural techniques on his property, where he introduced a policy of crop rotation, fine-fleeced sheep breeding, and horticulture.[6] Gagarin's father became vice-president of the Moscow Society of Agricultural Management in 1823. In 1844, he became president of the society. In 1862, he was named honorary president.[7]

We have little information on Gagarin's childhood and early life. According to V.A. Bil'basov, "As a child, his [Gagarin's] mother would force him 'to play in the Tuileries Garden with the French children, noisily amusing themselves'; as a young man, he avoided noisy diversions; did not play cards, or dance."[8] His parents placed him under the strictest supervision. He was required to study for ten hours each day and forbidden to read newspapers.[9]

Around 1820, the Gagarins went on a three-year journey to Germany, France, and Italy. The Dutch noblewoman Cornélie de Wassenaer, visiting the court of Dowager Empress Maria Fedorovna in 1824–1825 related the curious incident of a song recital given by some ladies of the court at which "the two little children of Princess Gagarin [he and his sister Mariia Sergeevna] appeared dressed as a gentleman and lady of the court of Louis XIV. They made us laugh a good deal."[10]

Gagarin received a "solid and pious 'Orthodox' education," and in the Gagarin house "a patriotic and patriarchal spirit reigned. . . . "[11] Clair argued that Ivan saw his mother as a deeply religious woman. She would only eat bread and water during Holy Week and abstained from food on all days she took communion. Icons occupied a particular place of honor in the Gagarin household.[12] An undated letter to Ivan Gagarin from his mother indicates to some degree the type of education he received from his family:

> Give some direction to your ideas: do not follow some vague dream. Dreaming diminishes the intelligence, erodes your abilities,

> makes them comfortable with small improvements. The more one feels attracted to these dreams, the more one should be devoted to real studies.
>
> One must have a will. It is important to discipline oneself, to establish goals, to accomplish them, to avoid complacency; the more one complains, the more one must assume the initiative, to cast off apathy.
>
> One must bend the heart to the will, to live, to need; suffering is often the price of becoming a remarkable man.
>
> The greatest misfortune is whirling from one thought to another, one preoccupation to another, incessantly, without having the time to breath. Such capriciousness is fatal to rest; the ideas and the sensations clash, torment you. One always profits by establishing seriousness in life. . . .
>
> Nourish useful work, study law and philosophy in its relation to society. Mark your progress here, if not by some results, at least by some effort. It is not a sphere so limited that one cannot do a little good.[13]

Gagarin's archives listed a variety of different texts in the Gagarin family library, including books on the travels of Columbus, Cortez, and Pizarro; philosophical works by Cicero and Socrates; Orthodox religious texts as well as Catholic writings such as the works of Dante, Joseph de Maistre, St. Augustine, St. Ambrose, St. Bernard, St. Jerome, and St. Francis de Sales, as well as documents of the Council of Trent and several Jesuit texts, including a Jesuit catechism of 1820. The library also contained the writings of Vico, Johann Wolfgang von Goethe, Heine, Shakespeare, Voltaire, Balzac, Montesquieu, and Dumas.[14] Books were available in Russian, French, and German.

Gagarin, like most nobility, was educated in his youth by a French tutor. He preferred to write in French rather than Russian. According to Father Clair, he only used Russian to express "that which could only be conveyed in the vulgar."[15] Christoff refers to the handicap that affected "gentry children brought up by foreign speaking nurses, governesses and tutors. . . . Speaking French and Latin at ten was admirable, but speaking and writing poor Russian was a heavy sacrifice."[16] The significant presence of Western texts and the French tutor indicate that from an early age Gagarin received a favorable presentation of the West and of Western intellectual scholarship. Furthermore, the family texts centered on issues of philosophy, history, and theology, those areas of importance to Gagarin in his desire to examine Russia's relationship with the West. It is possible that the significant presence of books related to travels outside of Russia inspired Gagarin's later interest in foreign service.

Gagarin attended Moscow University, which at that time played an important role in the development of Russia's intellectual elite. As Nol'de argued, "Russia's future cultural and political history" passed through its halls.[17] Some influential teachers were J. G. Buhle, who taught courses on Kant, Fichte, and Friedrich Wilhelm Joseph von Schelling; I. I. Davydov (1794–1863), who served as the chair of philosophy from 1822 to 1826 and taught logic, Latin, and the history of philosophy; M. G. Pavlov (1793–1840), who also expounded the ideas of Schelling; Nikolai Ivanovich Nadezhdin, who served as a professor of Russian literature from 1831 to 1836; and M. A. Maksimovich, who served as a professor of natural science. Their views on Russia's future would be influential on Gagarin. Nadezhdin argued that "Russia had no past . . . but only the present," which Peter had established and which was still being developed.[18] M. A. Maksimovich asserted that Russia needed to produce "patriotic youth who have received a Russian education." He praised Peter the Great but believed that the time had come for Russia to assert her independence, for "not everything done in Europe is also useful for Russia." He encouraged love of the fatherland and believed that "true enlightenment . . . requires also a religious-moral formation of the heart and will."[19] In addition to Gagarin, Samarin, Herzen, Vissarion Grigor'evich Belinskii, Ivan Aleksandrovich Goncharov, Mikhail Iurevich Lermontov, and Ivan Sergeevich Turgenev also attended Moscow University. Herzen wrote, "In its halls they [the students] became purified of all prejudices acquired in the domestic environment, reached common ground, fraternized, and once again flowed in all directions, and to all strata of society in Russia."[20] Gagarin's university education would prove important by providing his first exposure to the ideas of Friedrich Schelling, making him aware of his need as a patriotic son of Russia to seek enlightenment and moral formation, and linking him to other influential Russian thinkers concerned with the problem of Russia's relationship to the West.

From 1831 to 1832, Gagarin served as a member of the Moscow department of the Ministry of Foreign Affairs under the direction of Malinovskii. In 1832, Gagarin passed the university exams and attained the 14th class on the Table of Ranks.[21] On 4 May 1833, Gagarin was sent to serve in the Russian mission in Munich, at that time headed by his uncle Grigorii Gagarin.[22] Gagarin's memoirs, "Notes about My Life," give us some idea as to his character at this time. He wrote:

> . . . in the spring of 1833, when I was nineteen years old and a few months, I, for the first time, was separated from my family in order to enter into society. . . . I knew nothing of the real word, rather I lived in my own invented world, nourishing vague purposes and unclear goals. I saw before me a boundless ocean. Fearing to remain longer on the shore, I dreamed about the delights of the stormy seas. This mysterious future provided such fascination; this ideal world, engendered by my imagination, was opened to me through poetry, love, freedom—those divine delusions, which have such power over young souls.
>
> These were the streams of a life of poetry, in which I wanted to bathe—love, overflowing [my] heart with boundless delight, which not one human tongue could express; freedom, similar to nothing which existed in reality; happiness, the need which God invested in every one of us and in which everything was enjoyable, everything pleasing of this world satisfied.[23]

Gagarin was also disgusted by "everything that was connected to oppression and [tsarist] despotism, every time I witnessed it or heard about something like it, my heart overflowed with anger and indignation." For him, freedom from despotism meant the destruction of all external obstacles to happiness. At this stage of his life, he was a utopian. He wrote, "I dreamed about a republic no less fantastic than the republic of Plato, and I cherished in my burning heart hatred toward everything that did not resemble that image." He further argued that these ideas were not viewed favorably by his family.[24]

Ivan arrived in Munich in June 1833, where he found that he was forced to modify his image of life. He wrote, "I could be certain that here my political whims would meet still less understanding" and that, "gradually reality . . . began to demolish the fantastic structure erected by my imagination."[25]

At the time of Gagarin's sojourn in Bavaria, the country had become a repository of ideas that would play an important role in the development of Russian Western and Slavophile ideology. Louis I of Wittelsbach (1786–1868) was himself a poet and wanted to make Munich the artistic center of Germany. As Gagarin asserted in a letter to A. N. Bakhmetev: "King Louis made his capital, if not a new Athens, at least a remarkable city from the point of view of the arts. The university of Munich contained . . . men of great merit among the professors"[26] Louis transferred the University of Landshut to Munich in 1826; he gathered philosophers such as Görres and Friedrich Schelling (1775–1854); painters such as Cornelius, Schwind, Kaulbach; architects such as Klenze and Gärtner.

As Thomas O'Meara, O.P., remarked, Munich was a "special center because of the long-term union of Romanticism and Catholic life."[27] Ludwig wanted to make Munich "a new Florence": classical in art, Catholic in faith and life.[28] Influenced by the presence of Friedrich Schlegel, Adam Müller, and others hostile to rationalistic secularism, the ideas of Romanticism and Catholicism merged into an intellectual movement emphasizing both political conservatism and favorable views of medieval Catholicism.

One of the most important spokesmen of German Romantic thought was Friedrich Schelling. Schelling's ideas on the progressive nature of history and theology found a willing reception among Russian intellectuals.[29] He asserted that "Russia has a great mission" and that "one cannot determine to what it [Russia] is destined or its future but it is destined for something important."[30]

As early as September 1833 Gagarin attended meetings in Schelling's home where he became familiar with Schelling's views on Russia and her special mission as well as with the ideas of other French and German thinkers such as the French liberal jurist Jean Lerminier (1803–1859). Gagarin would later read Lerminier's *De l'influence de la philosophie du XVIIIe siècle sur la législation et la sociabilité du XIXe, Introduction générale à l'histoire du droit,* and *Philosophie du droit.*[31]

In addition, Gagarin was attracted to the eclectic philosophy of Victor Cousin (1792–1867) and Theodore Simon Jouffroy (1796–1842), as well as to the ideas of Friedrich Ancillon (1766–1837); he read, in the original, Titus Livy, Polybius, Dionysius (Aelius) of Halicarnassus. He also read Fitzer's *Briefwechsel zweier Deutschen,* books on Locke and the Scottish school, writings of Jean Baptist Say, the *Cours du droit romain* of Ferdinand Mackeldey, and *L'histoire du droit romain* of Gustave Hugo.[32] Tempest argued that "Gagarin tried to find in books some philosophical system, which explained to him the entire world and helped to create harmonic development and a complete personality (un homme complet); he dreamed about some high ideal, about some 'thought—strong and fruitful,' which filled his life with contemplation."[33]

Gagarin's diary noted that it was through a reading of Locke that he came to the eclectics, particularly the ideas of Cousin and Jouffroy.[34] Gagarin wrote, "In my understanding of philosophy, I want to begin with their doctrines."[35] He also wrote, "Jouffroy and Cousin advocated, in my opinion, philosophical reason."[36] The ideas of Cousin and Jouffroy would have appealed to Gagarin for several reasons, not the least of which was the connection of Cousin's ideas to those of Schelling. Jouffroy's belief that each man was created with a purpose, a destiny, would have appealed to Gagarin's desire to find a "direction to his ideas" as his mother had encouraged.

Gagarin also embarked on a study of law and jurisprudence. In addition to the texts of Mackeldey and Hugo, he studied Justinian and Mikhail Speranskii's recently published code of laws of the Russian empire, which, he asserted, would "establish an era of jurisprudence and serious studies, a thing which did not earlier exist. This publication is a good work, it is an eternal monument, a work comparable to Justinian."[37] After reading Ancillon's *Die Vermittelung der Extremen,* Gagarin came to support the primacy of law. He wrote, "Power, wielded by one man, if this man utilizes it only to enforce the laws, is a thousand times more legitimate than a democracy, if democratic government places itself above the laws. . . . In their origin, by their essence, laws have a divine origin."[38]

Gagarin's increasing support of law led him to renounce revolution as a means of governmental change. He criticized the French republicans for relying on force. He complained that "they were entirely disposed to sacrifice [individual] rights to assure the triumph of their party." He "renounced all the revolutionary schools putting force above law."[39]

Gagarin became enamored of Johann Wolfgang von Goethe.[40] Speaking of Goethe, he wrote, "I begin to know you, allow me to be your student, open in me everything! You have already made on me a deep impression and I answer your persistent call for exercise in some type of activity: only here is it possible to find the seed of the future and the seed of life."[41] In his journal, he strove to imitate the style of Goethe's *Aus Einer Reise am Rhein.*[42]

For Gagarin, undertaking an active life was very important. As early as 18 June 1834, he wrote, "The man who limits himself to study is like Don Quixote combating windmills; he hacks and chops with the sword and his blows only cut air."[43] Less than a month later, he wrote, "Where am I? What am I? What have I completed?" and "A need for activity devours me as a fever, as a poison."[44] For Gagarin, an active life meant choosing some goal, some objective for himself. Up to this point, he had become acquainted with a wide variety of different intellectual perspectives but had yet to formulate his own path. It was this need which inspired him.

As for Gagarin's religious ideas, despite his Orthodox heritage and Schelling's links to Catholicism, he began with vague theistic views and asserted that, under the influence of German ideas, he upheld the idea of an impersonal God.[45] In his diary he wrote, "In the century in which I have been born, the majority of men are fortunately not committed to the service of God, nor does the majority regard moral obligation as divinely sanctioned. In vain would I search for my duties in religion, we have been delivered from it and its voice is foreign to us. . . . There is no hope of finding a guide to life in religion, let us try to find it in philosophy. We must subordinate our desires and our fantasies to the will and our will to reason."[46] Gagarin looked for guidance from the "Muses of love, poetry, art, and philosophy."[47]

In 1834, at the age of twenty, Gagarin began to keep a journal. He soon began to think about his obligation to Russia and about Russia's place in Europe:

> Why, unreceptive to that which surrounds me, am I still not passionately committed to some noble end, to some good and useful idea, to make myself give my life every day, every instant, every faculty of my being? Oh! my fatherland, no, my faith in you is not extinguished; it begins anew to warm and enlighten my heart. *It is to you, my country, that I dedicate my life and my thought. My studies, my works, my efforts, my life, all are consecrated to you.*[48]

This decision demonstrated Gagarin's passionate character. He did not merely want to be of service to Russia, he wanted to devote his whole life to his country. However, before he could begin to work for Russia, he had to further clarify his goal:

> I began to compare Russia to Europe. I saw in Europe different nations, very distinct one from another, having searched their particular character; however, there was among them all some thing in common and something I did not find in Russia, or at least, Russia compared to other countries of Europe had a specific character which separated it from these countries by a line of demarcation incomparably more profound than that which one could observe between Germany and Italy, England and France, Spain and Sweden. From whence came this difference? What was common among the different European nations and yet remained foreign to Russia? That was the problem which confronted me in Munich . . . and which ended with my entrance into the Catholic church.[49]

From the very beginning, Gagarin focused on the religious question and the differences between Orthodox Russia and Western Christendom. Later, under Chaadaev's influence, he decided that Protestantism was of little importance in distinguishing Russia from Western Europe. Russia was as foreign to Europe in the nineteenth century as it had been in the fourteenth century. He began to suspect that Russian peculiarity was mainly rooted in Orthodoxy, or rather in the virtual absence of Catholicism in Russia.

It is important to remember, however, that in the early 1830s Gagarin was far from being a Catholic sympathizer. He was rather a Russian nationalist working for the advancement of his country. He hoped to facilitate progress in Russia by studying what distinguished Russia from the rest of Europe.

Despite its difference with Western Europe, Gagarin still considered Russia a European country. He called it "The youngest of the sisters of the European family."[50] For Gagarin, Russia had an important mission: to strengthen its links to Western Europe, to come into its intellectual inheritance, and to spread the benefits of Western civilization to its neighbors to the south and east. Russia was to become an "apostle of European civilization."[51]

At this stage Gagarin's weltanschauung was far from extraordinary. As Isaiah Berlin has noted, in both Russia and Germany there was "a romantic conviction that every man had a unique mission to fulfil if only he could know what it was; and that this created a general enthusiasm for social and metaphysical ideas."[52]

Gagarin's journal further indicates that during this time he became acquainted with many influential figures such as the exiled French king, Charles X, and members of his family.[53] Interestingly, Gagarin at this time did not view his future religious order favorably. He wrote that the Comte de Chambord was, "in the hands of a gaggle of frock-coated Jesuits who, full of reverence for this descendant of St. Louis and Louis XIV, are doing everything possible to keep him away from his mother and leave him to his own devices."[54]

His journal also describes a man struggling between hedonism and asceticism. He drew up a long list of strict rules which he often failed to obey. He was concerned over "temptations of the flesh" and wrote in his journal:

> No one must ever read this page! I pace my room restlessly in expectation of the fateful hour; I am approaching an important

> moment in my life. In a few hours I shall purchase experience with weakness. I do not know what to do: will I continue to stand on this slippery threshold or will I step over it—my heart shrinks, my blood boils, my feet grow cold; fear, hope, curiosity, desire, revulsion.[55]

In December 1834, he went on a gambling spree (apparently the only such time in his life). He lost all his winnings and criticized those who praised games of chance.[56]

While serving at the Russian embassy in Munich, Gagarin became acquainted with another diplomat, the great poet Fyodor Ivanovich Tiutchev (1803–1873). Correspondence suggests that Gagarin and Tiutchev developed a strong friendship. Tiutchev wrote:

> Believe, kind Gagarin, few can be so honest speaking with their beloved. . . . I feel that if I gave freedom to myself, that I would write you a longer letter only to demonstrate the inadequacy, the uselessness, the absurdity of letters. . . . My God, what is the point of writing? Look, here beside me is an empty chair, here is a cigar, here is tea. Come, sit down, let us begin to talk things over: yes, let us begin to discuss, as before, and as I will discuss no longer.[57]

It is clear that Gagarin felt the same toward Tiutchev:

> That time, my dear friend, when I discussed with you your notebook [of Tiutchev's poetry] . . . remains a time of blessedness. Besides the fascination of observing the poetic consciousness spread through all humanity; I, with pleasure, perceive on every page dear things which remind me of you, your spirit, things which we so often and so intensely discussed. . . . To me, nothing can be as pleasing as to give intellectual pleasure to people with talent and good taste.[58]

Gagarin and Tiutchev engaged in discussions on a variety of topics. They discussed the meaning of Pushkin for Russian poetry and the essence of the Don Juan type.[59] Tiutchev contended that Europe had been "flooded with lyrics" because language had become more supple and techniques of versification were more powerful. He thought intelligent men from all walks of life could demonstrate lyrical power if only they would unleash their tongues.[60] Gagarin and Tiutchev also discussed the nature of Russia and the place of Catholicism.[61]

Gagarin was one of the few individuals who truly valued Tiutchev's poetics from the beginning. It was through Gagarin's efforts that Tiutchev's poetry came to the attention of the general Russian public. As Ivan Sergeevich Aksakov (1823–1886) wrote, "Russian literature owes gratitude to I. S. Gagarin: he not only was the first to know the value of the poetical gift of Tiutchev, but he also turned it into the authentic property of Russia. Without his efforts, without his mediation, scarcely would these pearls of Russian poetry have seen the light in the Russian press."[62]

On 1 September 1835, Gagarin was recalled to Russia and made a state secretary with seniority. A dispatch from the Ministry of Internal Affairs on 25/13 November 1835 ordered him to Petersburg.[63] Gagarin brought with him Tiutchev's poetry and presented it to Vasillii Andreevich Zhukovskii (1783–1852), Petr Andreevich Viazemskii (1792–1878), and Aleksandr Sergeevich Pushkin (1799–1837).[64] All were impressed with Tiutchev's poems. Pushkin spoke of them with "a just feeling of appreciation."[65] He published twenty-four of Tiutchev's poems in the third and fourth volumes of his journal *Sovremennik* in 1836 under the title "Poetry Sent from Germany." Much later, Gagarin provided Ivan Aksakov with his papers concerning Tiutchev; these contained a collection of forty years of manuscript scraps, with poetry, some biographical information, and several letters exchanged between Gagarin and Tiutchev.[66]

Gagarin's friendship with Tiutchev ended after 1838, probably because of changes in Tiutchev's views on the Eastern question.[67] Tiutchev grew to support much of what Gagarin opposed in terms of Russia's mission and its relation to the West. For example, Tiutchev's article "The Papacy and the Roman Question from the Perspective of Saint Petersburg" accused Rome of creating a worldly kingdom and criticized the Jesuits for their aggressive conversion tactics. He also asserted that Protestantism and revolutionary thought were the direct result of Rome's assumption of secular functions into the church.[68]

In St. Petersburg, Gagarin played an active role in governmental and intellectual life. On 19 January 1835, he was promoted to the court-rank status of Kamer Iunker. Gagarin visited fashionable salons such as the one organized by Baroness Nesselrode, the wife of the vice-chancellor of the Russian empire.[69] In a letter to Tiutchev, Gagarin boasted: "I am almost constantly seen with those it is possible to call the literary world: with Viazemskii, Zhukovskii, Pushkin."[70] Along with his cousin, Grigorii Gagarin, Ivan helped Vladimir Aleksandrovich Sollogub on his work *Tarantas*.[71]

I emphasize the quality of the relationship between Gagarin and Pushkin to demonstrate the importance the tragic events of 1836 which led to the death of Pushkin and suspicion of Gagarin's possible involvement in that matter. On 4 November 1836, Pushkin received an anonymous letter calling him "coadjutor of the Grand Master of the Order of Cuckolds." Copies of the letter were sent to Viazemskii, Nikolai Mikhailovich Karamzin, Vilgorskii, V. A. Sollogub, the Rosset brothers, and E. M. Khitrovo. Angered by this letter, which accused his wife of unfaithfulness, Pushkin searched for the anonymous author. Both Pushkin and Viazemskii thought the letter had been written by a foreigner. Pushkin wrote: "In the morning of 4 November, I received three copies of an anonymous letter, insulting to my honor and the honor of my wife. In the type of paper, in the style of the letter, thus as it is constructed, I from the first minute understood that it came from a foreigner, from a man of high society, from a diplomat."[72] Pushkin later blamed Baron Louis von Heekeren and George Charles d'Anthes-Heekeren for sending the letters. In order to restore his honor, Pushkin challenged d'Anthes to the duel which would cost him his life on 27 January 1837.

After Pushkin's death, his friends and associates continued to look for the source of the anonymous letters. Suspicion also fell on Petr Vladimirovich Dolgorukov (1816–1868), Lev Sollogub, S. S. Uvarov, and Gagarin.[73] Of these, Dolgorukov and Gagarin were most often mentioned.[74] Pushkin's daughter, Countess N. A. Merenberg, wrote, "My mother [Natalie] always named as the author of the letter Petr Vladimirovich Dolgorukov, whom they called *le banacal* [bow-legged]—known for his extremely nasty reputation.[75] Another individual, to whom my mother pointed, as an author of the anonymous letter, was Prince Ivan Sergeevich Gagarin; in the opinion of my mother, he entered the Jesuit order to repent his sin against my father."[76] Aleksandr Ivanovich Turgenev (1784–1845) wrote in his diary on 30 January/11 February 1837: "Argument about Heekeren and Pushkin. Suspicion again on K[niaz'] I[van] G[agarin]."[77] According to the literary scholar Iashchin, at the Karamzins' the involvement of Gagarin was discussed.[78]

Since at this time Gagarin lived at Dolgorukov's, it was easy for suspicion to fall on them both. Gagarin had a long relationship with Dolgorukov. They had been acquainted since childhood. Dolgorukov's aunt and mother had close relations with Gagarin's mother.[79]

For his part, Gagarin denied any complicity in Pushkin's death. He claimed to have learned of the letters from K. O. Rosset:

> Once we [Dolgorukov and Gagarin] were eating lunch together at home as R[osset] arrived; before others he did not say anything, but as we got up from the table and went to another room, he took from his pocket the anonymous letter to Pushkin, which had been sent to him in an envelope bearing his name. The affair to him seemed suspicious, he decided to break the seal of the letter and found the famous libel. Then he began to converse with us; we discussed who could have written the libel, with what purpose, what could result from it. The details of the conversation I cannot remember now; only I know that our suspicions did not rest on anyone and we remained in ignorance. That evening I had in my hands this letter and examined it. I have never seen another copy.[80]

After Gagarin left for Paris, some friends of Pushkin continued to suspect him of writing the anonymous letter. N. M. Smirnov noted in her diary in 1842 that both Dolgorukov and Gagarin "were friendly with Heekeren and followed his example, spreading gossip." Also, there were certain details in the address on the envelope containing the anonymous letter that Gagarin and Dolgorukov would have known, but not Heekeren. Furthermore, Gagarin "appeared crushed by a secret distress after Pushkin's death."[81] Konstantin Karlovich Danzas wrote in 1863 that "The cause of the suspicion of prince Gagarin in the authorship of the anonymous letters was that they were written on a paper of a similar type to the paper of prince Gagarin." Danzas argued that even if Gagarin did not write the anonymous letters, since they were written on his paper, "the disgrace of participating in this dirty affair, participating, if not actively, then passively, confirmed in knowledge and admission—remains nevertheless on him."[82]

However, not all suspected Gagarin. S. A. Sobolevskii in a letter to S. M. Vorontsov on 7 February 1862 wrote that he considered Gagarin innocent and instead suspected Dolgorukov: "From my point of view, I love and esteem G[agarin] too much to have the slightest suspicion in this regard."[83] S. Abramovich has asserted that other important figures, such as A. I. Turgenev and Viazemskii, came to believe Gagarin innocent.[84] Even Pushkin's son considered Gagarin innocent in the affair.[85]

The blame of Dolgorukov and Gagarin first appeared in print in 1863 in a brochure of A. N. Ammosov, *The Last Days and the Death of A. S. Pushkin according to Konstantine Karlovich Danzas.* This accusation was republished in many Russian journals and newspapers and widely distributed.[86]

Shur called the brochure a "revelation for reading Russia."[87] Dolgorukov described the brochure as an attack by the Russian government and asked Gagarin to respond. Dolgorukov wrote that the brochure portrayed him and Gagarin as "the cause of the death of Pushkin!"[88] Dolgorukov published his response, denying his and Gagarin's involvement, in the journals *Sovremennik, Listok,* and *Kolokol.* In his response to Ammosov's claims, Dolgorukov asserted that both he and Gagarin were on friendly relations with those closest to Pushkin and were innocent of responsibility for the anonymous letter.[89] Gagarin did not respond because he was in the Middle East at the time and was unaware of the accusation.

In 1865, the journal *Russkii arkhiv* carried an article, "From the Reminiscences of Count V. A. Sollogub," in which Sollogub claimed that he met d'Anthes in Paris and received documents from him relating to the death of Pushkin. Sollogub claimed to have discovered the person or persons behind the anonymous letter. In the newspaper *Birzhevye vedomosti,* on 13 May 1865, Sollogub accused Gagarin and Dolgorukov of complicity in Pushkin's death. This accusation was forwarded by Prince Nikolai Ivanovich Trubetskoi to Gagarin's fellow Jesuit Ivan Matveevich Martynov. Martynov conveyed information about the article and a separate letter from Trubetskoi to Gagarin.[90]

Trubetskoi's letter informed Gagarin of the texts of Ammosov and Sollogub. He suggested that Gagarin issue a response which he would publish.[91] Gagarin responded by sending a letter to Trubetskoi which was published in *Russkii Arkhiv* in 1865 under the title "The Vindication of the Jesuit Ivan Gagarin Concerning the Death of Pushkin." In this text, Gagarin wrote "I solemnly assert and declare that I did not write these letters, that in this affair I had no part; who wrote the letters, I have never known."[92] Gagarin did acknowledge that the paper on which the anonymous letter was written was similar to that which he used, "but this means absolutely nothing: this paper carried no special sign, no coat of arms, no identifying initial. They made this paper especially for me: I bought it, as much as I can remember, in a British store, but probably half of Petersburg has purchased this paper."[93] He also asserted that his decision to enter the Jesuits in no way implied guilt, as "Pushkin died in February 1837, if I am not mistaken; I entered the Jesuit order in August 1843, six years later. During these six years no one noticed in me any despair, any sadness; until 1843, no one accused me of writing these letters; but as soon as I became a Jesuit, they began to discuss it."[94] Gagarin did not blame Dolgorukov in the letter, though he did indicate to Trubetskoi that Dolgorukov could have written the letter on his (Gagarin's) paper since the two of them lived together.[95]

Gagarin argued that he had very good relations with Pushkin: "I highly valued his genial talent and never had any cause for hostility."[96] In a letter to Tiutchev, he said, "We have already spoken of the place that Pushkin occupies in the poetic world."[97] In October 1836, Gagarin had sent a copy of the still unpublished "First Philosophical Letter" of Petr Chaadaev to both Pushkin and Viazemskii.[98]

In 1875, Nikolai Semenovich Leskov (1831–1895) visited Gagarin, and the issue of Pushkin's death arose during a discussion about Russian high society. Leskov wrote that Gagarin grew agitated and claimed to have been slandered by the accusations of his involvement in the anonymous letter. Gagarin further asserted that the slander was a result of the actions of Nicholas I and that evidence of his innocence was in Paris.[99] Leskov believed in Gagarin's innocence.[100]

Even after the fall of the Russian Empire, interest in Gagarin's role in the writing of the anonymous letter continued. In 1936, P. E. Shchegolev's *The Duel and Death of Pushkin* published conclusions based on an analysis of various copies of the anonymous letter to Pushkin; Shchegolev also analyzed the handwriting of Gagarin, Heekeren, and Dolgorukov. An examination of the handwriting by Alexei Andreevich Sal'kov concluded that the anonymous letter was written by Dolgorukov, not Gagarin.[101]

In 1962, L. Vyshnevskii attacked the conclusions of Shchegolev and Sal'kov in his article, "Petr Dolgorukov and His Letter to Pushkin." Vyshnevskii's article was to be part of a larger work entitled *The Union of Florence and the Historical Fate of Russia* which discussed "the anti-Russian plans of the Vatican and its faithful servants, the Jesuits." Vyshnevskii argued that the Jesuits wanted to force the Russian tsar to submit to their influence and were closely linked to the government of Nicholas I. Furthermore, Vyshnevskii argued that the supporters of Gagarin and the Nikolaevan government wanted to use the death of Pushkin to discredit Dolgorukov for his political acts, rather than to place proper blame on Gagarin for the anonymous letter. Vyshnevskii asserted that Sal'kov had followed the line of the "gendarmes" of Nicholas I and that he had "unscientifically" gathered material from Nicholas I's Third Section.[102] Vyshnevskii's article contained very little substance. The author was governed more by a desire to rehabilitate Dolgorukov and incriminate the Jesuits than to provide a factually based historical conclusion. At the time of Pushkin's death, Gagarin had no contact with any Jesuits.

In 1963, Mikhail Iashchin published the article "Chronicle of the Days before the Duel," followed by "A Portrait of a Spiritual Individual," in 1966. In these articles, Iashchin argued that Gagarin did not write the anonymous letter to Pushkin but did write the address on the envelope which contained the letter. Iashchin wrote, "The letter truly was not written by him, but he knew about it and with 'cadet-style irresponsibility' helped Dolgorukov address the letter. This 'joke' came to a tragic conclusion. For his entire life he [Gagarin] was burdened with the role which Dolgorukov forced him to play."[103]

Iashchin argued that the inscription "To Aleksandr Sergeevich Pushkin" on the envelope resembled Gagarin's handwriting. Iashchin asserted that Sal'kov had not examined the envelope, and so did not come to the correct conclusion regarding Gagarin's involvement in the Pushkin tragedy. In his second article, Iashchin also argued that Gagarin wrote the cursive signature at the bottom of the anonymous letter.[104] Iashchin further referred to the conclusions of V. V. Tomilin which supported his views about Gagarin's involvement on the basis of handwriting analysis.[105]

In 1967, Ia. L. Levkovich, in his *New Material for a Biography of Pushkin Published Between 1963-1966,* criticized the conclusions of both Vyshnevskii and Iashchin. Levkovich argued that Vyshnevskii did not reveal the basis for his conclusion regarding Gagarin's involvement.[106] As for Iashchin, Levkovich argued that "he constructs a system of evidence in order to lead the reader to a conclusion, reached *a priori.* Having previously decided that Gagarin had written on the letter, he considers much evidence about the relationship of Gagarin and Pushkin arising from the guilt of Gagarin." While not denying Gagarin's possible role, Levkovich claimed it remained a hypothesis requiring further study.[107] Furthermore, Levkovich argued that the conclusions of Tomilin, according to the objections of another handwriting expert, M. G. Liubarskii, could not be trusted. "The handwriting on the defective letter has gaps and does not give even the basis for reaching any conclusion about Gagarin's involvement."[108]

In 1969, A. S. Buturlin issued another article on the anonymous letter. He, too, criticized Iashchin's presentation: "Of course, in the article of M. Iashchin one will not find an unbiased assessment of Gagarin's personality or even an attempt to make such an assessment. On the contrary, all the acts, letters, opinions about him of contemporaries receive under the pen of Iashchin the most perverse interpretation."[109] Buturlin also criticized the conclusions of Tomilin.[110]

L. Vyshnevskii published a second attack on Gagarin in 1973. He asserted that the Jesuits wanted "a Russia in which the Roman pope and Jesuits would rule, joined by the Russian tsar and the gendarmes in suppressing the Revolution." Furthermore, he claimed, "The blood of Pushkin—'a poet of true blood'—obviously is on the black Jesuit cloak of Gagarin."[111] Again, Vyshnevskii's conclusions lacked any factual basis.

In 1976, S.A. Tsipeniuk published the conclusions of B.V. Tomashevskii. On the basis of the handwriting on the letter, Tomashevskii concluded that the two letters and the address on the letter were written by neither Gagarin nor Dolgorukov but by someone else.[112] This conclusion would later be supported by N. Eidel'man in 1987 and S. L. Abramovich in 1984 and 1989. As Abramovich wrote, "At the present time, we have insufficient information for answering the question about who wrote the letters. It is possible that it was not 'a man from society', but someone whose services were paid."[113] While the most recent evidence absolves Gagarin of responsibility in the writing of the anonymous letter, this entire incident is important as it demonstrates the strong reactions that Gagarin generated among both friends and enemies as well as the mixed reception that he received in Soviet historiography. Furthermore, since Pushkin was Russia's "National Poet," Gagarin's possible involvement could easily be used by his nationalist opponents to accuse him of hating Russia and seeking to subjugate Russia to Jesuitism and pernicious Westernism.

After the sordid events surrounding Pushkin's death, Gagarin remained deeply involved in governmental service and Russian intellectual life. He wrote to Viazemskii that:

> I am now located in the country, in a big room, where I am surrounded by the *Sbornik, Paterik* and other venerable works and from where I take pleasure to my heart's content in the fall landscape. Around me are three points, which attract me in turn. Uzkoe, where lady S. Apraksina resides; Valuevo, where Countess Emelia [Karlovna Mushchina-Pushkina] lives; and Moscow where no one lives, although there it is possible to meet a colossal collective of ravens and magpies, some pretty young people and a small number of men of sparkling wit [Ivan Vasilevich Kireevskii and Khomiakov]. They are distinguished by the enormous dignity of having preserved passion and vivacity in their ideas. . . .

> They assemble to organize balls and literary gatherings, but at this time, according to the witty remark of one Moscow *philosophe* [Chaadaev], have not reached the peak of their strength.[114]

Gagarin became acquainted with Petr Chaadaev in 1833 through Schelling. Gagarin spoke of Chaadaev:

> as one of the most remarkable men that he knew. Finding myself in Moscow in 1835, I pressed myself to put myself in rapport with him, and I had no difficulty convincing myself that Schelling had not exaggerated. I made the practice, every time that circumstances in Moscow permitted me, to frequently see this eminent man and to converse for a long time with him. These relations exerted on my future a powerful influence.[115]

A letter of Chaadaev to A.I. Turgenev in 1835 corroborated Gagarin's claim. He wrote, "I have recently obtained news about our illustrious Schelling through the young Gagarin."[116]

Petr Chaadaev (1794–1856) argued that Russia was not a European or an Asian country: "we are not related to any of the great human families; we belong to neither the West nor the East, and we possess the traditions of neither."[117] Chaadaev further asserted that Russians had never been motivated by a great universal spiritual ideal. Rather, they acted only out of caprice or violence.[118] For Chaadaev, Europe, unlike Russia, possessed a common Christian heritage. This heritage was rooted in Roman Catholicism.

The schism between Orthodoxy and Catholicism had separated Russia from the West and from the Western source of progress. For Chaadaev, Orthodoxy, unlike Catholicism, failed to prevent the establishment of serfdom in Russia and it supported un-Christian national prejudice.[119]

Chaadaev asserted that Russia needed to follow the example of Peter I and appropriate for itself the best aspects of Western culture. Russia was to serve as a new spiritual center for a rejuvenated Europe.[120] Furthermore, Russia needed to seek union with the pope both as a visible sign of union as well as for ensuring the independence of the church.[121] Chaadaev claimed:

> The day on which all the Christian sects will reunite will be the day on which the schismatic churches penitently and humbly decide to

> acknowledge, in sack and cinders, that by separating themselves from the mother church they rejected the effects of this sublime prayer of the Savior: Holy Father preserve in thy name those whom thou hast given me, so that they may be one as we are one. Were the papacy, as they suggest, a human institution—as if things of this stature could be made by human hands—what difference would it make? It is certain that in this time the papacy resulted essentially from the spirit of Christianity and that today, as a constant visible sign of unity, it is an even greater sign of union.[122]

Chaadaev condemned Protestantism for fostering disunity in the Western church.[123]

As for dogmatic disagreements between Catholicism and Orthodoxy, Chaadaev argued that papal temporal power was an issue only recently brought up by Protestants. The Orthodox had disputed primacy, not sovereignty. Whereas for the *filioque,* while the East was more faithful to the wording of the Creed, the West had only mentioned an idea already possessed by the faithful.[124]

Gagarin and Chaadaev developed an extremely close relationship. We have already seen Gagarin's role in the distribution of copies of Chaadaev's "First Philosophical Letter" to Pushkin and Viazemskii. In a letter to Gagarin on 1 October 1840, Chaadaev wrote, "But, dear prince, we really miss you, especially I do, since I like so much to follow with eye and soul your youthful and lively spiritedness."[125] Gagarin was deeply impressed by Chaadaev's intellectual abilities. He called him "The most remarkable man that Russia produced in the nineteenth century, though his compatriots are loathe to recognize [that].[126] He [Chaadaev] clearly explains how these peoples [the Slavs], from the very moment they fell under Byzantine influence, escaped the tutelary action of the papacy, remained estranged from the life of Christendom and as a result from all of the foundations of European civilization."[127] Gagarin would later write, "I owe the principle of my conversion to Chaadaev."[128]

Gagarin said, in 1835, that he saw the Catholic church as a human institution. He said, "I admired it as a great ruin, I even pitied it, not suspecting, that it maintained in itself all the principles of strength and life which conquer individual and nation. From this followed that it was not in my thoughts to confess the Catholic religion, and I could perceive as an absurdity, as an anachronism, the idea of bringing Catholicism into Russia."[129]

Yet, as we have seen, Gagarin, through Jouffroy and Schelling, believed in the idea of Christian progress. He wrote, "I saw in Christianity the path of human thought . . . but I was far from thinking that it had attained the limit of perfection of which it was capable, and I noticed a new progress in what I called the liberation [*osvobozhdeniem*] of thought; this seemed to me the goal of Protestantism."[130] Gagarin saw European Christianity divided into two camps: Protestantism and Catholicism. He thought the difference between the two was greater than the difference between either one and the religious views of Russia. He noted that Protestantism, as such, did not attract him, but that he was attracted to the idea of a dualism, "which supposed two opinions about every understanding: truth, it seemed, should be born of this opposition, and I saw in this dualism the source of this fruitfulness."[131] Gagarin could not find this notion of Protestant dualism in Russia and therefore concluded that dualism was not part of Protestantism and had begun long before Protestantism. Looking at the religious struggles of Europe—for example, between Jansenism and Jesuitism, Protestantism and Catholicism, Islam and the Crusaders—Gagarin came to the conclusion that only the Catholic church remained intact after all of these struggles. Therefore, the Catholic church was the "essential core of European civilization."[132] By 1838, the Catholic church, for Gagarin, had become the only means of ending despotism and barbarism in Russia.[133]

Chaadaev was most responsible for Gagarin's increasing sympathy with the Catholic church. From correspondence between the two it is clear that issues of Russian ecclesiastical history were at the forefront of their discussions. In a letter of 1 October 1842, Chaadaev noted that he and Gagarin were engaged in discussions on the question of the time of Russia's separation from the Vatican. Gagarin had argued that the existence of marriages between Eastern and Western Christians without evidence of conversions indicated that a period of union existed after the schism of 1054. Chaadaev agreed that primitive unity existed. However Gagarin asserted that the acknowledgment did not come easily for Chaadaev, since the premise behind his philosophical letters was that Russia entirely lacked the Catholic heritage of the West. Gagarin argued that Russia had a Catholic heritage, but had abandoned it.[134]

Additional proof of Chaadaev's profound influence on Gagarin can be seen in Gagarin's later decision to publish Chaadaev's philosophical letters. In 1860, in Paris, Gagarin received some of Chaadaev's documents from M. I. Zhikarev. Zhikarev wished to publish the writings of Chaadaev abroad, as it was impossible to do so in Russia.[135] Gagarin was extremely eager to have Chaadaev's writings and later published Chaadaev's "First Philosophical Letter" in the journal *Le Correspondant* under the title "Catholic Tendencies in Russian Society."[136] This was the first time the letter had been published in its original French. Two years later, Gagarin published *Oeuvres choisies de Pierre Tchadaief—publiées pour la première fois par le Père Gagarin de la Compagnie de Jésus.* This edition included the philosophical letters 1, 6, and 7 as well as "Apology of a Madman"; "Notes to Count Benkendorf"; a letter of Chaadaev to A. S. Pushkin, from 6/18 July 1831; and letters of Chaadaev to A. I. Turgenev, S. I. Meshcherskaia, Schelling, and Gagarin. Letters 6 and 7 of the philosophical letters were mistakenly marked by Gagarin as letters 2 and 3. Letter 4 in the publication was later identified as a part of another work, one not associated with the philosophical letters.

Gagarin's publication attracted much attention. Copies of the text were provided to several Russian intellectuals.[137] Michel Cadot has argued that these publications served to rehabilitate the image of Chaadaev after Nicholas's government had declared him insane.[138] A copy of the *Oeuvres* even came to the attention of Pope Pius IX.[139]

On 29 June 1837 the Russian government transferred Gagarin to London where he spent his time studying the political development of England. He wrote, "I strove to understand the causes of its greatness, to seriously, carefully and cautiously study, to discover why its essence consisted in such a powerful aristocracy, to explain that the difference between political parties divided it but did not weaken it."[140] Gagarin later went to Paris on 13 April 1838.

Having been made collegiate secretary with seniority on 12 December 1838, Gagarin returned briefly to the Dankovo estate outside of Moscow in December 1839, before traveling to Petersburg. During this time, Gagarin maintained his connections with Russian educated society. A. I. Turgenev wrote, "I am often seen here with Prince Ivan Gagarin. He quite rightly sees himself as a first-class citizen; possessing wealth, intelligence, civility and curiosity. Here he again breathes and is revived."[141] Gagarin was often seen at the house of Viazemskii and was considered as ". . . one of the most educated and outstanding young people of that time, belonging to that select circle of notables in wit and common European educational appearance."[142] Vasilii Elagin, younger half-brother of Ivan Kireevskii, wrote, "He is a most remarkable man. Gagarin is a diplomat and a dandy, and yet every day he goes to Nikolskaia Street to buy old books. I find that remarkable. His Russian is poor, but his French is so rapid and fluent that you can't understand a thing he says." Lev Sollogub, brother of writer Vladimir Sollogub, praised his "ability . . . to dispel one's apathy." Sophia Karamzina, daughter of the famous historian, said that Gagarin "knows how to talk."[143]

It was also at this time that Gagarin became involved with the circle known as *Les Seize* or the *Shestnadtsati*. This circle of sixteen met between the winter of 1838 and the spring of 1841.[144] Its membership was composed of intellectuals, diplomats, soldiers, all in their early or middle twenties. It had no formal organization, no membership roster, and no agreed-upon program.[145]

Historical information on the existence of *Les Seize* is scant. Polish soldier Ksavier Korczak-Branicki, in this letter to Gagarin in 1879, wrote:

> In the year of grace 1839, Saint Petersburg possessed a society of young men who had a nickname, because of their number, *Les Seize*. There camaraderie was formed, on the banks of the University, in the battalions of the army of the Caucasus. Each night, after leaving the theater or the ball, they would find themselves sometimes at the home of one, sometimes at the home of another. There, after a frugal supper, inhaling their cigars, they discussed the events of the day, chatted about everything, discussed everything, with perfect liberty of language: as if the *Third Section of the Imperial Chancellery* did not exist, so they depended on their mutual discretion.
>
> We belonged to that sincere and joyous association of *Les Seize:* you, my reverend father, who had been secretary of the ambassador, and I, who wore the uniform of a lieutenant of the hussars of the imperial guard.[146]

Valuev's diary noted that in 1838–1840, he [Valuev] "joined with Branicki, Dolgorukovs, Paskevich, Lermontov and others (*Les Seize,* to which I belonged)."[147] In a letter to Gagarin, Samarin wrote, "A short time after your departure, I saw parade past Moscow the entire faction of the sixteen, who held the path toward the south."[148] Gagarin referred to the *Les Seize* in two of his writings. In his diary entry of 6 April 1838, writing of Branicki, Gagarin noted that he "belonged to his circle for a long time."[149] In a letter of Gagarin to Stepan Petrovich Shevyrev of 11 January 1841, Gagarin referred to the joy of hearing news about "Moscow literature and the wise and beloved circle in which I spent so many pleasant hours."[150]

The only other indication of the membership of *Les Seize* were a pair of portraits done by Grigorii Gagarin (first cousin of Ivan). These pictures portrayed the members of *Les Seize* engaged in discussions.[151]

Historians disagree as to the nature of the organization. Some have argued that *Les Seize* was a neo-Decembrist circle; some have argued that the group was not an organized circle, merely a "crowd of golden youth." Eikhenbaum argued that the organization "grew in the soil of oppositionist moods to old ancestral thought and was exposed to the influence of the religious and historico-philosophical ideas of P. Ia. Chaadaev."[152] Gagarin served as an intermediary between Chaadaev and the other members of *Les Seize*.

In any case, it is clear that the group did not have a unified position. Gagarin represented the pro-Catholic view and supported a messianic idea of Russia. Korczak-Branicki supported alternatively Polish patriotism and loyalty to the tsar. Fredriks converted from Lutheranism to Orthodoxy at this time.[153]

In addition to discussing questions of religion and nationality (*natsional'nost'*), *Les Seize* also discussed Russia's place in the family of nations; its historical path; its presumed "youth"; and emancipation of the serfs.[154] From Gagarin's earlier writings, it is obvious that each of these issues was important to him. We have already noted Gagarin's opposition to serfdom; his desire to place himself at the service of Russia; his view of Russia's importance in European society; his desire to find the reason for the national differences between Western Europe and his homeland; and his desire to ascertain Russia's special place in history. Thus, it is not surprising that these ideas would also be discussed within *Les Seize*. It is also apparent that Gagarin had already attached himself to Chaadaev's ideas and wished to propagate them.

His discussions with Valuev allow us to see more clearly Gagarin's notions of nationality. Valuev asserted, "We in our arguments did not quite understand the word *natsional'nost'*." He went on:

> Taking this word in its domestic political connotation, organizing *natsional'nost'* by means of frontiers, institutions, a government, reducing it, that is to say only to a costume, a mask, under which people appeared in the political world, they forgot, it seems to me, the basic elements of *natsional'nost'*, they were occupied with reconstruction on the unsteady sand of diplomatic conversations, that is, the building, the fundamental [thing] which should be based on the internal

> life, customs, and history of the nation. I think that we forgot the word *natsional'nost'* in that sense, with which is marked the national spirit, national customs, national songs.[155]

In his *Notes about My Life,* Gagarin wrote:

> This question could be formulated thusly: all other peoples [*narody*] of Europe, whatever their original language, form of government [*pravleniia*] and religion, have something in common in their ideas, customs, means of existence and traditional modes of intercourse between people; between them, despite many perceptible distinctions, exists a spirit of kinship, a striking quality of unity. (It is worth while to put forward France, England, Germany, or Italy in the surroundings of the barbarian tribes of America).
>
> In the course of many centuries, the Russian people lacked almost any union with the other peoples of Europe; the result of this was that to it remained alien the defining unitary idea, expressed in customs, manners, literature, laws, in all relations of people among themselves, which could be found among all those peoples and which gave to them the spirit of kinship and character of unity, looking at the difference in their origin, language, customs, government and beliefs.[156]

Thus, both Valuev and Gagarin looked at "nationality" as something integrally linked to the internal life of the nation. However, it is important that nationality, for Gagarin, was not to be used as a method of division but of unity. He wanted to find those common elements of national culture which could be used to formulate European union.

At this point, the relationship between Iurii Samarin and Gagarin should be mentioned. Samarin and Gagarin were cousins, and their attachment grew during the period between 1835 and 1840. Gagarin told Samarin, "How many times, has it come to me to discuss ideas with you, to share my moods, to question you and to await your response?"[157] Samarin wrote, "Every time that I test some new emotion, vividly conceive something which occupies me . . . [I want you to join] this desire and make it part of you and to have your views."[158] Samarin, like Gagarin, was deeply interested in the relationship of Russia and the West. He wrote his dissertation on the history of the Roman Catholic, Protestant, and Orthodox churches.

Several archival documents of Gagarin's allow us to expound his views on the subjects of politics, history, revolution, and serfdom. In 1835, he wrote a text entitled "Réflexions sur la Démocratie en Europe, à propos de l'ouvrage de M. De Tocqueville, intitulé *De la Démocratie en Amérique*."[159] In this document, Gagarin presented his views on the subject of democracy and its applicability to the countries of Europe. Gagarin opposed universal democracy. He called it a "phantom" and a "chimerical" notion which threatened all government. Only in America had democracy acquired a stable and regular form. Democracy was possible in America because the country had been already populated by civilized individuals possessing fortunes of almost equal status. Gagarin said that, in theory, if a society was composed of people "having the same faculty of cognizance and following the rules of Reason and the same interests to coordinate with the prescriptions of eternal Justice, we admit that the means most simple, most just and most regular to fix the rapport which should govern them, would be to confide power to the numeric majority."

That type of situation did not exist in Europe. Rather, Gagarin argued, "The history of the struggles of class demonstrates that the power of government and the ruling elite always belongs to those who possess the light of intelligence, force, and property." Those in power may lose their monopoly over intelligence, force, and material interests and be replaced by a new governing group, but democracy will still not exist. As Gagarin wrote, "we see in the aristocratic countries, the families formerly powerful, fallen into misery and abasement and replaced by new families, which have acquired in their turn that which makes force [over] others." Gagarin argued that, in Europe, power initially belonged in the hands of the clergy (intelligence) and the nobility (force and material), but after the French revolution power shifted into the hands of the bourgeoisie, who had acquired education and control over material interests. However, he thought the domination of the bourgeoisie would also be temporary. Yet, to assume that democracy was inevitable was wrong and only discouraged those social forces that could oppose it.

In "De la puissance de la révolution en Europe," Gagarin, using the ideas of Guizot, addressed the problems of revolution.[160] Gagarin asserted, "We all know that these tempests [of revolution] are far from ending; they still threaten most of the European nations."

Exploring the history of revolution, Gagarin described how the unity of the Roman empire was replaced by Christianity, the head of which was the papacy. The revolution of the Reformation broke this Christian unity. A new revolution was now originating among the Slavic peoples, whom Gagarin compared to "plebeians of ancient Rome." The Slavs, once excluded from the ruling powers of Europe, now wished to become co-equals. For Gagarin, the Slavs were headed not by Poland or Austria but by Russia. He wrote, "No one can dispute the place which it [Russia] occupies at the head of the Slavic nation." He further noted the importance of political, religious, and national questions in Russia at this time.

In "D'un accord à établir dans les ideés philosophiques, religieuses, litteraires, etc. en d'un petit nombre," Gagarin expressed his ideas on the nature of society.[161] He wrote, "It is in the nature of man to search for agreement in his own views among his equals." He asserted that ideological consensus is the foundation of society. This consensus was based on an intellectual community and influenced by the ideas of school, church, and orthodoxy.

Political authority in society should be vested in the law.[162] Gagarin asserted, "*Laws should govern men and the human authority of society should be placed above that of those who reign. . . .* it is a pact between the decisions of universal Reason and the Truth of Eternal Justice."[163] He reiterated his claim that society was composed of individuals who had an unequal access to education and force; thus the idea of democracy "should be considered only as a cry of war." He asserted that there were legitimate representatives of education and force who should promulgate laws and enforce them, though, as he noted in his discussion on de Tocqueville, those representatives could change.

In Russia, Gagarin asserted, the nobility were called to exercise great influence. He further discussed Peter III's abolition of Peter the Great's law requiring service from the nobility in 1762.[164] He compared this act with the issue of abolishing of serfdom.[165] Gagarin argued that enfranchisement of the serfs would be a tremendous problem for the government, which would have to modify its internal administration and establish a new system of organization. He asserted that it would be best to concede ownership of the soil to the intermediate class of the nobility which could best use it. He feared that enfranchising the serfs might lead to the creation of a merchant class and the spread of democratic ideas.

Here we see Gagarin's strong emphasis on the role of the nobility in conducting governmental affairs. He opposed autocratic despotism, yet he equally opposed the violence and anarchy he associated with democracy. For Gagarin, the ideal holder of power was his own class, the gentry elite. This group already possessed the required intellectual ability for leadership; Gagarin hoped that the Russian autocracy would concede economic authority to them as well. It should be noted that although

Gagarin was opposed to autocratic despotism and supported the abolition of serfdom, he did not propose any means of providing the former serfs with the means of self-sufficiency, nor did he offer any means of preventing acts of oppression by the nobility.

Gagarin also presented his ideas on the enfranchisement of the serfs in his text "Affranchisement du serf à Russie."[166] Gagarin recognized the necessity of the liberation of the serfs through ukaz or constitution.[167] In "Affranchisement," he argued that maintenance of the status quo in Russia was impossible and contrary to liberty. He proposed the creation of a minister or ministers of domains. This minister would be called the *ministr pomeshchichikh del'* or something similar and would have the legal responsibility to make serfs fulfill their obligations without recourse to the bureaucracy (*chinovniki*). Gagarin also wanted to reorganize and develop the Russian commune (a peasant socioeconomic structure) with the municipal government; establish a judicial organization which would govern the relationship between the estate owner and the peasantry, to maintain civil relations; and to avoid all bureaucracy (*chinovniki*). A *ministr* would operate in each Russian province.

In none of these documents did Gagarin provide a detailed description of his political thought. However, together they present some key aspects of Gagarin's thought and allow us to see him as a man in support of a rule-of-law state and of more responsibility for the Russian nobility. He opposed serfdom, yet did not see in enfranchisement the beginnings of democracy. His support for legal authority over the arbitrary power of the government, his support for a government drawn from the social elites, and his reference to the need for some kind of constitutional arrangement show that Gagarin's ideas anticipated those of liberal Westerners such as Boris Chicherin.

During this period of time, Gagarin underwent a tremendous amount of intellectual development. His childhood and university education inspired in him an interest in the West as well as a belief that he was bound to use his educational gifts for the service of Russia. Through his contact with important thinkers such as Jouffroy, Ancillon, Schelling, Chaadaev, Tiutchev, Turgenev, Pushkin, and the members of *Les Seize,* Gagarin further involved himself in issues of Russian national identity—Russia's "special place" in history. As a result of this investigation, Gagarin came to the conclusion that he was personally obligated to work for the glory of Russia, to help it fulfill its special mission. That mission required an analysis of why Russia did not belong to the family of Europe, as well as an examination of Russia's role in the progressive evolution of Christianity. Like Chaadaev, Gagarin concluded that because Russia had separated itself from the Catholic unity centered in Rome, it had separated itself from the source of Christian progress. Yet Gagarin did not believe that Russia had always been separate from Roman Catholicism. Instead, he argued, Russia's separation came later than 1054 and Russia did indeed have a Catholic history.

In addition to Gagarin's religious views, he also developed his political views. His unpublished writings suggest a man deeply opposed to democratic revolution as something contrary to historical law. He was equally opposed to unlimited government. His desire to allocate more power to members of his own class also demonstrates his view that, as a noble, he deserved a foremost position of authority. He was part of an elite that possessed the necessary intellectual and economic qualifications to lead Russia in the future.

CHAPTER TWO

Paris: Conversion and Ordination

> Let us take the cases of [Mikhail Sergeevich] Lunin, [Petr Borisovich] Kozlovskii, Chaadaev, those other than Madame Svechina; certainly, neither spirit nor talent would be lacking; but none of these would have defended the Russian church, and because of that, what influence could they have? Lunin is dead in Siberia, Kozlovskii spent the great part of his life outside his country, Chaadaev was not exiled, he spent the rest of his life in Moscow, but he was declared mad by the emperor; his example shows us well that the climate of Russia is not favorable to those spirits who have the pretension to think for themselves.[1]

Gagarin first joined the Russian mission in Paris as the third secretary on 13 April 1838. After spending some time in Russia, he returned to Paris as the junior secretary of the Russian mission on 7 May 1840. He was promoted to the rank of titular councillor on 16 April 1841. According to the testimony of Gagarin's associates, he found the Parisian atmosphere very agreeable. Turgenev wrote, "I often see Prince Ivan Sergeevich Gagarin; he, it seems, again is as I knew him in Munich, where he amused me very much. Not avoiding the world, he looks at books and loves the salons of Svechina and her sort."[2] In Paris, Gagarin maintained his connections with Russian society, corresponding with Chaadaev and others.[3] He also met Count Louis-Mathieu Molé,[4] Antoine Pierre Berrier,[5] and literary figures such as Delphine Gay, Charles Nodier, and Eugène Sue. He attended recitals of Franz Lizt, which he liked, and Hector Berlioz, which he did not—calling them a "cacophany" and "bizarre." His struggles with hedonism continued as he found French cuisine too tempting and so resolved to eat but one meal a day of simple meat and vegetables. His journal portrays many interesting, if not scandalous, aspects of Parisian high society.[6] Gagarin attended Adam Mickiewicz's lectures on Slavic literature and continued his analysis of national identity.[7] His continuing desire to look for points of concord between nationalities can be seen in a section of his journal:

> All nations choose words with special care for expressing the friendly idea of parting, departure; in these words is expressed the popular genius of every nation. English *farewell* wishes you success, good journeys, fair winds; the French *adieu* fulfillment of faith, entrusting you to the heavenly patron, putting you under cover of the Almighty; the Russian *prosti* calls forth reconciliation, peace, to avoid leaving behind some hostility, some feeling of displeasure. But among all these words, full of poetry and feeling, the German pleases me the most. *Lebewohl* means—be happy, try to be happy![8]

In "La langage français en Russie," dated 1840, Gagarin further analyzed the connection of language and nationality.[9] He noted that the educated members of Russian society used French in familiar correspondence and for conversation. Since French culture had influenced Russian educated culture to such a degree and because the French had acquired their culture from Latin literature, Gagarin argued that Russia, too, must study foreign literature in order to acquire the benefits of Roman culture: "It cannot escape this universal law." Gagarin saw a link between the study of antiquity and the spread of Christianity: "the Christian civilization is not improvised but transmitted. The church in its admirable unity was the animating spirit and the intellectual property of all Europe. It used the native languages for preaching to the people and instructing them, while maintaining the usage of Latin for the regions more elevated in science and thought. It was also open to the study of the entire [field] of antiquity, not letting escape any vestiges of the human past, linking all times, the peoples of every nation and every profession." Unfortunately, since Russia had joined the Byzantine commonwealth, it never experienced in its formative stages the Roman influence which would have brought with it fundamental knowledge of antiquity and a share in Europe's animating spirit.

In this document, Gagarin further asserted that Peter the Great broke Russia's isolation from Europe but did not reattach Russia to Rome. Since eighteenth-century Europe was plagued by the disease of disbelief, Peter instilled this European disbelief in Russia and weakened the religious spirit of the Russian people. Gagarin called Peter's reforms "entirely external, entirely material." The Russian church, broken by Peter's reforms, was powerless to prevent the spread of Western European disbelief. In domesticating the French language, Russia imbibed the ideas of the French *philosophes* and skeptics. While some (the Slavophiles) wanted to return to the past and renounce European civilization, Gagarin argued that the only solution was to return to union with Rome. For Gagarin, French culture had both positive and negative aspects. On the one hand, French culture (as well as that of the rest of Western Europe) began under the progressive influence of Roman Catholicism and the Latin culture of ancient Rome. On the other hand, French culture had been distorted under the influence of the *philosophes* and the skeptics. Peter had grafted the dangerous aspects of French culture onto Russia. If Peter had seen the roots of Western civilization in Roman Catholicism, he would have adopted those traits instead.

Again, it is important to define Gagarin's Catholic sympathies at this time. He admitted in his memoirs, "At that time . . . I was not Catholic. However, without seeing where the flow of my ideas would carry me, I reflected more than once on the difference which existed, I would not say between the Catholic religion and the Greek religion in which I had been raised, but between the social condition of Russia and that of the other countries of Europe."[10] As for the papacy, he wrote, "I imagined the papacy as the point [of departure] for this entire [Western] society, of this entire civilization. But if the papacy struck me by the grandeur of the role that it had played in Western Europe, the immense void that its absence had made in Russia was even more astonishing."[11] Gagarin's sympathy for Roman Catholicism and the papacy was based on the conviction that they had played the key role in Christian progress and Western intellectual development; he did not admire the Roman church because it was the see of Peter established by Christ or because the Catholic church was the source of theological truth. He did not touch upon the dogmatic disagreements between the Russian Orthodox church and Roman Catholicism, rather he compared the intellectual sophistication of the Western European nations with the more primitive condition of Russia.

Through the influence of Ancillon, Schelling, Chaadaev, and others, Gagarin had arrived at this conclusion from his initial opposition to the despotism and barbarism in his native land. He did not see this barbarism and despotism in the West, except under the banner of revolution. Rather, he saw these problems resolved in the rule-of-law states such as France and England. Looking for a reason for this difference between his own land and Western Europe, Gagarin focused on religious differences between

Protestantism/Catholicism and Orthodoxy. He regarded Protestantism a recent phenomenon; therefore, he considered Catholicism the true foundation of Western civilization.[12] Since he viewed Catholicism as the source of Western development, not as the source of theological truths, conversion to Roman Catholicism as a theological system was not necessary. At this stage, Gagarin was interested in political and intellectual development, not the *filioque*.

While in Paris, Gagarin increased his knowledge of the theology of Roman Catholicism by participating in several salons at the homes of prominent French and Russian Catholics. The most important of these was the salon of Madame Sofiia Petrovna Soymonova Svechina.[13] Gagarin reported that the conversations at Svechina's salon involved political, religious, literary, and artistic themes from which the participants strove "to extract some higher, grave, serious ideas."[14] However, Gagarin did not participate in the salon discussions: "because he felt at that time too young and insufficiently informed on these questions, he listened with a rare curiosity of spirit. Those which touched on religion retained all of his attention."[15] Gagarin himself wrote that "I did not have any pretension to play a role there. My ambition was modest, I wanted to observe, study, look at the examples."[16] At these salons, Gagarin met well-known Catholic writers and thinkers such as Berrier, Baron Ferdinand d'Eckstein, Lammenais, Charles de Montalembert, Pére Henri-Dominique de Lacordaire, and Count Frédéric Alfred Pierre de Falloux, all of whom would have exposed him to a variety of Catholic ideas. Lammenais, Montalembert, and Lacordaire expounded the goals of Catholic liberalism, that is, the need to free the church from state control, encourage state support of religious freedom and greater political democracy. Baron d'Eckstein was a staunch ultramontanist.[17] However, the most important individual with regards to Gagarin's later conversion was Svechina herself.

Saint-Beuve called Svechina, "the older sister of de Maistre and the younger sister of Saint Augustine."[18] Gagarin wrote of her:

> That which touched me most in her, was the passionate love, the unswerving devotion to truth; one sensed, one saw that she could experience a true joy in the search, in the contemplation, in the possession of truth; this was her life. . . . She knew well that the Catholic faith alone could give the truth in its integrity; but she knew also that particles, bits, reflections of truth are found everywhere. She marvelously uncovered truth amidst the errors which surrounded it;

> she freed it, she showed all its brightness, she radiated everything which surrounded it. It is God himself that she saw in truth; also she accepted it with love, with respect, without stopping the hand which presented it to her. She rejoiced to find on the lips or on the pen of an adversary, a man who did not divide his beliefs and his opinions. She did not look to be right; she did not pretend to triumph over any party; she only wished the truth.[19]

Svechina's views regarding Russia appealed to Gagarin. Like him, she was critical of the Russian clergy, accusing it of passivity and ignorance.[20] She defended an expansionist, missionary Roman Catholicism as a bridge between Russia and Europe. She wrote, "Exclusive and proselytizing! And so preeminently proselytizing that the Word, in its present sense, has been fully comprehended and applied by the Catholic church alone! Exclusive! The church calls Greek and Scythian, barbarian, Jew, and Muslim; not only calls them, but goes to them, opening her arms to all, ready to clasp and press them to her maternal breast."[21]

Another important individual in Gagarin's conversion was the Jesuit father Gustave-Xavier de Ravignan (1795–1858), who preached at Notre-Dame de Paris.[22] Ravignan's views on the Roman Catholic church, its missionary activity, and the role of the Jesuits strongly appealed to Gagarin. Ravignan wrote, "Never in the world was a word more powerful and more fruitful than that which was pronounced one day from the top of a mountain in Judea, in order to change the destinies of the Universe: *Go ye, teach all nations.*" "But by thee, O Simon Peter, the Cross will be planted in the bosom of Rome itself. Watered by the waves of Christian blood, it is about to grow and flourish like an immense tree, whose branches will cover the earth. Under its tutelary shadow will soon come to rest all the nations which Jesus Christ has inherited; and Rome by the Cross, by the Pontiff who bears it, and who lifts it perpetually to the sight of the Gentiles, will extend her conquests farther than she did of old by the valor of her soldiers and the victorious force of her arms."[23] Ravignan saw that this missionary work could take place without threat to the national heritage of those evangelized.[24]

A third individual involved in Gagarin's later conversion was Count Grigorii Petrovich Shuvalov (1805–1859), like Gagarin, a member of the Russian nobility sympathetic to Roman Catholicism.[25] Shuvalov met Gagarin in Paris in 1841. He described Gagarin as a man "of a ready and cultivated mind and an active imagination; he possessed—and this was his most striking characteristic—a soul on fire, bent on overexertion, and which, unable to find in the world a field for its action, knew not how to satisfy the hunger that devoured it. It was a missionary soul wandering as one lost and consuming itself." According to Shuvalov, Gagarin was "gay, active, busied with a thousand projects destined to prove abortive, seeking and shunning the truth by turns."[26] Together, Gagarin and Shuvalov undertook reading Jean Louis de Leissègues Rozaven's *L'Église Russe et L'Église catholique,* Johann Adam Möhler's *Symbolique,* and Andrei N. Murav'ev's *Pravda vselenskoi tserkvi o rimskoi i prochikh patriarskikh kafedrakh.* Both Gagarin and Shuvalov noted that, while Murav'ev's text was written in justification of the Orthodox church, with them it had the opposite effect. Shuvalov wrote, "Happily for us, and for every impartial reader, this book fails in its purpose; for it proves in fact the truth, while seeking to defend error; and after studying it with care, we were almost thoroughly convinced that the church which calls itself Catholic is the only one which in fact is so."[27]

Gagarin also was moved toward Catholicism, again ironically, by the Orthodox apologetical writings of Moscow Metropolitan Filaret, particularly Filaret's *Razgovor mezhdu ispytuiushchim i uverennym o pravoslavnoi vostochnoi greko-rossiiskoi tserkve.* Other texts that Gagarin read were the *Memoires de St. Simon,* about Peter and the union of churches; materials on the Oxford movement;[28] the French Catholic liberal paper *L'Univers;* and several German texts on the relationship of the Catholic and Russian churches—*Strahl Kirchengeschichte, Die neuesten Züstände der Katholischen Kirche beider Ritus in Polen und Russland seit Katharina II bis auf unsere Tage,* and *Rückblick auf die russiche Kirche und ihre Stellung zum heiligen Stuhle seit ihrem Entstehen bis auf Katharina.*

The influence of the writings of Joseph de Maistre on Gagarin's religious transformation should also be mentioned. He wrote, "Everything concerning Count de Maistre has a claim to my respect and my gratitude, therefore I cannot doubt that in the hands of Divine Providence, his writings were an instrument of my conversion and salvation."[29]

Gagarin, who had previously admired the social contributions of Roman Catholicism to Europe, now found himself attracted to Catholicism theologically. He strove to understand and accept the papacy, and to fathom the theological disagreement between the Roman Catholic and Orthodox churches regarding the Holy Spirit. Gagarin's theological argumentation can be seen in his correspondence with Iurii Samarin and Ivan Kireevskii regarding differences between the Roman and Russian churches.

In his letters to Samarin, Gagarin accused the Orthodox bishops of "ambition and insubordination," for, he said, they had accepted papal authority at the councils of Lyons and Florence.[30] Relying on standard Catholic apologetics, Gagarin argued that the changing of Simon's name to Peter as well as the writings of the church fathers supported Petrine primacy.[31] As for the issue of the *filioque,* Gagarin argued that "No, not one canon, not one decision of the Eastern church, says that the Holy Spirit does not proceed from the Son, yet it is neither official doctrine nor a tenet binding on believers. The Holy Spirit either proceeds or does not proceed from the Son; that is a matter of free opinion, which anyone in the Eastern church is allowed to accept or reject." Gagarin added that Petrine primacy entitled Rome to add the *filioque* to the creed.[32] A third theme of his letters was the assertion that the Orthodox church had been silent since the seventh ecumenical council, yet the true church cannot remain silent, for faith must continue to grow and develop.[33] Despite all of this, Gagarin argued that "Both churches equally believe and confess one, holy, catholic [*sobornaia*], and apostolic church."[34]

In late 1842, Gagarin ruminated on these issues in correspondence with Ivan Kireevskii.[35] Again, Gagarin stressed the authority of the Roman Catholic church:

> the C[atholic] c[hurch] has passed through the furnace of science and criticism, already after three hundred years of an innumerable quantity of heretics and unbelievers of all types everyday attacking her from all sides, using all possible means, enjoying freedom to speak, write, publish, confess everything that is pleasing to them; most governments are hostile to her, not only in one area, but in the entire world, in the enlightened countries of Europe and America; yet the church, suffering intellectual persecution from the sixteenth to the nineteenth centuries, which could be compared with the bloody third century persecution of the Roman Caesar, not only survives but prospers, spreads, especially in the United States, England, and in Holland with such speed that her enemies are horrified by her successes.
>
> Acknowledge that these successes could scarcely be accomplished if the Catholic church were truly [as bad] as you imagine.[36]

Gagarin argued that the church should be "spiritual, united, universal, and independent."[37] He reiterated his comments regarding the lack of a pronouncement by an ecumenical council condemning the *filioque* and said that "If I knew the means to arouse in you a feeling of love for the Catholic church, I would with happiness abandon all books, all arguments, all commentary, because then all scales would fall from your eyes and you would at once understand everything that now seems to you so complicated and confused."[38]

Gagarin admitted that on the doctrine of the Holy Spirit he had submitted "to the judgement and the decision of the [Roman] church. When I had made this act of faith, I acquired on this matter a peace, a tranquility which has never been troubled."[39]

Gagarin had by now begun to support Catholic theology. He described the pope as the head of the church, as proven by the Bible and the writings of the church fathers. He believed that the Holy Spirit did proceed from the Son, as proven by the silence of the ecumenical councils and Rome's authoritative pronouncement. He thought that any new disagreement over doctrine could be resolved by an appeal to Rome. Yet Gagarin was afraid to convert to Roman Catholicism, fearing his parents' reaction and the Russian government's response.[40] He wrote, "How difficult it is to put away the things of this world! It seems to you that you are ready to make the biggest sacrifice, but when you think about the isolation in which you will find yourself, about breaking all ties joining you with the fatherland, and with society, shivers envelop you and you begin to doubt the means to find in your heart sufficient courage for such a great sacrifice."[41]

Gagarin's movement toward Rome continued in 1842. In January of that year, he was mentioned among the membership of the organization Cercle de l'Union along with Fyodor Alekseevich Golitsyn, Mikhail Aleksandrovich Golitsyn, Nikolai Ivanovich Trubetskoi, Andrei Pavlovich Shuvalov, and Petr P. Shuvalov.[42] On 10 February 1842, Gagarin and Grigorii Shuvalov received communion in the Orthodox church for the last time.[43] On that day, Gagarin wrote in his diary:

> God managed today to administer the Holy Mysteries to me. I pray and hope that they will help me to live a Christian life. I grieve that, having intellectual faith, I did not feel the ardent faith of a pure repentant heart. And it is this that I grieve, but I should not be depressed. A troubled heart hungering for purity is already the fruit of grace. I should ask for it by prayer, but I cannot be depressed, if it is not given to me instantly. With such sweetness I would follow the Divine commandments, if only my heart could experience aversion to the world and pure love of God. It is necessary to obey the law even in

the absence of these emotions and to hope that by obeying the law, by prayer and the sacraments, I will come to experience genuine happiness, the absence of which is the punishment of the sins of my life. I thank God that He gave me sincere tranquility and showed me the means to fulfill His commandments, in reading His word and in strong attachment to principles.[44]

When Gagarin finally decided to become a Catholic, he began to attend various Catholic churches and listened to the priests who preached there. The priest who filled him with the most trust was Ravignan.[45]

Although Gagarin was transferred to the position of junior secretary at the Russian mission in Vienna on 27 March 1842, he maintained his strong connections to Svechina and Ravignan and continued to harbor a desire to convert. On Easter Monday of 1842, Gagarin announced at one of the gatherings of Svechina that at six o'clock the next morning he would tell Ravignan his decision to convert. Svechina was greatly surprised and disturbed by this announcement, fearing a hostile Russian government response against the Russian Catholics in Paris. She persuaded Gagarin to wait twenty-four hours before he took this dramatic step. On 19 April 1842, Gagarin was received into the Catholic church by Ravignan.[46]

We must remind ourselves that Gagarin's conversion took several years: even after the influence of Schelling in 1832, Chaadaev in 1835, and participation in Svechina's salon in 1838, Gagarin only converted in 1842. This decision did not come easily for him: he began with a belief in the superiority of Western civilization, then identified Western civilization with the Roman Catholic church, and accepted Roman Catholic theology as the divine truth. Only then could he accept conversion. A testament written by Gagarin at this time provides an excellent description of his state of mind:

Our Savior Jesus Christ, whose infinite mercy has given me the grace to keep from wandering from the path on which I walk, who has made known to me that salvation and genuine happiness I can only find by doing God's will, which has been transmitted by and entrusted to the Holy Apostolic Roman Catholic Church outside of which there is no salvation. I have had the good fortune to be received and admitted into the communion of this Holy Church, the 19th of April this year 1842. Wishing to perpetuate the memory of this blessed day when I passed from the shadow of death to the awareness of the eternal Truth,

> and to render always to God, my Creator and my Savior, actions worthy of grace, I think I can do nothing more conforming to the Divine Will, nor more useful for my salvation, than to choose the 19th of each month to prepare for death and by directing all my actions as if I would appear that day before the final judgement of my Sovereign Judge. This is why, being of sound body and mind, I have composed the present testament and have written it with my own hand.
>
> My father and my mother are still unaware of my conversion or at least have only very vague suspicions. I entreat them to consider that I only undertook this act after a long inner struggle, after many years of indecision, and entirely so as to put my acts into harmony with my faith and so as not to jeopardize my salvation by a criminal resistance to the grace of God. I entreat them again to pardon me for all the voluntary and involuntary wrongs that I have committed against them and for which I feel in my heart a bitter sadness and terrible regret; I entreat them to examine and to weigh with the most serious attention the motives which hold them in schism and far from communion with the Holy Catholic Church, in which alone they can find true satisfaction in this world and in the next. I make the same recommendation to my dear sister, to her husband and in general to all the people who have had for me the sentiments of friendship and affection. I cannot stop here from making special mention of my friend Iurii Samarin who, I hope, will recognize one day the vanity of all the systems created by man and will find the peace of the soul and the true liberty of the spirit in the Catholic faith and in the practice that it teaches.[47]

On 19 June 1842, Gagarin returned to the Dankovo estate outside of Moscow for several months. At this time, he told no one except Iurii Samarin of his conversion. He feared persecution by the Russian authorities should his acts become commonly known. Moreover, Ravignan had ordered him to keep it secret. Gagarin wrote to Samarin, "You remember, how heavy was for me that secret, you know with what difficulty I obeyed the necessity to preserve silence and how from my mouth no seduction was ever uttered. . . . You did not forget how I was exposed then to danger and what might have resulted from one careless word pronounced by you at my expense."[48]

While in Moscow, Gagarin participated, along with Chaadaev, in the discussions of the Westerners and Slavophiles. Among other things, these discussions focused on the differences between Russian Orthodoxy and Western Christianity as well as the larger differences between Western and Russian civilization; in other words, the Westernizer-Slavophile debate dealt with the two questions most central to Gagarin's intellectual and religious mind-set. Samarin later testified that Gagarin "attacked the Orthodox church . . . scattering to the right and to the left extracts of the works of Count de Maistre and Father Rozaven; preaching openly, freely, without hindrance his Paris Latinism."[49]

During this period, Gagarin took preliminary steps on the path he would follow for the rest of his life—working toward Russia's conversion to Roman Catholicism. He wrote, "I decided to work for the conversion of Russia, to work to uproot the schism of the Slavic populations of Austria and Turkey which are united to the Russian people by the links of language and common origin. As soon as this thought appeared in the form I see now, I understood that an enterprise of that nature went beyond the forces and the limits of the life of one man or even several men. It required nothing less than a religious order to execute it."[50]

Here are the seeds of Gagarin's decision to enter the priesthood. His decision was driven primarily by the conviction that the assistance of a religious order would be required to achieve his main goal of converting Russia. Gagarin did not seek the priesthood as an end in itself, but as a means to an end—the salvation of his homeland.

Despite his effort to prevent discovery of his conversion, Gagarin confessed to Ravignan on 18 September 1842 that news of his acceptance of Catholicism had spread through those who had heard of it in Paris. "One young man who had not seen me for three years, stopped me in the middle of the road to ask me if it was true that I had changed religions."[51] Gagarin asked Ravignan's advice on whether he should remain in Russia or return to Paris. He wrote, "I know that I should take into great consideration both the age and the weakness and the fragility of my parents; but take also in consideration the state of my soul. . . . It is not my will but that of the Lord that I wish to follow; that is why I ask you to pronounce a decision: I will obey, and the obedience will give me calm and courage."[52] Ravignan told Gagarin to leave Russia and return to Paris.

After Gagarin's return to Paris, he began to contemplate entering the Society of Jesus. He was attracted to the Jesuits because of their expertise in missionary activity.[53] Perhaps his sympathies for the society also derived from his reading of Joseph de Maistre. The Jesuits constituted the antirevolutionary elites of Roman Catholicism and, as such, would have appeared compatible with Gagarin's own notions of himself. On 20 April 1843, Gagarin sent a letter to the Jesuit general Jean Philippe de Roothaan (1785–1853) expressing his desire to enter the Society of Jesus.[54] In this letter, Gagarin stated that conversion had sundered his ties to Russia. He declared he had "no other affiliation on the earth besides the church and the Society of Jesus." He added, "[it would be] too wondrous if one day I could be employed to preach that faith [which has been] abandoned by my compatriots, to those numerous Slavic populations whose affinity of language tends to hold in the same path of error as Russia and whose same affinity [of language] may permit me to open the way of truth [to them]."[55] Ravignan supported Gagarin's request and wrote to Roothaan that Gagarin "is a privileged, generous, constant, apostolic soul already; I think that God calls him to the Society."[56]

Roothaan responded to Gagarin on 13 May 1843. In his letter, he wrote "All that you told me, Prince, concerning your sentiments, your dispositions, and your desires, bear obvious signs of the spirit of God at work." Roothaan suggested that Gagarin make a retreat to determine the will of God on this matter.[57]

Gagarin's parents were deeply disappointed by his conversion and his decision to enter the Jesuits. His mother wrote, "I have suffered. . . . I do not hide it from you so that you will have pity on me! At least do not rush events, nor precipitate them."[58] On 20 April 1843, Gagarin wrote to Roothaan that "the profound sadness that my abjuration has caused them, has only made them more remote from the Holy Catholic Church."[59] His parents were anxious for several reasons. They knew that converting to Roman Catholicism meant Ivan Sergeevich would be punished severely by the Russian authorities; this punishment would only increase if Gagarin were to enter the Society of Jesus.[60] If Ivan Sergeevich were to escape punishment by remaining in Western Europe, his parents might never see him again. Still, the Gagarins reconciled themselves to their son's decision. Gagarin's father wrote, "You are far from your parents, but God is with you. . . . The sadness that I feel [over your conversion] does not efface the consolations that God has given me. . . . The first and greatest is the conviction that His mercy is equal to His power. Persuaded that He does and wishes every good for His creatures, I feel a great consolation in accepting from His hand all that He sends me."[61]

Gagarin loved his parents and hoped to lead them to Roman Catholicism.[62] The sadness that he felt he was causing his parents made his decision to enter the Jesuits even more difficult: "It seems to me that sometimes I may have more difficulty breaking the bonds of the world than I had anticipated; but I trust in the source of the Divine Providence; if God wishes the sacrifice, He will give me the strength to do it."[63] Gagarin saw his parents in Germany one last time in 1843.

In addition to the difficulties Gagarin had with his parents, both he and the Jesuits foresaw political difficulties stemming from his decision. They feared that his entry into the Jesuits might cause diplomatic tension between the Russian government and the French government, since the Russian government might attribute Gagarin's apostasy to French influence. To obviate this danger, Gagarin offered to accept a position in the Jesuits outside of France.[64] Roothaan decided otherwise. He wrote, "It is entirely natural that he [Gagarin] belong to the Province where he was received and in which he will make his novitiate, that is to the Province of France. The good Lord without a doubt will one day take pity on this unfortunate Russia; I am not surprised that He has now begun to prepare zealous missionaries. The vocation of the young prince demonstrates the truth of this consoling thought."[65]

On 12 August 1843, Gagarin entered the Society of Jesus and became a novice at the Jesuit center at St. Acheul.[66] Ravignan's notes provide details on the process leading up to Gagarin's entry into the Jesuits:

> We sincerely sought the will of God alone; although we may exercise our discretion and although we retain the liberty of conscience, the rules of the Society specify precisely how to proceed when pondering a vocation. . . . I have accordingly referred to the Book of the [Spiritual] Exercises; that holy book which our blessed father Ignatius bequeathed us. I have done no more than divide its pages into convenient portions. . . . The holy prudence of the Institute directed and instructed me, and six whole days of preparation and prayer were required. . . . I can still feel astonishment, struck by the abundance of calm grace and freedom of action that were secured under the influence of meditations of the most serious character. It seemed to me that all was settled. I met with nothing but marks that the final decision would be most reliable and perfect. St. Ignatius has himself pointed out these marks in his admirable rules on the Discernment of Spirits and on the Election of a State of Life. Then I set before our young friend [Gagarin] the full seriousness of the course he was

> contemplating. I drew his attention to all that the question involved, and I left him alone with God himself for twenty-four hours, without speaking to him, or even seeing him. . . . This morning, after Mass and Communion, he brought me his final decision in writing. After reading it attentively, I should be false to my conscience if I did not recognize in him a true vocation.[67]

Gagarin himself, in a later sermon preached to students at the Chapelle-Saint-Mesmin (Orléans), noted that God "desired that I become a priest, so that sinners might come to me with utmost confidence, so that they might open their hearts more freely, so that they might find in me a man who understands their troubles, who is not surprised at their weaknesses, who might cry with them over their infidelities and their ingratitude, who has in his heart an inexhaustible treasure of indulgence."[68]

One reason why the Jesuit order appealed to the Russian elite has already been mentioned: the Orthodox church had never developed a systematic theology, whereas the Jesuits represented a robust apologetical tradition. Gagarin hoped the Jesuits could bring the fruits of Roman Catholicism to Russia. He was also drawn to the society by Ravignan's charisma. In joining the society, Gagarin became part of a wave of new Jesuits in France. Between 1751 and 1836, 607 new novices entered the society; between 1837 and 1863, the number of new novices was 1,197.[69] Increasing traditionalist sympathies among the Catholics in France was certainly one reason for the increasing number of novices; a second and connected reason was the ongoing Catholic reaction against the anti-religious, revolutionary tendencies of the French left.

Other Russians soon followed Gagarin into the Society of Jesus.[70] The first was Ivan Matveevich Martynov, who entered the society on 12 September 1845 and would later become one of Gagarin's main collaborators.[71] He was followed shortly afterward by Stepan Stepanovich Dzhunkovskii, who became a Jesuit on 19 September 1845,[72] Iulii Konstantinovich Astromov on 8 November 1846,[73] Evgenii Petrovich Balabin on 27 June 1852,[74] and Pavel Osipovich Pierling on 5 December 1856.[75]

Gagarin's entry into the Jesuits caused great concern among the Russian Catholics in Paris. Jesuit father Clémént Boulanger wrote to Roothaan that "There is a great fear in the Russo-Catholic colony in Paris, among the new converts especially, that the Emperor will come to know of the conversion and the vocation of Father Gagarin, that his fierce anger will fall on the new converts, [that he will] send them the order to return to Russia."[76] As will be seen later, Nicholas I did learn of Gagarin's actions (as well as those of the other Russian Jesuits). Although angered by Gagarin's apostasy, he did not punish the other Russian Catholics.

Gagarin's actions prompted Ivan Aksakov to reflect on the phenomenon of Russian conversions to Catholicism, "As a general proposition, one can say the passage of Russians to Latinism is rarely the result of free conviction, more often it is a consequence of wholesale ignorance of the doctrine of the Orthodox church; besides, the Roman preacher does not actually *convert* individuals, he *seduces* them to Romanism."[77]

Some of Gagarin's friends, for example, A. I. Turgenev, tried to reconvert him. Turgenev visited Gagarin at St. Acheul on the 27th and 28th of September 1844. In his diary entry of the 28th, he wrote, "Seven o'clock at St. Acheul. Gagarin was waiting for me; he prepared the room, fire, chocolate, and coffee. We drink as friends in the hall. . . . Gagarin [talks] about [Barbara Juliane] Krüdener and [Aleksandr Khristoforovich] Benkendorf; apparently, he even hopes to convert him [Benkendorf]!![78] [He talks] about the Virgin Mary, about Schelling. . . . father and mother; tears well up."[79] In order to try to reconvert Gagarin, Turgenev sent him writings of Filaret and Murav'ev. He wrote to Viazemskii that "I wanted to make him an evangelical Protestant; otherwise it would be difficult to remove him from the Roman tenets. If Baron Protasov would send me for him everything coming out about the Russian church, I would deliver him: perhaps!"[80] Ironically, Gagarin tried to convert Turgenev as well by sending him a copy of an apologetic text by the Jesuit Rozaven.[81]

Three other reactions to Gagarin's conversion and entrance into the Jesuits deserve attention. Aleksandr Herzen wrote that Gagarin "fled into Catholicism, in order not to suffocate" in Nikolaevan Russia.[82] Herzen and Gagarin had become acquainted at the gatherings of the Westerners and Slavophiles in Moscow. Herzen's diary entry of 2 November 1844 suggests that he learned quickly of Gagarin's decision to become a Jesuit.[83] Despite sharing hostility toward tsarist despotism, Herzen and Gagarin had taken different paths. Gagarin rejected the path of revolution and atheistic socialism, while Herzen embraced it. Gagarin rejected mass violence, while Herzen rejected Catholicism as a "dead path."[84] Of course, Herzen and Gagarin were not close friends. Herzen said that Gagarin "did not receive a serious education, nor [did he have] talent—although he is intelligent and has a passionate heart." Herzen blamed Gagarin's conversion on this lack of education which caused him to be seduced by Roman Catholic scholarship and led Gagarin to abandon himself to "extinct principles."[85]

Herzen's comments on Chaadaev would have equally applied to his views of Gagarin: "It [Catholicism] formally contained all that was lacking in Russian life which was left to itself and oppressed only by the material power, and was seeking a way out by its own instinct alone. The strict ritual and proud independence of the Western church, its established limits, its practical applications, its inimitable self-assurance and its claim to resolve all contradictions by its higher unity, by its eternal *fata Morgana,* and its *urbi et orbi,* by its contempt for the temporal power, must have easily dominated an ardent mind which began its education in earnest only after reaching maturity."[86]

Still, according to N. P. Antsiferov, Gagarin made enough of an impression on Herzen to be included as the hero of the unfinished story *Dolg prezhde vsego.*[87] Antsiferov argued that there are enough similarities between the characters of Anatol' Stolygin in Herzen's story and Gagarin to justify the assertion that Herzen had Gagarin in mind when he wrote the text. Like Gagarin [in the mind of Herzen], Stolygin did not receive a serious education. Both Gagarin and Stolygin were converted to Catholicism by Jesuits.[88] Antsiferov also pointed to the similarity between Stolygin and a member of *Les Seize,* Stolypin. Antsiferov's argument was supported by M. P. Alekseev.[89]

Gagarin and Herzen did keep in touch after Gagarin's conversion. Herzen advertised Gagarin's text *Liubopytnykh svideitel'stv o neporochnom zachatii bogoroditsy* in his journal under the title "*Vol'noe russkoe knigopechatanie za granitsei.*"[90] In 1862, Gagarin sent Herzen a picture of Chaadaev and a copy of Gagarin's publication of Chaadaev's selected works. He wrote Herzen that "I know how distantly we are separated, but the memory of Chaadaev and your and my sincere affection for him serves between us as a bond; and it seems to me, this bond, if examined closer, is not the only one; in the face of evil and loathing, you do good and moral things. If you sometimes attack that which deserves neither your reproach nor your opposition, you do so, I am convinced, because in the heat of battle, you do not see clearly."[91]

I also wish to note the reaction of the Polish member of Gagarin's *Les Seize,* Korczak-Branicki. Korczak-Branicki praised Gagarin's conversion. He wrote that "Nothing kept you from obeying the voice of your conscience: neither the sacrifice of your vast fortune, nor perpetual expatriation, nor even the reproach of apostasy that most of your compatriots threw in your face."[92]

Viktor Balabin, who replaced Gagarin at the Paris mission when Gagarin went to Vienna in 1842, commented concerning Gagarin's novitiate, "If one is to believe the constitution of the Jesuits, published last year by Michelet and Quinet, novices are employed in menial functions inside the rectory; there are those who have the ineffable honor to sweep the rooms, the stairs, to prepare the soup, etc. . . . Forgive me, dear friend, but, at this image my blood freezes from horror! For my part, I sincerely and strongly regret what I regard as a deplorable aberration by one of the most cultivated spirits of our youth."[93] A. I. Turgenev wrote that Gagarin was "now at St. Acheul, fulfilling the duties of a cook's helper [half-dead] after having decided to give freedom to 3,000 serfs, leaving them in the care of a stranger and a weak father."[94]

The Russian government did not take Gagarin's actions lightly. Russian nationalists considered Orthodoxy an integral component of Russian identity. In their view, Orthodoxy was the one true religion instituted by Christ. Russia was the protector of Orthodoxy, the only truly Orthodox nation. For Russian nationalists, Catholicism was the antithesis of Orthodoxy.[95] The Catholic West was viewed by Russian nationalists as a violent and implacable enemy of the Russian people. The Jesuits, who were despised by many in the West, were viewed by many Russians as the epitome of Roman Catholic aggression and deception. Since their expulsion in 1820, no Jesuit had been permitted to reside on Russian soil. Tsar Nicholas I himself wished Orthodoxy, Autocracy, and Nationality to be the guiding creed for all his subjects. Furthermore, Russian law prohibited conversions. Therefore, Gagarin's decision to convert and enter the Society of Jesus was seen as a betrayal of the Russian state and nation. First, Gagarin had left Orthodoxy for the heretical religion of the West. Second, he had shifted his allegiance from the tsar to that of Rome. Third, Gagarin had chosen to live in France rather than to return to Russia and face his deserved punishment under Russian law.

The first indication of the government's displeasure was in 1845, when Gagarin's brother-in-law, General Sergei Buturlin, publicly denounced him. Buturlin had heard of Gagarin's conversion and wrote to him asking him to come back to Russia. Gagarin refused Buturlin's request. Buturlin used Gagarin's letter in order to convict him in the eyes of the Russian public and to gain the support of the government. Buturlin appealed to Nicholas to hinder "the transmission of large Russian capital abroad into the hands of the Jesuits."[96] Gagarin's father believed that Sergei

Buturlin deliberately wrote this letter to provoke a hostile response to Ivan's actions. He wrote, "To his [Sergei Buturlin's] hateful and violent character he joins an audaciousness which augments his deceit and shows his folly."[97]

Sergei Gagarin was sending Ivan money from the Gagarin estate.[98] Since Sergei Buturlin was married to Mariia Gagarina, the only surviving daughter of Sergei and Vavara Gagarin, and since Ivan Sergeevich was the only son of Sergei Gagarin, Buturlin knew that if Ivan were disinherited, that he, Buturlin, would gain control of the Gagarin estate. Motivated by greed and a hatred of the Jesuits, Buturlin wrote to Mariia and demanded that Ivan Gagarin be punished for his crimes against Russia:

> I propose a property settlement that is just and equitable. I would have the place of your father concurrent with the arrangement that I propose, drafted by hand, an agreement privately witnessed . . . but with the signatures of respectable sources, such as Volkov, Chertkov, the marshal of the nobility, and two or three others, among them the confessor of your father, by which agreement you would promise under oath, praying before these witnesses . . . to make restitution to Ivan of all the property that he would also return to you . . . if Providence should direct that he return to Russia and enter the bosom of the Orthodox church . . .
>
> Your brother, a Catholic priest and Jesuit, an enemy of our Holy Church and our institutions, has rights to nothing, and to give him anything would be a crime of treason, since the property would [in fact] be not given to him, but to a foreign monastic order. I remain and will always remain in seeing this as an outrage and an injustice without equal.[99]

Loss of inheritance was not the only price that Gagarin paid for his actions. The Russian government also took steps to punish him and the other Russian Jesuits. Gagarin, Martynov, Dzhunkovskii, and Balabin were sentenced for "unauthorized residence abroad and entering into a monastery of the Jesuit order."[100] According to Article 354 of the criminal code, Gagarin and the other Russian Jesuits were to be "deprived of all rights of [noble] status, recognized as eternally exiled from the boundaries of the Russian State and in the event of their unauthorized residence in Russia, to be banished to Siberia for perpetual exile." Nicholas approved this sentence on 2/14 December 1853 for Balabin and on 25 February/9 March 1854 for Gagarin, Martynov, and Dzhunkovskii. If Gagarin's decision to convert and enter the Jesuits caused a sensation, so did his sentence. V. I. Shteingel', in a letter to I. I. Pushchin, wrote, "Have you heard: four junior officials—Prince Gagarin and Balkashin [sic], Martynov, and Dzhunkovskii, son of a privy councillor, went abroad, found themselves in Paris, in Roman Catholicism, and finally in the Jesuit order. They have been deprived of their rights and exiled from society; should they return to Russia exile in Siberia awaits them. About that, see the ukaz, recently published; it could not be believed."[101]

By choosing to enter the Jesuit order, Gagarin had lost his inheritance, he faced exile to Siberia if he returned to Russia, he was rejected by family members, he would never see his parents again. Despite all of this, Gagarin never rejected his homeland and continued to love it. He wrote, "My heart bleeds profusely when I think about Russia. I ardently love Russia; but no one can understand my love, no one can credit it; because I do not love her as a son, proud of a beautiful mother; but as a son, clearly seeing the deadly illness in her blood."[102]

In his desire to serve Russia, to make her an equal of the nations of the West, Gagarin identified the source of Russian inferiority vis-à-vis the West as Russia's separation from Rome. He came to believe that Orthodoxy had separated itself from the dogmatic truths of the West, particularly papal primacy; thus, Russians had separated themselves from God's established church. Arriving at these conclusions through the influence of Schelling, Chaadaev, Svechina, Ravignan, and others, Gagarin was forced to either remain tied to the (perceived) errors of Russian Orthodoxy and the Russian government or to completely move into the Roman Catholic camp at the expense of separation from his native land. Gagarin chose the latter.

Gagarin chose obedience to God's will, as he understood it, over nation, parents, friends. But he hoped one day to bring friends, family, and his fellow Russians back into union with Rome. To realize this hope he joined the Jesuit order.

The disappointment of his family and friends and the hostile response of the Russian government were not surprising for Gagarin and did not cause him to change his mind regarding either his own need to be in union with Rome or the need of his country to follow that example. Nor did hostility to Gagarin end his deep love for his native land. He chose to work for Russia's reunion with Rome, not out of a traditional Jesuit desire to convert all lands, but out of a personal desire to be of service to Russia itself. Russia was Gagarin's "sick mother," and just as he loved his real mother enough to pray for her conversion, he could do no less for the land of his birth.

CHAPTER THREE

The Beginnings of the Mission to the Slavs

> The force of Providence upon me, the insights that I have drawn from the diverse retreats that I have done and that the voice of obedience has always confirmed, all make me think that, if I am faithful to the designs of the mercy of God on me, I shall be employed in one manner or another for the great work of the conversion of the Slavs and the extinction of the schism.
>
> Since the resolution I have made with the approbation of my superiors, I can consider as my mission an apostolate to the Slavs; I shall therefore prepare myself to be an apostle to the Russians and the Slavs. That is for me the glorification and the service of God: to make God known, loved, and served by all peoples, to work for their salvation and their perfection—that is my mission.[1]

Ivan Gagarin began his Jesuit novitiate at St. Acheul, near Amiens, on 12 August 1843.[2] From the beginning, he felt called by God to work for Russia's conversion. While aware of the sorrow he had caused his parents and knowing that the "doors of Russia were closed" as a result of his conversion, he wrote, "it is impossible to believe that my great attraction to the religious life comes from a human source."[3]

Gagarin participated actively in the life of St. Acheul. In a letter to Roothaan, Jesuit father Ambroise Rubillon wrote, "I must speak about dear Gagarin. The care of the lights, the writing of the *Diarium*, the consultations and teaching catechism to sixty some prisoners is for him now an affair more important than all his great diplomatic activities of the past."[4] Fellow Jesuit Dzhunkovskii wrote, "My guardian angel was a very pleasant companion, none other than prince Ivan Sergeevich Gagarin. The novitiate did not improve his diplomatic habit of talking about politics and telling anecdotes."[5] Gagarin himself wrote that at St. Acheul "I find incomparably more pleasure than in the sparkling festivals of

Petersburg or among the garrulous and wise of Paris [society]."[6] From 1845 to 1849, Gagarin resided at Laval, where he studied dogmatic theology. In September 1848, Gagarin was ordained into the diaconate. In 1849, he became a priest at the hands of Jean Baptiste Bouvier, bishop of Mans.[7]

Gagarin's correspondence with N. N. Sheremeteva during this period between 1843 and 1849 provides some insight into his thinking about the Slavs and Russia. He wrote: "I love to remember Saints Cyril and Methodius and our Russian saints Boris and Gleb."[8] He continued to think that he would return to Russia "when it will be pleasing to God." Gagarin imagined himself to be "a simple, happy soldier in one of the many regiments of the spiritual army of our Lord and Savior."[9]

Already in this first year at St. Acheul, Gagarin submitted to Roothaan his first plan for converting Russia. Not surprisingly, however, this proposal was rejected by Roothaan who believed that Gagarin was not yet ready for such a step.[10] On 13 November 1844, at St. Acheul, Gagarin took his tonsure.[11] Sometime in 1844, Father Ravignan put Gagarin into contact with Albéric de Foresta.[12] De Foresta offered Gagarin his first real chance to put his goals into action. In his letter of 22 August 1844, Ravignan wrote, "Here is a precious memorial of de Foresta, scholastic at Vals, fourth-year theologian, deacon . . . he nourishes constantly the desire to work for the conversion of the peoples of the North. I have spoken to him of you, of your thoughts: this dear and holy brother has been quite touched. Send me promptly a word of response and acceptance for him. May you both be blessed if God calls you to the foreign missions!"[13] In a second letter to Gagarin in February 1845, Ravignan wrote, "The excellent Brother de Foresta comes to write me that his house at Vals will furnish you with apostles. Write to him sometime."[14] Gagarin was happy to learn of de Foresta's desires.[15] In his response, Gagarin told de Foresta:

> There are, in effect, three great evils to end, much good to do, millions of souls to save.[16] At some time, it seems to me, Divine Providence will prepare an answer for these vast countries, plunged for so long a time into darkness. Persecution has always extended and affirmed the church of Jesus Christ on the Earth. The source of graces is not lacking and six hundred confessors who moan at this moment under the tyranny of persecutors, send to heaven prayers which fall again on

> those countries in a dew of blessings. Some converts quietly, during these last years, have come to form a nucleus of Russian Catholics.[17] This *pusillus grex* [weak flock] will become, one must hope, the germ of the church of Russia. Obliged to flee and hide themselves, these new members of the church retrace in themselves the history of the Divine infant, flying to Egypt to escape the fury of Herod.[18]

Gagarin told de Foresta, that in working toward the conversion of Russia, they must bear two things in mind: the history of the Greek schism and the significance of using the Russian language. Concerning the first point, Gagarin asserted that the best theological treatment of the schism could be found in Rozaven's book, *L'Église catholique justifiée.* He added, however, that the schism's significance went far beyond theological debate, for, by revolting against the "unity and universality of the church," the Greek church fell into slavery and oppression. This same slavery and oppression now afflicted the Slavs.[19] In Russia and other Orthodox Slavic nations, Gagarin argued, the suppression of the church by the secular power occurred just as it had in Byzantium. Conversion of the Slavs, therefore, would require the liberation of the church from state tutelage.[20] Gagarin told de Foresta any attempt at conversion would require the use of the Russian language.

More specifically, he told de Foresta:

1. pay attention to previous attempts by the Jesuits to convert Russia;[21]
2. look at the historical research on the conversion of the Slavs in Moravia, Bohemia, Poland, Hungary, and Russia; and examine the history of the church from the ninth to the eleventh century;
3. research the Greek schism; study the Greek fathers on this issue.

Gagarin wrote, "The most crucial step is to create an institutional center to coordinate attempts at conversion and scholarly investigations, a center in which such attempts would acquire momentum and life. . . . History is, I believe, the most powerful warrant against the schism."[22]

As a result of Gagarin's suggestions, de Foresta established the *Oeuvre de Saint-David et de Saint-Roman.* While Gagarin did not collaborate with de Foresta in this work, de Foresta had given Gagarin a pretext to clarify his thinking regarding practical steps toward Russia's conversion and the intellectual foundations of his ecclesiology.

In 1845, Gagarin took his first vows of poverty, chastity, and obedience and sent Roothaan new plans for the conversion of the Slavs.[23] Gagarin asserted that his main goal was to save the Russian soul. He hoped that "the time will come when all of Russia takes the Roman faith and the most distant descendants will consider me as a patriarch like Abraham, as a new founder of a pure Christianity in Russia."[24] In *Mémoire sur le schisme des russes,* Gagarin wrote: "Of all the steps that one can take to work for converting Russia and extinguishing the schism of which this country is the principal source as well as the principal victim, one of the most efficacious would be, I think, the foundation of a scholasticate joining Russians, Poles, Bohemians, Dalmatians, Croatians, Serbians, Illyrians, etc., etc.; this scholasticate would be neither Russian, nor Polish, nor Bohemian, but Slav." Those gathered in the scholasticate would use the local vernacular to preach, confess, teach, and write in the Slavic areas of Austria, in the European part of Turkey, in Prussia, and in Russia.

Gagarin argued that the Jesuits should initially focus on the thirty million Slavs outside of Russia, since they could draw on twenty million Catholic Slavs for teachers and apostles. By addressing all the non-Russian Orthodox simultaneously, Gagarin felt, the Jesuits would demonstrate, "the catholic or universal nature of the church." Gagarin proposed the following steps for establishing missions to the Slavs:

1. In all the countries where Slavs live with members of another nationality, such as in Austria, there would be separate and distinct colleges for those of Slavic heritage.
2. Missions would be expanded from Catholic areas to Serbia, Bulgaria, Bosnia, and much later into parts of Russia.
3. The literary movement would be examined as it manifested itself among the Slavs. The Jesuits would work to direct the movement on a Catholic path.

Within the scholasticate, Gagarin proposed:

1. Teaching four or five subjects designed to teach the religious history of Russia and to combat the teaching of the Russian seminaries and universities. Subjects would include history, theology, and apologetics.
2. Reinstituting measures taken by Skarga, Bobola, and Possevino.

3. Study of the Slavic version of the Bible, the use of Slavic in the liturgy, the existence of two rites, the best means of conversion.
4. Preparing a good history of the schism which could be widely distributed.

Gagarin identified some problems that would have to be addressed. First, a knowledge of Slavic languages would be required for some tasks. Second, the Jesuits would have to overcome the mistrust of the Orthodox Slavs toward the Catholic church and the Jesuits in particular. This would be especially difficult in Austria, where the Jesuits were long-time allies of the secular authorities.

In a second proposal, *Mémoire sur le schisme et la nationalité slave,* Gagarin went into further detail on the reasons for working toward conversion of the Slavs. He wrote, "One cannot meditate too much on the links which exist between the Slavic nationality and the schism. These are the two bases on which rest the spiritual and secular authority of the emperor of Russia. By turns cause and effect, each of these three forces—the autocracy, the schism, and the Slavic nationality—exacerbates the [deleterious influence of the] others."[25] Gagarin further asserted that should the unity of autocracy, Orthodoxy, and Slavdom ever be fully realized, it would form the base of a gigantic empire comparable only to the Islamic empire of Mohammed. A schismatic pan-Slavic autocracy would pose the gravest dangers to Europe, since it would cause the suffering of all those nationalities under its yoke. The only remedy for such a problem would be a crusade, a holy war pitting Catholic West against Orthodox East.

For Gagarin, the primary cause of the schism's continuation in the modern world was the subordination of the catholic/universal principle to the national principle. The abandonment of Latin as *lingua franca* had contributed to the growth of nationalist movements. Conflicts between Germans and Slavs had also fueled national desires among both nationalities. Finally, Russia had "an immense national vanity and a profound indifference to the truth." A secondary cause of the schism's continuation was the subservience of the spiritual to the temporal power. In schismatic nations, unscrupulous governments identified the Roman church as their adversary. They feared papal authority, which, Gagarin contended, represented spiritual power free from secular control.

While Protestantism exalted the rights of reason and placed the individual above society, Orthodoxy exalted society at the expense of the individual. Thus, the Orthodox nations lacked the benefits of genuine civilization; they were mired in barbarism, despotism, and slavery. Unfortunately, the inhabitants of schismatic nations, seeking political power and national grandeur, confounded the nation with the church. Rather, they put the national cause "under the protection of heaven," a step that Gagarin considered a grave error, a "vain chimera!"

He advised the Jesuits to work first for the conversion of individuals and to provide an indigenous clergy linked by language and nationality to the flocks that they served. Gagarin called for a "peaceful crusade" using preaching and education among the Poles, Bohemians, Illyrians, and Russians.

Taken together, these two proposals help us to understand the fundamentals of Gagarin's mission to the Slavs. He depicted the schism as a threat to both Slavs and the West. Among the Orthodox Slavs, the schism destroyed the independence of the church and the individual, placing them under a despotic, nationalistic autocracy. This autocracy, identifying national glory with satisfaction of its own expansionist desires, was a threat to the independence of its neighbors and to the universal church. To address these problems, Gagarin called on the Jesuits to enlist missionaries of Slavic heritage familiar with Slavic languages. These missionaries should be prepared to present the laity an accurate history of the schism, its causes and effects, and to make an educated defense of the Catholic church.[26]

Roothaan again rejected Gagarin's plan. He wrote, "Your project seems well conceived, and I desire to begin to execute it. The moment does not yet seem to have arrived; the Savior appears to want to prepare the way little by little."[27]

During the period between 1843 and 1845, Gagarin maintained his connections with other Russian Catholics and received advice regarding the best means to convert his homeland. Svechina encouraged Gagarin: "When, dear friend, in the passion of my hope you dared to call forth thoughts for the conversion of our poor country, I thought that God would not forget such a great compassion and I even began to believe in the possibility of realizing these wishes."[28] Svechina discussed with Gagarin the writings of Theiner on Peter the Great and the reunion of churches, and also problems of nationalism in Russian Orthodoxy.[29]

Gagarin also conducted an extended correspondence with fellow Russian priest, the Redemptorist Vladimir Sergeevich Pecherin (1807–1885).[30] With Pecherin, Gagarin discussed ideas for the distribution in Russia of

Catherine Labouré's Miraculous Medal with a Slavic inscription, problems of Russian nationalism and issues of religious freedom. Like Gagarin, Pecherin found great fault in Orthodox nationalism:

> The poor Slavic people! They are always enslaved: enslaved to despotism on account of politics, enslaved to delusion on account of religion. Thus, is it not a new scourge that God has sent it, this miserable *panslavism* of which you speak! It is the very same national spirit, this narrow national pride which destroys nations. It is a spirit entirely pagan, it is this which makes a people set itself up as a divinity, prostrate itself before the idol of the fatherland, and adore itself; it is this spirit which has separated all the peoples from the Holy See; which has created the national churches—Anglicanism, Gallicanism, the Greco-Russian church, and recently the Greco-Athenian and German Catholic church. May God ever preserve us from this national spirit! Our fatherland is an eternal and unchanging truth: our fatherland is Rome.[31]

However, Pecherin disagreed with Gagarin's view that freedom of conscience might soon be achieved in Russia. Pecherin predicted that religious freedom would remain impossible in Russia "as long as Peter the Great with his politics lives in his successors."[32] Gagarin and Pecherin also discussed the Oxford movement, particularly Puseyism, and whether or not a similar movement could occur in Russia.[33] Pecherin believed that a move away from Protestantism toward Catholicism could take place only in England.

Like Gagarin, Pecherin believed that Russia should unite with Roman Catholicism. In fact, Pecherin asserted that Russia must choose between Rome and death.[34] However, despite the similarities in their desires to see Russia become Catholic, there were important differences between the two Russian converts. Whereas Gagarin saw the Russian empire as a threat to Rome, Pecherin saw it as Rome's possible savior. He wrote:

> The Russians are called to complete the task of the earlier barbarians, to destroy the last remains of the Roman Empire which still languish in Western Europe. The East will yet have the upper hand; its mission is to regenerate by blood and fire the contentious civilization which has corrupted Europe. . . . A new Attila will come at the head of the Slavic hordes, but before the walls of Rome he will recognize another Leo. . . . There will be a great Russian emperor . . . he will proceed to

> Rome. He will kneel at the feet of the Sovereign Pontiff. He will receive homage to his crown, to his Empire. He will make Russia fief of the Holy See. Thus, the great wall of separation will fall, the revolutions will be vanquished forever, the world will be Catholic.[35]

Whereas Gagarin saw the Jesuits as the only religious order that could serve to convert Russia, Pecherin wrote that "The very name of 'Jesuit' is odious to me . . . if someone in Russia identified me as a Jesuit, I would find it shameful and ignominious." Unlike Gagarin, Pecherin opposed the political authority of Rome as an "offense to reason, an injurious sacrilege to the dignity of man." Pecherin supported democracy within the church.[36]

Gagarin was not the only individual who desired the conversion of Russia and worked toward achieving that objective. Abbé Louis-Eugène-Marie Bautain (17 February 1796–15 October 1867) worked with A. N. Murav'ev, whom he met in 1836, to secure religious union by persuading the Roman church to renounce papal primacy.[37] He wrote, "What a beautiful day it will be when the East and the West embrace, renouncing their pretensions . . . one abandoning a spiritual power placed in the hands of a prince of the world, the other renouncing a temporal power placed in the hands of a prince of the church." Bautain's program failed due to papal opposition.[38]

Abbé Hippolyte Terlecki also worked to bring about ecclesiastic reunion.[39] On 4 June 1847, he sent to Pope Pius IX a memorandum entitled *Mémoire sur les moyens de réléver l'église Greco-Slave et sur le rétablissement des Basiliens Greco-Slaves.*[40] In this document Terlecki wrote, "The most dangerous enemy of the Catholic church in our time is the Russian schism. It extends one hand to protect all the heretics and the schismatics of the East while with the other it gathers under its auspices all the Slavs. Unfortunately, the deplorable state of religion in which it has plunged this immense population can only favor the spread of this evil [the schism]." In order to combat Orthodoxy's expansion, Terlecki called for the revitalization of the Byzantine rite among the Byzantine Catholics. Terlecki considered the Byzantine rite invaluable because it conformed to apostolic tradition and enjoyed popular support. He believed that Byzantine Catholic priests might more easily engineer mass conversions than could Roman rite priests. Since secular clergy were mostly married and missionary activity would require a prolonged period of activity, Terlecki believed that religious clergy would play the largest role in the conversion of the East. Terlecki proposed the following:

1. The Basiliens would propagate and affirm the faith in the East through missions, texts, seminaries.
2. Missionaries would serve as curés of parishes.
3. Missions would begin with the Slavs, then spread to the rest of the East.
4. The center of this work would be at Rome. This center would publish texts on the liturgy, dogma, religious controversy, and propaganda.
5. "The spirit of faith, abnegation and devotion the most generous for God, for His church, and for the salvation of souls" would form the basis of the religious education.
6. A trip to the East to find youth appropriate for this congregation.
7. Terlecki himself would pass to the Byzantine rite to gain the confidence of the Slavs.
8. The need for strong papal protection of the Byzantine rite.
9. Full liberty and reparation for the past wrongs done to the Byzantine rite church.
10. Naming a member of the Byzantine rite to the cardinalate and a promise that there would always be at least one member of the Byzantine rite in the Sacred College.
11. Admitting to the calender and offices the saints venerated in the Slav Catholic church and working toward the canonization of "Venerable Josaphat, martyred by the schismatics."
12. Making bishops of certain sees always members of the Byzantine rite.
13. Creating a patriarchal see for the Greco-Slav church.

Terlecki's second memorandum had to do with the Société orientale pour l'union de tous les chrétiens d'Orient, in which he served as vice president.[41] This organization was founded in Rome on 17 June 1847 under Cardinal Giacomo Filipo Fransoni, prefect of the Sacred Congregation of Propaganda. On 1 July 1848, in Paris, it formed a Comité des rites orientaux under the archbishop of Paris. Its charter was to preserve national rites, work for the reunion of churches, defend the Holy Places, and propagate the faith among the Jews and "infidels." This organization regarded prayer as the most powerful means of action, so its members promised to pray for the Eastern Christians, "asking God to maintain in unity those who are now faithful, that he gather the separated and that he touch the heart of the Jews and infidels, in order that there only be one flock and one pastor." The society was placed under the protection of Mary, the Archangel Michael, John the Baptist, St. Andrew, St. Jacob, St. Louis, all patron saints of the Eastern churches, and under all canonized popes who had worked to maintain or restore unity. The society also held public prayers at l'Établissement Slave Catholic, at the Chappelle de Notre Dame de Sion, and in the Collége Arménien. Finally, the society promoted indigenous schools, sent missionaries to the East, published texts in native languages and produced periodical publications. Under the leadership of the titular bishop of Hesbon, Monsignor Jean Félix Onésime Luquet (1810–1848), the society published the *Revue religieuse d'Orient.*

During this period, Gagarin's fellow Russian Jesuit Stepan Dzhunkovskii began his own work toward religious reunion of East and West. On 21 June 1847, Dzhunkovskii wrote a document entitled "Observation sur quelques moyens à prendre pour la conversion des herétiques et des schismatiques."[42] In this text, Dzhunkovskii wrote, "The preparation of devoted men who have an intimate knowledge of the history of the church in Russia can be served by oral apologetics to that end as well as written texts.... One might even press for permission to open a college of the Company in Odessa or even St. Petersburg; the social stratification of the Russians and the danger that the education in Russia will be influenced by German philosophy may facilitate winning this permission." Dzhunkovskii believed that each social class in Russia required a different approach by Catholics seeking to obtain conversions.

Dzhunkovskii noted that since the Jesuits had been instituted "ad defensionem et propagationem fidei," the Society of Jesus had a special responsibility to spearhead Russia's conversion. However, he noted the Jesuits faced problems stemming from Russian nationalism. The masses recalled religious persecutions at the hands of the Poles in the sixteenth century and were responsive to anti-Polish rhetoric. Furthermore, the Russian masses had fallen prey to bad texts from the West, i.e., texts critical of or misrepresentative of Catholic teaching. The masses were also unable to distinguish rite from dogma. Despite these problems, Dzhunkovskii saw opportunities in Russia for Catholics because the law permitted proselytization among the non-Orthodox. Moreover, Catholics held as much political authority as did the Protestants.

In 1853, Dzhunkovskii published a pair of articles in *L'Ami de la religion* describing his views on the reunion of Russia and Rome. The first, "De l'opportunité de travailler actuelement au retour de la Russie à l'unité catholique" appeared on 3 March.[43] In this article, Dzhunkovskii wrote: "We come to prove as we have promised in speaking of *the new crisis of Catholicism in the East and especially of Russia,* that if one has a sincere zeal for the return of Russia to unity and for the conservation of the faith among the Russian Catholics, one cannot fail to find in learning, in charity, etc., the means of reaching this end."[44] Dzhunkovskii argued that the time had arrived to work for conversion. Morals would only be weakened by delay, for Orthodoxy's influence was growing rapidly. A favorable situation for successful conversions also supported immediate action.

Because Dzhunkovskii considered Protestantism more distant from Catholicism than Orthodoxy, he wanted to convert Russian Protestants first to Orthodoxy and then to Catholicism. He argued that converts must first believe in the existence of a true church which, he alleged, Protestants did not. The only solution to these problems for Russia was the conversion of Russia to Roman Catholicism, which meant the acceptance of the fruits of civilization and knowledge. Acceptance would return Russia to greatness, would lead to "honesty in business transactions" and the abolition of serfdom. Rejection of Catholicism would cause Russia to revert to its primitive past, or worse—succumb to revolution, disbelief, or communism.[45]

Dzhunkovskii thought that Russia's conversion should begin with the nobility, whom he sought to proselytize by using French literature. After the nobility were converted, mass conversions in Russia would be possible.

In "Des chances du rétour de la Russie à l'unité catholique sous le rapport de l'état actuel de la littérature de ce pays" on 2 April, Dzhunkovskii continued his critique of Protestant influences in Russia. He called for the translation of Catholic documents for distribution in the Baltic provinces in order to combat Protestant influence. He also recommended publishing in the Russian press pro-Catholic articles representative of historical truth.[46]

The pope himself worked actively for union. In 1847, he established the Society for the Union of All the Christians of the East. On 6 January 1848, under the influence of Niccolò Tommaseo (1802–1874) and Monsignor Luquet, Pius IX issued an encyclical letter to the Byzantine Catholics and Orthodox.[47] Monsignor Innocenzo Ferrieri, titular archbishop of Sidon, was ordered to distribute the letter to as many Orthodox as possible.

In the encyclical, the pope stressed the importance of the East in Christian history. Jesus had appeared in the East; there preaching of the Gospel had begun; and there many holy bishops, martyrs, and saints had lived. However, the pope added, "a great part of the Christians of the East are now separated from communion with the Holy See, and, by this, from the unity of the Catholic church."[48] The pope promised the Byzantine

Catholics to “preserve your Catholic liturgies, which you truly honor though different in certain things from the liturgy of the Latin church.”[49] He then went on to address the Orthodox “because the love of Jesus Christ inspires us to try . . . to seek the lost lambs on the steep beaten path and to aid their weakness so that they finally return to the fold of the flock of the Lord.”[50] The Orthodox would be required to accept papal/Roman primacy. The pope supported his position with references to the scriptures and the writings of the Holy Fathers.

The Orthodox quickly issued a response signed by the patriarchs of Constantinople, Alexandria, Antioch, Jerusalem, and twenty-nine other bishops. They objected to Rome’s distribution of thousands of copies of the encyclical to the Orthodox masses; they saw this as an attempt by Rome to bypass the Orthodox clergy. They called the encyclical “a plague coming from without.”[51] The Orthodox leadership rejected union with a Rome they accused of changing church practice through the failure to baptize by immersion, denial of the communion cup to the laity, use of unleavened bread, exclusion of married men from the priesthood, papal authoritarianism, etc.[52] The Orthodox leadership accused Rome of changing doctrine when it inserted the *filioque* into the Creed, contrary to the decision of the Ecumenical Councils. They said this altered the correct understanding of God by casting doubt on the true nature of the unity of the Trinity.[53] The Orthodox asserted that the church was not founded on Peter but on Peter’s confession that Jesus was the Son of God. They observed that Antioch, not Rome, was the oldest and most esteemed see. Finally, the Orthodox lambasted Roman Catholic evangelization which corrupted the authentic Orthodox teaching and was motivated by a “lust for power.”[54]

Others who worked for union were Father Victor de Buck (26 April 1817–23 May 1876), a Bollandist who worked for Roman Catholic reunion with the Anglicans and the Orthodox, as well as Aleksandr Golitsyn and Fedor Golitsyn.[55]

While there were several Roman Catholics working to establish union between the Catholic and Orthodox churches, the programs and the purpose varied. There were important differences between these proposals and those of Gagarin. Bautain hoped to form a union based on mutual concessions by the East and the West, whereas Gagarin was unwilling to concede papal authority. Terlecki wanted to revitalize a declining religious order (the Basilians), whereas Gagarin wanted to rely on the Jesuits, an order with an established history of success in the area of conversions.

Dzhunkovskii believed conversions in Russia would be easy, whereas Gagarin saw Russia as territory hostile to Rome and believed the first conversions needed to occur amidst non-Russian Slavs. The pope apparently hoped that an encyclical to the Orthodox masses would engender mass conversions, whereas Gagarin knew that the conversion process would take a long time. There were also important similarities between Gagarin's approach and those of the others working for union. They all believed union was not only the will of God but a secular imperative, necessary to obviate revolution and disbelief. All agreed on the need to use the Byzantine rite to promote conversions. All worried about secular control over the Russian church.[56]

Despite Orthodox hostility to the pope's encyclical, Gagarin continued work toward reunifying the churches. From 1849 to 1851, Gagarin was at the Jesuit College in Brugelette, Belgium, where he taught moral philosophy, religion, and history. It was here that he began work on what would later become his most important work, *La Russie sera-t-elle catholique?* In a letter dated 27 December 1850, Gagarin described his teaching. He wrote:

> I am writing a treatise on the church, since I consider all the facts as proofs in favor of our religious and philosophical doctrines or as objections to be met; it is in this spirit that I examine a diverse period. . . . My intention is to make of the course a polemic against the most widespread and widely believed errors of our day, since these errors are almost always based on a historic foundation, I will combat them on that terrain. I sense each day how I am inadequate to my task, but I take up some ideas each day, examine them, and I am educated. For my part, I only wish one thing, that is to continue this double education through teaching and reading during these long years; being forced to reexamine and reread all the same things, I might produce a manual with the indications of the authors to consult, the sources, etc., etc.

Gagarin noted that he wished to use the writings of de Maistre, Balmés, Muzzarelli, Klee, and Wiseman in his course. In the lower classes, the students were required to recite lessons in ecclesiastic history; the upper-class philosophy course would demonstrate the truth and confirmation of Catholic religious and philosophical teaching as opposed to Protestantism.[57]

While at Brugelette, Gagarin published a series of articles in *L'Univers* under the pseudonym *La Puséisme moscovite.*[58] The first article appeared on 12 April 1850. In response to the rise of Panslavism espoused by Tiutchev and Aksakov, Gagarin warned of the threat emanating from the Orthodox churches. He claimed that the Slavic Orthodox considered themselves "a new Israel," chosen to bring the truth to a declining Europe. He wrote, "One cannot contemplate the faith that they have in this path, with what confidence they have calculated the day and hour of this triumph."[59] Gagarin added that the national basis of Slavic Orthodoxy served as a justification for territorial expansion. In his second article, on 15 April 1850, Gagarin criticized the religious "reforms" of Peter the Great. Although institutional changes in the Russian church were necessary, Peter had not chosen the path of genuine reform but that of "bloody and impious" revolution. Gagarin wrote, "If, instead of shaving off beards, which is puerile, and chopping off heads, which is horrible, he had worked sincerely and seriously toward the reunion of churches, he would have ended the religious schism, the schism which has held and which continues to hold Russia separate and distant from European civilization." Gagarin also stressed the benefits of church reunion: Russia would preserve its discipline, liturgy, rites, and receive the benefits of Western knowledge. Furthermore, the Russian church would acquire independence from the state. Religious unity with the West would increase the prestige of the Slavs.[60]

In 1851, Gagarin went to Notre Dame de Liesse for his tertianship.[61] On 25 August, he submitted a new type of proposal for the conversion of churches entitled *Union de prières pour la Conversion de la Russie et l'extinction du Schisme chez les peuples Slaves.* Gagarin began this text by writing, "One prays for the conversion of England, we see every day the fruits of salvation that these prayers provide; why do we not obtain the same results by praying for the conversion of Russia and the extinction of the schism among all the Slavic peoples? What hopes could not be conceived for the church, in Europe, in Asia, in the entire world, if Russia and England were Catholic?"[62] Gagarin wanted to establish places of education for men and women; to organize among the Catholic Slavs associations such as Confraternities of St. Vincent de Paul and living rosaries; to propagate good books; to republish out-of-print texts; to make translations; to establish Catholic journals in Slavic dialects; and to establish new libraries.[63] He placed this work under the guidance of Saints Cyril and Methodius. Gagarin even urged the Orthodox to pray for union with the

Catholics.[64] Finally, he assured that there would be no need for a change in rite in order to achieve his goal.[65] Gagarin's archives suggest that this brochure was distributed in Brussels and attracted some measure of attention among the Belgians.[66]

The August 1851 proposal was the first occasion when Gagarin referred to the need for journals and libraries to facilitate unionist activity. When he suggested this idea to Roothaan, the latter responded by asking for more details.[67] Unpublished documents in Gagarin's papers make it possible to ascertain the types of journals which interested him. In one undated document, he wrote, "For a long time I have thought that a journal was lacking in Europe. . . . I would like that the title be *Nouvelles de Russie* or something similar."[68] He wanted to publish this journal in French. It would contain the principal articles of the Russian press in translation or extract; the principal correspondence and articles relating to Russia from the French and Belgian journals; translations of important articles from other Western European journals; and editorial pieces responding to other journals. Gagarin's proposed journal would examine the opinion of Europe on Russia and the opinion of Russia on Europe. This was the seed of an idea which would later come to fruition in *Études de théologie, de philosophie et d'histoire.*

The new proposal suggests that Gagarin was expanding his audience from the Slavs to the general European public. The journal was to be published in French, not a Slavic dialect. Its audience would most likely be Western European and Roman Catholic. The planning of the journal proves Gagarin had recognized that union between churches would require persuading Roman Catholics as well as Orthodox Christians. His sensitivity to this point explained his assurances to the Orthodox that union with Rome would not mean a change in rite: he knew that past Roman efforts to Latinize the East had not respected the integrity of the Byzantine rite.

In November 1851, Gagarin undertook a retreat at Notre Dame de Liesse. At that retreat, he meditated on the means necessary to obtain Russia's conversion. He wrote that he would propose to his superiors such things as the publication of a life of Pope Nicholas the Great, a life of Josaphat Kuncevich or some other saint who had worked for union. He vowed to combat schism and "all the other sins that followed it." He argued that the schism was a sin against charity; since it involved rebellion against the pope, it was also a sin against obedience.[69]

From 1852 to 1853, Gagarin lived at the Jesuit College on rue de Vaugirard 391 in Paris where he acted as superior.[70] He was asked by nine young men who were former students from Brugelette to serve as director for the newly founded association of the Congrégations de la Sainte Vierge. The congregation took the title of *Sancta Maria, auxilium christianorum.*[71] It organized itself according to the rules of congregations blessed by the popes. Its first meeting was 5 December 1852. Gagarin directed the association for seven years, except for one year when he was at Laval. He continued to direct the association even after he moved to the École préparatoire de Sainte-Geneviève (rue de Postes) in 1853. Later the congregation moved to rue de Sèvres (1867). By 1857, the association included a hundred members. At Sainte-Geneviève, Gagarin founded another association devoted to Mary that had three hundred members.[72]

From 1853 to 1854, Gagarin returned to Laval where he taught Jesuit scholastics as a professor of ecclesiastic history. A note from Father Armand Jean in Gagarin's archives provides details on this period. Father Jean noted that Gagarin's lessons were "very creative and interesting."[73] His lessons examined the origins of the Greek schism and the current status of religious practice in Russia. His principal points of criticism against Orthodoxy were those that would later be published in articles in *Études* and in *La Russie sera-t-elle catholique?* These included the social disrepute of the rural Orthodox priest, mistaken popular adoration of the tsar, the Russian law's mandate to reveal the secrets of the confessional when crimes against the state were at issue, the differences in religious practice between the Russian elite and masses. Father Jean mentioned that, while Gagarin was highly critical of Russian religious practices, he deeply loved Russia and the Russians. During the Crimean War, if the Russians were beaten, Gagarin was sad. If the Russians obtained a victory, "the old blood warmed and only the refinement which was strong in him and fear of offending the French prevented him from rejoicing quite loudly." Jean also noted that Gagarin loved France "as his second country," and he also liked the Austrians and the Germans. However, Gagarin despised the Italians, even those of Rome and the pontifical court.[74]

At Laval, Gagarin became acquainted with the Anglican priest William Palmer (1811–1879) of Magdalan College, Oxford University.[75] During his novitiate, Gagarin had read Palmer's works on the procession of the Holy Spirit.[76] We do not know when Gagarin and Palmer first met, but Palmer referred to him in a letter to Alexei Khomiakov in 1853.[77] Like Gagarin, Palmer opposed the subjection of the Russian church to the crown and urged the restoration of the patriarchate. In his major work, *Dissertations on Subjects Relating to the "Orthodox" or "Eastern-Catholic" Communion,* Palmer urged reunion between the Orthodox church and Rome through an ecumenical council. He claimed that religious union would help the tsar win the allegiance of his Roman Catholic subjects and would put the tsar into a position to act as emperor of a united Christendom. Palmer wanted to eliminate civil control over the Russian and Greek church hierarchy. He also called for union with the pope. He thought this union would offer Rome military protection against the threats from Protestantism and democracy.[78]

In an unpublished archival work, "Notes sur les tentatives de réunion entre l'Église russe et l'Église anglicane," Gagarin discussed the failure of Palmer's attempts to promote ecclesiastical union between England and Russia.[79] In an article entitled "Varietés" in *L'Univers* on 24 April 1853, Gagarin reviewed Palmer's book and his proposal for the union of churches.[80] In this article, Gagarin noted Palmer's support of the branch theory and his abortive attempts to receive communion in the Russian and Greek Orthodox churches.[81] He noted that Palmer's text showed the important points of discord between the Greek and Russian churches over the baptism of heretics and the problems of ecclesiastical servitude in the Russian church. Gagarin claimed that Palmer's ideas on reunion would do much good in Russia, "if it wished or if it could adopt them." He further claimed that, if Palmer's program were ever realized, "the barriers which separate today the Russian church and the Roman church would fall in the same blow."[82]

In his article, "M. Palmer et l'Église russe," published in *L'Univers* on 10 May 1853, Gagarin further analyzed Palmer's program of union through an ecumenical council composed of the pope, the Russian tsar, and the Russian bishops. He agreed that under such a union the Russian bishops would obtain liberty from civil authority. The tsar would pacify various religious dissenters in Russia and enhance his influence in Europe. Gagarin warned that if Russia did not seek union with Rome, it would be infected by revolution and unbelief. Only the Catholic church could successfully resist these forces.[83] In these articles Gagarin first posed the dilemma *Catholicism or Revolution.*

Palmer was a very important influence on Gagarin, as we shall see below in greater detail. Palmer's proposal for union by means of an ecumenical council would be repeated in Gagarin's later work *La Russie sera-t-elle catholique?* and in other writings.

On 20 May 1852 a letter of Gagarin referred to his desire to write a life of Father Bobola.[84] Gagarin believed that such a biography would help show the peaceful intentions of Jesuits in Russia. A later letter from Father François Guilherny to Gagarin noted that Gagarin's idea to publish historic documents on the Jesuits was "an excellent idea, in which the realization would be of great interest, if the selection is done by a man of tact and taste."[85] In 1855, Gagarin and Martynov published anonymously a spiritual treasury entitled *Sokrovishche khristianina ili kratkoe izlozhenie glavnykh istin very i ob'iazannostei khristianina.* The treasury was a Roman Catholic catechism that discussed such issues as the Immaculate Conception, the procession of the Holy Spirit, and the role of St. Peter as the head of the church.[86] This work was also the first Catholic catechism in Russian. The publication was in accord with one of Gagarin's earlier proposals to publish materials in Slavic languages which could be used to promote and prepare conversions. The audience for this work was clearly Russian and, in fact, the text was distributed in Russia by Roman Catholic missionaries.

Gagarin also began to look at the Orthodox and Byzantine rite Catholic churches in the Middle East. In 1855, Gagarin, Charles Lenormand, and Baron Augustin Louis Cauchy formed an organization called L'Oeuvre des Écoles d'Orient.[87] Xavier de Montclos wrote that Gagarin formed the organization because he was "aware of the advantages to Catholicism posed by the recoil of Russian Orthodoxy following the Crimean War" and by the growth of nationalism within the Turkish Empire. Gagarin wanted to develop Catholic schools in the Middle East to prepare Orthodoxy's return to union with Rome.[88]

At the time of its formation L'Oeuvre aimed to raise money for various religious congregations in the Middle East. Lazarists worked in Egypt, Syria, and Constantinople. The Jesuits had a small seminary for the formation of Maronite clergy in Lebanon. The Sisters of Saint Vincent de Paul were in Alexandria, Beirut, Smyrna, and Constantinople. From 1855 to 1856, L'Oeuvre played a small role. Sums acquired were not more than sixteen thousand francs.[89] In 1857, through the influence of Ravignan and Gagarin, Charles Martial Allemand Lavigerie (1825–1882) became director of L'Oeuvre. Gagarin wanted someone with a large appeal who could raise money. With Lavigerie, L'Oeuvre spread to Belgium, Italy, and Ireland. Between 1859 and 1860 it raised sixty thousand francs. After the massacre of the Christians in Lebanon in 1860, L'Oeuvre raised several million francs to aid the victims' families.[90]

Gagarin returned to issuing grand proposals for reunion with his "Notice sur l'action de la Société de Jésus sur la conversion de l'Orient et notamment de la Russie" (1855).[91] Gagarin began his proposal with a brief historical analysis of Russian church history. This was the first proposal by Gagarin to analyze the history of the schism in Russia. The inclusion of this analysis was probably a spin-off from the courses Gagarin had taught at the Jesuit colleges. He asserted that Russia had once belonged to the universal church and had been in union with Rome. While the proposal itself did not elaborate on this argument, Gagarin's notes clarified his emerging views on Russian religious history.

Of course, Gagarin's conversion to Catholicism came largely as a result of his belief that the Catholic church had been the source of Western civilization. He lamented Russia's separation from that source. In his notes on the history of Russia, Gagarin wrote, "Russia is situated between Europe and Asia. To speak properly, it has never been integrally part of one or the other, but has oscillated between the two."[92] Russia's initial ties to Europe could be seen in a comparison of the genealogies of prominent Russian families and by studying intermarriages between Russian and Roman Catholic nobility where neither spouse changed religion. Gagarin divided his research into an early period that spanned the late tenth century to the early thirteenth century and a late period that extended from the seventeenth century to the nineteenth century. In the early period, he examined intermarriages between the princes and princesses of Scandinavia and Russia. He noted that no spouse had to abjure his or her religion, even though Scandinavia was religiously tied to Rome and Kiev was tied to Constantinople.[93] For Gagarin, this demonstrated that the Russian/Ukrainian church maintained its unity with Rome during this period.[94] The intermarriages also demonstrated that "Hellenism was completely indifferent and foreign to Russia," that is, that Russia did not follow a path of hostility to Rome as Constantinople did.[95] During this period, Kiev's unity with Rome kept it free from the despotism that would come later when the tsars moved Russia into the Asiatic sphere.[96]

Despite Russia's earlier unity with Rome, it was now in schism. However it should be noted that Gagarin, despite earlier using the word *schisme* in his published articles, now wanted to "teach our truths, while avoiding all expressions which wound too keenly, such as the word *schisme*. The Russians are, for the most part, only in material error, that is, without recognizing the truth."[97]

Gagarin divided Russia's path from unity to schism into five stages:

862–1015	Idolatrous Russia.
1015–1054	Catholic Russia.
1054–1238	The beginnings of the schism.
1238–1462	The first chastisement of the schism.
1462–1605	The second chastisement of the schism: Asiatic despotism is installed in Moscow.[98]

He urged that works be published in Russian to prove that the Russian church had once been united with the Roman church, demonstrating that the Roman church had not departed from the traditions of the early church, and showing that Saints Ol'ga and Vladimir belonged to the Catholic church.[99]

Gagarin repeated his earlier contention that schismatic Russia had become dangerously expansionist: "the Russians extend the schism more and more toward the West and within a space of fifty years they have advanced their domain to the shores of the Dnieper near Kiev and the frontiers of Vitebsk to the shores of the Dneister and the Bug."[100] This schism was "the most dangerous enemy to the church; it has affected more millions than the heresies of Luther and Calvin and Islam had done in the past two centuries." Gagarin included in these millions the ten million Byzantine Catholics who had been forcibly rejoined to the Orthodox church by Catherine II and Nicholas I.[101]

Now was the time to eradicate the schism. Gagarin argued that the diminution of Islamic power in Europe permitted Roman Catholics to focus their energies on the conversion of the Orthodox; the forced amalgamation of Catholics with the Orthodox in Russia exposed the Orthodox to Catholic theology; and the influence of France on the moral development of Russia opened Russia to Western ideas.[102] Thus, Gagarin wanted to work immediately in Galicia, northern Hungary, Transylvania, Wallachia, Moldova, Bukovina, and Bessarabia.

Union would be facilitated by several means that Gagarin had suggested in earlier proposals. He called for the publication of political, religious, and literary journals; the use of the native language in missionary activity; sensitivity to Slavic culture; and the preservation of the Byzantine rite.[103] Furthermore, both France and Poland would have key roles in the reunion project. The first houses for the Byzantine rite religious would be in Poland, and Gagarin noted, "It is necessary to profit from the immense prestige that France has in Russia to catholicize [catholiciser] the Russians."[104]

Of course the Jesuits would have the primary role in the promotion of union. They had worked earlier to end the schism in Russia; they could exert influence on the upper classes in Russian society; many members of the society were capable of working in the target nations.[105]

During this period, Gagarin and others issued a variety of proposals for promoting the union of churches, from the establishment of missionary societies to the establishment of prayer organizations. Gagarin's own proposals contained several common elements. He viewed the Orthodox as sinners who had deliberately violated God's will by separating themselves from Rome; they were guilty of sins against charity and obedience. He asserted that Russian nationalism had contributed to the schism by emphasizing Russian uniqueness over Catholic universality. The schism had led to barbarism, slavery, and despotism in his homeland: in a sense, Russia had been punished by God for its disobedience. Still, Russians were a threat to other European peoples and would remain so as long as the schism persisted.

Influenced by his contacts with de Foresta and Palmer, Gagarin made a number of concrete suggestions to his superiors regarding the conversion of the Orthodox Slavs. He called for missionary activity, the use of native priests, and vernacular languages for education and publications. He believed that over the long run, Jesuit efforts in Slavic Europe would be successful. He claimed that the conversion of Russia would obviate dangers to the West, restore Christian unity, and also benefit Russia.

The language Gagarin used in his formal proposals for union often conflicted with statements in his private correspondence and the confidential report of Father Armand Jean. Privately, Gagarin presented himself as a faithful, patriotic son of his homeland. Publicly, however, he called Russia a barbarian threat and "the most dangerous enemy of the church." The tensions between Gagarin's private sentiments and public declarations were a consequence of the two different audiences he had to address. He believed his superiors were less interested in saving Russian souls than in averting the Russian threat to Western Europe. Hence, he obediently depicted Russia as an oppressor nation bent on spreading apostasy in the West.

Gagarin advocated a tremendous undertaking, involving the creation of missionary houses throughout Europe, the establishment of publishing centers, and other steps that would have required massive financial and human investments—all without any sign of genuine Orthodox interest in conversion or reunion. He truly believed that the West harbored the one true church and the world's most advanced civilization. He hoped that, if Russians finally came to understand this, they would quickly join the Catholic church. Gagarin's task was to make the Slavs comprehend what he himself had grasped on his personal road to Damascus.

CHAPTER FOUR

Signs of Hope

> Russia will always remain the first of Slavic nations; it will always remain the first of the nations of the Eastern rite. . . . [T]o what place can it not attain within the Catholic nations?[1]

In June 1854, Gagarin requested permission from the new Jesuit general, Peter Beckx, to come to Rome for a discussion of his plan to promote the reunion of churches.[2] Early in 1855, Gagarin sent a similar request to French provincial Father Frédéric Studer.[3] Beckx responded on 24 February 1855, "The conversion of Russia and the extinction of the schism among the Slavs have for a long time been the focus of my prayers." However, Beckx wrote that he had presented Gagarin's proposals to the pope and that they both believed one could only "pray to see what God would prepare."[4] He further added, "Everyone seems to believe that the critical moment approaches. But perhaps the moment in question has already come, and maybe it is time for us to act?"[5] In March of 1855, Beckx approved Gagarin's request to meet him.[6]

Gagarin immediately left for Rome, where he found himself in an optimal situation for his work. He wrote:

> Here I accomplish more in one day than I did in six months at Paris: from morning until night I am immersed in the issues of the Eastern rite, the reunion of churches, etc., etc. Here there are the Jesuit archives, German pamphlets, memoirs, notices, and especially colleagues. Each day I see Pitzipios[7] or Terlecki or Palmer or someone else who speaks on these subjects. The question involves everyone. In Germany, they discuss the reunion of churches, here the question of rites is the order of the day, the *mass of projects* presented to the Pope exhaustes him: but he will certainly select something and the place best chosen in Europe for studying the question, for preparing it, for working for a solution—is Rome.[8]

In his meetings, Gagarin reiterated points from his earlier proposals: the need to use missionaries of the Byzantine rite and the need to do initial work in Austria and Turkey before entering Russia.[9] He wrote that he believed his ideas to be "a major innovation" in the means of promoting church reunion. Due to previous negative responses to his proposals, Gagarin fully expected "to see my proposals rejected, possibly many times, before the evidence finally convinced everyone." Now, although he encountered some opposition, it was "much less than I expected and I must especially remark that the welcome was more favorable the higher up I went."[10] In a letter to Father Augustin Carayon, Gagarin added, "I made carefully conceived proposals which were readily accepted in principle; their implementation is to be left to another generation, but if I do not eat the apples, I must at least sow the seeds and when they have grown a little, keep them from being destroyed by vandals."[11]

Although Beckx responded positively to Gagarin's initiative, he did not approve the establishment of Slavic centers in Austria and Turkey. Instead, Beckx asked Gagarin to establish a journal and a library to work for the conversion of the Slavs. Gagarin wrote to Father Guilherny that:

> Father Martynov and I are discharged of all our other occupations and consecrated entirely to the conversion of Russia; we are charged with forming a library called the *Bibliothèque de S. Cyrille et de S. Méthode*, apostles of the Slavs; this library is to be composed of texts in many languages which are required in our special work; an annual sum of 8000 francs is apportioned for that work and our pensions are taken from that sum; I have the principal direction, Father Martynov is procurer; also we will publish a collection of memoirs, dissertations, brochures, unpublished documents, reprints, translations, etc., everything which relates to the future reunion of churches and is destined to prepare a future council of Florence or negotiations concerning the end of the schism. But as this motivation would be too narrow for France and would be somewhat threatening to Russia, we disguise our intent by speaking of everything which is connected in general to theology, philosophy, history, and literature. The publication should consist of one or many volumes each year, without any obligation, except that it be a journal. . . . Father [Charles] Daniel and Father [Jules] Tailhan are both attached to the work through the Father Provincial, I have even consented to pay them from the fonds of *S. Cyrille* to sustain their work, their publications.[12]

Beckx's letter to Studer on 12 October 1855 provided more detail on Gagarin's project: "You know Father Gagarin well enough to understand how much political-religious events must preoccupy him at this time, and I must say that the situation in Russia, of which my old relations with many persons of that country have made me aware, interests me vividly and has been a frequent subject of serious reflections."[13] Beckx wanted Gagarin, with the assistance of Jesuits in France and the rest of Europe, to establish a library and publish works while waiting and investigating the possibility of establishing missions. The published works were to "prepare hearts and remove prejudice"; to provide information on the schism and on the ecclesiastical history of Russia; and to be handbooks for conversion. Gagarin was to avoid provoking hostility among the Russians; to do so, he would discuss aspects of the Byzantine rite rather than the fundamental errors of the schism.[14] The combination of the library and publications would be called l'Oeuvre des SS. Cyrile et Méthode.

Gagarin established the Bibliothèque Slave, or Musée Slave, in Paris at 18 rue des Postes. The purpose of the library was to make Russia familiar to the people of Western Europe and address the Slavic question, that is, the means of returning the Orthodox Slavs to union with Rome. Gagarin accepted Slavic antipathy toward Roman Catholicism as a fait accompli and aimed only at the "reconciliation of all Slavic tendencies with the condition that there not be any violence to personal conscience." The Bibliothèque Slave was to offer "a practical demonstration of the truth that, whether one is Orthodox or Catholic, one can be a good patriot and that one can love Russia and be faithful to his religion."[15]

Shortly after the establishment of l'Oeuvre des SS. Cyrile et Méthode, Gagarin published his most famous work, *La Russie sera-t-elle catholique?* It appeared on 29 June 1856, the feast day of Saints Peter and Paul.[16] He chose to publish the text at this time because he believed that Russia's defeat in the Crimean War and Alexander II's coronation speech asserting that "everything in the social order rests on religion" guaranteed a receptive audience for his ideas. From the beginning of the text, Gagarin stressed his links with his native land. He noted that "exile has not broken the ties which attach my heart to the country. Profoundly stirred in my soul by its great and noble language, I asked myself what I could do to respond [to Alexander's proclamation]."[17] Gagarin responded by presenting "the idea which uniquely occupied me after my youth and to which I have devoted all my life," that is, the reunion of churches.[18] By reunion, Gagarin meant not the absorption of Orthodoxy by Rome, but reconciliation between them. The Russian church was to maintain its rite and its liturgy.[19]

Gagarin's text was divided into four sections: *le rite oriental, l'Église et l'État, le clergé russe,* and *Catholicisme ou révolution.* He added an appendix containing the decrees of the Council of Florence and the papal bulls of Clement VIII and Benedict XIV on the Byzantine rite. From the beginning, he asserted that the Russian church need not fear Latinization. Gagarin was aware that Orthodox Russians mistrusted the Roman church because of the historical association of *Polonisme* and *Latinisme.* He admitted "that the progress of the Catholic religion is equated in Russia with the progress of the Polish nation, and that, by another association of ideas, all that is favorable to the Polish nation is considered as favorable to the revolutionary spirit."[20] However, Gagarin assured the Orthodox they had nothing to fear, since the popes had repeatedly declared their support for the preservation of the Eastern rite. He cited as evidence Benedict XIV's bull *Allatae sunt* on 26 July 1755; the writings of Innocent IV, Leo X, Clement VII, Clement VIII, Benedict XIII; and most recently the encyclical letter by Pius IX in 1848. In Gagarin's opinion, "the Russian bishops are true bishops, the Russian priests are true priests, who offer truly on their altars the sacrifice of the body and blood of Jesus Christ."[21] Furthermore, Gagarin argued that with reunion, prospects existed for a rollback of Latinization. For, if Russia became Catholic, "without any violence, without any intervention of the Russian bishops, by the sole force of things, the Byzantine rite will make rapid progress and a number of families will pass from the Latin rite to that of the dominant nation."[22]

Gagarin then followed a pattern used in his earlier writings and proposals by stressing the earlier ties between the churches of the East and West. He advocated a return to that earlier unity under the authority of the pope, a unity that the East had broken in two areas: the universality of the church and the independence of the church. Gagarin asserted that from the very beginnings the church of Jesus Christ had emphasized its unity, as demonstrated at Pentecost when the Apostles "preached the same truth in many languages to the representatives of different peoples of the universe that Providence joined at Jerusalem for aiding in this miraculous prediction."[23] For Gagarin, the church's catholicity allowed for and required the comity of all nations within the unity of the church.[24]

Unfortunately, Orthodoxy had succumbed to political influences and national antipathies. Orthodox churches had overemphasized local languages and customs. By exalting the principle of nationality, they had broken the unity of the universal church.[25] As Gagarin would later note, these were "national churches, local churches confined to a particular country or race, rather than expanding their powerful branches over the entire globe; they propagate themselves only through the material support of the nation to which they belong, they are not Catholic."[26]

The Catholic church, in Gagarin's mind, could exist without threatening national particularity, for to be Catholic was to embrace diversity. Furthermore, he pointed to the inherently evangelical character of Catholicism. The Orthodox churches violated his conception of catholicity because, in his mind, they rejected universality. The very terms of "Russian Orthodox church," "Greek Orthodox church," "Serbian Orthodox church" implied the primacy of nationality over religion. Orthodox churches confined themselves within national boundaries and had lost Catholicism's required evangelical properties.

The Russian church, Gagarin wrote, "needs its independence [from the state], it knows this."[27] The submission of the Orthodox church to secular authority began in Constantinople, as the Byzantine Empire began to conflate the affairs of church and state without determining the limits of the two with sufficient precision. The process by which the national church separated itself from the universal church and fell under the control of the political administration Gagarin called *byzantinisme*, because it occurred first in the Byzantine Empire.[28] *Byzantinisme* did not itself constitute schism but was "the cause that produces it, as poison is not death, but causes it." A sign of *byzantinisme* was "the exaltation and the triumph of the Greek church, the Greek empire, the Greek nationality." In the long run, however, rather than assuring the triumph of the Greek church, empire, and nationality, *byzantinisme* caused their ruin.[29]

Despite the fall of Constantinople, Gagarin argued, the Russian church had been able to resist the poison of *byzantinisme* until the fourteenth or even fifteenth centuries.[30] Gagarin argued that the emperors of Constantinople did not have any political authority over the princes of Kiev and that the differences between Slavic and Greek nationality created an entirely different relationship in Russia between the Orthodox church and the government. The characteristics which led to the development of *byzantinisme* in Constantinople did not exist in Russia, therefore "one can say that, for a considerable time, there had been between the Russian church and the Roman church only a purely material schism."[31]

However, this condition did not last. Gagarin blamed the advance of the schism and of *byzantinisme* in Russia on the influence of Greek clergy "who deeply hated the Latin church." According to Gagarin, the end of Russia's ecclesiastical independence began with the fall of Patriarch Nikon, brought about by Tsar Alexei in 1666–1667, and was completed with the acceptance of the establishment of the Holy Synod by Peter I in 1721.[32] Gagarin described the patriarchs of the Orthodox church who accepted Peter's ecclesiastical reforms as *Judases* who had "as always, betrayed the Russian church for gold."[33]

For Gagarin, the true church of Jesus Christ needed to be independent of all secular control. The ministers of the heavenly kingdom could not be subordinate to the ministers of the secular kingdom, for each possessed a particular jurisdiction with prescribed limits. The submission of the Russian church and the creation of the Holy Synod meant, for Gagarin, the establishment of a new church authority not instituted by Christ, but by man. Only union with the pope, the personification of the church's independence, could serve as a means of ensuring that the Russian church would regain its autonomy.[34]

Gagarin, following the ideas of Palmer, argued that union could come through an ecumenical council composed of the pope, the emperor of Russia, and a synod of the Russian bishops.[35] He wrote, "The pontiff who occupies the chair at Saint Peter is animated by the most conciliatory dispositions toward the East. The Russian bishops feel threatened by Protestant and Febronian currents [in Russia].[36] Finally, when did a sovereign more capable of leading such an enterprise come to the throne of Russia?"[37]

While Gagarin was aware of the theological differences between the Russian Orthodox and Roman Catholic churches, he found those differences minimal and "superficial": they could be resolved through an ecumenical council which would "in the eyes of both parties have infallible authority."[38] With particular regard to the *filioque* clause and to papal authority, Gagarin argued that the Roman Catholic understanding of the procession of the Holy Spirit had not been condemned by an ecumenical council and should be acceptable to the East as a "simple opinion" that one could accept or reject. He saw papal authority as necessary to inoculate the body of the church against the poisons of *byzantinisme.*[39]

Gagarin was convinced that the Orthodox clergy desired union. Of course, the lower clergy were often poorly educated in theological matters and very docile toward the national government. Gagarin considered the high clergy—priests, monks, and bishops—to be very learned, to respect the tradition of the early church, and to desire ecclesiastical independence. He assumed that the desire for independence from the Russian state would fuel the desire for reunion with Rome.[40]

In union with Rome, Russia would resolve several problems. First, it would rejoin the source of Western civilization, "the work of the Catholic church."[41] Second, the Russian church would obtain an ally against "the exaggerated pretensions of secular authority" and the emperor would find an ally against "the exaggerated pretensions of ecclesiastical authority."[42] Third, with reunion, Russia would find a defender against the revolutionary tendencies which had infected that country. As Gagarin had argued earlier, Russia had to choose between Catholicism and revolution. Only Roman Catholicism provided a "social principle diametrically opposed to the revolutionary principle."[43]

Gagarin found revolutionary tendencies all over Russia:

> the movement initiated by Peter I introduced into the country ideas favorable to the progress of revolution. Unbelief had already greatly ravaged the Russian upper class prior to the reign of Catherine II; the spirit of her [Catherine's] epoch aided the enyclopedists to weaken the foundations of the social order in France and prepare the triumph of revolution, to dominate the court at Petersburg; at the present time, it can be seen in the countries of Europe among the Voltairians.
>
> Under Emperor Alexander I, the ideas of liberty which were fermenting in the young minds of France, Germany, Italy, and Spain did not remain foreign to Russia and secret societies began to become numerous and powerful. Under the reign of Nicholas, the progress of the revolutionary spirit, though hidden, did not become less rapid or terrifying. German philosophy, particularly the ideas of [Georg Wilhem Friedrich] Hegel—which were the most radical and extreme, was propagated in Russia through the assistance of universal education and the protection of the government.[44]

According to Gagarin, the personification of the revolutionary spirit among the Westerners was Herzen. Though he recognized Herzen's exceptional talent and had a certain sympathy "for this vehement and angry spirit, for that high intelligence and that untamed heart," Gagarin was appalled by Herzen's atheism. Furthermore, whereas Herzen preached the radical program of Alexandre Auguste Ledru-Rollin, Jean Baptiste Victor

Proudhon, and Guiseppe Mazzini, Gagarin decried revolutionary changes of any sort.[45]

Gagarin was even more alarmed by revolutionary Slavophilism and Panslavism. These ideologies promoted the expansion of the Russian Orthodox church in this world. Gagarin saw seeds of violence in the Slavophiles/Panslavists' desire to establish an Orthodox Slav national unity.[46] Furthermore, he argued, in order to be convinced of the revolutionary tendencies "one only needed to see the ease with which these partisans, so vehemently Orthodox, adopt the philosophy of Hegel on the connection between the church and state."[47] He added, "If you compare the old Moscovite party with the party of Young Italy, you will be struck by the resemblance. There as here . . . political, religious, and national unity is pursued."[48] However, Gagarin doubted that the revolutionaries of Italy had ever proposed "anything better calculated to act on the masses and to carry them away." He responded with skepticism to Slavophile declarations of loyalty to the autocracy. He said the Slavophiles would remain loyalists only so long as the autocracy served as a useful tool for uniting Russian Slavs with other Orthodox Christians. "When the moment comes, it will not be difficult to get rid of the autocracy, to find in the principles of nationalism political doctrines that are very radical, very republican, very communist."[49] In fact, Gagarin presented "only one sole barrier" which could oppose revolutionary panslavism—Catholic panslavism which would seek free and spontaneous union with Rome while preserving its own rite.[50]

Gagarin sympathized with the Slavophiles' hostility to Peter I and with their desire to return to a pre-Petrine Russia. Like the Slavophiles, he found Peter's reforms brutal and damaging to his homeland: he called them "antinational" and "anti-Christian."[51] However, Gagarin opposed the Slavophile primacy of nationality, its appeal to the masses, and its opposition to union with Rome. When he said that he wanted a return to a pre-Petrine Russia, he meant a return to the pre-Petrine unity of Russia and the Roman Catholic church.

Gagarin closed *La Russie* with a reference to the benefits that Russia would obtain through union. First, it could obtain the rank of first place among Catholic nations. Second, union would give Russian missionaries the strength to evangelize Asia and repel the advances of Islam.[52]

Gagarin's proposal was innovative in its method and ideas. It was a program for union which did not require Russia's theological conversion, since he saw no theological differences between Orthodoxy and Catholicism. His program justified ecclesiastical union by its political consequences. Union with Rome would protect Russia from revolution. Gagarin's justification for Russia's union with Rome recalled his own reasons for conversion to Roman Catholicism: he cited the historical vitality of Latin civilization and Rome's opposition to revolution rather than Rome's theological position on papal authority and the *filioque* clause. This method was intentional. In a letter to Balabin, Gagarin wrote:

> I have avoided all which could injure and only insisted on that which caters to our poor Easterners. It is by virtue of these motives that I avoided saying that which you wished to see developed or at least indicated—the necessity to belong to the Catholic church to be saved. Tell a Russian that he must absolutely become a Catholic and all the difficulties immediately come to mind: he must renounce his country, family, fortune, future, and immediately his will exerts itself to keep his intelligence from seeing the truth. However, leave in the dark this question of individual conversion, do not speak of what the reader should do, the sacrifices he should make; but speak to him of a concordat, a reconciliation for which the Russian government and Russian bishops should work; this is an act which does not ask of him any hardship or sacrifice, but, to the contrary, will procure great advantages. At peace, he will move without defiance toward the truth, and in any given moment, it is certain that he will think, "but if the Russian government does not fulfill its obligation, is that a reason I will not fulfill mine?"[53]

Gagarin's *La Russie*, despite its innovativeness, was naive in its perspective and presentation. It was preposterous to assume that theological differences which had separated the Roman Catholic and Eastern Orthodox churches for hundreds of years could be resolved at a council in a fashion amenable to all participants. As demonstrated by the 1848 Orthodox response to Pius IX's encyclical, the Orthodox were in no mood to accept the Roman Catholic teachings on the *filioque* or papal jurisdiction. Ecclesiastical union could hardly be built on dogmatic disagreement, and papal jurisdiction could certainly not be relegated to a matter of "simple opinion." Furthermore, as Gagarin knew, his method had been attempted before at Lyons and Ferrara-Florence. The reason it failed then was not a lack of a desire for union among the Orthodox elites, but opposition from the Orthodox masses. Gagarin called for a repetition of those two earlier councils without any indication that the Russian masses were any more prepared for or desirous of union.

Second, Gagarin did not offer the Russian church real independence. He would have had the Russians exchange their secular masters for a papal master. He consciously tried to deceive the masses as to his true intention so as to obtain their support.

Third, Gagarin's invocation of a revolutionary threat was unlikely to persuade the Russian government of the desirability of supporting church reunion. Of course, the Russian authorities fretted about the danger of a peasant uprising, but there is no evidence that the reunification of Orthodoxy and Catholicism would have diminished this peril. On the contrary the last major problem for the Russian crown had come from Catholic Poland in 1831–1832. In 1848, France and Austria, two countries with sizable Roman Catholic populations, had experienced revolutions whereas Orthodox Russia had escaped an uprising. If Roman Catholicism could not prevent the rise of revolution in its own territory, how could it be more successful in Russia? Thus, Gagarin failed to adequately respond to Tiutchev's accusations of Roman Catholic culpability in the spread of revolutionary ideologies.

Although Gagarin had claimed that the Slavophiles paid more attention to secular affairs than to spiritual matters, his own slogan—*Catholicism or Revolution*—presented the same problem. He justified Russia's union with Rome mainly in secular terms. Since he saw no doctrinal differences between Roman Catholicism and Orthodoxy, the advantages of reunion had nothing to do with saving Russian believers.

With regards to Polish Latin rite Catholics, Gagarin's suggestion that many of them would join the Byzantine rite as a result of Russia's conversion could only be seen as an attack on their nationality as well as their religion. Gagarin's hint that the Byzantine rite might spread to the West was offensive to Polish nationalists fearful that Gagarin was willing to sacrifice Polish independence to obtain Russia's conversion.[54]

The publication of *La Russie sera-t-elle catholique?* was celebrated by the Jesuit and Russian Catholic communities. Father Ivan Fiorovich wrote, "I have been confounded and edified by receiving your book. . . . You press your adversary hard with arguments and data that are impossible to reasonably refute, and this is a great merit of your work. Truly the method of attack is completely new." Fiorovich also asserted that Gagarin's book could serve missionaries working for reunion.[55] Ravignan wrote of the book, "You have planted a fertile seed which should produce a great tree.... Truly your brochure has completely satisfied me; I only complain that it is too short a pleasure."[56]

Even Pope Pius IX read and approved of Gagarin's ideas in *La Russie.* Beckx informed Gagarin that "You should be aware that for a long time... the Sovereign Pontiff has been very content with your work on Russia."[57]

The Redemptorist Pecherin wrote, "It appears, my dear Father, that the good God has chosen you to be the valiant and untiring champion of the Catholic truth against the Eastern schism. Continue, under the blessing of heaven, your meritorious and brilliant work. The ongoing transformation in Russia may be greatly facilitated by your writings."[58] Svechina wrote, "Pure love shot through with benevolent zeal permeates each line, and no one will deny to your work a spirit of reconciliation."[59] Fellow priest Grigorii Shuvalov: "The question there is approached from perspectives that neither politics nor mere human sentiments could have inspired. When he [Gagarin] returned to the religion of our fathers fifteen years ago, this noble young man solemnly vowed to devote himself to God and his country. He kept his word."[60] John Henry Newman was also pleased with the work, which "treats of the most important and interesting subjects."[61]

La Russie was translated into German (two editions), Spanish, and Russian.[62] Father Martynov translated the text into Russian in order to use it in missionary activity and to "distribute it in Galicia among the Ruthenians and even the Serbs."[63] The Russian translation appeared in 1859 under the title *O primirenii russkoi tserkvi s rimskoiu* (On the reconciliation of the Russian church with Rome). In his introduction, Martynov justified the translation by arguing, "would it not be strange not to have in our language a book written especially for Russians, particularly one involving a question of such importance—for all are equally affected and no one can remain unmoved."[64]

One of the German translations was done by Baron August Franz Ludwig Maria von Haxthausen (1792–1866), known for his book *Studies on the Interior of Russia.*[65] Deeply sympathetic to Gagarin's work, Haxthausen asserted that it "could be considered as an official church document, the church's first manifesto on a subject regarding a question that interests the entire world, the most important assessment of the time."[66] Impressed by Haxthausen's translation, Gagarin wrote, "It is very important. His name does not arouse any revulsion; under his name my brochure will go to persons who would never have seen it."[67]

In a letter on 26 November 1856, Gagarin introduced himself to Haxthausen. He wrote:

> For a long time I have wanted to write to thank you for the good reception that you deigned to give my brochure as well as for the kind suggestion of your memoir on the means to purify Poland. . . .
>
> I do not, however, have any illusion as to the immensity of obstacles. . . . The greatest of which . . . is that which prevents Emperor Alexander from hearing the truth. . . .
>
> It seems that the time has come to involve public opinion with these questions; the more one speaks of them, the more one discusses them, the more there will be the opportunity to make the truth triumph and the light shine.
>
> Monsieur le baron, Providence has admirably situated you for aiding this great work of reconciliation of churches and for hastening its desired arrival. Of all the writers who occupied themselves with Russia, there is not one who has more understanding than you; and at the same time you have never threatened national pride and have recognized the immense importance that the reconciliation of the two churches would have, not only from a spiritual perspective, but from a secular perspective as well.
>
> Divine Providence has called me to the same work. With all my strength, I urge you to not neglect the formidable resources you have for achieving the end that we propose. I take only the liberty to call your attention to the great role that the Catholic cause can play amidst the present circumstances with a large and continual publicity.[68]

On 18 January 1857, Haxthausen responded with a proposal that Gagarin establish a program for the Catholic German press to follow in its relations with Russia and that Gagarin visit him in the fall.[69] In responses dated 20 and 26 February 1857, Gagarin suggested that he meet with Haxthausen at the beginning of Lent in Brussels, where there is a "priest [Victor de Buck] of our company who is occupied with the question." He added that a meeting in Belgium or Germany would be best as it would avoid the anti-Rome attitudes in France.[70]

Between 11 and 13 March 1857, Gagarin met with Haxthausen and de Buck at Brussels. There they examined means to prepare the conversion of

Russia and judged that the most opportune method was through a daily press, a journal to be edited by Haxthausen in German.[71] By 12 April 1857, Haxthausen had obtained commitments from the bishops of Paderborn, Münster, and Fulda to attend a meeting with Gagarin on the prayer union. He wrote to Gagarin suggesting that the prayer union for the unification of the Orthodox and Catholic churches be put under the patronage of the Virgin Mary and that contact with the Russian bishops be made to establish a similar union.[72] Gagarin responded on 29 April 1857 that while he was in favor of establishing the prayer union and seeking the assistance of the German bishops, he feared that directly asking the Russian bishops for assistance would force them to say no. Instead he urged a more indirect route. He believed that if a prayer union were established among Catholics, it would be possible to suggest in the press that the Russian bishops do the same without requiring them to agree or disagree.[73]

Haxthausen sent copies of *La Russie sera-t-elle catholique?* to the German bishops, and on Pentecost in 1857 Gagarin and Haxthausen met at Paderborn with the bishops of Münster, Hildesheim, and Paderborn. They decided to form an association under the German episcopate to pray for reunion of the churches.[74] On 4 June 1857 at Haxthausen's estate in Theinhausen, in Westphalia, the three bishops signed an agreement to establish an organization called the Union of Prayers for the Reunion of the Holy See with the Separated Christians of the East. The bishops also established a provisional committee and wrote a circular letter to all the German bishops. These actions signaled the birth of a new pious association under the protection of St. Peter—the so-called *Petrusverein*.[75] Branches of the *Petrusverein* were to be established in all parishes. A special revue would treat all the questions regarding the unity of the church. In the autumn of 1857, Haxthausen carried the circular to all the German bishops and to Rome, where he presented it to Cardinals Giacomo Antonelli and Allesandro Barnabo.[76] He also had two long meetings with Pius IX. On 3 May 1858, the pope issued a brief of approbation for *Petrusverein* including indulgences to be granted to those members who prayed for church union. On 21 March 1859, the bishop of Münster, Johann George Müller, promulgated by pastoral letter the prayers which would be used in the association. He chose Eastern prayers used prior to the schism.[77]

Gagarin and others had previously considered founding prayer societies to facilitate union.[78] The *Petrusverein* was the most extensive prayer society for the conversion of Russia yet established. According to the documents of *Petrusverein*, every Sunday, in all parishes of the dioceses in

Germany, adherents were to pray for the reconciliation of the Russian and Orthodox churches with Rome. As Gagarin had previously done in his 1851 proposal for the establishment of a prayer society, he now justified the creation of the *Petrusverein* by noting that similar organizations had been formed to pray for the conversion of England, "Why would we not obtain the same results by praying and making prayer for the reunion of the Orthodox church with the Catholic church?"[79] The *Petrusverein* also called the faithful to a variety of pious activities designed to promote union: "One must pray, one must offer for that intention [for union] masses, communions, novenas, chaplets, penance, offerings, visits to the Blessed Sacrament, all sorts of good works." The prayer proscribed for recitation by the *Petrusverein* was:

> O God, who searches the errors of man, who gathers those who are dispersed, and preserves in unity those who are joined; we implore you to lavish on the Christian people the grace of your holy union, so that it will be given them to reject all division, to be in union with the true pastor of your church and your worthy servant. Through Our Savior Jesus Christ. Let it be. Amen.

Gagarin also wanted to establish a prayer association in France, but this did not occur.[80] Later, as a result of articles published in the *Journal de Bruxelles,* prayer societies were established in Belgium.

Both Gagarin and Haxthausen took the *Petrusverein* and the whole idea of prayer societies one step further, in that they sought to establish a parallel organization among the Orthodox in Russia.[81] They approached the tsar through Grand Duchess Elena Pavlovna, who, though not a Catholic, was sympathetic to Catholic social practice.[82] On 22 August 1857, Haxthausen spent six weeks at Wildbad as a guest of Grand Duchess Elena. There he met with Konstantin Dmitrievich Kavelin, Count V. V. Tarnovskii, and Baron Pavel Dmitrievich Kisselev. He discussed the *Petrusverein* with the grand duchess.[83] Later, Haxthausen sent Elena Pavlovna translations of materials on *Petrusverein* written by Gagarin.[84] In November 1857, Haxthausen spent four weeks at Baden-Baden with the grand duchess who promised to deliver Haxthausen's and Gagarin's requests to Alexander II.[85] Haxthausen also suggested sending a letter to the metropolitan of Moscow, Filaret. If Filaret approved of the *Petrusverein,* he might influence favorably the decision of the Holy Synod. With the synod and the emperor in support, the project would be realized.[86]

Haxthausen and Gagarin had reason to hope for a positive reaction from Filaret. While Filaret did not accept Roman Catholicism as the true church, neither did he condemn it. He said, "I leave the particular church of the West to the judgement of the universal church . . . In that I strive to obey faithfully the spirit of the Orthodox church which begins each office praying not only *for the prosperity of the holy churches of God, but also for the union of all.*"[87]

On 7 March 1859, Haxthausen sent a letter to Filaret.[88] Though signed by Haxthausen, the letter was written by Gagarin. The letter was sent over Haxthausen's name because it was thought that a letter from him might be viewed more favorably by the Russian authorities due to the favorable response to Haxthausen's earlier visit to Russia. Since Gagarin was an apostate, sending a letter under his name was not advisable.[89]

The Haxthausen/Gagarin letter informed Filaret that German Catholics were praying for church unity. It added: "Oh, what a sublime spectacle for Heaven, if all the Russian people, so numerous and powerful, directed at the same time toward God their prayers for obtaining the same grace, especially if they could adopt a formula of that prayer in the same words that we have adopted."[90] The Haxthausen/Gagarin letter justified this request by referring to Alexander II's views that the end of the Crimean War had started Russia on a new path. The letter insisted that the establishment of mutual prayer societies for union was an important part of that future.

Haxthausen/Gagarin acknowledged Russia's interest in preserving its own traditions and rites. They argued that establishing an organization similar to *Petrusverein* would pose no risk to these traditions and rites since the Orthodox would only repeat prayers already spoken in their own services.

Haxthausen/Gagarin concluded the letter by asking Filaret to urge the Holy Synod to adopt their program. "I know the immense authority in which your word is invested and with what respect and veneration it is heard. I do not doubt that such a good and holy cause would easily triumph in the deliberations of the Holy Synod, if it were presented under your name."[91]

Filaret received the letter, then transmitted it to the Holy Synod and to its procurator, Count Dmitrii A. Tolstoi. Filaret preferred not to respond in his own name; he gave that responsibility to A. N. Murav'ev.[92] From the perspective of church unity, Murav'ev was a disastrous choice, for he vehemently hated Roman Catholicism. In his response on 6 June 1859,

Murav'ev argued that the adoption of a parallel organization to the *Petrusverein* was pointless. First, since the Orthodox already repeated these words three times a day at Vespers, Matins, and the Divine Liturgy, "what good is asking authorization to pronounce them again? Repetition three times a day is not sufficient?" Second, Murav'ev argued that praying about the "holy churches of God" would imply that the Roman church was holy, but the Orthodox church could not assert that the Roman church was holy at the same time as it accused it of error. Third, Murav'ev asserted that Gagarin/Haxthausen did not understand the true meaning of the prayer. The reference to the union of churches in the Orthodox liturgy of St. John Chrysostom did not entail the union of the Orthodox with the non-Orthodox; it referred to the preservation of the current union among the Orthodox churches. Murav'ev also took the opportunity to directly attack the Roman Catholic church. He reiterated earlier Orthodox claims of heresy regarding the *filioque* and the Immaculate Conception. He said that the true cause of the schism was Roman error.[93]

Haxthausen wanted to respond to Murav'ev's attack but did not consider himself sufficiently knowledgeable on theological issues. He initially turned to Gagarin. However Gagarin saw no point in engaging in correspondence with Murav'ev, whom "no one takes seriously" and given that he had "many more adversaries more serious than him."[94] Therefore, he turned to de Buck, who responded to Murav'ev in a letter over Haxthausen's signature. In this letter Haxthausen/de Buck asserted that Murav'ev did not truly represent the sentiments of the Russian church. "I never anticipated that his Eminence, Monseigneur Filaret, would make you his secretary, and still less do I believe that you have faithfully expressed his sentiments." Furthermore, Haxthausen/de Buck argued that the very fact that Filaret was unable to respond demonstrated the oppressed condition of the Russian church: "you represent it [the church] as a slave who cannot even open his mouth without the permission of the master; according to you, the lips of priests . . . cannot move in Russia without the permission of the government."[95] As for the issue of the *Petrusverein*, Haxthausen/de Buck again asserted that there would be no inconvenience in reciting the prayer one more time in order to obtain the invaluable benefit of church union.[96] Finally, the pair reiterated that union with Rome would not mean a change in Russian rite or discipline. Rather, it would be a union of equals.[97]

On 15 April 1860, Murav'ev wrote to Haxthausen again. He justified his actions on Filaret's behalf by observing that Haxthausen was only a layman who had no official standing to address the metropolitan. Besides, Murav'ev noted, Filaret was "a prelate who does not represent the Russian church." Furthermore, Murav'ev wrote, Filaret's silence did not imply that the Russian church was any more subordinate to secular authority than was the French church, "in which the bishops do not always correspond freely with their spiritual head" and where "[the distribution of] papal bulls is sometimes stopped by the lay government." Finally, Murav'ev reiterated his objections to the Roman Catholic method of union. With regards to the *filioque,* Murav'ev asserted that the desire of the Roman church to require it among Roman Catholics and to permit its absence among the Eastern rite Catholics recalled the adjudication by King Solomon of the argument between the two women fighting over the child, except that, in this case, the child would indeed be cut in half.[98]

Haxthausen recognized that there would be no convincing Murav'ev. In 1860, he sent a final letter, in which he defended his position as spokesperson for the Roman Catholic church, since both the pope and his bishop had permitted him to write to Filaret. While Haxthausen recognized differences between the Eastern and Western churches, he described the papacy as "the common patrimony" of both. Finally, he said he accepted a difference between the institution of prayers for union in the churches of the East and West. He only asked that they each simply ask for union while leaving to the will of God the means of answering that prayer.[99]

In his zeal to oppose the *Petrusverein,* Murav'ev publicly accused Grand Duchess Pavlovna of harboring Roman Catholic sympathies. Count Tolstoi later reprimanded Murav'ev for this slander against the grand duchess.[100] Alexander II did not involve himself in the matter.

The controversy aroused by the proposed *Petrusverien* in Russia threatened to compromise Elena Pavlovna's authority at court. Conservatives in Russia opposed to peasant reform could use the controversy to undercut her position by linking Elena Pavlovna and her supporters to "foreign and anti-Russian" forces. Since she was more interested in the success of peasant reform than in effecting church reunion, she informed Rahden that she would no longer talk to Haxthausen about the prayer organization.[101] Haxthausen also became disillusioned with the possibility of *Petrusverein* in Russia. He wrote Elena Pavlovna that he now believed church union would take a very long time.[102]

Opposition to the *Petrusverein* also developed among the Roman Catholics in the West. A letter of de Buck to Gagarin on 20 July 1858 noted that the journal *L'Univers,* after initially strongly supporting *Petrusverein* because of its ties to the German bishops, came to oppose it as a bad means of achieving union.[103]

The end of the *Petrusverein* did not mean the end of attempts to form organizations for union by means of prayer. Charles Lenormand offered a mass for union every Saturday at Notre Dame des Victoires.[104] In 1860/61, in Paris, the Union of Holy Communion for the Feast of St. Michael, Protector of the Russians, was formed to seek the conversion of the Russians. In June 1862 in Milan, the statutes of the *Association of Prayers for the Triumph of the Immaculate Blessed Virgin by the Conversion of the Eastern Schismatics and Especially of the Russians to the Catholic Faith* were published.[105] This organization was the idea of Father Grigorii Shuvalov and had received papal approval in 1862.[106] In his brief, Pius IX, who had already established indulgences for the organization in Italy, extended those indulgences to the rest of the world. He noted that he did not desire "anything so passionately" as "the reconciliation of the Christians of every country with the Holy See, which is the center of unity."

Shuvalov's program was no more successful than Gagarin's in obtaining mass conversions among the Orthodox; however, it did arouse their ire. In an article in the Orthodox publication *L'Union chrètienne,* Vladimir P. questioned the veracity and consistency of those praying for "conversion of the Orthodox." Defenders of unity like Shuvalov referred to the Orthodox as "schismatics," but schismatics could simply rejoin the "universal church" without conversion. If the Orthodox were heretics, however, then they would need "conversion." *L'Union chrètienne* implied that Shuvalov actually regarded the Orthodox as heretics instead of as schismatics. The author also claimed that if the Orthodox church converted to papism and its innovations, it would lose its status as part of the universal church. The author pointed to the lack of success of organizations praying for the conversion of England as a sign that God did not answer the prayers of the Roman "heretics." The author concluded by asserting he would pray that one day Roman Catholics would return to the true Orthodox Catholic church.[107]

The *Petrusverein* was an innovation in Russo-Catholic relations because it was the first organization to search for union with the Orthodox rather than to polemicize against them. The *Petrusverein* sought union between Russia and Rome without specifying how that union might take place. In its lack of specificity lay its main appeal to the Orthodox. But the lack of clarity that made the *Petrusverein* acceptable to some Orthodox did not allay the concerns of those such as Murav'ev, who rightly questioned how a reunion acceptable to both East and West could occur when the differences which separated the two churches were so great. Nor did it address the concerns of Catholics such as Martynov who feared violations of church canons. The *Petrusverein* did not bring the two churches any closer to reunion, because it assumed a desire for union that did not exist in either church apart from a few individuals.

During this period between 1856 and 1860, Gagarin also worked on a second project designed to facilitate church union. Joined by Fathers Balabin and Martynov in 1856, Gagarin published the first volume of *Études de théologie, de philosophie et d'histoire* in 1857. The journal's purpose was to "deal with the entire complex of questions that may usefully occupy a priest." These questions included "Holy Scripture, patristics, and other principle branches of the sacred science," philosophy ("the science of principles") and history ("the science of facts"). The journal would concentrate on those religious questions "which immediately relate to the needs of the times in which we live." As for philosophy and history, they were "equally necessary to solidly establish and to reveal the very foundations of the Christian faith."[108] The preface did not speak of Russia, conversion, or the union of churches, because the editors wanted to avoid provoking Russian hostility and because they wished to disguise the journal's intent.[109] Thus, in addition to containing two articles by Gagarin, the first volume also included three articles unrelated to the subject of Russia and church union, on the subjects of rationalist exegesis, moral philosophy, and the authenticity of the Gospels.[110]

Gagarin's article, "De l'enseignement de la théologie dans l'Église russe," analyzed theological education in Russia by examining the writings of Bishop Makarii. Gagarin began his discussion of the Russian clergy by asserting his desire for reunion of the churches. He wrote, "What I want and desire most dearly is to see the reconciliation of the Russian church and the Holy See brought about not through absorption [of the Russian church] into the Latin church, but under terms established previously at Florence."[111] He added about himself that he was a "Russian by birth and by heart, raised in the Russian church." "If I separated myself from my countrymen and my fellow believers, I did it in order to obey my conscience; but I always preserve the hope that I set an example and that the Russian nation and the Russian church will follow, with truth, light, and peace."[112]

Gagarin observed a literary revival among the Russian clergy. While encouraged by this activity, he did not expect it to lead to rapid growth in the Russian church itself "as long as the Russian clergy and the European public remain estranged." He said that there needed to be an intermediary between Russia and Europe to present information about each to the other. *Études* was to take that role.[113]

Gagarin recognized the validity of the Russian Orthodox priesthood and the Orthodox sacraments. He proclaimed that the distance between the two churches was small. Still, in spite of the short distance between the two churches and the intellectual revitalization of the Russian higher clergy, the educational and social differences between the churches remained marked. He argued, "the ignorance of the [common] clergy, its depravity, its debasement pass all measure." The unfortunate condition of the Russian lower clergy, Gagarin claimed, was a result of separation from Rome.[114]

Gagarin then criticized certain points of Orthodox theology. He attacked Bishop Makarii and other Orthodox priests on their attachment to St. Gregory Palamas, because Gregory belonged "to one of the most extravagant sects that false mysticism has ever engendered." Gagarin singled out for censure the Orthodox practice of hesychasm, since he thought it associated with "propositions contrary to the first tenets of the Christian faith."[115]

Examining Makarii's sources, Gagarin pointed out that several Orthodox authors held ideas in agreement with Roman Catholic theology. On the other hand, many of Makarii's theological sources—one example being Feofan Prokopovich—opposed Roman Catholicism. In these cases, Gagarin attributed the divergences from Roman Catholicism to the Protestantization of Russian theology.[116] For Gagarin, there seemed to be little distinctive about Orthodox theology. He contended that Russia borrowed much of its theology from the West. It was in the West, for example, at Roman Catholic theological academies, that important Orthodox theologians, such as Petr Moghila, conducted their studies. Russia's ecclesiastical renaissance had begun in the West, particularly in Poland.[117]

Of course, not everything borrowed from the West was good. The Protestantization of Russia began with "the influence of the German party" under Peter I and Anna Ioannovna. Peter did not borrow appropriately from the West, Gagarin wrote: "Very often, instead of grafting branches; he tore down, uprooted, and instead planted a land of clippings deprived of roots, scarcely able to produce; often he imitated the evil instead of imitating the good; finally, Peter became attached more to consequences than causes, to the surface of civilization rather than to that which gave it strength and life."[118] Gagarin asserted that the best way for Russians to assure the importation of healthy ideas from the West was reunion with Rome. He claimed that this union would regenerate Russian Orthodoxy. Gagarin laid much of the practical burden of promoting church unity on Poland, which "Providence has destined . . . to reattach all Slavic people to the center of Catholic unity." Although Poland was, formally speaking, a subjugated state, Gagarin gave tribute to the Polish national greatness: "who knows if during these twenty-five last years, the Poles, dispersed over the entire surface of Russia, and even to Siberia; have not done more for the triumph of Catholicism than during the ages of [Polish] domination?"[119]

Although Gagarin's analysis of the Russian church was not entirely negative, his criticism of St. Gregory Palamas and hesychasm was an attack on a theological system integral to Russian Orthodoxy, just as Thomism was integral to the Roman Catholic theological system. In spite of the allegedly "small" differences in rite or tradition, the criticism of Orthodoxy's core theological/philosophical assumptions indicated a real, perhaps unbridgeable, gap between the two churches.

In this connection, it is interesting to compare Gagarin's thoughts regarding the comparisons of Roman Catholic, Protestant, and Russian Orthodox theology with those of the distinguished Orthodox theologian Father Georges Florovsky. Gagarin looked for similarities between Russian Orthodox catechisms and Roman Catholic theology as evidence of the earlier theological unity of the two churches. He ascribed any differences to the Protestantization of Orthodox theology and thus implied the differences were not reflective of distinctly Orthodox beliefs. Florovsky strongly disagreed with Gagarin's view. While concurring with Gagarin that Prokopovich's theology was "Protestant," Florovsky interpreted the theology of Moghila as "pseudo-Orthodox," or heavily Latinized; therefore neither truly represented Orthodoxy.[120]

The second volume of *Études* contained two more articles by Gagarin. The first, "Les Starovères, l'Église russe et le pape," analyzed a book by Bishop Grigorii of Saint Petersburg, *Istinno drevnaia i istinno pravoslavnaia Khristova tserkov', nalozhenie v otnoshenii k glagolemomu staroobriadstvu.* Gagarin mined the book for evidence that the schism between the Old Believers and the established Russian Orthodox church demonstrated the need for Orthodox union with Rome. The second article, "Le feld-maréchel comte Boris Chérémétev à Rome en 1698," analyzed unionist tendencies during the reign of Sophia. Other articles connected with the reunion of churches were "Origines catholiques de l'Église russe jusqu'au XIIe siècle" by Verdière, "Essai de conciliation sur le dogme de la procession du Saint-Esprit" by de Buck, and a "Notice sur Mme Élisabeth Galitzin."

Gagarin began the article "Les Starovères, l'Église russe et le pape" with a description of the Old Believers. He asserted that "while difficult to precisely count their number" they numbered in the millions and continued to grow each year.[121] The Old Believers were united in their opposition to the reforms of Peter I and to the Westernizing tendencies of his successors. As such, Gagarin claimed, the Old Belief indicated "the Russian people's opposition to the official [state] church. It [the Old Belief] is a protest against the condition of dependence in which that church is placed vis-à-vis the temporal power."[122] Gagarin then noted that the Russian Orthodox church moved to end the schism with the Old Believers by promising to respect the rite and liturgy of the Old Believers in return for recognition of the authority of the Synod.[123]

Bishop Grigorii had argued that the Old Believers should rejoin the Orthodox church because it alone was the true church established by Jesus Christ. Gagarin compared this assertion with that of Bishop Makarii on the nature of the true church. He said neither was correct.

According to Bishop Makarii, the true church is "that which preserves exactly and without alteration the infallible teachings of the ancient universal church and remains completely faithful to them."[124] Gagarin rejected this definition. First, the definition was too broad since many groups have claimed to preserve faithfully the ancient teachings of the church. Second, Gagarin asserted that doctrinal rigidity "is not and cannot be an attribute of the true church of Jesus Christ."[125] Ironically, the Old Believers had earlier accused the Russian church of "innovations." As a result, in 1667–1667, they had made apparent their own rigidity and "Orthodoxy" in contrast to the Nikonian church's "flexibility." Third, Gagarin contended that the Holy Synod was an innovation not known to the early church.[126] Thus, Makarii's definition was inadequate, but if accepted it would mean that the Russian church, having altered the infallible teachings of the ancient church, was not the true church of Christ.

Having responded to Bishop Makarii's definition, Gagarin now addressed the definition of Bishop Grigorii. In attempting to persuade the Old Believers to rejoin the Russian church, Grigorii argued that the true church was that which had and would always have an authority distinct from the civil authority as well as a hierarchy composed of bishops, priests, and deacons. Since Old Believers did not always have bishops, he said they could not be the true church of Christ.[127] Gagarin faulted this definition as well. The assertion that the Old Believers' lack of an episcopate proved that they were not the true Church of Christ struck Gagarin as an *ad hominem* argument. He thought the Old Believers' lack of bishops purely accidental. Moreover, he pointed out that many heretical groups, such as the Arians and Nestorians, had an ecclesiastical hierarchy of bishops, priests, and deacons.[128] Therefore, Gagarin rejected the notion that a simple ecclesiastic hierarchy necessarily marked a church as genuinely Christian.

In place of the two definitions of Bishops Makarii and Grigorii, Gagarin postulated his own definition of the true church. He said the true church must be defined by reference to scripture, to the writings of the Holy Fathers, and to Russian Orthodox catechisms. This true church had a hierarchy instituted by Christ composed not only of bishops, priests, and deacons; it also contained the pope.[129]

Gagarin acknowledged Orthodox arguments against this definition of church authority. The Orthodox church did not deny to the pope a primacy of honor, rather it denied the primacy of papal jurisdiction. Furthermore, the Orthodox church argued that the pope's authority came from earthly, not divine, sources. The Orthodox said that the pope possessed no authority outside the West.

Gagarin said none of these arguments was valid. Church history demonstrated that the pope exercised an authority outside of the West. Popes condemned and deposed the patriarchs of Constantinople, Antioch, and Alexandria; they received the appeals of the patriarchs from these sees, and heard the appeals of people against the sentences of those sees. Furthermore, papal primacy was an institution inaugurated by Christ himself.[130] St. Peter received primacy from Jesus Christ and then transmitted it to the successive bishops of Rome.[131] This primacy in no way detracted from the authority of Christ, just as the authority of the bishops within their dioceses did not detract from Christ's authority.[132]

Gagarin went on to argue that this idea was an authentic teaching of the Russian church, justified by the scriptures, by writings of the Holy Fathers, and by the Russian Orthodox liturgy. As for scripture, Gagarin made reference to traditional Roman Catholic apologetical arguments ("You are Peter, and on this rock I will build my church and the gates of Hell will not prevail against it"; Christ's charge to Peter to "feed his sheep").

For Gagarin, these texts proved Peter's divinely instituted authority. He appealed to selections from the writings of St. Gregory of Nicea, St. John Damascene, St. John Chrysostom, and St. Theodore Studite which supported a divinely instituted Petrine authority and a succession of that authority into the hands of later popes.[133] As for Russian liturgical texts, Gagarin wrote that they described Peter as:

> the first of the apostles (*pervii apostolov*), the prince of apostles (*verkhovnii apostol*), he who occupies the first see in the church (*pervoprestolnii*), the doctor (*nastavnik apostolov*), the foundation (*osnovanie*), the guide (*vozhd*) of apostles, the pastor of the apostles who exerts authority over them (*pastir vladichnii apostolov*). He is the source and the principle of Orthodoxy (*nachalo pravoslaviia*); from him comes all Christianity (*nachalo khristian*); he is the foundation, the column of faith, the rock on which it is supported (*kamen' very*); he is the rock on which Jesus Christ has built his church and against which the gates of Hell will not prevail.[134]

Such authority could not perish with Peter: it had to have an inheritor.[135] Furthermore, Russian liturgical texts supported a succession of this authority with such phrases as "Clement, holy martyr, disciple of Peter, You imitate his divine virtues and you show that you are the true inheritor of his throne," and "You [Saint Sylvester] are head of the sacred council, you occupy the exalted throne of the prince of the apostles."[136]

For Gagarin, therefore, the evidence for papal primacy as a necessary characteristic of the true church of Christ was overwhelming. In order to rejoin the true church, the Russian church was therefore required to rejoin Rome. This was proven by the very texts which the Russian Orthodox church considered authoritative.

Gagarin's presentation of the Old Believers as exponents of the Russian Orthodox church's independence from the state was greatly in error. Old Believer opposition had nothing to do with the loss of ecclesiastical independence in the Holy Synod, since the synod did not exist at the time of Nikon's reforms. In fact, the Old Believers suspected that Nikon's reforms had, in fact, been contaminated by Roman Catholic beliefs and that the Russian church had submitted to "papist" errors. There were absolutely no indications that the Old Believers had any desire to accept papal primacy to secure ecclesiastic independence.[137]

The third volume of *Études de théologie, de philosophie et d'histoire* included a small review-article by Gagarin entitled "Publications Russes sur le marriage," which analyzed J. Bazarov's text *Die Ehe nach der Lehre und dem ritus der orthodoxen russichen Kirche*[138] and Iosif Vasil'ev's *Office du mariage selon le rite de l'Église catholique orthodoxe d'Orient.* In this article, Gagarin criticized the differences in the marriage rite between the Greek and the Russian Orthodox churches.[139] Furthermore, he accused the Orthodox church of hypocrisy since it claimed marriage was a binding sacrament, yet it permitted divorce.[140] The third volume also included an article by Martynov on the Slavic manuscripts in the Bibliothèque Impèriale de Paris.

These first volumes of *Études* met with approval from the Catholic public and Gagarin's superiors. Sebastian Laurentie, in the Catholic paper *L'Union,* wrote, "The authors of *Études de théologie, de philosophie et d'histoire* continue their knowledgeable work; the second volume contains works which fully justify our characterization of them as serious intellects working toward Catholic unity." Laurentie also called it a "great and wonderful journal," "a wise critique and a sparkling exposition," and "an admirable defense of the church and science."[141] Beckx wrote, "The *Études* has already surmounted the first difficulties inseparable from all undertakings; they have acquired status in the scholarly world and have done much good in Russia, I am assured. I should thus sustain and encourage it."[142]

By November 1858, the Jesuits were forced to find a new publisher for *Études* and to modify the schedule of later volumes of the journal. They now projected one volume of 640 pages a year, to be published in four books of 160 pages each. The editorial board would consist of Fathers Gagarin, Daniel, Ambroise Matignon, Victor Mertian, and Hilarion Taupin.[143]

Gagarin's writings were far from consistent on the feasibility of achieving union between Rome and Russian Orthodoxy. Early proposals to Gagarin's superiors said that vast missionary activity would need to take place and that hostility to the Jesuits would require that initial missionary work take place outside of Russia. On the other hand, in *La Russie sera-t-elle catholique?* Gagarin suggested that a formal church union required only a simple agreement with the Russian authorities. In Gagarin's grand schemes for the establishment of union there was more propaganda than substance. Sadly, his articles demonstrated that he was willing to distort aspects of Russian religious history in order to fit them into his arguments for union. This was especially the case in his interpretation of the Old Believers, but was also demonstrated in his arguments on "Catholicism or Revolution." While Gagarin's activity sometimes met with favorable reviews from his associates, from Jesuits and Russian Catholics, it generally irritated the Orthodox. Murav'ev's hostile reaction to *Petrusverein* was just one indication of this antipathy.

CHAPTER FIVE

Signs of Failure: I

> O Company of Jesus, my mother, when I consider so vehemently the ignominy the world gives you; when I see the shame, the calumny, the outrage amassed against you from all sides; I raise a heartfelt cry, without stopping to refute the falsehood, without wishing to find the earthly source of it. I raise my eyes toward God crucified and cry out full of love and confidence: Ah! The world did not know from whence came this scorn against us, it ignored the causes of these affronts. It is to your name, Jesus, alone that we owe everything![1]

While Gagarin's text *La Russie* met with the approbation of his fellow Jesuits and Roman Catholics it was condemned by French secularists, Polish nationalists, and Orthodox critics.[2] This hostile response demonstrated to Gagarin his error in expecting imminent church union. It also made clear to him that issues of Roman Catholic/Russian Orthodox reunion necessarily concerned a wider audience than the one he had specifically addressed in his work so far.

French secularists attacked both Gagarin's program and his allegiance to the Jesuits. As one writer noted about Gagarin's proposal for a union between the pope, the tsar, and the Russian clergy, "Only a disciple of Loyola would be so naive as to make a question of faith into a question of politics and transform a matter of conscience into an issue for the police."[3] The French socialist Izalguier accused Gagarin of underestimating the significance of dogmatic differences between Roman Catholicism and Orthodoxy regarding the *filioque,* the pope, and married priests. He predicted that any ecumenical council between the East and West would prove unable to resolve questions defined as dogma by Rome, yet viewed as opinion by Orthodoxy. As one might expect of a republican dedicated to secular control of the French church, Izalguier defended the Russian government's authority over the clergy on the ground that a clergy independent of the state would likely overburden the people. He argued that the best way to free peasants from superstition was not church union but popular education.[4]

Gagarin did not respond directly to Izalguier or other French secularists, perhaps because he knew they would oppose his plan in any case. "They do not want the reunion of the Eastern church with the Western church, because they like neither one nor the other, and because they imagine it would be more easy to get rid of the Russian church isolated, separated from Rome, than [to discard it after it has been] reconciled with the Holy See and reattached to the great body of the Catholic church."[5]

While opposition from the French left could have been anticipated, the attacks from the Poles caught Gagarin by surprise. We noted earlier that the Poles feared that Vatican accommodation with Orthodoxy might further compromise Polish national independence because such an accommodation would force Polish Catholics to accept the legitimacy of the Russian state. Indeed, Gagarin was plainly ready to sacrifice Polish autonomy for the sake of a Rome-Moscow union.[6] The Polish journal *Czaz* warned Gagarin that a Catholic-Orthodox reunion could and should never occur so long as the Russian government controlled the church. According to the journal, a genuine church union would have to be preceded by the reestablishment of the ancient kingdom of Poland, by the appearance of a new Stefan Bathory to lead a national uprising against Russia.[7] The journal characterized Polish reaction to Gagarin's text as universally negative. It described Gagarin himself not as a priest but as a "diplomat, a Russian."[8] The response of the Polish journal *Przeglad Poznańskii* was also critical. Like *Czaz, Przeglad Poznańskii* criticized Gagarin's willingness to accept the authenticity of Russian Orthodox clergy and Orthodox rites.[9] It asserted that, by claiming Russian Orthodox rites to be authentic, Gagarin would "shake yet again those souls already affected by the treacherous propaganda of [Russian] government agents, and strengthen the impression of the faithful that the difference between the two rites is of little importance."[10] In the journal's view, Gagarin's emphasis on church union was dangerous for it might divert attention from the "sufferings and needs of the church in Poland."[11] The *Przeglad Poznańskii* also condemned Gagarin for not taking account of Russian coercion of the "unfortunate Ruthenian church." Above all, it complained that Gagarin had not planned a role for [an independent] Poland in establishing any eventual union.[12] *Przeglad Poznańskii* concluded with the assertion, "In Poland, we will preserve our religious faith without alteration; that is permitted to us, just as it is permitted to the Russians to be patriotic. Reverend Father Gagarin is a Russian patriot; he should not be astonished that we are Polish patriots."[13]

Gagarin tried to find common ground with his Polish critics.[14] He wrote, "We respect the Poles, we love them, we hope to find in them allies and brothers." Still, he admitted that "they have regrets, griefs, interests, which are not ours."[15] Gagarin described his goals as different from those of the Polish nationalists, yet not in conflict with them. His program of church reunion was a spiritual objective, whereas Polish independence was "a purely political and temporal issue."[16] He wrote, "They [the Poles] do not want to see a Catholic Russia because they desire Polish sovereignty." He accused Polish nationalists of using rhetoric about Russian persecution of Polish Catholics to provoke a Polish popular uprising against Russian rule. According to Gagarin, Polish nationalists would certainly be "very disappointed" if the Russian government became Catholic because this would remove the masses' primary motivation for making a revolution against Russia.[17] Gagarin refused to support Polish independence, because he did not want his Russian readers to suppose that Roman Catholicism was the property of a particular nationality. Of course, Gagarin credited the Polish church for its historical role as "the citadel of Catholicism in Eastern Europe," but he did not think it necessary for Poland to place itself in opposition to Russian Orthodoxy. Therefore, he argued, "without the intermediation of Poland," Rome should accept the Russian church with "its bishops, priests, rite, liturgy" into the Catholic church.[18]

Gagarin's polemics with the Polish nationalists of *Przeglad Poznańskii* lasted from January 1857 to May 1857. On 30 April 1857, Beckx ordered Gagarin to suspend the debate, since "They [the Poles] fundamentally agree with you: they call everyone to the desired conversion of Russia." Beckx added the reproof that "Silence appears to me more Christian, more religious, more dignified, more apt, more useful to the Catholic cause than the continuation of an endless polemic."[19] Gagarin obeyed Beckx's order, although he did observe in a later article that conflicts with the Polish nationalists would disappear as soon as the Poles recognized that "the reunion of the Russian church with the Holy See on the foundations indicated by us cannot do any harm to the Polish church."[20]

Orthodox critics blasted Gagarin and *La Russie* from a variety of directions.[21] First, they rejected any association with the Roman Catholic church. As Abbé René François Guettée wrote, "With Rome, you are a *schismatic;* with the innovations of Rome, you are a *heretic.*"[22] Khomiakov considered Gagarin's proposal for union with Rome the equivalent of union with Arians, Nestorians, or "any other heresy."[23] Many of the errors the Orthodox critics ascribed to Rome had already been noted—among them, the *filioque*, papal primacy, the Immaculate Conception of Mary, a misapprehension of the nature of the Eucharist and Baptism. Now the Orthodox leveled new accusations. For example, S. Baranovskii condemned what he called the papal prohibition on reading vernacular-language Bibles. Baranovskii believed "that the testament of Jesus Christ revealed their falsehoods [i.e. false doctrines]."[24]

Behind Gagarin's desire for church reunion, the Orthodox saw Rome's secular ambitions. Khomiakov described Gagarin's proposal as a politically motivated deal between the pope, the tsar, and the Russian bishops, rather than as a religious conversion of the Russian populace. He wrote that Gagarin envisaged not spiritual conversion of the Russians but "negotiations and sending of plenipotentiaries. Romanism shows itself in all the nakedness of its terrestrial character."[25] Orthodox writers reminded the faithful of papal aggression against the Orthodox church.[26] They blamed Roman Catholic errors for the creation of Protestantism.[27]

Orthodox authors disagreed with Gagarin's claims about the weakness of the Russian church; instead they praised Russia's loyalty to its faith. The history of the Russian emperor's defense against the opponents of Orthodoxy was invoked, as was the memory of Russia's refusal to accept the decrees of the Council of Ferrara-Florence. Karatheodores noted, "The history of Russia confirms our assertions by more than one example, and we cannot conceive how Gagarin, who is Russian and who knows the Russians' steadfast attachment to their rites, to their liturgy, to the ancient and pious customs of their church, has not remarked that the Russians consider the dogmas of their church as a thing most essential and more important than the rites so artificially put at the first rank by the Jesuit priest."[28] The conversion of the peoples of Siberia to Orthodoxy was also mentioned as a sign of Russian Orthodoxy's continued strength.[29] The Orthodox refused to rally around Gagarin's banner of Catholicism as an alternative to revolution, for they regarded Orthodoxy as the answer to revolution. Khomiakov wrote:

> Should the sovereign of Russia let himself be seduced (this is outside all probability!), should the clergy be treacherous (that which passes all limits of possibility!), there would be millions of souls who would remain steadfast in the truth; millions of arms would raise the invincible banner of the church; millions of people would form a lay order. In the immensity of the East, at least two or three bishops, remaining

> faithful to God, would bless the lesser orders and would compose of them alone all the episcopate. The church would lose nothing of its force and its unity and would still be the universal church as in the time of the apostles.[30]

Murav'ev predicted, "if one of the members of the [Russian] higher clergy . . . were to propose seriously a union with Rome, the congregation would stone him on the spot: this is the degree of aversion the West has inspired in the Russian people, which is gentle by nature but which has not forgotten the intrigues of the Jesuits at the time of the false Dmitrii and the oceans of blood which they cost us."[31]

The Orthodox critics used the occasion of Gagarin's proposal to attack the Jesuit order, accusing it of secrecy, calumny, falsehood, and treachery. Samarin asserted that the Jesuits wanted religious freedom only where they lacked the power "to oppress their adversaries or to control their opinions."[32] Dmitrii Tolstoi asserted that the Jesuits hypocritically advocated liberty while criticizing liberalism.[33] Baranovskii claimed that Jesuit propagandists often tried to persuade potential converts that there was no difference between their own religion and Roman Catholicism.[34] Youssov provided a most graphic description:

> Like a spider, the Company of Jesuits spins an artistic web; they almost always toil in shadow and in mystery. It is all too easy to fall into their clutches, to be taken in by their kind words. But scarcely is one in their web, when they manifest the spirit of domination which guides them; they enlace their victims and only release them after having removed from them all spirit of life, only after having made them cadavers.[35]

The Orthodox also criticized Gagarin himself. Like Artamov, some believed that all of the Jesuits in Paris were under Gagarin's leadership.[36] Others wondered whether Gagarin was merely doing the bidding of his society: Youssov asked whether the work of Gagarin "is due to the inspiration of the Company to which he belongs, or if it is a product of his own personality."[37]

Some critics doubted that Gagarin could be both a Russian and a Jesuit, for they considered those two concepts mutually exclusive. In *L'Union chrétienne,* an anonymous author wrote that Gagarin could no longer be a Russian, "because he is a Jesuit."[38] Another wrote:

> in entering into the Company of Jesus, he [Gagarin] should have known that he would find himself under the proscription that the Jesuits have merited. His resolution was free, his removal from his country cannot be classified as *exile,* for exile presupposes coercion, persecution. Gagarin loves justice and truth too much not to admit that the only word which can characterize his separation from Russia is *emigration;* he preferred the Company of Loyola to his country, and left the latter for having the mark of honor of being a Jesuit.[39]

Several Orthodox questioned the integrity of Gagarin's conversion to Roman Catholicism. Unable to imagine how a conversion to Catholicism could be based on conviction, they accused Gagarin and other Orthodox converts to Catholicism of ignorance regarding their national faith. For example, Dmitrii Tolstoi attributed Svechina's conversion to her lack of religious education.[40] As for Gagarin, Khomiakov wrote:

> It is said (although I dare not affirm it) that he left Russia profoundly ignorant of his religion and was soon seduced by clever missionaries; not completely carried away, he returned for some time to his country. There, it is said, he had the misfortune of meeting with harsh and rude defenders of the church, doing more to inspire repugnance than love of the truth. This meeting confirmed his departure. Whatever may be, his career is not finished: his age promises him many long days. Let us hope that, with more light and repentance, he will finally return to the tranquil ranks of his countrymen or possibly may even join a monastic order. He must repent a life of intellectual errors that has tossed him into a monastery of Jesuits, where he has learned to equate religious Machiavellianism with zeal and unscrupulousness in the choice of means as proof of faith.[41]

By denying that there could be spiritual justification for Catholic conversions, the Orthodox attempted to minimize the scandal resulting from the decisions by prominent Russian nobles such as Gagarin, Svechina, Shuvalov, and Golitsyn to leave Orthodoxy. The Orthodox assured themselves that future defections from Orthodoxy could be prevented by better religious education.[42] Since they attributed Gagarin's conversion to ignorance, they could then assert that his subsequent religious maturation might lead to his eventual return to Orthodoxy, however unlikely such a return might appear.[43] The attribution to Gagarin of ignorance also made it possible for the Orthodox to refrain from addressing his substantive criticisms of the Russian church. Finally, by presenting Gagarin not as a Russian with inside knowledge of Orthodoxy but as a Jesuit and "foreigner" ignorant of the Russian church, the Orthodox minimized Gagarin's credibility on issues involving the Russian church.

Yet, even Gagarin's critics sometimes credited his intelligence. Youssov commended Gagarin for his "patriotic sentiments," "good intentions," and the fact that he presented his arguments "more politely" than other "adversaries of the Russian church."[44] Another author commended Gagarin for recognizing the character and intelligence of the Russian clergy.[45] One Russian went so far as to write that "He [Gagarin] does not need councils or long negotiations, but [only] sincere explanation, based on the evidence of our liturgical texts, a thousand times more eloquent than all our doctors with their arguments borrowed from Protestants and Jansenists."[46] However, most of the responses to Gagarin's arguments were reflective of Murav'ev's comments that "none are so harsh in condemning a cause as those who have left it" and that "the true duty of a zealous son of the church is to endeavor by all possible means to correct its abuses, if there be any, and not because of them to desert to the opposing camp."[47]

On more substantive issues, such as the dogmatic distinctions between the Orthodox and Roman Catholics, the Orthodox insisted on the seriousness of their differences with Rome. Khomiakov, for whom dogmatic issues (papal primacy, *filioque*) were of paramount importance, did not accept Gagarin's attempt to minimize the distinction between the churches.[48] Gagarin's concept of *byzantisme* was ridiculed as "a child of his fantasy."[49]

The Orthodox also found fault with Gagarin's proposal for an ecumenical council involving the pope, the tsar, and the Russian bishops. The Orthodox believed that such a council would be incapable of reuniting the churches. They felt that the disagreements between the two churches were too extensive to be resolved.[50] They suspected such a council would place the Orthodox faithful in a position of having to sacrifice or alter their beliefs, while the Roman Catholics could retain their own faith, since it would be assumed that Roman Catholic teachings on the pope and the procession of the Holy Spirit would have to be accepted at any council.[51] As Guettée wrote to Gagarin, "Why do all the bishops of the East bear the weight of reunion with those of the West by recognizing *first of all, necessarily,* as a preliminary and as a condition *sine qua non* of a council, that which is precisely the principal object of discussion?"[52] Orthodox critics of Gagarin suspected that even if an ecumenical council achieved agreement between churches, that agreement would be more formal than substantive. It would place the churches of the West and the East in a difficult position, where one church might regard disputed issues as matters of dogma and the other might think the issues matters of opinion. Khomiakov put forward the following example:

> An Easterner adopts the Roman faith: he remains in communion with the entire church, one monk receives him with joy and another dares not judge him because it is not a point of decided faith. Let us take the contrary. A man of a Latin diocese adopts the Eastern opinion: he is necessarily excluded from the communion of his diocese for having rejected an article of faith and he is also excluded from the communion of the East. The West excommunicates the man because he believes the same as their brothers [the East], with whom they are in communion and the East excommunicates the unfortunate because he shares their belief. It is difficult to imagine something more absurd.[53]

The Orthodox argued that union could only come if Rome renounced "its errors." According to Karatheodores, "only the return to the past and respect for ancient Christianity can return us to the time when East and West formed one church."[54]

As for Gagarin's argument that reunion would lead to the freedom of the Russian church from secular authority, the Orthodox critics responded that the Russian clergy was already freer than the Roman clergy.[55] They thought union with Rome would only diminish their freedom: "A Christian clergy is necessarily free: a clergy viciously separating itself from the church and entering schism removes the blood and word of Christ from the faithful; it invents new dogmas; it violates conscience. It cannot be free, it can only be tyrannical."[56] Because of previous poor treatment of Byzantine rite clergy at the hands of Roman Catholics, the Orthodox critics believed that, if union did occur, their priests would not be accepted as equals by the Roman Catholics; instead, the Orthodox would be accepted "only as children, with a privilege of ignorance . . . of stupidity."[57] Youssov wrote: "For Rome, union is nothing other than the annihilation of everything not in complete uniformity with it."[58]

As has been mentioned earlier, the Orthodox critics found great fault with Gagarin's slogan "Catholicism or Revolution." They argued that should the tsar and the Russian bishops convert to the faith of Rome, as Gagarin wished them to, a revolution would take place among the Orthodox faithful. Furthermore, the Orthodox critics claimed that it was in the West, under the eyes of the papacy, that revolution was born and grew:

> Revolution was born in the land of the Roman Catholics. The first throne destroyed by it was the papacy itself. The pope crowned the emperor [Napoleon], the son of revolution.[59] When the new revolution destroyed the throne of the so-called Restoration and the Charter took from France the character of a Christian power: then the pope commanded the French clergy to support a new revolution to create a new kingdom. In 1848, the Roman Catholic clergy in France gave its support to the forces of freedom. In Rome itself, the mouth of revolution opened and would have swallowed up the pope if he had not escaped. And now, why is there a foreign army in Rome? Because in Rome *Catholicism and Revolution* are together.[60]

Orthodox critics argued that an Orthodox Russia was immune to revolutionary uprisings. Since the Russian government was carrying out its sacred duty, "revolution is impossible; yes, now in Russia revolution is decidedly impossible." According to Baranovskii, so long as the Russian state continued to protect Russia's distinctive national identity [*narodnost'*], the country will develop tranquilly "without disruption, without revolution."[61]

Gagarin's charge that the Slavophiles were revolutionaries provoked that group's anger.[62] The Slavophiles believed that Gagarin wanted to encourage the Russian government to persecute them. Iurii Samarin, who had been a close friend of Gagarin, wrote that Gagarin should have known that his accusation of a Slavophile connection with revolutionary ideas was false. In the spirit of a former friendship, Samarin was willing to believe that Gagarin himself had no responsibility for the charge: "his hand was guided at this moment by a foreign will."[63] The Slavophiles' irritation was understandable. The Third Section and the Russian Ministry of the Interior had long considered the Slavophiles advocates of "radical, communistic views and convictions."[64] Since Gagarin's *La Russie* was published soon after the end of the "seven dark years" (1848–1855), they feared that the text might lead to return of governmental censorship of Slavophile publications.

Orthodox writers also reacted to Gagarin's attacks on the canonicity of the Holy Synod and to his accusations of Orthodox persecution of non-Orthodox. The Orthodox claimed that the establishment of the Synod had met with the acceptance of all the patriarchs. Even Peter I had "proved more than once his pious obedience to all prescriptions of the universal church."[65] The Orthodox denied that the Russian church had persecuted religious minorities. They put forward Russia as a model of religious tolerance: "In Russia, as all of Europe knows, there are millions of Roman Catholics who today continue to enjoy complete liberty of religion; as members of the civil service, they are on equal footing with all the Orthodox faithful."[66] Furthermore, Orthodox critics argued that, unlike Rome, "The Russians hold to their rite, but do not want to suppress other forms of Christian belief; in that they follow the rule of the early church which admitted local differences in discipline but believed that these differences are indispensable."[67]

Gagarin's later articles on Petrine primacy were also condemned, most strongly by the Orthodox journalist Sergei Petrovich Suchkov (1816–1893). In a series of articles in *L'Union chrétienne,* Suchkov attacked Gagarin for interpreting Russian hymns and prayers as support for Roman Catholic doctrine. Suchkov wrote that "one cannot search for the dogmatic teaching of a church in its songs and canticles," which are poetic compositions with hyperbolic language. Suchkov insisted that dogmatic teachings should be found in the creeds, catechisms, theological works, and the writings of the Holy Fathers.[68] Still, Suchkov took up Gagarin's challenge to look at the content of Russian Orthodox hymns.[69] Suchkov accused Gagarin of mistranslating, misrepresenting, and misinterpreting the Russian hymns as well as the writings of the church fathers. For example, though Gagarin translated the phrase *pervo-verkhovnye apostoly* as indicating that the Russian church truly taught Petrine primacy, Suchkov argued that similar phrases had been applied to Saint Peter, Saint John, Saint Andrew, Saint Philip, and others.[70] Suchkov further argued that several other titles such as "Head and Prince of Apostles" were also given to apostles besides Peter and were purely honorific.[71]

As for Gagarin's attempts to find the roots of the doctrine of Petrine primacy in early Christianity, Suchkov argued that if such an important doctrine existed it should have been evident in a period noted for the deaths of so many martyrs. Suchkov claimed that Gagarin's concept of the papacy differed significantly from the concept embraced by first-century Christians.[72] Suchkov found unpersuasive Gagarin's attempt to trace Petrine primacy to the Gospel text indicating that Peter was "the rock" upon which Christ built his church. Suchkov said that Peter was considered "first among the apostles" because he was chosen first, not because he possessed any special authority.[73]

Other Orthodox writers also criticized Gagarin's position on papal primacy. Guettée argued that if Gagarin had studied "with a little more care" the ancient theologians of France, he would have seen that papal primacy was not a matter of divine ordination, for even Benedict XIV had taught that papal authority was a matter of church law.[74] Vasil'ev claimed that the Orthodox fast before the feast of the martyrdom of Saint Peter proved that the Orthodox had a greater love of Peter than did nonfasting Roman Catholics.[75]

As for Gagarin's article on the Old Believers, one author writing in *Pravoslavnyi sobesednik* said, "We do not know by what sources Gagarin studied the *raskol* [Russian schism], but his opinions about it are directly opposed to the opinions of the [official] Russian church and the Old Believers themselves." The author claimed that Gagarin failed to take into account explicit evidence from the writings of the Old Believers which indicated that they were in no way sympathetic to Roman Catholicism and that they believed the pope to be the anti-Christ.[76]

As could be expected in debates involving such deeply held personal convictions, some of the Orthodox responses were insulting and petty. For example, Suchkov wrote that Gagarin's arguments inspired "a profound pity."[77] Guettée wrote, in response to one of Gagarin's homilies, "His [Gagarin's] style is not good; the reverend father speaks poor, very poor French. Another time, he may preach in Russian; this would be better, I am certain, because he is of a noble family, I am told, and he should know perfectly the language of his native country. As for his French, he should not trot it out in public, he makes too sad a figure in the chair of Saint Thomas Aquinas."[78]

Gagarin, too, often resorted to personal attacks on the character of his opponents. For him, Karatheodores was merely "the Sultan's doctor." Karatheodores's proposition that an ecumenical council could occur without Rome's presence was "bizarre."[79] As for Murav'ev, the "habitual champion of the Russian church," Gagarin wrote that he was a writer of talent who had written a useful work on the Russian saints. However, "as for his works of polemic, it is better not to speak of them; and if Murav'ev has succumbed to the weakness to take himself for a theologian, he is certainly alone in his views, even in Russia."[80]

Gagarin saved most of his attention for Khomiakov, for whom he had some respect. He called Khomiakov "one of the most able and most dangerous champions of the Eastern schism" and assigned him "the first place among the poets that Russia possesses today."[81] However, rather than consider Khomiakov a real authority on authentic Russian Orthodox teaching, Gagarin classified him as a representative of a deviant, Protestant wing of Orthodoxy. Gagarin saw Protestant influences in Khomiakov's views regarding the Immaculate Conception and on the relationship of the clergy and laity. According to Gagarin, during a meeting with Khomiakov in November or December 1842, the latter "pretended to find in the Gospel, I do not know how many sins of which the Holy Virgin would be culpable."[82] Khomiakov also repudiated the distinction between the clergy [the teaching church] and the laity [the learning church] by asserting that an ecumenical council had no authority outside of that which was attributed to it by the people. In this respect, Gagarin said, Khomiakov ignored a fundamental distinction which had always been admitted by the Orthodox church. Gagarin even accused Khomiakov of introducing the concept of universal suffrage into the Orthodox church.[83] Of course, Gagarin was aware that Khomiakov drew support for his ideas from the 1848 response of the Eastern patriarchs to Pius IX, but Gagarin claimed the patriarch of Constantinople and his synod were themselves in error.[84] He noted that the Russian Holy Synod itself had refused to permit publication of Khomiakov's texts in Russia.[85]

Gagarin wrote several articles in response to Orthodox objections. He developed his earlier arguments that the Russian church and the Roman Catholic church were generally in accord on matters of dogma, that these dogmas had developed throughout the history of the church, and that the pope was needed for union. For example, Gagarin claimed that it wasn't only he who believed that the Orthodox and Catholic churches were in accord on matters of dogma, but that the Russian Holy Synod did as well. For, Byzantine Catholic bishops did not repudiate the Council of Florence, yet they were accepted into the Russian Orthodox church. By accepting the Byzantine Catholics without requiring them to repudiate Florence, Gagarin said, "the Synod has solemnly declared that there was no dogmatic difference between the Roman church and the Russian church; that is incontestable."[86]

On the question of papal primacy, Gagarin said that the pope's authority was divinely instituted, that the pope was a crucial figure in the early church, and that church reunification would require a center of unity.[87] Gagarin repeated his views that papal primacy was supported by the writings of the church fathers as well as by Russian liturgical texts and hymns. He argued that Suchkov's citations were misrepresentations and did not really contradict Gagarin's arguments.[88] Suchkov had tried to attack Gagarin's ideas by pointing to a Russian text which stated that "Christ transmitted to James the see of the church." Suchkov then stated that "The see which is in question . . . is not simply the see of a local church, it is that of the entire universal church, because he employs the word transmit [*predal*]." Gagarin thought that it was highly ironic that the opponent of Petrine primacy would show that such primacy had been duly transmitted to another apostle, thereby confirming its existence.[89] Finally, Gagarin argued that other patriarchs had accepted the idea of primacy. He noted that at the time of the deposition of Nikon by Tsar Alexei, the tsar had addressed to the patriarch of Constantinople a series of questions on the matter. The patriarch responded that he had a true primacy over the church and that "while this privilege had belonged previously to the bishop of ancient Rome, the pope, *as a result of his pride*, had departed the universal church; the bishop of the New Rome, that is to say the patriarch of Constantinople, had inherited his rights."[90]

Gagarin continued to emphasize the advantages which would occur with reunion. He predicted that the Russians would have their own cardinals and possibly a Russian would become pope one day.[91] He thought union would broaden the exercise of religious liberties in Russia.[92]

There were many signs of hope for Gagarin after the publication of *La Russie sera-t-elle catholique?* He had finally received approval from his Jesuit superiors for the establishment of an organization which, even if it could not directly address the issue of Russia's conversion, could at least serve as means of advancing Gagarin's lifelong goal. The responses of the other Jesuits to Gagarin's writings also encouraged him, particularly when they observed that his arguments were "unanswerable." However, Gagarin quickly learned that, while it was easy to obtain the support of people who were already in general agreement, dealing with his real opponents was much more difficult.

The hostile response of the Poles was a surprise to Gagarin, who had previously not concerned himself with the issues of Polish independence, because he perceived any Russian oppression as based on religion, rather than ethnicity. Gagarin's attacks on revolutionary movements were seen by the Poles as attacks on their attempts to obtain freedom from Russian occupation. They saw his project of church unity as a Vatican policy to sacrifice Polish freedoms for the sake of a better relationship with the Russian government. While Gagarin wished to separate the issues of nationality and religion, the Poles considered these concepts just as interconnected as did the Slavophiles.

Gagarin was, therefore, forced to deal with unexpected opposition from a group of Roman Catholics. He could not support Polish independence without arousing the anger of Russians who already linked Catholicism, Polish nationalism, and revolution. He could not submit to Polish requests and still present himself as a loyal Russian. He was forced to try to persuade the Poles that a Catholic Russia would cease its persecution of Polish Catholics; however, for the Poles this was not enough.

The response of the Orthodox critics was more severe than that of the Poles, due to Gagarin's status as a former member of the Russian Orthodox church and as a Jesuit. By accusing Gagarin of ignorance and of treachery, by recalling past Roman Catholic/Jesuit persecutions of the Orthodox, the Orthodox critics attempted to discredit Gagarin as well as his proposals. Since Gagarin's proposals were essentially those which had been tried before, this response should have been anticipated. What the critics demonstrated was that their hatred of Roman Catholicism and the Jesuits was so great that they would not admit in public that Gagarin's views on the Russian clergy, issues of free speech, and the independence of the Russian church were to varying degrees similar to their own. Of course Gagarin's accusations of revolutionary ideas among the Slavophiles did not help his relationship with this group, even if there were aspects of the peasant commune which could serve as the basis for later revolutionary uprisings.

CHAPTER SIX

Signs of Failure: II

> Is it not amazing, that Prince Gagarin, apostate, and what is more, a Jesuit, reproaches others for treachery? This is understandable, for an apostate, a deserter, is in a terrible position of having to flatter his new masters and the country which is the home they give him. It is only through zeal and ardor that he can drive away mistrust and any doubt concerning his sincerity; it is only in the noise of his own words that he can stifle the remorse of his conscience.[1]

Nationalism and nationality were very important themes in Gagarin's polemics with the Orthodox. The link between national and religious identity figured in the discussion whether or not Russia could be defined as an "Orthodox nation."

Slogans of Gagarin's opponents—for example, the Russian government's cry of "Orthodoxy, Autocracy, and Nationality"—and the Slavophile equation of Russianness and Orthodoxy implied that anyone born in Russia who renounced the Orthodox faith, also renounced Russianness. For the Slavophiles, who believed that the Russian peasantry embodied nationhood as well as faithfulness to Orthodoxy, the renunciation of Orthodoxy was also a renunciation of the Russian common people. The Slavophiles could only imagine such a repudiation issuing from a member of the Russian nobility who had fallen prey to Western "corruption."[2]

Gagarin's opponents saw a contradiction between "Russianness" and membership in the Jesuit order. It may seem absurd to assert that Gagarin renounced his national identity when he decided to enter a Roman Catholic religious order, but the illogic of the assertion is loosely analogous to that in the declaration in 1950s America that "Communists" were un-American because they had repudiated quintessentially "American" values of liberty and independence. Gagarin's Orthodox critics believed that the Jesuits were un-Russian, because the Jesuits attacked Orthodoxy, which was integral to their conception of nationality. For many Russians, the Jesuits symbolized inimical aspects of Western Europe and Roman Catholicism. The Jesuits had links to Polish aggression against Russia; the Jesuits had participated in the forcible conversion of Russians; the Jesuits supported papal authority over Russia. Since Gagarin had joined the Jesuits believing that they were the Roman Catholic order most dedicated to Russia's conversion, Russian Orthodox hostility toward Gagarin was understandable.

Indeed, it was Gagarin's aggressive commitment to the conversion of Russia that differentiated him from many other Russian converts to Catholicism. Although they prayed that Russia might one day convert to Roman Catholicism, neither Svechina nor Shuvalov did much to make those hopes a reality. When Svechina heard of Gagarin's desire to convert, she tried to change his mind or at least postpone his decision. While Shuvalov established a prayer society for the conversion of Russia, he limited membership to Western Europeans, whereas Gagarin's *Petrusverein* sought to penetrate Russia itself. Neither Svechina nor Shuvalov wanted to conduct missionary activity in Russia; neither published texts with the sole goal of causing conversions. Therefore, Gagarin was perceived by Russian Orthodox as an "evil Jesuit," not so much because the Orthodox detested all Roman Catholics but because they objected to his decision to actively work for the conversion of his homeland.

Of course, Gagarin saw himself as a loyal son of Russia striving to save it from "wretchedness." He never saw his entry into the Jesuits as apostasy against Russia, even though entering the Society of Jesus meant physical separation from his homeland. As for his definition of national identity, he wrote, "I also highly value nationality [*narodnost'*], but in my eyes it does not consist in common beginnings and in the maintenance of old, outdated forms. I base national identity on independence; on the exercise of this independence in scholarship; the achievement of enlightenment [*prosveshchene*] does not diminish us, when we gather the fruit placed before us by friendly peoples."[3] By Gagarin's reckoning, he was the patriot and his critics were the betrayers of Russia's interest.

Gagarin's conception of nationality was sharply at odds with Orthodox views on the subject, but it could claim at least some justification in Russian legal practice. Orthodox assertions that religious apostasy meant a renunciation of national identity implied that any Catholic should be classified as non-Russian. Legally speaking, however, neither Gagarin, nor Svechina, nor Shuvalov was ever classified as non-Russian, despite their adherence to Roman Catholicism. Even an atheist like Herzen was never classified by law as non-Russian. Under Nicholas I there was a difference between Russia's religious self-conception and its juridical practice.

Gagarin's views on nationality were also perhaps more consistent than the views held by the Slavophiles: if peasant status were made a requirement for Russian nationality, as the Slavophile Konstantin Aksakov implied it should be, the Slavophiles, being gentry themselves, would no longer be Russians.[4] The Slavophiles could not very well apply to Gagarin criteria they failed to meet themselves. Also, obedience to the tsar was not a consistently applied criterion for Russian nationalism; Gagarin was at least as supportive of the tsar as were the Slavophiles, and even more supportive than Westerners such as Herzen.[5] Neither the Slavophiles nor the Westerners were condemned for being non-Russian as a result of their desires to increase certain freedoms within Russia.

My objective here is not to decide whether Gagarin should be defined as a Russian but to explore the differing conceptions of national identity held by Gagarin and his opponents and to grasp what those national conceptions tell us about the two parties. Gagarin's definition of nationality was both civic and religious: it was civic insofar as it involved a commitment to the nation's welfare, a hope of making Russia equal to the countries of Western Europe; it was religious insofar as Gagarin believed that Russia's welfare depended on ecclesiastical union with Rome. According to Gagarin, this union would lead to a new era in Russian history, religiously, socially, and intellectually. It would serve as a means of protecting Russia from the harmful forces of revolution. Orthodox conceptions of nationality shared Gagarin's civic commitment to Russia's welfare but repudiated his religious ideas.

The profound differences in conceptions of national identity informed the debate between Khomiakov and Gagarin over Khomiakov's notion of *sobornost'*. Scholars such as Berdiaev, Christoff and Walicki have recognized the centrality of *sobornost'* in Slavophilism.[6] In spite of recognition that Khomiakov's most explicit treatise on *sobornost'* was written in response to Gagarin's initial claim that the Orthodox church was not catholic, nobody has examined Gagarin's views for the light they cast on this crucial concept.[7]

The debate between Khomiakov and Gagarin began on 27 January 1860 with a speech by Gagarin at l'Église de Notre-Dame des Victoires. Gagarin asserted that in the Slavonic translation of the Nicene Creed "the world *catholic* has been replaced by a vague and obscure expression which does not convey the idea of [the church's] universality, of its amazing expansion to all regions, to all peoples."[8] He asserted that, by using the word *sobornaia* rather than *kafolicheskaia* in the Slavonic translation of the Creed, in the phrase "I believe in one holy, *catholic*, and apostolic church," the Russian Orthodox translators failed to convey the sense of unity contained within the word *catholic.* Gagarin claimed the word *sobornaia* implies that the church is "synodal" or "conciliar," not "universal" in the sense of being "unbounded geographically."[9]

Khomiakov thought Gagarin's objection ludicrous. He rejected Gagarin's idea that *catholic* denotes a church existing throughout the world in all places and among all peoples. After all, nobody had yet located the Roman church "among *the Turks in Turkey, among the Persians in Persia, among the Negroes in the interior of Africa.*"[10] If Gagarin's definition were valid, Khomiakov thought, then the church was not *catholic* at its Pentecostal beginnings when it was surrounded by paganism; nor was it *catholic* when threatened by the forces of Islam which spread "from the Pyrenees to the frontiers of China"; neither was it *catholic* at present since the world harbored more Buddhists than Roman Catholics.[11]

Although all original copies of the Slavonic translation of the Nicene Creed had been lost, Khomiakov assured Russians that current translations were authentic. He agreed with Gagarin that the word *sobornaia* was "vague and obscure," but he found it no more obscure than the Greek word καθολικός.[12]

Khomiakov recognized the words *catholic* in the West and *sobornaia* in Russia had acquired different connotations. He claimed these connotations reflected the authenticity of the Orthodox church and the error of the Roman Catholic church:

> *Sobor* implies the idea of assembly, not necessarily joined in some place but existing virtually without formal reunion. It is unity in plurality. Thus, it is evident that the word *katholicos* in the thought of the two great servants of God that Greece sent to the Slavs [Cyril and Methodius] came not from *kath'ola,* but from *kath'olon. Kata* is based on the word *according to* (*kata Loukan, kata Joannen,* according to Luke, according to John). The Catholic church is the church *which is based on all,* or *based on the unity of all,* the church of free unity, of perfect unity, where there are no more nationalities, neither Greek nor barbarian, where there are no longer differences in conditions, no masters or slaves; this is the church prophesied by the Old Testament and realized by the New, the church that finally Saint Paul defined.[13]

For Khomiakov, *sobornaia* meant that the members of the church were united in a free and organic fellowship in a perfect or *catholic* union.[14] The

Russian church was truly *catholic,* because all members of Orthodox society lived in a communal setting; Western churches lacked this free community, so they were not truly *catholic* in the Greek sense. Khomiakov argued that the Protestant churches, though free, lacked unity, as witnessed by the diversity in their dogmatic teachings. Meanwhile, the Roman church was united but not in free community, for its members experienced the tyranny of the papacy. In Protestantism there was diversity of beliefs, in Orthodoxy there was a union of faith. In Roman Catholicism there was a formal, compulsory unity based on involuntary submission to papal tyranny, in Orthodoxy there was a free unity created by voluntary submission to the community. Ivan Aksakov further clarified this idea in a letter to Gagarin in which he wrote, "In the church, rulership is not a matter of external, juridical administration; rather it is something spiritual and moral—not a matter of numbers but of content. The church's unity consists in a common consciousness. Therefore, although Ivan [the Terrible], Peter [I], Biron succeeded in perverting the church's external, administrative status, although they could and did bind her external freedom, they could not affect the inner unity of the universal church."[15]

Khomiakov was not the only Orthodox writer attacking Gagarin's interpretation of church universalism. Suchkov, Guettée, and Baranovskii all argued that "The Catholic is the *complete Christian;* for to be Catholic and to belong to the true church of Jesus Christ, it suffices to accept the revealed doctrine, without removing anything, without adding anything to that which has been admitted by the apostolic and universal church."[16] Suchkov added some additional qualifications to his definition of *catholic.* He further argued that "The adjective *sobornaia,* the noun *sobor,* and the verb *sobirat',* express the double idea of the action *to assemble* and *to reunify; sobornaia* denotes one church *composed of the reunion of all the particular churches,* that is to say *catholic* (according to the Greek sense of the word)."[17] To this, Suchkov added the definition of the Academy of Saint Petersburg in its 1847 dictionary, *Ecclesiastico-slavo-russe,* which defined *sobornaia* as "universal, catholic."[18] Suchkov further noted that in French texts containing the teachings of the Russian Orthodox church, the world *sobornaia* was always translated as *catholic.*[19] Finally, Suchkov wrote, "I belong to the Russian people, and I assert that the Jesuit father seeks to give a false idea of it; surely these people understand their own language and religion better than Father Gagarin understood them when he entered the Roman church."[20]

Guettée, writing on this issue, accused the Roman Catholics of altering the Nicene Creed by adding the word "Roman." He wrote, "This word is not in the Creed, my reverend father. And note when a church is *Roman* or *of Rome,* it loses the character of *catholicity* or *universality.*"[21]

Like Suchkov and Guettée, Gagarin understood *catholic* to mean "universal." His point was that Orthodox churches were local or national rather than universal. He wrote, "One only has to use one's eyes to see that the churches of this communion [Orthodox] are local or national churches, that they do not form a universal church. In this case, they are in a situation inferior to Protestantism; Protestants are everywhere, but one cannot say the same of the Easterners."[22]

While the translators of the Creed into Slavonic may have believed that the word *sobornaia* conveyed the meaning of the Greek word καθολικός, Gagarin believed that *sobornaia* only expressed "the idea of collection, of assembly" not the idea of universality contained in καθολικός.[23] To prove his point, Gagarin looked at various ecclesiastical uses of the word *sobor.* He noted that the word could mean "council" (in the phrase *vselenskii sobor* [ecumenical council]) or "cathedral" (in the phrase *uspenskii sobor* [Cathedral of the Assumption]). While καθολικός may have been translated as *sobornaia* in the Creed, outside of the Creed the word *sobornaia* was never synonymous with "universality." It simply did not connote universal expansion in the sense contained within καθολικός. Gagarin also observed that Russian translations from Greek, Latin, French, German, English, and Spanish, never used *sobornaia* in place of *kafolicheskaia.* The phrase *sobornyi sviashchennik* did not mean "Catholic priest," but "a priest attached to a cathedral"; the phrase *sobornoe postanovlenie* meant a "conciliar decree."[24]

Gagarin believed that, despite the attempts of Orthodox elites to convince themselves of the contrary, the Russian faithful reciting the Creed in Slavonic did not have the concept of universality in mind when they said the word *sobornaia;* instead they thought of "conciliar" or "synodal." Fellow convert Vladimir Pecherin agreed with Gagarin's position: "I am completely of your view on the sense of the word *sobornaia.* I recall well the impressions of my childhood: I always thought that this signified 'the conciliar church.'"[25]

In trying to compare the various definitions and understandings of *kafolicheskaia* and *sobornaia,* we must face a problem regarding the Orthodox understanding of *catholic.* Suchkov and Guettée believed that the church must be universal, but Khomiakov apparently did not. He cited the presence of a non-Catholic majority in various parts of the world as evidence against the church's universality. Khomiakov's attacks on Gagarin's conception of *catholic* therefore applied equally to the conceptions of Suchkov and Guettée.

Still, there were similarities between Gagarin's perspective and that of the various Orthodox writers. Gagarin, Suchkov, and Guettée all recognized the church's universality. Suchkov and Guettée were less concerned to ridicule the Roman Catholic church's lack of universality than to show how the Orthodox church met that definition.[26] Guettée's argument that Gagarin's church was *Roman* rather than *catholic* is similar to Gagarin's view that the Orthodox churches were *Russian, Greek*—that is, national rather than *catholic.* All disputants agreed with Khomiakov's view that in the true church "there are no more nationalities."

Other aspects of the various definitions are less easy to reconcile and, in fact, support Gagarin's arguments. Suchkov's idea that *sobornaia* meant the "reunion of all particular churches" lent support to Gagarin's argument that *sobornaia* meant conciliarity rather than universality. Guettée's comparison of the word *Roman* in *Roman* Catholic church with the word *Russian* in *Russian* Orthodox church could be turned against him: the word *Roman* plainly referred to the Roman rite, whereas *Russian* contained the idea of nationality.

It is difficult to define what Khomiakov meant when he defined *sobornost'* as "perfect unity." Khomiakov proudly insisted that Westerners were entirely incapable of understanding the term and he himself never published a monograph, treatise, or essay to explain *sobornost'*—even though it was a central concept for the Slavophiles. The term *sobornost'* remained the property of Orthodox believers. Indeed, it is doubtful that Khomiakov's idea had any connection whatsoever with the universality which Suchkov and Guettée implied in their ideas of *catholic.*[27] Khomiakov's idea of *sobornost'* only reinforced Gagarin's accusations that the Orthodox church was a national church.

Like Khomiakov, Gagarin failed to fully present his ideas in this polemical exchange.[28] Gagarin's earlier correspondence with Kireevskii and Samarin indicated that the idea of *catholic* contained within it the ideas of expansion and the possibility of separate nationalities coexisting within a universal church. This correspondence proves Gagarin recognized that, at the time of Pentecost, the term *catholic* did not mean the church existed everywhere, only that the church could exist everywhere without an end to differences in nationality. If Gagarin had reminded the Slavophiles of his earlier positions, he might have been more persuasive to them.

Gagarin saw the church as a supranational entity, a cosmopolitan organization that encompasses all peoples without destroying their national peculiarities. He saw himself as a "Russian" who had become "Catholic" without abandoning his "Russianness." In the same way, he believed that Russian Orthodoxy could join the Roman church without sacrificing its national character. However, if the Orthodox insisted on isolating themselves from other Christians, they would forfeit their place in the universal church. In isolation, they would never achieve equality with the rest of Europe.

Before leaving the theme of national identity, we must investigate the disagreement between the Slavophiles and Gagarin over whether Slavophilism was a revolutionary ideology. The Slavophiles presented themselves as conservatives loyal to the Russian autocracy. In a memorandum to Tsar Alexander II, Aksakov proudly proclaimed that, in Russia, revolution was inconceivable.[29] Yet, the Slavophiles desired changes in various aspects of Russian society. Like Gagarin, they deplored the ignorance of the Russian clergy. Sergei Timofeevich Aksakov wrote, "Our clergy is fit for nothing; it is decidedly harmful to the religious convictions of the people and arouses them against itself."[30] The Slavophiles also worried about the state's heavy-handed interference in matters of conscience. Khomiakov wrote, "The general aspect of things, at least in matters of religion is very favorable in our country, and would be still more so if we had not so much of political religion, and if only the state were more convinced that Christian truth has no need of constant protection, for faith is weakened by an excessive solicitude."[31] Like Gagarin, the Slavophiles desired greater freedom of religious expression, and they claimed that "this absence of freedom of speech more than anything else is harmful to the Russian Christian world."[32]

The changes recommended by the Slavophiles were far from revolutionary. Still, Gagarin accused the Slavophiles of at least indirect support for revolution.[33] He saw the roots of revolution and communism in the principle of communal ownership supported by the Slavophiles. Although the 1861 emancipation of the peasants had eased dependence on the landowner, the commune itself remained intact. Gagarin was concerned that the commune would lead to revolution because it would place the will of the masses over the will of the established government. In the commune, Gagarin saw the specter of democracy and the possibility of a violent attempt by the commune to place itself in power.[34] Gagarin also worried about the Slavophile phobia of the West. He was concerned that

Slavophile contempt for Western learning might exacerbate the uneducated masses' hatred of the upper classes. Because of this, he argued that the Slavophiles merited the name "Europophobe."[35] He saw in the Slavophiles' advocacy of universal suffrage an end to the separation of clergy and laity; hence, he concluded that Khomiakov's teachings were the "teachings of Lamennais" in Russian disguise.[36]

Gagarin found support for his views of the Slavophiles from other Russian converts. Father Leontii Nikolai wrote:

> I am sure that the Slavophiles are honest. Yet, I do not doubt that they are pioneers of the plague that today ravages every country; the mania of nationalities is only a phase; it strokes the passions and ignorance, it undermines the terrain very softly, removes from the regular authorities their initiative, and creates for the profit of the masses a certain omnipotence of opinion, which exploited by men without faith or law, becomes, one fine day, revolution.[37]

The Slavophiles did not perceive themselves as a revolutionary group. They were just as concerned as Gagarin was with the possibilities of a peasant uprising. In a memorandum to the tsar, Samarin wrote, "three-hundred-thousand landowners are, not without grounds, alarmed by the expectation of a frightful revolution."[38] Those ideas which Gagarin thought "revolutionary" were not considered to be revolutionary by the Slavophiles but rather a return to a Russian culture uncontaminated by Western influences. Furthermore, the Slavophiles did not want a return to this "truly Russian culture" to be brought about by violent means but by gradual, peaceful change.

Gagarin ascribed revolutionary ideas to the Slavophiles because he saw similarities between the Slavophiles and the radical Westerners, particularly on the peasant question. He failed to consider that the Slavophiles, as serf-owning members of the gentry, had a material interest in preventing a violent revolution. He also failed to note his common ground with the Slavophiles on matters such as the dependence of the clergy and the advance of secular values. For their part, the Slavophiles were shortsighted not to recognize their agreement with Gagarin on the need for greater freedom of speech and a church independent from the Russian state.

On many issues the Slavophiles and Gagarin were closer to each other than the Slavophiles wished to admit. As Gagarin wrote of the Slavophiles, "One sees that there is nothing [in Slavophilism] essentially opposed to

Catholicism, nothing which makes rapprochement impossible. When the misunderstandings which exist today will have disappeared, nothing will prevent this party from becoming the most ardent promoter of union."[39] In a similar fashion Khomiakov wrote that "the greatest obstacles to unity are not in the visible and formal differences of doctrine (as theologians are apt to suppose), but in the spirit which pervades the Western communities, in their customs, prejudices, and passions, but more than anything else, in a feeling of pride which hinders a confession of past errors, and a feeling of disdain which would not admit that divine truth has been preserved and guarded for many ages by the long-despised and benighted East."[40] Both Gagarin and the Slavophiles saw their first duty as service to their native land and a desire to make Russia serve as an intermediary between East and West; the differences between them arose in regard to what direction Russia should take to reach that point.

As has become obvious, Gagarin's writings, particularly *La Russie*, generated a tremendous reaction, both positive and negative. Such a reaction was neither entirely unintended nor unwanted. Through publications, particularly in Russian, Gagarin and the other Russian Jesuits hoped to achieve the greatest influence in their former land. As Martynov wrote: "It is my deepest conviction that we need to have a Slavic press with Russian, Cyrillic and Glagolitic characters. . . . Of course, we have in mind certain works which absolutely require a Slavic press, that is, the reprinting of manuscripts or, even, scholarly works where Slavic text is necessary."[41] Fellow Jesuit Balabin even talked of publishing a Russian translation of Ignatius' *Spiritual Exercises*.[42]

Gagarin took advantage of every chance to express his ideas in Russian. For example, in his projected response to Iakhontov's attacks, Gagarin noted that he would achieve several advantages from responding in Russian because "M. Iakhontov could not dispense from mentioning my response in his own, and by this he would make those in the seminaries and clergy aware of its existence; many persons would procure it and despite all prohibitions they [Gagarin's ideas] would succeed. They would be incomparably better understood than my French brochures." He further noted that his earlier publications would have had a larger impact "if they had not been done in French."[43] Beckx agreed that publication in Russian was necessary, "an entirely natural labor." He approved of the Jesuits' desire to publish in that language.[44]

The Orthodox were unsure how to evaluate Gagarin's status as a spokesman for Roman Catholicism. One author attributed to Gagarin's

La Russie an increase in Europe's interest in issues of church relations.[45] The Jesuit journal *Feuilles historico-politiques* claimed that the Orthodox church perceived Gagarin to be so dangerous that it was forced to establish a journal (*L'Union chrétienne*) to refute him.[46]

Gagarin's writings entered Russia in various ways. Dzhunkovskii published Gagarin's catechism, *Sokrovishche,* at his press in Norway. The text was spread by Roman Catholic missionaries into the hands of Russians in the Arkangelskaia guberniia of northwest Russia; these missionaries placed particular attention on distributing the text among the Old Believers.[47] *La Russie* entered Russia with relative ease, perhaps because the authorities under Tsar Alexander II were preoccupied with the peasant emancipation. Gagarin believed that *La Russie* "was read by many educated people." He noted that "in this first moment the impression was not profound." He was assured "that the men most opposed to it believed that it was useless to respond."[48]

La Russie was spread by Roman Catholics in Saint Petersburg and Moscow who "began to cite it in their discussions with schismatics." The Catholics "commented, they applied it, and by this method they produced much more fruit than it could have produced by itself."[49] One priest, Vasilii Grechovlevich, became the propagator of *La Russie.* Charged with teaching the catechism in a boarding school for young women, he distributed sheets detached from Gagarin's text and told the women to make many copies.[50]

Gagarin was fully aware of the impact his text was having among Russian Roman Catholics. A Polish priest wrote that Gagarin's text "has made a sensation in Petersburg."[51] He was equally aware that his writings had generated conversions among the Russian Orthodox. A letter of Countess Anne Apponyi to Gagarin stated:

> The brochures that you have had the goodness to send me have made a quite profound impression, the one about the *Staroveres* especially. It seems to me difficult to refute it, however a Russian priest that I have seen this winter has tried. What can one oppose to your arguments? I do not understand them and I am more shaken then ever since I read your writings.[52]

Beckx was equally aware of the effect of *La Russie* and was happy that "the attention of Russia was excited on this question without causing irritation on the part of the Russians."[53]

However, Beckx was wrong. The Russian government was irritated and had been irritated for some time with the activities by Gagarin and the other Russian Jesuits. The government's decision to sentence Gagarin and the other Russian Jesuits to exile had already given one indication of its concern. Further indications of governmental hostility are evident in an 1852 letter to the Russian Third Section which described Gagarin, Pecherin, Martynov, Dzhunkovskii, and Balabin as "all Jesuits." The letter written complained that "without any doubt, there is no possibility for us to presently put an end to this *evil*."[54]

Many important Russian officials were unhappy with what Vasil'ev called Gagarin's "war against Orthodoxy."[55] Metropolitan Filaret asked, "What is the goal of the nest of Jesuits? Falling away from Orthodoxy, they attack Orthodox texts and even write a *shameful* book against Orthodoxy." Filaret asserted that the "Jesuits wish to *cripple* us."[56] Andrei Murav'ev was equally concerned; he wondered, "How many such books [like *Sokrovishche*] has Gagarin written?" He wanted to present Gagarin's texts to the Holy Synod and Russian clergy so that they could respond appropriately.[57]

The reason for the Russian authorities' concern is given by Vladimir Fedorovich Odoevskii:

> The calm, nonargumentative activity of the Jesuitic texts of Gagarin, Martynov, and others may be even more dangerous [than the writings of Herzen and Petr Dolgorukov], for these texts, published in the form of spiritually edifying discussions, even as types of prayer books (as for example *Sokrovishche Khristianina*), have penetrated the hearts of those people who would be angered by anarchic ravings. It is also said that the existence of Jesuitic texts was widespread among the Raskolniks [Old Believers].[58]

In addition, the Russian government was worried about the status of those former Byzantine Catholics in Western Russia who had been forcibly converted to Orthodoxy and who now were returning in large numbers to Catholicism.[59] Vasil'ev further argued that Gagarin's writings, in particular *O primirenii russkoi tserkvi s rimskoiu* and *Pis'ma o neporochnom zachatii bogoroditsy,* might be dangerous "for the uneducated and soft Orthodox." These texts were "dangerous" because Gagarin's methodology of using selections from Russian liturgical texts to support Catholic doctrines such as papal primacy might be convincing to some Orthodox faithful.[60] Gagarin himself noted that his publications had produced a great effect in Russia and caused many Russian journals to become focused on his works and on the issues of church union.[61]

The Russian government responded in various ways to the perceived threat from Gagarin. A flat prohibition against publication of Gagarin's writings was issued.[62] The police maintained a constant watch on his activities. The letters of Iosif Vasil'ev (1821–1861), chaplain at the Russian embassy in Paris, to A. P. Tolstoi, the procurator of the Holy Synod, suggest that one of Vasil'ev's responsibilities was to keep the Russian government informed about Gagarin's activity.[63] The Orthodox authorities sometimes responded to Gagarin's texts with publications of their own. Murav'ev's critique has already been mentioned. Murav'ev called on the Holy Synod to distribute texts throughout all of Russia reiterating the "true beliefs" of the Orthodox church and attacking the Jesuits.[64] V. F. Odoevskii urged publication in the West of unflattering biographical works about Gagarin.[65] Vasil'ev also wanted to publish criticisms of Gagarin in Western languages. He argued that the Jesuits published their "venomous arrows" in Russian because it was safe: "The Sons of Loyola think that the response to their works will also be in Russian, which is not understood by Western Catholics." Thus, Vasil'ev argued, when the Orthodox pointed out the weaknesses in the Roman church, their arguments would not be noticed in the West.[66]

Another interesting example of the Russian government's support for published attacks on Gagarin was its decision to issue an official thanks to Karatheodores for his text attacking Gagarin.[67] Note also the publications of texts at this time which implicated Gagarin in the death of Pushkin. The Russian government apparently believed that they would serve a purpose in discrediting Gagarin.

The chief response of Russian propagandists was the creation of the journal *L'Union chrétienne*. Published from 1859 to 1870 for the Russian mission in France, *L'Union chrétienne* proclaimed as its goal to serve "as the center and as the organ for true Christians who wish to participate in the work of fostering religious unity that Our Savior Jesus Christ established on the earth."[68] Vasil'ev's presence on the editorial staff of the journal, as well as the presence of Suchkov and Guettée, who had strong Russian Orthodox connections, indicates that the Russian religious authorities had a significant role in the publication. This explains the large amount of space in the journal's early issues dedicated to criticism of Gagarin; it also explains the rumor that the journal had been founded with the sole purpose of attacking Gagarin.

Evidence of the irritation caused by Gagarin's *La Russie* can be seen in the government's response to Gagarin's petition to see his dying father. On 29 November 1856, Gagarin sent Beckx a draft of a letter to Tsar Alexander II asking for permission to visit his father. In this letter, Gagarin told the tsar that while he "never regretted what I have always considered as the discharge of a duty [to join the Jesuits], it is no less true that the sacrifice has been heavy and that my heart has bled more than once."[69] Gagarin appealed to the tsar's kindness by citing the aid of previous tsars to the Jesuit order, by mentioning the death of his mother and the age of his father, who was "at the gates of death." Gagarin hoped that the tsar would permit him to visit his father one last time.[70]

Alas, filial piety was not the only reason for which Gagarin wanted to return to Russia. Gagarin subordinated all things to the goal of converting Russia. A letter to Beckx indicated that Gagarin also sought permission for Balabin to return to Russia. He would later petition for permission to act as a priest, and finally would ask Alexander's permission for the other Jesuits to enter Russia.[71] Beckx approved only a request to visit Gagarin's dying father; no approval was given to Gagarin's other suggestions. Gagarin sent the letter to Alexander II in December 1856.

On 13 December 1856, Prince Vasilii Dolgorukov, head of the Third Section, wrote to Gagarin's father, Sergei, that Ivan wished to see him for a few days.[72] Sergei responded with joy at the prospect of seeing his son: "As a father, how could one not wish it? I am deeply grateful to His Imperial Majesty for graciously permitting me to respond to the request of my son."[73] On 29 December 1856, the Russian Ministry of Internal Affairs asked the Third Section to inform the Russian embassy in Paris that Ivan had been permitted to spend fifteen days with his father.[74]

Unfortunately, several Russians opposed Gagarin's return to Russia. We have already mentioned the hostility of Gagarin's brother-in-law and sister.[75] More seriously, Filaret wrote to Murav'ev that "Surely he [Gagarin] will not be permitted to come? They assure me that this will not be."[76] Gagarin himself wrote, "there is in Moscow an outburst of public opinion against me; it is said that I asked to come not to see my father, but to initiate conversions."[77]

The opposition to Ivan Gagarin's prospective return frightened Sergei Gagarin, who asked the tsar to "excuse his excitement" and to rescind his request to see his son. Sergei emphasized his love of country and of the tsar. He thanked Alexander for "permission to embrace once more my unhappy son." However, the hostile response, particularly from Gagarin's sister and brother-in-law was too great to permit Ivan to return.[78] On 9 January 1857, the Third Section sent a telegraph to Paris rescinding permission for Gagarin's trip. The decision was motivated by the change in his father's desires.[79] On 28 February 1857, Beckx informed Gagarin that his permission to return home had been revoked. Beckx attributed the revocation to *La Russie* and to an uproar in Russia generated by this text.[80] The unhappy Gagarin blamed neither his family nor the tsar. Alexander II, Gagarin wrote, "has shown that he is a most tolerant man." Gagarin attributed the decision to unnamed Muscovites who "give me too much honor."[81] Beckx would later tell Gagarin that it was probably good that he did not return to Russia: "in Russia they would put you on trial or confine you to the estates of the prince, your father; they would not permit you to visit Petersburg; they would prohibit the exercise of the ministries of confession and of preaching." Beckx consoled Gagarin with the thought that "in Paris, by your demeanor and your writings, you serve more efficaciously the cause of Catholicism in Russia than you could in Petersburg or Moscow."[82] Gagarin's father died on December 9/17 of 1863 without again seeing his son.

Gagarin's polemics with the Orthodox and his problems with the Russian government demonstrated the degree of mistrust and anger which he generated through his writings and ideas. Despite moments of agreement between Gagarin and his Orthodox opponents on the need for Orthodox ecclesiastical independence vis-à-vis the Russian state, Gagarin's desire to convert Russia clashed with Orthodox conceptions of national identity. The Orthodox mistrusted the Jesuits too deeply to find a modus vivendi with Gagarin; this mistrust was only exacerbated by Gagarin's verbal aggressiveness and occasional deceptiveness.

Meanwhile the Russian government took Gagarin seriously enough to subsidize a journal (*L'Union chrétienne*) to refute his arguments and to award a medal to a Greek Orthodox opponent of Gagarin. The Russian government kept Gagarin under police surveillance in Paris. Finally, the government did nothing to alleviate the atmosphere of hostility toward Gagarin among the Russian Orthodox elites. In fact, the government used this hostility as a lever to move Sergei Gagarin to rescind his invitation asking Ivan to return home to Russia.

Gagarin's activities fueled this hostility. He had his texts smuggled into Russia. He intentionally sought the support of the Old Believers against the existing church-state dispensation in Russia. He tried to take advantage of his father to engineer the return of the Jesuit order to Russia. Worst of all, he accused the Orthodox church of violating the Nicene Creed.

For all these reasons, Gagarin's suggestion that church union could be achieved through the simple agreement of pope and tsar received little support from the Russian government. Significant differences between Orthodoxy and Catholicism prevented achievement of union.

CHAPTER SEVEN

Byzantine Catholics and the Middle East

> It is quite true that there is something transitory and provisory in the actual situation of the Uniate church, but the goal for which one must work is not the absorption of this church by the Latin church, but the absorption of the Greek church in its entirety by the Greek-Uniate church. Our efforts should not aim at causing some thousands of individuals to embrace the Latin rite, but [rather] at making some seventy million [non-Catholic] Christians enter the Catholic church.[1]

Just as Russian hostility prevented Gagarin from promoting church union in his native land, opposition by French Jesuits limited Gagarin's effectiveness in Paris. After publishing two large articles and two book reviews in the 1859 volume of *Études*, only two book reviews by Gagarin appeared during the years 1860 and 1861. He was increasingly estranged from the journal he had so recently founded. The problem was a sharp disagreement between Gagarin and French Jesuits over the direction of *Études*. While Gagarin saw the journal as a tool for achieving union with Orthodoxy, his coeditor, Father Daniel, strove to broaden the journal's focus and to appeal to a wider French audience. After a time, when it had become apparent that these two visions were impossible to reconcile, Father Daniel decided to force Gagarin and the other Russian Jesuits from the journal's editorial board.[2] The danger that Father Daniel's coup de main might succeed was increased by Gagarin's isolation in the Jesuit order: only a handful of Jesuits, either in the company at large or on the editorial committee of *Études,* was really interested in issues involving Russia or Orthodoxy.

Among those uninterested in Orthodoxy was the French provincial, Michel Fessard, a figure who disdained Gagarin. Fessard thought Gagarin difficult to work with, a man of "irascible character" and "acerbic tongue."[3]

Even Beckx, in response to Gagarin's decision to undertake a retreat at Liesse in January of 1860, wrote:

> Yes, my Father, the Divine Master you love, who has called and added you to his service in the company, has spoken to [your] heart: one recognizes this in the way you acknowledge your defects and especially the resolution that you have to work with all your strength and with the help of divine grace to become a contemplative man [homme intérieur]. Doubtlessly, that is a work for every religious of the company, but this obligation is somewhat more urgent for you, my Father; because, for your very extensive activity to be constantly and entirely directed to God's greater glory, it must be directed by a spirit of faith and by a powerful interior life; and also because God alone can tame the tongue of man.[4]

Because of his French orientation and a personal dislike for Gagarin, Fessard assumed that the best way to deal with the conflict between Daniel and Gagarin was to separate the two. Thus, in autumn 1860, Gagarin was sent to Strasbourg to work in pastoral ministry. He now feared that *Études* was being taken from him. Gagarin wrote to Beckx that he was the "sole Russian against four French." He complained about "secret intrigues" against him. He suggested that l'Oeuvre des SS. Cyrille et Méthode be suppressed and replaced with a new organization in which Balabin and Martynov would serve as members and not advisors.[5] Beckx responded to Gagarin that there were no real problems with *Études*. Martynov and Balabin would be able to replace him while he was in Strasbourg. Beckx also advised Gagarin to remain calm. He noted that Gagarin had been heard to say with respect to an opponent, "One must remove that Father!"[6]

However, Gagarin's fears were not allayed. On 12 October 1860, attempting to separate *Études* from the French Jesuits, Gagarin sent another letter to Beckx. He now asked for permission to move l'Oeuvre des SS. Cyrille et Méthode to Jerusalem. He observed that Jerusalem was the center of the East, the site of pilgrimages from Russia; in Jerusalem, he claimed, there was a possibility to meet and influence Russian monks, priests, even bishops, and to establish contacts with Old Believers. Gagarin also asserted that Russians no longer came to Paris.[7] Beckx responded that, though he was favorable to an annual visit of two months to Jerusalem, since l'Oeuvre des SS. Cyrille et Méthode had been established in

Paris, it would remain there barring some very grave development.[8] This, of course, did not satisfy Gagarin. He left Paris without being on speaking terms with Fessard.[9]

The French Jesuits pressed their attempt to obtain control over *Études.* Some Jesuits complained to Fessard that the *Études* was too soft and compromising, others complained it was not very compromising and, as a result, was colorless and inferior to what Jesuits should produce. Father Fessard charged Father Daniel with drafting a memoir in support of *Études;* however the memoir backfired. Daniel ended his presentation by submitting his resignation. Fathers Mertian and Matignon voiced their support for *Études.* Fessard came to the conclusion that *Études* should continue and advised Beckx of that.[10] Beckx agreed that *Études* would continue to exist and be dedicated to the work begun by Gagarin. On 25 January 1861, Father Mertian wrote to Gagarin in Strasbourg about the decision of Beckx:

> The *Études* are not to be separated from l'Oeuvre des S. Cyrille, the Father General wishes that it be attached to you and as you would wish. There will be a collective directorship which will operate by majority vote. Fathers Balabin and Martynov are to be members of this group, but entirely *ad honores.* The voting members will be you, Fathers Matignon, Daniel, Dutau, and me.

Mertian went on to inform Gagarin that the directorship would contain a president, procurer, and librarian. Furthermore, there would be no superior other than the provincial, to whom the president would answer. Neither the president, nor the procurer, nor the librarian could act unilaterally; all decisions required approval of the directorship. Mertian concluded, "Thus, although the two works will not be truly separate, I do not see that they will have anything in common except for you, dear Father, who are a bright ring binding St. Cyrille to the *Études.*"[11] Although Beckx's decision represented a formal victory for Gagarin, he feared that the peculiar composition of the directorship would reduce to zero his actual control over the journal. Gagarin's letter to Mertian, thanking the latter for his assistance in keeping the *Études* focused on Russian church union, fairly breathes resentment at the French Jesuits:

> If one ever decides to write the history of *Études de théologie* and *l'Oeuvre des S. Cyrille* your letter of the 25th will certainly be one of the most curious pages of this history. It exceeds all that I would have

> imagined. . . . We thus constitute a chapter: five titular canons, two honorary canons, and you, the oldest member. This is a marvel.[12]

Gagarin wrote to Beckx at the same time, not to thank him for his intervention in the conflict, but to state his fears that the *Études* would lose its original mission.[13]

To understand Gagarin's motive for transferring l'Oeuvre des SS. Cyril et Méthode to Jerusalem, we must look back at his 1859 trip to the Middle East. Early in 1859, l'Oeuvre des Pèleringages invited Gagarin to serve as chaplain on a pilgrimage to the Middle East. The invitation excited Gagarin, who said it "has hit me like a bomb."[14] He asked Beckx for permission to accept the invitation; the approval was given on 22 January 1859.[15] Gagarin wanted to see the Holy Land for two reasons. First, he saw the trip as a culmination of the Ignatian practice of mental prayer called "composition of place."[16] By this, Gagarin meant that to truly understand the biblical texts, it was necessary to "transport oneself by thought to the place which serves as the setting for the evangelic writings." For Gagarin, it would be much easer to create this mental picture if he could actually see the place imagined. Secondly, he hoped to meet Russian pilgrims in the Holy Land and study the Byzantine rite. He wrote, "A mass of ideas has come to me on this subject. But I must first see what one can do. I should, however, say that Providence seems to be at work and is preparing something by it [his journey]."[17] After leaving Paris in May 1859, Gagarin visited Beirut, Malta, Jaffa, Jerusalem, Bethlehem, Jordan, Jericho, Naples, Nazareth, Carmel, and many other famous pilgrimage sites. He returned to France on 19 July 1859.

In an article entitled "Trois mois en Orient," Gagarin commented on the status of the Catholic church in the Middle East.[18] He argued that the Byzantine rite of the Catholic church was under attack from two directions. On one flank, the Orthodox church and "the ancient schism of Byzantium" threatened to separate the Byzantine Catholic church from Rome.[19] On the other, Protestantism "works to seduce and corrupt" Byzantine Catholics.[20] To deal with this double threat, the Byzantine Catholics needed a strong clergy.

Gagarin believed that the problems confronting Byzantine Catholicism could be resolved by the establishment of better seminaries for the education of clergy and by the unification of all Arabic speakers in one church. According to Gagarin, in spite of differences in nationalities and beliefs, Middle Easterners were linked by the Arabic language. If one could bring all Arabic speakers together in an Arabic church, one would change the historical direction of the entire region. "Give these men religious unity, as they already have unity of language, and you will immediately create a powerful nationality capable of playing a great role in the world."[21] Gagarin proposed an Arabic church that would be a Byzantine rite Catholic church. With its creation, the Byzantine rite would again dominate most of the Middle East, just as it had in the past. Meanwhile the Maronite rite would flourish in Lebanon; other rites would be preserved so long as there remained congregations to practice them. Membership in a Byzantine rite would therefore be no obstacle to pan-Arabic unity. "Speaking all the same language, reading all the same books, possessing all the same literature, the same civilization, they would form an intelligent, sparkling, rich and powerful nation."[22]

A great Arab church could not exist without a strong clergy, and such a clergy could only be created through proper education. Gagarin argued for the establishment of several different types of schools for the preparation of clergy. He supported the effort by l'Oeuvre des Écoles d'Orient to create a network of public and primary schools.[23] This work, which Gagarin called "a true crusade, a peaceful crusade," had already resulted in the creation of primary schools in Beirut, Bikfayya, Zahleh, and Sayda.[24]

Colleges and seminaries also needed to be established "to prepare a clergy equal to its mission."[25] Colleges would be designed for the upper classes of Arabic society, while seminaries would cater to persons from all social backgrounds who wanted to enter the clergy. Gagarin pointed to the Jesuit college and seminary at Gaza as a model.[26] He also proposed a new school at Jerusalem "to combat the challenge of German theology."[27] He argued, "Two or three able professors would be sent to these places, they would quickly attract numerous disciples. After a few years one would have a center whence true exegesis could radiate throughout the world."[28] Though these seminaries would train indigenous Arab-speaking clergy, Gagarin hoped they would "plant some seeds of European civilization" and bring about the conversion of non-Christians and the Orthodox.[29]

With the accomplishment of these things, the once-divided Arabic peoples would become unified in a single Arab church and become "the nucleus of a great Arabian and Christian nation." It goes without saying that Gagarin understood this church would be Catholic and under the authority of the pope.[30]

Gagarin's article betrayed his habit of formulating vast programs promising speedy and dramatic results. On the basis of only three months in the Middle East, he had decided that the reform of education among the Byzantine Catholics would bring about the unification of all Arab peoples into a Byzantine rite Catholic church. This would be accomplished by sending "two or three professors" to Jerusalem.

Despite the naiveté of his proposal, Gagarin was supported by Guiseppe Valerga, the Latin rite patriarch of Jerusalem. In a letter to Gagarin of 15 July 1860, Valerga wrote:

> I can only encourage you, my Reverend Father, to persevere on the excellent path you have entered so as to effect the reunion of the Eastern church to the Catholic church by taking advantage of the points of contact between the former and the latter. This method appears to have at least the advantage of being the most conformed to the spirit of Christian charity; at the same time, it shows with evidence that the points of contact are infinitely more numerous than the points of dissidence. In religious controversies, one is not necessarily wise to confine oneself to refutation and to propagandizing one's adversary; one must also touch and bring him back to the truth, one must make him see that the distance which separates him [from the truth] is not as great as he may imagine.[31]

Valerga also supported Gagarin's plan to move l'Oeuvre des SS. Cyrille et Méthode to Jerusalem in October 1860, at least on a temporary basis.[32]

In December 1860, events occurred which would greatly affect Gagarin's proposals for the Byzantine Catholics. In Constantinople, on 24 December 1860, a group of Bulgarian Orthodox approached Primate Anthony Hassoun of the Armenian Catholics and asked his permission to enter communion with the Roman Catholic church. The Bulgarians agreed to conform to the decisions of the Council of Florence, so long as they could maintain their liturgy, ceremonies, and religious customs. In return for recognizing the pope as "the true successor of Saint Peter and the supreme head of the Roman church," they asked for the creation of a Bulgarian patriarchate. The new patriarch would "conserve the Orthodox faith in its purity as received from the holy apostles and the ecumenical councils." Hassoun responded favorably to the Bulgarian petition. Later that year 120 deputies, two archimandrites, a priest, and a deacon acting in the name of 2,000 of their compatriots presented their act of union to Mgr. Paolo Brunoni (1807–1875), the apostolic delegate.[33]

In January 1861, a Bulgarian delegation headed by Archimandrite Joseph Sokolski arrived in Rome with the Bulgarian petition. Pius IX approved the petition. He promised to respect the maintenance of Bulgarian religious customs. On 8 April 1861, the pope ordained Sokolski as archbishop for Bulgarian Catholics of the Byzantine rite. The Bulgarian church initially included about 60,000 members.

While the Bulgarian initiative was completely unexpected by Gagarin, he saw it as a hopeful sign of impending church union and a symbolic reversal of Nicholas I's violent absorption of the Ruthenian church in 1839:

> If the Bulgarian Uniate church succeeds in surviving and organizing not only all the Bulgarians and rallying them, this example will bring along the Serbs, the Moldovans, the Wallachians, all the schismatics of European Turkey. The Greeks will hesitate for a long time, but they will end by equally attaching themselves. The Greek Uniate church in Austria will have a new vigor, a new life; and it is permitted to believe that all the Eastern schismatics outside Russia will accept union. Will this Greek Uniate church, once constructed on such a foundation, not certainly exert a great influence on Russia, torn apart by sects which can only multiply outside of Christianity?[34]

Gagarin hoped for nothing less than that the Bulgarian union would galvanize the entire Orthodox East to seek union with Rome. He also saw in the Bulgarian desire to place themselves under the "the supreme pastor" a conservative, catholic movement which would be "the sole barrier and sole defense that one could use to prevent the expansion of revolutionary panslavism."[35]

While the Bulgarian act of union was encouraging, Gagarin should have realized that the Bulgarians sought union with Rome to achieve ecclesiastical independence from Constantinople, i.e., to enhance their ecclesiastical stature through a national patriarchate, not because of agreement with Gagarin's arguments regarding the historical and theological validity of the Roman Catholic church. The Bulgarian act of union was rooted in nationalism, not theology. The Russian church, which was already autocephalous, lacked such motivations.[36]

On 26 January 1861, Beckx recognized the significance of events in Bulgaria by writing to Cardinal Barnabo of the College of Propaganda. Beckx encouraged Barnabo to contact Gagarin on Roman relations with the Bulgarians, because Gagarin had demonstrated his ability to work on these matters.[37]

On 9 February 1861, the council of l'Oeuvre des Pèleringages asked Father Fessard to allow Gagarin to accompany an Easter pilgrimage going to Jerusalem. Lavigerie explained that "Father Gagarin totally succeeded in the first trip in winning the esteem and affection of all; the council believes it cannot make a better choice."[38] Fessard approved the petition. He wrote Gagarin, asking him to return to Paris to prepare for the pilgrimage. Fessard added, perhaps ironically: "I would like to give you more time for solitude."[39]

Gagarin and Balabin went to the Holy Land. There he met with Valerga and discussed his projects for the conversion of the Bulgarians, for the conversion of the East, and the union of churches. He wrote:

> I think I have a good sense of the situation and I believe that the moment has come to act. One must not proceed under any illusion. The Bulgarians detest the Greeks and have no sympathy for the Russians. This is the root of their Catholicism. What they want is a hierarchy independent of the Phanar [Ecumenical Patriarch]. They are extremely attached to their rite. . . . What they especially want is a patriarch. Pius IX has refused them because they are not sufficiently numerous. The Uniate patriarchs of the East have even smaller flocks. This is the central question. There is much to say in favor of a patriarch. He will attach to him all the Bulgarians and possibly the Serbs. I repeat, one must not wait to find among the Bulgarians another Catholicism than that which I have outlined; but one must not stop at that. The great point is education and especially the formation of a good indigenous clergy.[40]

Recognizing that his ideas regarding Bulgaria and the Byzantine rite were not those of Rome, Gagarin separated his proposals on Bulgaria from his goal of achieving overall church union. He wrote to Beckx, "Suppose that the enterprise in Bulgaria fails, that is no reason for me to abandon this great cause." In fact, Gagarin said that he would prefer to work for the conversion of the entire Orthodox church at one time.[41]

As he had suggested earlier, Gagarin saw that the best means of addressing both his goals and the issue of the Bulgarians was through education:

> one must give them above all else an instructed, edifying, zealous clergy: that is to say one must build seminaries. My idea is to establish a central seminary for all the churches of the Greek rite; one would not receive there Latins, Maronites, or Armenians, but all those of the Greek rite would be received without distinction—Ruthenians, Moldovans, Bulgarians, Greeks, Arabs . . . I would like this seminary to become a central light which shines on all the Greek Uniate churches and must later [shine] on all the churches enveloped today in the schism.

This seminary would be established in Jerusalem. Gagarin also wanted to establish a college in Jerusalem for students of the Byzantine rite, to publish Russian texts in Jerusalem, and to receive permission to celebrate mass according to the Byzantine rite. Gagarin told Beckx that Valerga was favorable to his project and that he and Balabin wanted to go to Constantinople to talk with Brunoni and Hassoun.[42] Beckx responded:

> The plan to establish in Jerusalem a central seminary for young men of the Greek rite is a good idea, and I am not surprised that this idea has come from you. But its realization offers some difficulties; it would bear careful consideration even supposing these obstacles were lifted, if the place would be well chosen. At the moment such a project cannot be undertaken in view of the decision taken by [the College of] Propaganda to permit only Franciscans to establish in Jerusalem.

Beckx added that Cardinal Barnabo had permitted Gagarin to go to Constantinople.[43]

On 6 June 1861, Gagarin and Balabin arrived in Constantinople where they met with Brunoni, Hassoun, the French ambassador Boré, Archbishop Sokolski, and some influential Bulgarians. The group resolved to establish a Bulgarian college under the direction of the French Jesuits. Gagarin wrote to Beckx again about the need for an indigenous clergy and about his desire to celebrate mass according to the Byzantine rite under the rubric established by the brief of Benedict XIV, *Allatae sunt*.[44]

Gagarin also sought permission for the Russian Jesuits to be the guiding influence on the Bulgarians:

> our nationality does not expose us to any difficulty on the part of the Russian ambassador. The Russian government will struggle against the Bulgarian Uniate church, but will not take any official steps against us personally. One must of course remark that the Lazarists were known to Constantinople as in the Levant in general, under the name of Jesuits; it is to the Jesuits that the conversion of the Bulgarians is generally attributed and it is not likely that the schismatic Bulgarian journals will rage against us more than they do today. Providence seems to have chosen the Bulgarian Uniate church to attach the entire Orthodox church to Rome. This great hope sustains us in the trials that surely await us.[45]

Upon his return to Paris in late June 1861, Gagarin reassured Beckx that his Russianness would not impede work with the Bulgarians: "In my soul and conscience, I am convinced that it is only we Russians who can go at this moment into this country; all the problems that are attributed to our Russianness are figments of the imagination . . . we will open the doors to others, when the others, especially the French, will succeed in nothing." He added that he wanted to work with Balabin and Martynov on the Bulgarian issue.[46]

While Gagarin was continuing to formulate grandiose projects of reunion, his fellow Jesuit Balabin approached the issue much more cautiously. He wrote, "In his solicitude for the salvation of our brothers of the East, Gagarin has conceived of many projects for the seminary to be established at Jerusalem, in Syria, and we speak often; but these projects seem impractical."[47] Balabin's caution was echoed by other Roman Catholic clergy. In Beckx's letter to Balabin on 6 July 1861, Beckx instructed Balabin to wait in establishing a college for the Bulgarians. Cardinal Barnabo believed that Balabin and Gagarin had "possibly invested too much confidence in the Bulgarians."[48]

Suspicions regarding the Bulgarian Catholics had been raised by an unusual event. On 18 June 1861 in Constantinople, Archbishop Sokolski mysteriously disappeared. He was taken to Odessa on a Russian ship and spent the last eighteen years of his life at the Monastery of the Caves at Kiev. It has never been established whether he was kidnapped by the Russian government or went willingly to Ukraine. Despite this setback, the Bulgarian Catholic church survived, especially thanks to the inspirational Panteleimon Zhelov.

Gagarin responded to Beckx's urge for caution in a letter of 14 July 1861. Gagarin said he was not disturbed by inimical words, because he had heard them earlier when he converted and became a Jesuit. He argued, "I know perfectly what to believe. If the Bulgarian enterprise succeeds, as I strongly hope, I know that it will bring on more difficulties, more sacrifices, more of the cross than my conversion and my vocation have furnished me." Gagarin believed that God had appointed him to work for the reunion of churches and that "the Bulgarian enterprise is the door by which I must enter." In fact, he indicated a growing impatience to begin work with the Bulgarians: "in some weeks, I will attain the age of forty-seven, and it will have been eighteen years since I entered the Company; I have waited for the moment marked by Providence and I believe it has now arrived: the obstacles and opposition do not scare me."[49] Gagarin later added, "It is not my fault if I see in the entire Catholic church that only we three [Gagarin, Martynov, and Balabin] form the group called for by the necessary conditions. It is supremely important that at the moment when Russia is open to us, there be a Catholic church of the same rite, fully organized and capable of providing apostles to Russia."[50]

Let us note where Gagarin placed himself. Not only was his mission so important that he felt called by Providence, but it could only be accomplished by the Russian Jesuits: the other Jesuits would "succeed at nothing." Again, Gagarin demonstrated, through a variety of proposals, a deep desire to convert his homeland; at the same time, he displayed a trust in his own abilities not completely shared by his superiors, who alone were in positions to approve those proposals.

As part of the means of achieving his goals, Gagarin again asked for permission to establish a journal separate from *Études*. Again, Beckx refused, citing practical difficulties. Beckx wrote, "The good God does not forget you; you know this; He created you to do His work. But is it a journal?"[51]

In a letter to Beckx on 20 November 1861, Gagarin again voiced the need to establish a seminary in Bulgaria and asked for permission to move l'Oeuvre des SS. Cyrille et Méthode to Syria. He argued, "If we do not go to Gaza, the poor Bulgarian children, very numerous, far from their country, will be lost amidst the foreign element."[52] He later added that he wanted to establish a seminary in Gaza which would receive some

Bulgarians. He wanted to prepare students in the manner of the Jesuit colleges and use the Bulgarians as apprentices in the work of l'Oeuvre des SS. Cyrille et Méthode. Furthermore, he wanted to publish texts in Russian and send the texts to Constantinople for distribution in Russia.[53] Beckx again responded negatively, saying that there were not enough Bulgarians for a seminary in Gaza and that it would be difficult to move the entire l'Oeuvre.[54]

Beckx's rejection did not dissuade Gagarin from seeking to move the center of his work to Syria. He wrote again to Beckx that "It would be possible to form a Russian nucleus for aiding pilgrims; in this connection, Syria offers us an advantage that Bulgaria does not present. L'Oeuvre de Saint Cyrille et de Saint Méthode would have at the same time a Russian press, a Bulgarian seminary, Russian pilgrims from Jerusalem, and the hope of forming a small nucleus of Russian converts." He added, "I fervently believe that God has destined me to engage in the great work of the reunion of churches and that this Bulgarian enterprise is the place one must begin."[55] Gagarin noted that he had been approached by a Father Agapius Honcharenko (1832–1916), who wanted to operate a small Russian press in Smyrna or Beirut.[56] Again Beckx chose not to approve Gagarin's requests. He wrote, regarding his objections to moving l'Oeuvre to Gaza, "If the question is whether to move [the society] immediately [to Syria], the objections are the precarious position of other Catholic establishments in Syria and the condition of the existing [Jesuit] college. . . . If this is a question for the future, I foresee definite difficulties, but I also see advantages. I have not yet sufficiently weighed the advantages against the disadvantages to be able to decide."[57]

By December 1861, Balabin was the only Russian Jesuit on the editorial staff of *Études,* though Gagarin still had some input. By 1862, the journal ceased to carry the title *Études . . . publiées par les PP. Charles Daniel et Jean Gagarine;* now it simply said *publiées par des Péres de la Compagnie de Jésus.*

Gagarin's continuing interest in working on the issue of the Byzantine Catholic churches can be seen in his submission to Beckx of a memorandum entitled "Sur l'utilité de l'adoption du rite Grec par quelques péres de la Compagnie." This document was reprinted with some changes in *Études* as "L'Avenir de l'Église grecque-unie."[58]

To understand the scope of the issue of the Byzantine Catholicism with which Gagarin was dealing in these texts, the statistics in Table 7.1 below should be considered.[59]

Table 7.1 Catholics of the Byzantine Rite (1865)

Total Number of Byzantine Catholics	4,312,992
Greek Catholics	3,810,447
in Galicia	2,000,000
in Transylvania	900,000
in Hungary	520,447
in Poland	250,000
in Syria	50,000
in Prussia	40,000
in Italy	30,000
in Croatia	20,000
Armenians	200,000
Maronites	150,000
Chaldeans	119,000
under the patriarch	20,000
in Malabar	99,000
Syrians	30,000
Copts	3,445
Abyssinians	100

Gagarin began his discussion of the Byzantine Catholic problem with an historical outline of the development of the Latin and Greek rites. Beginning with Alexander the Great, the Greeks exercised the dominant cultural role in Asia Minor, Syria, Egypt, and Thrace. According to Gagarin, the East remained Greek "even after the Romans had conquered it." Since Gaul, Spain, and Africa knew only the Roman yoke, while the East retained its Greek culture, the Roman Empire contained two languages, two civilizations, "or, as one says today, two nationalities"—the Greek and the Latin.[60]

When apostolic evangelism began, the church did not attempt to change the linguistic and national circumstances prevailing in the Roman Empire; instead the evangelists "cast the seed of the divine word among the Greeks and among the Latins and left it to rise there among the one and among the other without being preoccupied with questions of languages or nationalities."[61] As a result, the church assimilated into itself the national character of the Roman Empire—its two languages, two cultures, and two liturgies. At this stage, the simultaneous existence of the Greek and Latin rites "did not create any barrier to the unity of faith or to the unity of the church."[62] The two rites were united under the supreme authority of the pope, with whom they were obliged to be in communion and to whom they appealed regarding points of controversy.[63]

Next Gagarin discussed the current problems in the Byzantine Catholic church. He condemned the lack of unity among the Byzantine Catholics: "Not only are the faithful of this church dispersed among so many different states, among so many different nations and languages, not only are they foreign to one another, but especially they are a minority and in a state of relative inferiority."[64] Gagarin saw this inferiority primarily in the Byzantine Catholic clergy which had suffered when its most educated youth had left the church. The Byzantine Catholic clergy "scarcely includes among its children more than the poor and the ignorant . . . in its entirety, it is inferior to the Latin clergy in education, in zeal, in sacerdotal spirit; in a word it is inadequate."[65]

Gagarin warned against the Latinization of the Byzantine Catholics. He said that any attempt to Latinize the Byzantine Catholics in order to strengthen their links to the Roman church would achieve the diametrically opposite result. He argued, "Some think that a sincere and durable reconciliation will be possible only if the rites, customs, and regulations of the Eastern churches are totally destroyed. It is not surprising that men animated by this spirit do not find among the Easterners favorable dispositions, and, that after some interval, they give way to discouragement."[66] As evidence, Gagarin pointed out that the Byzantine Catholic church of Syria had become alarmed by an attempt to introduce the Gregorian calendar.[67] He also pointed to the situation in Bulgaria, where "union has not made progress as rapidly as one would hope, because here also, the emissaries of the Greek patriarch and the Russian government frighten the people by making them believe, despite the promises of Monseigneur Hassoun, . . . promises guaranteed by a brief of the pope, that the Latin rite will later be imposed on them."[68] Furthermore, Gagarin wrote, attempts at Latinization were contrary to Benedict XIV's brief *Allatae sunt* which condemned that policy.[69]

Later Gagarin discussed the issue of a married clergy. [70] He feared that a married clergy leads "almost inevitably to formation of a hereditary caste." He admitted that a married clergy might be necessary for those Christians who wished to select priests from their own village; in such a case a priest would remain tied to a particular community. He wanted to supplement the married clergy with a group of celibates whose responsibility would be evangelizing.[71]

To obtain for the Byzantine Catholics an "instructed, pious, zealous clergy," Gagarin urged the publication of books adapted to the needs of the people; the establishment of hospitals, hospices, associations of aid; and the foundation of schools for both sexes, from primary school to college, as well as seminaries. Each Byzantine Catholic diocese would eventually have its own seminary, but the immediate need was a central seminary "common to the entire Greek-Uniate church, without distinction of nationality, to furnish professors and directors for all the diocesan seminaries." This would reduce disunity among the Byzantine Catholics. Gagarin also called for the creation of patriarchates for each of the churches of the same rite in Turkey, Syria, Greece, Austria, and Russia. Here he followed the path he had previously blazed for the Bulgarians.[72]

Since Gagarin did not want the directors of these seminaries to be Latin rite priests and since there were not sufficient numbers of Byzantine rite priests to fulfill the need, he looked to the writings of the Carmelite father Thomas de Jésus (1564–1627) for a solution.[73] This approach was to create Byzantine rite "branches" of the various Roman Catholic religious orders—Benedictines, Dominicans, Franciscans, Jesuits, Carmelites—without changing their institutions or rules.[74] By this means, the dual-rite nature of the various religious orders would mirror the dual-rite nature of the Catholic church. The Byzantine rite members of the various orders would remain faithful to their superiors yet conform to the rite of the country in which they served. Religious missionaries would establish novitiates, submit novices to the discipline of the religious life, and form them in a European fashion. Meanwhile, the novices would learn their own rite, language, usages, and national sentiments.[75] Religious services would be celebrated in Greek, Syrian, Arabic, Slavonic, Armenian, and Latin as appropriate. They would follow the same rules, the same spirit, and create unity among themselves.[76] Furthermore, these missionaries would recruit among the indigenous people in order to form an indigenous clergy and an indigenous ecclesiastical hierarchy.[77]

Gagarin cited several precedents for this approach. "From the thirteenth or fourteenth century the Dominican Fathers gave the rule of their order to the Armenians, who preserved their rite; only, instead of making these Armenians a branch of the order under the authority of the superior general and the general magistrate, the Dominicans formed a distinct and independent congregation under the name of the United Brothers."[78] Gagarin pointed again to Benedict XIV's brief *Allatae sunt,* which placed the Byzantine college of Rome under the Jesuits. There the Jesuits practiced the Byzantine rite "so that the students would not remain strangers to the practice of this rite which was and should be their own."[79]

There were some additional comments on reforming the Byzantine Catholic church which Gagarin added later. He suggested the Byzantine Catholic liturgical texts be purged of the errors and mistakes which had entered them. He insisted that the Byzantine Catholic church retain papal authority.[80]

Unlike previous writings, which implied an immediate solution to the issues of church union, Gagarin now stressed that the reform process would be slow: he compared it to "drops of water eroding rock."[81] Gagarin still saw a reformed Byzantine Catholic church as key to the reunion of churches, for it would facilitate "absorption" of the Greek Orthodox:

> When one sees this church flourish and prosper, observing its venerable rite in all its purity and possessing an instructed, pious, zealous clergy, having nothing to envy in the Latin clergy; when one sees schools open to both sexes, in all conditions, from the nursery, the boarding school and the humble primary school through the colleges, seminaries, faculties; when hospitals, hospices, associations of charity come to the aid of all the poor; when the word of God is proclaimed with force and simplicity from the pulpits, when the texts adopted to the needs of the populations are put in their hands, it is inconceivable that Greek non-Uniates, in considering this spectacle, at the sight of its devotion, its charity, its zeal, its light, will not be brought to recognize that the spirit of God is there.[82]

Gagarin's ideas on the Byzantine Catholic churches were not without influence in Vatican circles. Lavigerie supported Gagarin's views on the problems of Latinization and the need for Latin rite priests to enter into the Eastern rite. He planned to present Gagarin's ideas as his own in dealings with the pope and the College of Propaganda. He wrote to Gagarin that "I have attracted to our ideas the principal halls of Rome."[83]

In January 1862, Pius IX divided the College of Propaganda into two sections. One section, the Sacred Congregation for the Oriental Churches, had special members and a secretary devoted to the affairs of the Byzantine church. Lavigerie was named as a councillor in this special section. Unfortunately, his influence was minimal, since the head of this section until 1874 was Cardinal Barnabo, a Latinizer.

On 8 April 1862, Piux IX issued the encyclical *Amantissimus*. This encyclical began by addressing the unity and catholicity of the church with "one spirit, one faith, one hope, one love joined and firmly held together by the same bonds of sacraments, religion and doctrine." It asserted that the church would "embrace all peoples and nations of the whole world."[84] Pius IX then went on to address the Byzantine rite churches. He argued that "a variety of legitimate rites obviously in no way oppose the unity of the Catholic church; rather, indeed, such a diversity greatly enhances the dignity of the church itself." Pius condemned Latinization.[85] Finally the pope referred to the establishment of the Sacred Congregation for the Oriental Churches and asked for the Byzantine Catholic churches to "send us an accurate report on the status of your dioceses in which you carefully explain whatever pertains to the dioceses themselves that we may attentively provide for the necessities of the faithful residing in them." In this light, Pius IX suggested aid in the field of religious education, in providing books, in renewal of families.[86] While this brief in no way accomplished all of Gagarin's program for the Byzantine Catholic churches, its emphasis on the need for increased education, its opposition to Latinization, and its praise for the Byzantine rite give some indication that the ideas of Gagarin, as presented by Lavigerie, had an impact on the pope.

In addition to feeling concern over the internal problems of the Byzantine rite church, Gagarin felt anxiety over the influence of the Russian government in the Middle East. While the Arabic Orthodox were under the authority of the Greek Orthodox church, the Greek leadership did not know Arabic. This anomaly developed in the seventeenth century when the Arabic Orthodox bishops recognized the authority of the pope: the Orthodox laity, having no bishops, had to quickly select new bishops who were Greek.[87] By the nineteenth century, the Greek Orthodox hierarchy had become nervous about losing their hold over the Arabic-speaking laity. Their fear increased when the Russian government sent Russian monks and bishops to minister to Orthodox pilgrims in the Middle East. Gagarin argued that the Greek clergy feared a growing incursion of Russian power, particularly since the Russians might intensify the Arabic populations' desire for an indigenous clergy.[88] He wondered why the Russian Orthodox clergy had invaded the ecclesiastical territory of the Greek Orthodox since they were of the same communion.[89]

Gagarin's articles on the Byzantine Catholics and on Russian activity in the Holy Land did not escape the notice of his Orthodox critics. Many of the same type of arguments which the Orthodox had used in their previous attacks on Gagarin continued to be voiced. Guettée, in his article "Les Églises orientales unies," attacked Gagarin's Jesuit heritage, saying, "He [Gagarin] is a Jesuit, an arch enemy of the Orthodox church; this is all that we have need to know to evaluate his diatribes against the Orthodox clergy and his plans to corrupt that which remained good in the Eastern [Catholic] churches which had the misfortune to submit to the yoke of the pope." Guettée also attacked Gagarin for not discussing dogmatic differences between the Orthodox and Catholic churches such as the *filioque.*[90] Ieromonakh Iuvenalii's text, *Neskol'ko slov po povodu stat'i Gagarina—"Russkiia uchrezhdeniia v sviatoi zemle,"* accused Gagarin of ignorance: "It is a pity that the former prince did not acquaint himself before now with the dogmatic faith of the Orthodox, for he has not understood what an invaluable treasure is possessed by members of the Eastern Orthodox church."[91]

Guettée also attacked Gagarin's proposals concerning the Byzantine Catholic clergy, but not without resorting to blatant misrepresentations of Gagarin's position. Guettée claimed that Gagarin wanted to abolish all married clergy and that he wanted to abolish the Eastern rite through Latinization—palpably false claims.

Ieromonakh Iuvenalii attacked Gagarin's claims of Russian clerical invasion of the Holy Land. While the Orthodox hierarchy in the Middle East consisted of Greek speakers, Iuvenalii said that the newer clergy were all Arabic and performed services in Arabic. Furthermore, Iuvenalii described the Russian bishop in Jerusalem not as an invader but as "an honored guest." He wrote that Gagarin's apprehension might have been justified before the Russian presence in Jerusalem, but he insisted that the current situation showed the Russians' respect for the unity of the Greek church. Iuvenalii complained that Gagarin's accusations were part of a "common Jesuit practice of sowing doubt and discord."[92]

During this period in which Gagarin worked on the problems of the Byzantine Catholic churches, his problems with *Études* continued. He attempted several times to get l'Oeuvre des SS. Cyrille et Méthode transferred to Syria or to Jerusalem. The French Jesuits also continued to work to press for Gagarin's separation from his creation.[93]

To escape the conflicts over *Études,* Gagarin returned to the Middle East. In September 1862, he left France for the Jesuit seminary at Gaza, where he began working on 16 October 1862. In a letter to Beckx, Gagarin wrote, "I find myself blessed and content and am satisfied to have escaped from the uproar in Paris, from which I was recently fatigued."[94]

In Gaza, Gagarin served as a director of studies, professor of dogmatic theology, director of the library, confessor, and an advisor. At the start of his teaching, he had eight students: two Maronites, one Armenian, one Greek Melchite, and four Bulgarians—ages ten, fourteen, fifteen, and sixteen. Gagarin taught catechism and Bulgarian grammar.[95] As for his work with the Bulgarians, he wrote that he wanted "to foster understanding and love of their native language and rite." "Not knowing the Bulgarian dialect, I study their Bulgarian grammar and explain to them the Bulgarian catechism, in the hope that from their number will develop some sort of Cyril or Methodius who again will enlighten the Russian land that has been submerged in pitch darkness by the Holy Synod and overwhelmed by the lies and deceptive learning of today's atheistic youth."[96] Thus, Gagarin's work in the Middle East was not an end in itself: he considered it a step toward the conversion of Russia. Even studying the Bulgarian language was a means of achieving this purpose.

In Gaza, Gagarin prepared to work with Arabic Christians. His archives indicate that he had purchased the following in Arabic: a Bible, copies of the Epistles of Paul and Acts of the Apostles, and a copy of the rule of St. Bernard of Clairvaux. He also obtained Arabic/Latin interlinear Gospels, an Arabic/Latin dictionary as well as an Arabic grammar.[97] It was probably at this time that Gagarin became a full member of the committee of l'Oeuvre des Pèleringages.

In 1863, Gagarin, Martynov, and Balabin again attempted to publish a Russian journal. Acting under orders from the pope and in hopes of creating a journal that might refute the arguments of *l'Union chrétienne* and that could reach a Russian audience, the three Russian Jesuits founded the *Kirillo-Mefodievskii sbornik.*[98] The first volume of the journal contained some Ruthenian texts published by Martynov. In its preface, the three Jesuits expressed their rationale for the new journal. They noted that the thousand-year anniversary of Saints Cyril and Methodius was approaching, but that the anniversary would be sad, because the churches founded by the two men were troubled. Besides decrying the schism that had broken the "common faith and love of Rome," the three Russian Jesuits condemned the "solitude, division, discord, and lack of any unity" among the Slavic churches. They also discussed problems affecting particular Slavic churches. The Bulgarian church was "held down under the heavy dominion of the Byzantine clergy, which was suppressing the church's ancient liturgy." The Russian church had lost its ecclesiastical independence to the Holy Synod, was beset by the schism of the Old Believers, and endorsed religious persecution. The Byzantine Catholic churches were fragmented, possessed poor leadership, and were threatened by Latinization. The Russian Jesuits' mission was to point to the true teachings of Cyril and Methodius, to "walk on the path of the Holy Apostles of the Slavs," to work for unity with Rome and to maintain the Greek rite and liturgical services in Slavonic. They promised the journal would contain "everything which will serve to develop and clarify the foundational thought of the holy evangelists to the Slavs, but principally works of historical and theological content."[99]

In the introduction we see clear evidence of Gagarin's ideas: his antipathy toward Christian disunity, his desire to maintain Byzantine Catholic clergy and customs, and his commitment to promote unity with Rome. Whether he intended this journal to replace *Études* is unknown; in any case the journal published one more volume in 1867, then ceased publication.

Gagarin remained in Syria until August 1864. At that time, Beckx ordered him back to Paris, saying, "I do not see what profit the prolongation of your sojourn in Syria will provide l'Oeuvre des SS. Cyrille et Méthode. You have remained there a sufficient time to become current concerning the many points upon which you desired to be enlightened in these places."[100]

After Gagarin left Syria, his interest in Bulgaria diminished. He refocused on his primary goal of church reunion. Giot rightly claims that the refusal of the College of Propaganda to create a Bulgarian college in Constantinople and the support for Latinization by Valerga, Brunoni, and Hassoun prevented the success of Gagarin's proposals for the Bulgarians (or the other Byzantine Catholics).[101] Yet Gagarin's advice on the establishment of a Bulgarian patriarchate proved prophetic when, in 1870, the Ottoman government, under Russian influence, established an independent Bulgarian Orthodox exarchate. In the absence of a Byzantine rite patriarch, three-quarters of the Bulgarian Catholics returned to Orthodoxy by the end of the nineteenth century.[102]

Another interest for Gagarin at this time was the issue of language differences between the Orthodox and Catholic Slavs. This was a complex problem since language differences reflected the different national and cultural heritages of the two different ethnic groups. As Peter Christoff has argued:

> It would have been virtually impossible for anyone to have raised the question of an all-Slav language and literature without getting bogged

> down in millennial passions aroused by the division of the Catholic Slavs, who used the Latin alphabet, and the Orthodox Slavs, who used the Cyrillic. In fact the alphabet issue, like the two confessions, Orthodox and Catholic, were daily reminders to the Slavs of the different cultural traditions which had separated them down through the centuries while their ethnic and linguistic similarities persisted and are noticeable to the present day.[103]

In addressing this question of Slavic linguistic unity, Gagarin was following the path previously blazed by P. J. Šafařík, J. Kopitar, and Ljudevit Gaj (1809–1872). Šafařík's text *Geschichte der Slawischen Sprache und Literatur nach allen Mundarten* related the history and development of Slavic literature. Assuming that all Slavs belonged to one nationality and spoke dialects of one language, Šafařík condemned the use of Latin by Catholic Slavs in place of the Cyrillic that would permit Slavs to learn each other's literature. J. Kopitar in his texts *Grammatik der Slawischen Sprache in Krain* and *Kärten und Steyermark* called for the reformation of the Latin alphabet so that it could clearly and simply express Slavic sounds. He also suggested the creation of an all-Slavic literary language composed either entirely of Cyrillic characters or a dual-alphabet system of Cyrillic and reformed Latin.

Ljudevit Gaj, a member of the Illyrian movement and a nationalist, elaborated on the ideas of Kopitar and Šafařík. He called on the Croatians to replace the Latin alphabet with Cyrillic since the latter had more letters and was better suited to Slavic sounds. He also suggested that if all the Slavs were to use Cyrillic, an all-Slavic literary language might develop. Later, Gaj modified his beliefs and supported maintenance of Latin among the Slovenes and Slavonians in order to increase cooperation among them. He believed that a common Slavic literary language would take several thousand years to develop.[104]

Gagarin first addressed the issues of the differences between the Latin and Cyrillic alphabets in an unpublished document entitled "Le rite latino-slave et l'alphabet glagolitique."[105] Here he presented a brief historical overview of the development of the Glagolitic alphabet and the Latino-Slav rite.[106] In the document there is little analysis, and it is obvious that the piece was intended to be the introduction to a much larger work. Most of the information in this text reappeared in his later article entitled "L'Alphabet de Saint Cyrille."[107]

In this second article, Gagarin observed that, despite their division, Slavs "aspire very ardently toward unity, so much so that they have created a new word: *panslavism.*" For Gagarin, the strongest barrier to union between Slavs was "neither the political antipathies nor the religious dissidence" but rather "the differences of alphabets and orthography."[108]

Gagarin went on to identify active literary movements in Poland, Russia, Bohemia, and among the Slovaks, Croatians, Serbians, and Bulgarians. However, scholarly works in these vernacular languages were not available to other Slavs without translations: "The Russians, for example, remain completely estranged from the intellectual life of Poland, and the Poles are, in general, little aware of the current of ideas which circulate in Russian society."[109]

Gagarin concluded that, if only all the Slavs had adopted and preserved the alphabet of Saint Cyril, "we would today be in possession of all the advantages which the unity of an alphabet would assure us."[110] Since this was not the case, a new common alphabet needed to be developed. For Gagarin, this alphabet could not be either Greek or Latin, since neither alphabet could approximate the sounds of the Slavic language. He added, "One must necessarily either complete these alphabets with new characters, or render the sounds which have no equivalents by the combinations of letters or by some signs added to letters, such as cedillas, umlauts, etc."[111] Furthermore, Gagarin argued, "If this [common Slavic alphabet] is Latin, the Easterners do not want it; if it is derived from the alphabet founded on the Greek by Clement, the people who after all this time know only the Latin alphabet will not consent to learn new characters."[112]

The problems with the Latin and Greek alphabets led Gagarin back to his earlier research on the differences between the Cyrillic and the Glagolitic alphabets.[113] He noted the use of the Cyrillic in the Orthodox churches and the use of Glagolitic in those churches following the Latino-Slav rite and present among the Czechs, Poles, and Dalmatians. For Gagarin, a common Slavic alphabet could be constructed on the Cyrillic and Glagolitic alphabets.

Gagarin commended the approach of Ljudevit Gaj and the approach adopted in some part by the Illyrians and the Czechs. Gagarin did not call for a change in languages, but for a change in orthography. He called for texts originally published in Cyrillic in the East to be republished with Latin characters in the West; texts originally published with Latin characters in the West would be published using Clementine/Glagolitic characters in the East.

> Thus, if Poland consented to sacrifice its somewhat antiquated orthography, success would be assured and Poland would gain the advantage [of this change]. Who can calculate the influence that Polish literature and the Polish press might exert on the Czechs, the Moravians, the Slovaks, the Croatians, the Illyrians, the Dalmatians? All these peoples are today almost completely ignorant of Polish thought; the misunderstandings which exist now will disappear the day when the Polish publications become accessible to all the Slavic populations of the West.
>
> There will be a similar growth of understanding among the Eastern Slavs, if they all adopt the Clementine alphabet with which they have been familiar from time immemorial. Of course, to provide a common orthography for the Russians, Serbs, and Bulgarians, some small indispensable modifications will be necessary.
>
> There would now be two alphabets in use among the Slavs; but there would remain one other important thing to do. While preserving the two distinct alphabets, they should be provided a similar orthography, so that each letter from the Glagolitic alphabet will correspond one-to-one with a letter of the Latin alphabet, and there should be no difference except in the form of the characters.[114]

For Gagarin, adoption of this system would permit the publishing of the poetry of Pushkin in Latin characters for distribution into Poland, Bohemia, and Dalmatia. It would facilitate the distribution in Russia, Bulgaria, and Serbia of works of Mickiewicz in Glagolitic characters. This exchange of literature would foster greater cultural and eventually religious unity among the Slavic peoples.

Gagarin would later expound on his views of the Slavic languages in a letter to Beckx:

> There is no Slavic language; the Slavic languages form a group of different languages; in this number there are some I do not want to give the name of *patois*—they have the pretension to be literary languages, but are not in reality and probably will never become such. In effect, they have struggled against obstacles which seem insurmountable. They are dialects spoken by small elites that are known outside these elites by a very small number of individuals; these dialects have no literature or literary language.[115]

Gagarin believed that these dialects would soon disappear as a result of the advancements made in communication. He argued that among the Eastern Slavs there were only two literary languages—Church Slavonic and Russian. Church Slavonic, or Paleoslovene, he called "a dead language," yet he insisted it was very important due to its liturgical usage among all Slavs who followed the Greek rite as well as among the Dalmatians who followed the Latino-Slav or Glagolitic rite. It was also the language of the Slavonic version of the Bible.

Gagarin explained that Slavonic had served in Russia as a foundation for the literary language. Russian resembled Church Slavonic as Italian resembled Latin. Since Russian was spoken by almost sixty million people and was the official language of the Russian empire, Gagarin argued that it was understood by all educated Eastern Slavs. It had a considerable literature and a large periodical press. Gagarin predicted that Russian "will quickly become the literary language of all Eastern Slavs, by way of assimilation." The different Eastern Slavic dialects were "too weak to struggle against this formidable development."[116]

Gagarin's view that the best means of promoting linguistic unity was to adopt common orthographies gradually yielded to a belief that Russian orthography would eventually be adopted by all Eastern Slavs. Since Cyrillic and Glagolitic contained the same number of letters and identical sounds, differing only in letter form, attempting to establish a common orthography was possible. The problem was attempting to adopt a common orthography among all the Slavic dialects. Gagarin attempted to establish a common living orthography based on similarities between two languages used neither in civic or literary life.

Some curious questions arise from Gagarin's interest in a unified Slavic orthography. Was this not an attempt by Gagarin to accomplish peacefully what he accused the Panslavists of desiring to achieve militarily, that is, to create a Slavic culture unified by language and religion? Whether that unified orthography developed after mutually agreed upon changes in the Eastern and Western Slavic alphabets or through widespread assimilation of Russian by non-Russian Slavs, the objective was similar. Just as Gagarin believed that an Arabic state unified on the basis of language and religion would play an important role in world affairs, so would a unified Slavic state play a much greater role in world affairs than any Slav state could separately.

It is not surprising that Gagarin later changed his views on linguistics to predict the gradual acceptance of Russian, a living Slavic dialect, among the Eastern Slavs. With Russian, Gagarin already had a base of "sixty million" people and a language understood by "educated" Slavs. Russia's genuine importance would eventually force non-Russian Slavs to learn it to understand events in Russia as well as to reach a larger audience for their own ideas.

Gagarin's interest in Pan-Slav nationalism went beyond intellectual inquiry. In 1863, he approved and participated in Bohemian Catholic pilgrimages to Brno in commemoration of the millennial anniversary of the arrival of Cyril and Methodius in Moravia. These celebrations acquired a nationalistic tone because the priests dressed in traditional costumes rather than their usual cassocks. Gagarin hoped that the Brno pilgrims would aid him in his unionist efforts among the Slavs.[117] He also familiarized himself with Bishop Josip Juraj Strossmayer's (1815–1905) work in support of nationalist movements among the South Slavs. With Strossmayer, Gagarin discussed his ideas of publishing books in Cyrillic.[118]

Gagarin's acerbic character, his unwillingness to sacrifice control over *Études*, and his perception of himself as chief spokesperson for the conversion of Russia led to personal conflicts with his fellow Jesuits, and especially with his superiors. Of course, the French Jesuits themselves were far less concerned to affect the conversion of the Eastern Slavs than to bolster the French readership of *Études*. Furthermore, Beckx's fear of provoking Russian hostility toward the Jesuits further limited the extent to which Gagarin could publicly express his views.

These conflicts led Gagarin to attempt to separate *Études* from the French Jesuits and seek its transfer to various locations around the Middle East. He wanted to regain control of his journal and take advantage of the unexpected event of the Bulgarian union. The time he spent in the Middle East permitted him to look in greater detail at the condition of the Byzantine Catholic churches and to explore them as a possible means for achieving church union. Gagarin's decision to seek the reform of the Byzantine Catholic churches through education and his call to the Roman Catholic church to protect the distinctiveness of the Byzantine Catholic rite demonstrated that he no longer sought church reunion from the top down as he had in *La Russie sera-t-elle catholique?* Now, instead of anticipating a union initiated by the pope and the tsar, he engaged in missionary activity designed to promote popular support for union. Improving the status of the Byzantine rite clergy would serve as a sign to the Orthodox East that its traditions and its members would be respected through union. The establishment of dual-rite religious orders would make Catholic missionaries more acceptable to the Orthodox masses. Furthermore, Gagarin's work with Valerga, Beckx, and Lavigerie indicated his greater willingness to seek outside assistance to accomplish his objectives.

Gagarin's proposals for reform essentially came to naught. He faced opposition from those such as Balabin and Beckx who feared that such proposals were too ambitious and incautious to succeed. He also faced opposition from those who disagreed with him and saw Latinization as the best means of improving the Byzantine Catholic clergy.

Gagarin's comments on the Slavonic languages demonstrated his belief that ecclesiastical union might be promoted through cultural unity. Just as Gagarin argued that a unification of the Arabic-speaking peoples into one church would greatly strengthen that culture, so would linguistic unification strengthen the bonds between the Slavic peoples. Though Gagarin later saw that unity coming less from a modification of Slavic orthography and more from cultural assimilation of Russian, obtaining linguistic unity was still the desired end.

CHAPTER EIGHT

The Vatican and the Russian Church

> . . . no one is more convinced than I that in Russia it is very difficult to have a just idea of the Catholic church.[1]

Upon his arrival in Paris in late 1864, Gagarin returned to Laval, where he served briefly as professor of church history. Meanwhile, in Rome, Catholic church leaders made decisions that affected the feasibility of Gagarin's plans for Russia. On 6 December 1864, Pope Pius IX expressed the intention to convoke a worldwide council of Catholic bishops, a gathering that would become Vatican I. In 1865, several cardinals suggested using the council to facilitate reunion with the separated churches. In response to Pius IX's desire to learn the views of Eastern bishops, the primate of the Armenian Catholics, Hassoun, wrote:

> As for the spirit of schism, thanks to the incessant paternal solicitudes that the Holy Father, since the beginning of his glorious Pontificate, has shown for the East, one sees a notable change in their spirits: the Eastern schismatics' inveterate aversion to the Holy Roman church has greatly lessened, especially among the Armenian schismatics and generally more among the laity than among the clergy, so that if the respective clergy of the Eastern schismatic churches were a little more instructed in the sacred sciences, they would be more open to the voice of truth, and the oppositions of that part of the population against the reunion *en masse* with the Roman church would not be as great as they were before.

Hassoun argued that inviting the entire Orthodox episcopate to union would be more efficacious than invitations to the patriarchs alone.[2]

During this period of papal activity, Gagarin continued to promote education as a means of establishing union. For example, he proposed the establishment in Paris of a Jesuit school for young Russians. He observed that, in Russia, a large number of Catholics of various nationalities were without schools. All Catholic children, except for those who aspired to the priesthood, were trained in "schismatic" [i.e. Orthodox] or even atheistic (i.e. secular) schools.[3] He admitted that opening the Jesuit school to Orthodox children might "excite the fears" of Russian Orthodox "fanatics." If the school accepted only Catholics, however, Gagarin predicted that the Russian government would not raise objections. Rather, "it would be seen with a certain satisfaction."[4]

In late 1864, Gagarin's proposal was approved. Since it would take time to acquire students, Gagarin suggested opening a boarding school in which the students would receive lessons in Russian. The students would follow the courses of the Jesuit college of Vaugirard. The first student Gagarin planned to invite to this school was a young Russian convert who returned with him from Syria, but Gagarin hoped to add several young Bulgarians whom he had instructed at Gaza. Unfortunately, nothing came of the idea. Martynov wrote, "I cannot yet believe that this [idea] is serious and that it will not soon end."[5]

The school project showed that Gagarin and other Jesuits continued to be anxious to avert hostile public reaction by the Russian government. Whether concealing their goals during the publication of *Études* or focusing solely on Roman Catholic Russians, the Jesuits' purpose was the same: to obtain the conversion of Russia without offending the Russians. This policy, however, had no chance of success. The Russian Jesuits' effort to bring about Russia's conversion could only be viewed by the Russian government as an attack on Russia's national identity.

At this time, Gagarin became aware of a new Anglican attempt to establish union with Orthodoxy. He did not believe it would be successful. He wrote, "The perseverance with which the Protestants have always worked to obtain a rapprochement and fusion between them and the Easterners is remarkable. . . . Protestants have rejected the authority of tradition and the hierarchy, the cult of the saints, icons and relics, ceremonies and all which can be called the exterior aspect of religion; the Greeks, far from rejecting these things, have exaggerated them."[6]

Gagarin believed that the Anglican church sought union as an escape from its own "doctrinal anarchy": hence, the Anglican's longing toward the "ancient and unmoving church of the East."[7] Meanwhile, the Orthodox church sought to escape having to identify itself with a small number of nations.[8] While all attempts at union had failed in the past, prospects for such a union had much improved. Within Anglicanism, Pusey and his followers emphasized the importance of tradition, the church fathers, and the ecumenical councils. In Russia, Gagarin thought, "the attachment to Orthodoxy has lost something of its profoundness, of its sincerity, of its inflexibility." As a result of Protestantization, Gagarin thought, the Christian faith in the East "has been cooled, shaken, diminished."[9] Despite these improved possibilities for success, Gagarin believed that the new attempt at Anglican-Orthodox union would fail. The Anglican church was interested in *intercommunion* with Orthodoxy—that is, that both churches would retain their beliefs, yet members would be allowed to participate in each other's sacraments. The Orthodox church would accept nothing less than dogmatic union.[10]

Gagarin's realization that the Orthodox church sought catholicity through union with the Anglican church represented a new turn in his understanding of Orthodoxy and of catholicity. Earlier he had argued that catholicity had nothing to do with geographic expanse; now, he seemed to suggest that catholicity did indeed have some geographical dimension. Yet, his new view was riddled with inconsistency, since he did not offer to use the criterion of geographical extension to critique Anglicanism.

A third matter of interest to Gagarin was the status of the Catholic church in Georgia. He wrote to Beckx, "Your Paternity knows how much I desire that the Company recruit in Russia. For some time, Georgia particularly has held my regard, because there are millions of Latin Catholics there."[11] In his article "Les missionaries catholiques en Géorgie," Gagarin offered a historical presentation of the problems of Catholics in that nation. He contended that, like Russia, Georgia had been historically united with Rome but had become separated as a result of the Byzantine schism. However, Georgia had preserved "a certain autonomy and did not show itself hostile to the Catholic church."[12] In the seventeenth century, Roman Catholic missionaries, the Theatine Fathers, arrived in Georgia. They later departed and were replaced by the Capuchins. On 12/24 September 1801, Tsar Alexander I agreed to protect religious freedom in Georgia. However, Gagarin argued, "the Russian government did not delay in regretting having confirmed the ancient privileges of the Catholic mission, and all the works of the Capuchins were the object of a jealous and malevolent surveillance. The plan of banishing them was shelved, but only until after the ascension of Nicholas."[13]

Upon the ascension of Nicholas I, persecution of the Capuchins returned. They were forbidden, under pain of exile to Siberia, to receive into the Catholic church any member of the Orthodox church or to personally instruct anyone in the Catholic faith. They were also forbidden to convert any non-Catholic, to take the title of missionary, to receive aid from Europe, to recognize the authority of a superior who resided outside of Russia, to ordain priests by a bishop who was not a Russian subject, to baptize any child of a mixed marriage of a Catholic and an Orthodox, to oppose mixed marriages, or to build churches in places where the Catholic population did not number at least four hundred. They were also obliged to preach sermons of fidelity to the emperor and declare in writing that they were not Jesuits.[14] The Capuchins were eventually expelled.

Gagarin expressed concern over the persecution of the Georgian Catholic church. He argued that Georgian Catholics were only persecuted "because Catholicism is identified with Polonism." He thought the Russian government would be served better by maintaining priests who were not Polish than by expelling Western European clergy.[15] He thought Russia would profit by promoting the establishment of a strong Catholic presence which would assist it in "combating Islam and developing the foundations of a true civilization."[16]

Gagarin believed that Georgia was destined to play a great role in the East and that in the past it had been "the model of a Catholic country." To combat Russian persecution of the Catholic church in Georgia, Gagarin suggested the creation of the Société de Marie which would provide assistance to Georgian Catholics.[17] The goal of the society would be to propagate the Catholic faith in Georgia through the publication of Georgian books, missionary activity, the establishment of schools, orphanages, and religious communities. Chapters of the society would be created in each town or city in Georgia. Finally, prayers would be used to assist the society: each Saturday its members would say one Hail Mary for the society, and each month masses would be celebrated.[18]

Nothing came of this idea. Gagarin's Georgian project was predicated on the assumption that, from the Russian perspective, the Catholic question had been mistakenly understood as part of the larger Polish problem. He sought to separate Catholicism as a religious issue from Polonism as an ethnic and national dilemna for Russia. Meanwhile, the Russian authorities stubbornly interpreted Catholicism, whether in Poland or Georgia, as a threat to the empire.

Throughout this period, Gagarin's problems with *Études* continued. He wrote a memoir accusing Fessard of breaking the connection between l'Oeuvre des SS. Cyrille et Méthode and the *Études.* Fessard had "destroyed the character that the Father General had given it" and "wished to make [*Études*] a purely French work." Gagarin asked that the *Études* continue its association with l'Oeuvre des SS. Cyrille et Méthode and that he be given complete direction of the journal.[19] Gagarin's resentment over losing control of *Études* became known to other Jesuits. Father Carayon wrote, "Truly, I cannot be of your opinion concerning *Études.* . . . You are upset and I understand this, but does resentment, however legitimate, excuse the virtual absence of dialogue?"[20] Carayon faulted Gagarin for being "no voice of compromise."[21]

If Gagarin could not control *Études,* he wanted to found a biweekly Russian-language journal to refute the arguments of *L'Union chrétienne.* The journal would discuss reform of the Russian clergy and seminaries, the affairs of the patriarchate of Constantinople, events in Bulgaria and Romania, the Polish and Catholic questions, projects of union with the Anglican church, and dogmatic differences between the Orthodox and Catholic churches. While Gagarin did not want the journal to be political, he pointed to actions by the Russian government that needed to be addressed.[22] He thought these contentious matters could be explored without irritating the Russian government—a task that was difficult, if not impossible. Since, *L'Union chrétienne* was sponsored by the Russian government and Russian officials participated in its publication, any polemic with *L'Union* would be a polemic with the Russian authorities.

Beckx refused to grant Gagarin's demands regarding *Études,* but he did consult Balabin and Martynov on the possibility of a new Russian-language journal.[23] On 8 May 1866, Balabin claimed that a new journal might be very useful for responding to the attacks of the Russian journals against the Catholic church. This was also the belief of Martynov. The Russian Jesuits suggested editing the journal in Paris and publishing it in Brussels. The journal might even appear weekly. On 18 May 1866, Beckx asked the French provincial, Ponlevoy, and his Belgian counterpart for their opinions. Ponlevoy supported the new journal. He suggested that it be headquartered in a new Russian residence at Versailles, a venue that would be separated from the Paris headquarters of *Études,* thereby giving l'Oeuvre des SS. Cyrille et Méthode some autonomy.[24] Ponlevoy wrote, "Without this move, because of the inconsistencies of the good Father Gagarin who often starts but does not quite finish, the Fathers might encounter a few inconveniences in their enterprise; [the move] would have the not insignificant advantage of disentangling [l'Oeuvre from the *Études*]."[25] In spite of his support for the project, Ponlevoy feared that Gagarin's obduracy would doom it to failure:

> The lack of measure, of manners . . .. in this brave Father Gagarin, and also the lack of agreement with his collaborators give me reason to doubt in the result. But despite all that, I cannot find many great risks in the enterprise. . . . I have difficulty believing that God called these Russian fathers, so generous in their sacrifice, so desiring and so devoted, to do nothing definitive in the Company. . . . Thus, it appears to me good to knock on this door . . . perhaps it will open. . . . Father Gagarin is in a state of anticipation. This time he can be occupied, utilized . . . this man, where he should serve more, where he can embrace more.[26]

Note again the criticism of Gagarin's ability to complete projects, of his lack of manners, and of his inability to work with others. These accusations were not without foundation. During this two-year period after his return from Syria, Gagarin had suggested the establishment of a college and the foundation of a multinational organization of assistance for Georgian Catholics, neither of which had any appreciable results. Gagarin's accusations against Fessard, while not baseless, cast doubts on his ability to reconcile the Jesuit ideal of obedience to one's religious superiors with his desire to obtain Russia's conversion. Gagarin's preference for complete authority as opposed to conciliar control over the projects of l'Oeuvre des SS. Cyrille et Méthode further irritated his superiors and his fellow Russian Jesuits.

On 15 June 1866, Beckx gave his approval to Ponlevoy to establish a residence in Versailles at rue St. Honoré 30. On 5 August 1866, Bishop Pierre Mabille of Versailles granted his approval of a new Russian residence. On 25 September 1866, Gagarin, Martynov, Balabin, and Pierling arrived in Versailles at the new residence, where Pierling was named superior. On 18 August 1866, Beckx gave his approval to publish a new Catholic journal in the Russian language. The journal would be established in

Paris instead of Brussels, probably due to the Jesuit general's fear of provoking a hostile Russian reaction. Beckx left it up to Gagarin "to examine if you did not have to fear even in Paris some opposition on the part of the Russian government." Gagarin was to abstain from touching political questions and from speaking of Poland "in a manner which could bruise the susceptibility of Catholics of that nation."[27]

Just as Russia's connection of religion and nationality posed an obstacle for Gagarin, so the connection of Catholicism and Polonism posed an equally serious hindrance. Thus, Gagarin cast about for some means of persuading Polish Catholics to accept union with Russian Orthodoxy even if union should mean sacrificing national independence.

Ponlevoy rightly expected nothing to come of Gagarin's plan for a new journal, yet Gagarin's draft editorial statement for the proposed journal gives us a clear understanding of his objectives at this time.[28] Gagarin began this document by saying, "This is an age in which we set questions of every sort before the public. A tremendous revolution has been accomplished before our eyes; it now expands its sphere of influence to encompass all men and all humanity; on the one hand, it seeks to destroy all barriers between people; and, on the other hand, it moves them more and more to recognize their deepest spiritual needs." This revolution had affected the Eastern church where "everywhere life begins to boil, everywhere with every day more clearly is expressed the impossibility of maintaining the past." This revolution was also felt in Russia where "every thinking man feels the approach of a new epoch in which the relations of the ecclesiastical and civil authorities should be completely different."

Gagarin welcomed the Russian clergy's educational attainments, its deeper appreciation of spiritual refinements, and the expansion of Orthodox theological journals. Despite these favorable signs, however, the Russian civil authority did not permit the clergy to express its beliefs without secular supervision. Russian seminary education still hindered intellectual enlightenment. Gagarin argued, "If there were not these two obstacles, many clergy could of course understand that the only means of reconciling old traditions and the unchanging teaching of Christ's truth with the new needs of our time is joining with the believing and Christian West." Furthermore, "The restoration of this precious and salutary unity of faith and love would offer the Russian church legal independence from the state, of which it is now deprived to such an extent; it would offer the Russian clergy an abundant means of intellectual and clerical education, which it needs; it would disperse the prejudices which darken the clergy's eyes; it would permit the clergy to acquire the means of influencing society which every day becomes more necessary for the education of its highest appointments."

Repeating many of his earlier arguments, Gagarin stressed that the dogmatic beliefs of the Catholic and the Orthodox churches were essentially the same. He said that "opposition to reconciliation is a sinful deed and opposed to God." Gagarin also repeated his assertion that many Russian clergy sincerely wished for reconciliation but believed that there was no possibility of success.

The new journal would address these issues, Gagarin promised. It would explain possibilities of reconciliation. It would encourage reconciliation of the sort established at the Council of Florence and in the examples of the Byzantine Catholic churches:

> Our goal is the reconciliation of the East with the West, the union of churches. To attain this goal, we will try to put forward as clearly and strongly as possible the reasons obliging us to promote this reconciliation, we will try to lay the foundations on which it is possible and proper, we will try, finally, to counter the prejudices and misunderstandings which we find in our path. As far as possible, we will avoid debates, since usually they do not persuade and everyone remains convinced of his view. Rather, by the exposition of our convictions and foundations of our opinions we hope to attract the attention of the reader and show that agreement with us is not as difficult as has been previously imagined.

Gagarin's preface repeated many arguments from his earlier work, especially *La Russie sera-t-elle catholique?* Among these arguments were his desire to eliminate civil jurisdiction over the church, the need to promote a developing church, and the need for Russian church union with the West. Gagarin was no longer proposing a speedy end to the schism separating the Orthodox and Catholic churches, nor was he advocating a specific means of achieving such a union. He limited himself to promoting a favorable relationship between East and West.

The failure to establish a new journal did not stop Gagarin from making additional suggestions. Disappointed as a result of the continuing persecution of Russian Catholics under Alexander II, he proposed establishing a prayer society to come to the aid of his cobelievers, "At the beginning of the current regime, everyone believed that a new era of calm and peace would begin for the unfortunate Catholics so cruelly tested under the preceding reign."[29] He complained of the persecution in Vitebsk of Catholics who were forced to join the Russian church. He now argued, "It is no longer possible to live in illusion. There exists a long-standing plan to destroy the Catholic church throughout the empire."[30] Gagarin now suspected that the Russian government cared little about dogmatic differences between Orthodoxy and Catholicism: the Russian authorities merely wanted to place the Catholic church under civil authority.

Gagarin noted that the Russian church was isolated more than ever from Constantinople. "The see of Constantinople is more and more isolated, it collapses under the weight of its faults and the hate it inspires in its proper communion. The Slavic peoples recognize that the cause of their weakness is their disunion, and they do not hesitate to see that this disunion is the result of the schism."[31] Chief of the problems facing the Russian church was the threat of nihilism, which promoted materialism, atheism, lack of belief in the soul, and opposition to authority, property, and family. Gagarin argued, "The church should reign over its members' souls, their minds, and their hearts; it should be a queen, but their [the Russian] church is a slave; the church should be a mother, their church is a harlot; the church should be living, their church is dead."[32]

Gagarin called for constant prayer to save the few remaining Catholics in Russia. "One must pray, pray for those who remain in the Catholic church in these lands that they not be destroyed and for all the peoples who are separated from the center of unity, that they not be in schism." He called for an association of prayer under the protection of Saints Cyril and Methodius "who died in communion with the Holy See at the same time Photius raised his revolt." He also asked for the special aid of Saints Peter and Paul. The patroness of the association would be "the most holy and glorious Virgin Mary who has never ceased to be honored and invoked by the Russians, the Slavs, and the Easterners." He also called for prayers to Jesus Christ.[33] The center of the association was to be the chapel of the Jesuit residence at Versailles. On the first Thursday of the month, three masses would be celebrated in intention of the association. Every Sunday, five Our Fathers and five Hail Marys would be recited with prayers appropriate to the purposes of the association. Gagarin also planned to contact the pope to obtain various privileges for the association.[34] As with his other proposals, this, too, came to nothing.

Gagarin's most important work in 1866 was a series of articles published in *Études* suggesting major reforms for the Russian clergy. His main sources of information about the condition of the Russian clergy were texts written by Russian priests and published covertly in the West: D. Rostislavov's *O belom i chernom pravoslavnom dukhovenstve* and *Ob ustroistve dukhovnykh uchilishch v Rossii;* and the landmark text by Ioann Stefanovich Belliustin, *Opisanie sel'skago dukhovenstva.*[35]

Belliustin's work was most important to Gagarin and the Russian Jesuits. It related the life of a typical Russian parish priest and criticized various aspects of the Russian clergy: it attacked seminary education, deplored the poverty of the typical parish priests, highlighted religious oppression by the bishops, and exposed the clergy as a hereditary caste. The most learned historian of the church reforms, Gregory L. Freeze, wrote of the text, "Although its sarcastic and polemical style may suggest a distorted and one-sided account, the substance of the description is essentially accurate, conforming to that given not only by other well-informed observers but also to the data and conclusions of numerous official commissions in the late 1850s and early 1860s."[36] Publication of this text outraged the Russian Holy Synod. Belliustin was saved from exile to the far Russian north only by the personal intervention of Alexander II.

The Jesuits were greatly interested in Belliustin's text. Balabin wrote, "A brochure has appeared, published in Leipzig in Russian, on the actual state of the rural clergy; it was written by a Russian priest who was a curé and who knows perfectly the subject he treats. One cannot imagine anything more terrible. The effect that this brochure has produced in Russia is immense."[37] A copy of Belliustin's book, published in Paris in 1858, bore an epigraph from Gagarin.[38] The Jesuits also followed the reaction to the publication of Belliustin's text in Russia and were fully aware of Alexander II's support for the ideas contained within *Opisanie sel'skago dukhovenstva.*[39] Belliustin himself was greatly upset over the Jesuits' use of his text. He wrote, "[My] composition is now in the hands of those who tirelessly seek all opportunities to ridicule that which we revere in the depths of our soul! . . . New food for malice and calumny!"[40] While Gagarin made use of Belliustin's work, he did not agree with everything in it, such as Belliustin's hostility toward Latin or of the need to increase clerical salaries.

Even though Belliustin's text appeared in 1858, Gagarin did not publish his work on the Russian clergy until 1866. His occupation with *Petrusverein* and the reforms of the Byzantine clergy as well as a desire to await Alexander II's reaction to Belliustin's text postponed his response. When Gagarin determined that the tsar's proposed reforms failed to address the fundamental problems of clerical education and ecclesiastical subservience, he chose to publish his own observations and suggestions for the reform of the Russian clergy.

As in *La Russie sera-t-elle catholique?* Gagarin began his series of articles on the Russian clergy with a reference to the ascension of Alexander II, which "inaugurated a new era for that vast empire."[41] Despite this new era, "among the Russian clergy there is such a mass of abuses, and these so interlaced one with another, that the subject cannot be touched without revealing the necessity of radical reform, and of a new organization in the church itself."[42]

La Réforme du clergé russe was divided into five sections: on the White or secular clergy; on the Black or religious clergy; on Russian ecclesiastical schools; on Russian bishops; and on the Holy Synod. Analyzing the distinction between the White and Black clergy, Gagarin observed, "The history of the Catholic church reveals traces of a rivalry between the secular and the regular clergy . . . its most lively manifestations cannot be compared with the profound hatred with which the secular clergy of Russia regards the regular."[43] Gagarin defined the difference between the two as follows, "If one said that the White clergy has Protestant tendencies and the Black clergy Roman, he would not express himself exactly; but, in comparing the Russian church to the Anglican, one might say that the White clergy somewhat resembles the low-church and the Black the high-church party. The former has a Presbyterian cast, while the latter defends the rights of the hierarchy."[44]

Gagarin's text listed several problems facing the White clergy. The hereditary nature of the clerical *soslovie* or caste virtually compelled sons of priests to follow their fathers' paths and the daughters of the clergy to marry priests.[45] A second problem was the influence of nihilism among the clergy, those "who deny everything and believe nothing." Gagarin argued, "Nihilism is rapidly spreading in the universities, but if we may believe the *Moskovskie vedomosti,* it has committed still greater ravages in the seminaries."[46]

Gagarin suggested several solutions to the problems of the White clergy. First, he argued that "The most important of all reforms is the abrogation of the measures which have resulted in making the clergy a hereditary caste." Thus, he called for the priesthood to be open to all and for the children of priests to be free to follow any vocation.[47] He also suggested that the creation of a secular celibate clergy might "extinguish the hostility which now reigns between the White and the Black clergy, and it would at the same time be a new barrier against *Leviteism*."[48] An unmarried clergy might be easier for the state to support, might have more time to devote to the parish, and might be more able to face dangerous situations.[49] Second, he called for reform of the Orthodox liturgy. He thought Sunday services too long, and he believed that priestly offices were often read too quickly. He asserted, "The first reform in this matter would be to abridge the offices, to retain only that which can be read and sung with edification."[50] Third, Gagarin called for more efficient collection of funds to support the White clergy.[51] He admitted, however, that none of these steps could easily be taken.

> Who will execute these reforms? The Russian church, had it the will, has not the necessary authority to cause their adoption. Will the government? It would obviously transgress the limits of its sphere and trespass on the rights of the church. This shows the radically false situation in which the Russian church is placed, and proves to us that it is outside herself and outside the government that she can alone find a remedy for the evils which ruin her.[52]

Gagarin's second section discussed the Black or regular clergy. He noted that, because the Russian government had seized monastic land in the eighteenth century, contemporary monasteries and churches "are guardians of it [wealth] rather than proprietors."[53] Therefore, the Black clergy could neither effectively support itself nor discharge its charitable office. Yet, since the religious can more directly aid the needy than can the government, the government should return confiscated property to the church.[54] Meanwhile, Gagarin condemned the clergy's misappropriation of funds that might assist the poor, hospitals, schools, colleges, or libraries.[55] A second problem affecting the Black clergy was a shortage of vocations. Shrinking numbers of religious were not able to adequately discharge their many responsibilities. The life of solitude, prayer, penitence, self-denial, perfection, and devotion was increasingly rare.[56] A third problem affecting the Black clergy was the bureaucratic interference in monastic affairs. Government-appointed bishops named the heads of Russian monasteries, generally picking types submissive to the Holy Synod and the government ministers. Gagarin decried the government's "excessive guardianship" over the church.[57]

To resolve the problems of the Black clergy, Gagarin suggested the establishment of Western-style religious houses. He claimed, "if the community-life were everywhere introduced, if [religious] superiors were subject [to community rules], if they could misappropriate nothing of the [community's] revenues for themselves or their relations, it would not be difficult to find a useful purpose for the resources of the religious houses."[58] Gagarin suggested the establishment of religious congregations focusing on peculiar needs of Russian society. He argued, "The formation of orders, composed of many houses, bound to a common center, is completely misrepresented by some Russian authors as an innovation coming from the Latin church. We have before seen that [they] formerly existed in Russia, and that [their] abolition has been for the interests neither of the monasteries nor of the church."[59] Gagarin also suggested testing vocations for a year or two before enrolling people into a religious order, giving people complete freedom to enter or leave an order, and having superiors selected by members of a congregation.[60]

In the third section of *La Réforme du clergé russe,* Gagarin addressed problems attending ecclesiastical education. Here he cited earlier work on the history of Russian religious training. In the seventeenth century, he claimed theological education was much closer to Catholic teaching. At the Kievan Theological Academy, Petr Moghila used a catechism that was "Catholic" except for issues concerning the pope and the *filioque.* The academy even incorporated elements of the Jesuit *ratio studiorum.* In the eighteenth century the Moscow academy used the grammar of Alvarez, the educational methods of the Jesuits, and the *Summa Theologica* of St. Thomas Aquinas.[61] However, under Feofan Prokopovich education became Protestantized. Gagarin accused Prokopovich of "tak[ing] his doctrines from Protestantism" and of "stray[ing] noticeably from all the traditions of the Eastern church."[62] Protestantization had persisted into the nineteenth century. Gagarin cited various instructions of the Holy Synod which seemed to follow the Protestant logic of resting belief on Scripture alone:

> In presenting the dogmatic teaching of the Greco-Russian church, one must explain with the greatest care that this church recognizes the word of God contained in the Holy Scriptures as the *only* and *perfectly sufficient* rule of faith and of Christian life, and as the *sole* measure of truth; that it doubtless reverences the tradition of the primitive church, but only so far as that tradition is found to be in harmony

> with Holy Scripture; and finally, that from this pure tradition it draws not new dogmas of faith, but edifying *opinions* as well as *instructions*, for ecclesiastical discipline.[63]

The Protestantization of Orthodoxy, Gagarin contended, had generated conflicts between "pro-Catholic" and "pro-Protestant" churchmen and thus had fostered tension within Russian Orthodoxy.[64]

Although he was cognizant of the powerful anti-Catholic currents in Orthodoxy, Gagarin insisted that scholastic education was needed to combat Protestantization and nihilism in the seminaries. He recommended that the Orthodox establish teaching congregations consisting of secular celibate clergy to direct the seminaries.[65] He also urged the Russians to permit greater religious freedom in education:

> Renounce frankly your traditional policy in matters religious; break all the fetters with which you have loaded alien worship; allow Catholics and Old Believers to have their seminaries, their academies, their faculties of theology, as you freely allow them to Protestants; do not burden these establishments with your administrative tutelage; leave the bishops free to organize their seminaries as they desire, to entrust the direction of them to whom they will; grant all the religious orders—not excepting the Jesuits—permission to have colleges; remove from your law code the laws which forbid Russians to convert to any other religion aside from Orthodoxy: free competition can alone save you.[66]

The fourth and fifth sections of Gagarin's tract addressed questions confronting the bishops and the Holy Synod, especially the church's submission to civil authority. In his opinion, the church's dependence upon the state had begun with Peter I's suppression of the patriarchate and its replacement by the Synod. Gagarin argued, "He [Peter I] shook the organization of the church to its foundations; he effected in it a *true revolution*."[67]

In these sections he made his most serious accusation against the Russian church. Gagarin asked if there was any Russian bishop who did not owe his position to the secular authority. At least one bishop, Feofan Prokopovich, was consecrated on Peter's direct orders. Yet, Gagarin noted, the third canon of the Second Council of Nicea (787) and the thirty-first apostolic canon "*declares null the election of a bishop when it has been made by the prince.*"[68] In Gagarin's opinion, the Orthodox church had violated its own canons when it consented to the establishment of the Holy Synod. Orthodox canon law strongly implied that all bishops in communion with Prokopovich should have been excommunicated: in other words, canon law, if taken literally, should have led to the formal condemnation of the entire church of Russia.[69] Not surprisingly, Gagarin failed to explain from what body the Russian church could have been excommunicated. The Russian church had already separated itself from communion with the Vatican before the consecration of Prokopovich, so excommunication from Rome would have been superfluous. If Gagarin meant that the Russian church ought to have been excommunicated from the larger Orthodox community, then his logic would have condemned those patriarchs who maintained communion with Russia after Prokopovich became a bishop. Surely, his rhetoric about excommunication was the sort of hyperbole that could never be taken to heart by Russian churchmen.

Gagarin also cited the Romanian Prince Couza's decision to establish his own version of the Holy Synod in July 1864 as evidence of Orthodox inconsistency. All Orthodox churches, including Russia and Constantinople, condemned Couza's act. The Orthodox had criticized the Romanian government for replacing its liturgical language with Latin, but also for subjugating the Romanian church to civil authority. The other Orthodox churches told the Romanian bishops to "place themselves in the presence of the thirtieth apostolic canon and to examine their consciences." This canon stated, "If any bishop, making use of the secular power, thereby obtains a church, let him be deposed and separated, and all who communicate with him." For Gagarin, this was the height of hypocrisy—Constantinople and Russia had condemned Prince Couza for repeating the actions of Peter I.[70]

The only way to end such hypocrisy and the subjugation of the Russian church was to abolish the Holy Synod and to reestablish union between the Russian Orthodox church and Rome.[71] Gagarin argued:

> Suppress despotism, the church recovers its independence, and there no longer exists any motives for maintaining the schism. Suppress the schism, and the action of the church, without shock, without revolution, will put limits to the arbitrariness of the prince. In this way one will establish laws which the prince will not be permitted to transgress, that there will be a sphere placed outside his power.[72]

In addition, Gagarin asked for the establishment of a patriarchate outside the authority of Russian imperial power, that is, outside of Russia. He pointed out that the pope had historically been the head of the patriarchs. Unity under the pope was crucial, he wrote, because "There exists no other means of having a church that is free without being fractious, and that yields obedience to the laws without suffering enslavement."[73] As he had done previously, Gagarin cited the example of the Old Believers who recognized the need to have an independent hierarchy and who had also established a head outside of Russia.[74]

Thus, Gagarin pointed to a variety of problems in the Russian church. Some of them, such as nihilism, Protestantism, and ecclesiastical dependency, he had previously explored. Now, for the first time he raised the difficulties affecting the Russian clerical *soslovie.* Although he continued to insist that the problems of the Russian church could be finally resolved only in union with Roman Catholicism, he proposed several reforms that did not require church union: the establishment of a celibate clergy, the adoption of Western-style seminary education, and the establishment of religious freedom.

The Russian authorities—including Tsar Alexander II—also showed an interest in improving the Russian clergy's status. As early as 1858, the Holy Synod commissioned a study of Western seminaries with the goal of improving clerical education.[75] The minister of internal affairs, P. A. Valuev, a former associate of Gagarin in the Circle of Sixteen, declared the Russian clergy to be inferior in status, education, economic condition, and effectiveness to the Catholic and Protestant clergy. Valuev wanted to dissolve the clerical *soslovie,* and he called on the government to satisfy the clergy's material needs.[76] The government's decision to seek reform was, in part, defensive: it wished to answer a perceived Catholic threat. P. A. Batiushkov argued, "One should not limit oneself to one-sided measures to preserve things but must adopt measures that can place our faith on firm foundations, and that can be achieved in no other way than by placing our clergy—in terms of education and material support—on a level equal with the Latin [Catholic] clergy."[77] D. A. Tolstoi argued that reform was essential to "combat the Catholic menace in Russia's western provinces."[78] However, progressive church reform proved extremely difficult to engineer, largely because Orthodox church officials remained suspicious of Western experience and traditions.[79]

D. A. Tolstoi's program of May 1867 was designed to abolish the clerical *soslovie* and "create a new class of parish clergy, adequately supported, experienced, and dynamic." No longer were the sons of clergy forced to follow in their fathers' paths, nor were clergy forced to marry within their class.[80] Even after these reforms, however, problems in the seminary remained. No longer forced to follow in their fathers' careers, many students fled the seminaries for secular schools. Within seminaries, academic problems such as a lack of rigorous courses continued to retard the quality of religious education.[81] Nihilistic activity continued, leading conservative bishops to blame Western theologians for the flood of young people "leaving the seminary as atheists."[82]

Gregory Freeze has asserted that the Orthodox commitment to maintaining a married clergy made it very difficult for the state to subsidize the parish clergy at an adequate level.[83] He wrote, "In contrast to the Catholic clergy, who were celibate and required more modest support, the Orthodox clergy were married and needed far greater income to support their families."[84] The government also discovered that the abolition of the clerical *soslovie* was a more complex task than it had anticipated. Thus, despite its support for far-reaching reforms in the state church, the imperial government failed to reinvigorate Russian Orthodoxy in the manner that Gagarin had hoped.

Of course, Gagarin had little hope of influencing the course of Russian church reform. Orthodox suspicion of "Western" innovations probably doomed his suggestion that the Russian Orthodox reorganize their seminarians on Western lines. Also, the tendency of Russian authorities to attribute the rise of nihilism to Western ideas undercut Gagarin's program from the start. Finally, his argument that Russian Orthodox theology was faulty because of the Protestant ideas incorporated within it was not persuasive to the Orthodox, and hence it could not serve as a justification for the kinds of church reform Gagarin advocated.

Acquaintances in Russia kept Gagarin informed of the consequences of D. A. Tolstoi's 1867 reform program. Prince S. Obolenskii wrote him, "The caste has been abolished by law, but in reality the Russian tribe of Levites remains in its closed circle, just as it was earlier, [and] there is no influx of new elements."[85] Gagarin himself wrote in the preface to the 1872 English translation of *La Réforme du clergé russe* that:

> We by no means call in question the good intentions that prompted these reforms; but we must remark, that some have been decreed on paper without any sensible and real change, and the others leave untouched the foundations and the roots of evil we have sought to

> disclose. In any case, many years must elapse before any substantive change can be felt as their result. After these reforms, the clergy is still a caste separated from the rest of the nation, and the church is still in absolute dependence on the state.[86]

Gagarin's later writings on the subject indicated a growing doubt as to the impact of such a reform:

> . . . but the hour of mercy has not yet rung for Russia. Following the prediction of Count de Maistre, it must exhaust all its errors to arrive at the truth. The work is progressing. The classes of society are schools producing sceptics, nihilists, materialists, and atheists. Those who escape that dangerous education find refuge in the constantly multiplying sects. Faith is extinguished in the clergy who are finding it more and more difficult to recruit future priests. The tutelage that the government exerts on the church saps its life. One can foresee the day when that church will collapse in ruins. We will not see it disappear without regrets. If only it had not remained in schism and if only it had really taught the catechism, if only it had contributed somehow to maintaining in the masses some notions of positive Christianity. But we can do nothing. Its death is inevitable and imminent. What will become of its millions of followers? Will they fall prey to the *raskol* or to nihilism? Or [will they follow] the example of Emperor Alexander; after having run the circle of errors, having become tired and disgusted with everything, will they turn toward the West and ask the successor of Saint Peter to send them priests to instruct and receive them in the ranks of the one, holy, catholic, and apostolic church, of which the center is Rome? *Fiat! Fiat!*[87]

As he had done with earlier works, Gagarin shared this text with fellow Russian converts. Father Nikolai wrote that he read *La Réforme du clergé russe* "with much interest, but not without a certain sadness." Nikolai expressed sadness because he agreed with much of what Gagarin had written, and believed "as you do that the evil is too inveterate to be corrected, at least under present conditions." Nikolai was particularly pleased by Gagarin's references to the problem of Protestantism. He wrote, "In making the parallel between the two churches, I have always compared the Catholic church to a vigorous oak, beaten by the tempest, but which resists and serves as a support for others, whereas the Russian church is like an ivy supported by a wall and which falls with it."[88]

After finishing his analysis of the Russian clergy, Gagarin conducted a similar examination of the Byzantine Catholic clergy. His article "Les Églises orientales unies" was conceived as a companion to *La Réforme du clergé russe.*[89]

Gagarin began by expressing concern that the married clergy in the Byzantine Catholic church might one day come to constitute a hereditary caste. He feared that the creation of a hereditary caste of priests might vitiate true vocations: "When a son follows in the path of his father, this is a career, not a vocation."[90] He quickly added that he did not want to suppress the married clergy, since under some circumstances it may be "an advantageous institution and difficult to replace."[91] He repeated many of his previous arguments regarding reform of the Byzantine Catholic churches: the need for religious education, the importance of links to religious congregations and the Holy See, the importance of an indigenous clergy, his opposition to Latinization and the need to follow the ideas of Thomas de Jésus. Gagarin also voiced his desires for the establishment of a Bulgarian college and seminary, possibly in Constantinople, and the establishment of patriarchates for the Eastern rite churches so that they would not be in a position of inferiority vis-à-vis the Orthodox churches.[92]

Not surprisingly, the Orthodox did not favorably receive Gagarin's suggestions for Russian church reform. A. Lopukhin accused Gagarin of using "typical" Jesuit techniques of "politics, economics, mathematics, and prophecy," rather than theological arguments to attack the Russian church.[93] *Russkii arhkiv* called Gagarin's *La Réforme du clergé russe* a "Jesuit diatribe against the Russian church."[94]

The most vitriolic attack against Gagarin's text came from Abbé Guettée in his article "Lettres au R. P. Gagarin sur la réforme du clergé russe." Guettée began by asserting the superiority of Russian Orthodoxy over all religions: "the Orthodox church does not know jesuitical methods, and yet it prospers. It does not fear comparison to Protestant, Roman, and even jesuitical doctrines, for it knows that the comparison will prove favorable to it. It does not have an *Index* [of prohibited books], yet does not fear that error will ever win over truth when this truth is well taught."[95] Then Guettée attacked Gagarin himself, asserting "One knows well that jesuitism eradicated in you respect for the traditions of your own noble family." Guettée added: "If you had remained Orthodox and in the career of attaché to the ambassador, you would have been considered, you know this well, as a man of mediocre capacity, despite your title of prince, by these 'sovereigns, ministers, synods and bishops,' over whom you now place yourself as solemn judge."[96] Guettée claimed that as a diplomat not connected with the church, Gagarin had learned nothing about Orthodoxy; indeed, Guettée suggested, Gagarin only learned about the Russian church through the hostile writings of de Maistre, Rozaven, and Theiner.[97]

Guettée attacked Gagarin's analysis of the Russian clergy without having read Belliustin's text and without studying the history of its reception by the Holy Synod. Guettée wrote, "I tell you quite frankly, I do not have [a copy of] this book [by Belliustin]; thus I shall not use these letters to attack it. I do declare that, using your work as a basis, one cannot begin to evaluate Belliustin because I assume that you have chosen [from Belliustin] only that which is convenient for your case, indeed, I am tempted to say, in correct French, *que vous en avez abusé.*"[98] Guettée refused to accept Gagarin's word that the Holy Synod was upset with Belliustin's book; Guettée claimed that Bellustin had retained his position after his criticism of the Russian church, which would not have been the case in the Roman church.[99]

Turning to the content of Gagarin's *La Réforme du clergé russe,* Guettée attacked Gagarin for underestimating the importance of the married clergy.[100] He criticized Gagarin for claiming that the Russian clergy is a caste. Guettée noted sons of priests were free to marry outside the clerical *soslovie.* He stated that Gagarin had been wrong to say that sons of priests were destined to become priests as well.[101] As for the issue of clerical celibacy, Guettée noted that celibacy had been condemned by church councils, and that establishing a universally celibate clergy, as Gagarin wished to do, would create an even more rigid caste system than the one Gagarin now attacked.[102] Guettée rejected Gagarin's proposal to shorten Orthodox liturgical services; Guettée said that the services were the result of sacred tradition itself, and therefore the Russian church "should not cut them as the Jesuits think, nor add new services and offices as the Romanists do."[103]

Turning to the celibate Black clergy, Guettée claimed that all of Gagarin's attacks could be equally applied to Roman Catholicism.[104] Guettée defended the principal of state control over church wealth, because only the government could ensure that priests would possess sufficient funds to practice their ministry.[105] Guettée accused Gagarin of being interested only in obtaining the church's wealth for the Jesuits: "One can truly say that you hope one day to see this money deposited in the hands of the disciples of Loyola!" Guettée claimed that Gagarin's plan to build schools and hospitals in Russia was only a cover for his desire to obtain money.[106]

Guettée defended Russian ecclesiastical education against Gagarin's attacks. He observed that Roman Catholic seminaries had similar problems with nihilism, as demonstrated by the secularism of Proudhon, Renan, and others. Guettée thought that Russian seminaries were offering much better theological education than were Catholic seminaries.[107] He asserted that most Western seminaries were based on Jesuit teaching and were, therefore, "heretical, schismatic, and on many points, *anti-Christian*."[108] Addressing Gagarin's claims that Speranskii contributed to the Protestantization of Russian ecclesiastical education, Guettée argued that Gagarin had maligned Speranskii only because Speranskii came from a poor family.[109]

Guettée concluded by arguing that the Jesuits and the Roman Catholic church needed to be reformed first of all.[110] He presented Russian Orthodoxy as an exemplar of freedom: "Russia does not persecute anyone, all the denominations are respected within it."[111]

For the most part, Guettée's attacks were based more on his hatred of the Jesuits and Roman Catholicism than upon an accurate portrayal of the condition of the Russian clergy. His ignorance of Belliustin's text and his false characterization of the Holy Synod's reaction to its publication cast doubt on his ability to depict accurately the Russian church. His denial of the existence of a clerical *soslovie* and of Russian religious persecution further diminished his credibility. However, some of Guettée's criticisms of Gagarin were valid. Freethinking within Western seminaries did suggest that Western theological education was no antidote to the nihilism in Russian ecclesiastical education.

Operating against the background of preparations for Vatican I and Pius IX's desire to use the council as an opportunity for union, Gagarin made several new proposals: the establishment of schools for Russian Catholics, a new focus on Georgia rather than Poland as the site from which to catholicize Russia, pressing Russia to increase freedom for Catholics, and suggesting Russian clerical reform to end problems of church subjection and nihilism. While many of these proposals aimed to promote church union in the immediate future, Gagarin retained his belief that the only permanent solution to the problems of religious persecution, ecclesiastical subservience, and the spread of revolutionary ideology was through the union of the Russian Orthodox church with Rome. Gagarin's various plans yielded no significant immediate results. It is obvious that he lacked the self-discipline to see his programs through to the end, but a lack of perseverance was not the only obstacle to be overcome. The schemes themselves were often too grandiose to be implemented by anyone, whatever his disposition.

CHAPTER NINE

Ends and Beginnings

> When Russia renounces its blind prejudices and unjust legislation, the schism which separates it from the Catholic church will disappear as a cloud in the first rays of spring. One will remember well the small group of men devoted to their country and at the same time to their faith, who worked to hasten that blessed moment.[1]

After Gagarin's return from the Middle East, his reception by other Jesuits was very cordial. According to Ponlevoy, "The little Russian house of Versailles is truly good. Father Pierling is the best of men. . . . Father Gagarin is tranquil and content."[2] Unfortunately for Gagarin, this situation did not continue. By August 1867, problems had arisen between Gagarin and Pierling. A letter from Beckx told the Russian fathers to persevere despite difficulties and the misunderstanding between them.[3] In a letter to Pierling, Beckx wrote, "You find that your work does not measure up to your aspirations. No doubt many stand in the way of what we desire to do in Russia. However, I hope you will not fall prey to discouragement . . . have patience and be of good heart." In a letter to Balabin, Beckx wrote, "I see with pleasure that you do not despair of l'Oeuvre de S. Cyrille. Despite current difficulties, the work has born real fruit and I believe it will continue to do so in the future: it stirs the spirits and, little by little, the truth will appear."[4]

Tension also developed between Gagarin and Martynov. In 1865, the Oratorian Augustin Theiner had called Martynov to Rome; there Martynov was to serve on a Vatican I commission concerning the fate of the church in the East. Gagarin had wanted to participate in the council and was upset at not being chosen. The jealous Gagarin wrote sarcastically that Martynov "must not forego his speciality. Searcher of libraries, publisher of unpublished texts, connoisseur of reprintings, maker of annotations—that is his concern. . . . His translations leave much to be desired from the standpoint of style, and it would not be proper to make finished works of his materials."[5]

Furthermore, Gagarin continued to face criticism from Polish opponents who portrayed him as a supporter of Poland's Russian persecutors. As one Pole wrote, "It is easier, I suppose, for a Pole to be impartial in speaking of Russians, than for a Russian to be in speaking of Poles; at root this is natural, because who is more victim than the Poles?"[6] In a letter to Ponlevoy, Gagarin wrote that, to his great regret, he felt defiant and angry toward the Poles who, "I know not why, perceive me as an enemy . . . they accuse me of wanting to achieve the conversion of Russia on the ruin of the Polish church."[7]

The most intensive Polish response to Gagarin came in a series of letters from a fellow *Les Seize* member, Xavier Korczak-Branicki. Korczak-Branicki defended Poland's cultural superiority over Russia, a superiority rooted in Polish allegiance to the Roman church. "In preserving the writing that Cyril and Methodius gave to them and in receiving, with the Greek rite, the schism of Byzantium, [the Russians] held fast to the decadence of the vile [Byzantine] empire and closed their eyes to the light which, in Christianity, did not come from the East, but from the West. Without taking account of this fundamental linguistic and religious distinction among the Slavic nations, one cannot explain why [the Poles] have been so superior to [the Russians] in intellectual development." Korczak-Branicki noted the appearance of "brilliant literatures" in Poland and Bohemia two centuries before the appearance of prose and poetry in Russia, under Catherine II.[8] He called the contemporary West "the world of the future" and the East "the dying world." According to him, the East was moribund because Russian civilization modeled itself on Byzantine decadence and cut itself off from the Roman Catholic impulse to progress.[9] In view of the distinction between West and East, Korczak-Branicki argued that a union among the Slavs was impossible.[10] As for the future, he argued:

> The question is thus posed—and, if one reflects, one cannot pose it otherwise—there are only two alternatives: either the autocracy will evolve into a civilized regime, repudiating all Asiatic barbarism and placing itself in the sphere of Western Europe; or, as one extreme provokes another, Russia will become the scene of a terrible anarchy, followed probably by a demagogic dictator. Evolution or revolution, there exist no other alternatives. The first alternative is certainly preferable to the second. In either case, the crisis passes, the Russian nationality will find itself vital and strong. Well, will Russia be Catholic, as you hope, my reverend father? Certainly the authoritarian faith of Rome will

> gain many adepts; but the philosophic faith, that of Socinus, Channing, Coquerel, will equally open a vast field to its propaganda.[11] It has already rooted itself among the twelve million sectarians, as demonstrated by statistics. It is destined to reconcile faith with science; and that is why its adepts will multiply soon with rapidity. In the religious domain, despite the diversity of cults, mutual tolerance, born of absolute liberty of conscience, will establish concord and peace. In the political domain, the European federation, to which Russia will cease to be an obstacle, will establish a unitary civilization while preserving national autonomy.[12]

Korczak-Branicki's views were similar to those of Gagarin, in that he recognized the historically progressive nature of Roman Catholicism as opposed to Orthodoxy, the impoverished nature of the Russian state, and the likelihood of future revolution in Russia. However, there were significant differences between the two—not only regarding perspectives of democracy and Protestantism, but also especially in the interesting alteration that Korczak-Branicki made of Gagarin's slogan *Catholicism or Revolution.* Korczak-Branicki, being hostile to "authoritarian Catholicism," made Russia's alternatives *Protestantism or Revolution.* His notion of Protestantism was a society based on the ideas of Socinus, Channing, and Coquerel. He believed Protestantism, particularly in this "dissident form," much more compatible with the discoveries of modern science than was Catholicism.[13]

Polish opposition upset Gagarin. He complained, "I do not believe I have ever rejected a Polish hand offered to me in friendship, in contrast to the Poles who too often turn away from me. . . . I left my parents and my homeland, I raised between them and me unbreakable walls, I created [between them and me] an abyss. I was exiled, banished, I am overwhelmed by the Russians' calumnies and attacks against me because I am Catholic; yet the Polish Catholics [dare to] say that I am from a family of executioners."[14] Gagarin did respond to Korczak-Branicki in a series of letters. While sympathetic to Poland's condition and noting, "the most cruel trials weigh on it, it endures the most terrible suffering," he criticized Korczak-Branicki's view that the salvation of Poland lay in Protestantism.[15] He wrote:

> You seem to believe, my dear Branicki, that if Poland had been Protestant or Socininian, it would have avoided its present misfortunes and would today be a powerful and prosperous state. That is possible.

> We have seen Sweden and Holland, we see today England and Prussia form powerful states in full prosperity. This might have happened in Poland, but that is only a supposition, a conjecture which is not based on any proof.[16]

Gagarin reiterated earlier arguments that Catholicism was the true source of the Protestant nations' progress: the Protestant nations were initially Catholic; they grew under the influence of Catholicism; only when they attained maturity did they "repudiate the religion of their fathers and their grandfathers."[17] Gagarin claimed that the root of Russia's problems was that "unlike all nations of Europe, Russia was not formed and educated by the Catholic church."[18] Ironically, the Russian Gagarin instructed the Pole Korcazk-Branicki that Poland's glorious intellectual history owed much to Catholicism.[19]

Gagarin's testy response to his friend Korczak-Branicki illustrated how sensitive he was to criticism from Poles. Several of Gagarin's articles during this period suggest that he wanted at all costs to persuade the Poles of his sympathy for their national and religious suffering. In the article "Mgr. Lubienski—Évêque d'Augustowo" and in the introduction to August von Haxthausen's work *La question religieuse en Pologne,* Gagarin condemned the current effort to Russify Polish culture and the Russian persecution of the Polish Catholic church.[20] He laid the onus for Poland's most recent persecution on Nikolai Miliutin, state secretary for Poland from September 1863 to December 1866.[21]

Gagarin attacked Miliutin's attempt to replace the use of the Polish language with Russian, "which is odious to them." He wrote, "This substitution of one language for another takes time: in other words, the generations which succeed each other familiarize themselves little by little with the language that they feel the need to know; they begin by speaking two languages simultaneously, they end by forgetting that which to them is least useful."[22] Rather than persuading the Poles to learn Russian, Gagarin argued, Miliutin's policies would have the opposite effect: "How can a Pole be attracted toward a language in which he can scarcely open a book without finding there outrages against his patriotism and his faith?" Furthermore,

> history tells us that it is the vanquished who are the most often successful in making their language prevail over that of their conquerors. The Bulgarians do not speak Turkish, but a Slavic language, and that language is not that of the conquerors, it is that of the vanquished.

> Rurik and his companions, did they impose on Russia the use of Scandinavian? And when Gedymin and his descendants had gained control of Byelorussia and of Ukraine, was it Lithuanian which became the language of the country?[23]

The root of this persecution of Poland, Gagarin argued, was the Russian government's mistaken perception of a link between the Catholic opposition to Orthodoxy and Polish nationalism: "The Russian government pretends that Catholicism is identified in Poland with Polonism, hence it [the Russian government] subjects the Catholic church to tyrannical controls, which, when all is said and done, may end in the complete destruction of the [Polish Catholic] church."[24] Gagarin observed that the perceived link between Polonism and Catholicism had not always existed. "One does not see any trace under Catherine II, under Paul, and under Alexander I.[25] This perceived link dated from the ascension to the throne of Nicholas." Nicholas's "triple hatred" of liberty, the Catholic church, and Poland, displayed in the slogan of Official Nationality—*Orthodoxy, Autocracy, and Nationality*—was the source of the Russian government's conflation of Polonism and Catholicism.[26] According to Gagarin, attacking Poles because of their religion only guaranteed a defensive nationalistic response. He asked, "Why is it astonishing that Polish Catholics, simultaneously experiencing an attack on their faith and on their legitimate [national] aspirations, have taken for a slogan God and Country and have committed themselves to defend two causes both of which are dear to them and which are under simultaneous attack from the same enemy!"[27]

Gagarin directed his angriest words at the Russian government, the persecutor of the Polish and the Russian Catholic church. "For a long time," he complained, "the Catholic church in Poland and Russia has born suffering beyond words."[28] The oppression of Polish clergy by the Russian government and limitations on the Catholic bishops and the Vatican imposed by the Russian government exacerbated relations between Catholics in the empire and the Russian government.[29] Gagarin condemned the establishment of the Roman Catholic ecclesiastical college under governmental control, and he accused Russia of wanting to make the Polish church "as schismatic as the official church of the Greek rite."[30]

Gagarin consoled himself that Russia's persecutions would not be successful. Historically, Russian attempts to compel its citizens to enter the Orthodox church had always failed: "During all the centuries, it [the Russian Orthodox church] has not achieved the conversion of the Muslims,

Buddhists, or the pagans; if today it organizes some missions, the results are very meager, if there are any at all."[31] So-called "conversions" to Orthodoxy were illusory. According to Gagarin, such changes of confession "cannot be attributed to the zeal and the preaching of the Russian priests; they are the work of the bureaucracy, of tax officials, and the police."[32] Gagarin noted that in Ireland, the British had failed to convert the common people to Protestantism. In spite of British persecution, he said, "Ireland is more Catholic than it was before persecution began."[33] In the same way, Russian persecutions had made Poland "more Catholic today than it has been in a century; all the efforts undertaken to separate it from the [Catholic] faith have had no other result than to make the roots of that faith deeper in the hearts of the people."[34] To the extent that Russian policies had succeeded in shaking individuals' religious beliefs, to that degree the imperial authorities had encouraged nihilism and revolution. Gagarin claimed that Miliutin's policies had undermined "all conservative elements" in Polish society and contributed to the impending "triumph of anarchy, impiety, and atheism" in Poland: "Nikolai Miliutin, when he inaugurated this system, was promised a respite [from revolutionary uprisings] of twenty years. More than half the time is gone. We will see in six years. Possibly in 1883, the masses will have forgotten the catechism of the Catholic church and they will have ripened to the catechism of Bakunin and the cadres of the International."[35]

Gagarin urged that, instead of persecuting the Polish people and the Catholic church, the Russian authorities should grant religious liberty to the Poles and permit the Catholic bishops to establish schools and congregations: "Leave the Poles free to practice their religion, show them that their faith and their church have nothing to fear under your government and be assured that you will have contributed significantly to the pacification of [angry] spirits and hearts."[36]

Gagarin's attempt to present himself as sympathizing with oppressed Poles did not truly entail a change in his views regarding Poland. He stopped short of advocating Polish national independence from Russia, though he did attempt to convince his Polish opponents that he understood their reasons for seeking self-determination. Gagarin's main argument continued to be that it was in Russia's self-interest to grant religious liberty to the Poles, for religious liberty would dampen desires for political independence and would permit the Catholic church to act against the forces of revolution.

Meanwhile, Gagarin's program continued to draw criticism from the Russian Orthodox. The Polish uprising of 1863–1864 generated a burst of

Russian nationalism and increased Orthodox anger toward the Catholic church and toward the Jesuits, who were perceived as the main enemies of Orthodoxy and Russia. In 1864, when a rumor circulated that the Russian government might permit the Jesuits to return to Russia, I. S. Aksakov published an editorial in the Slavophile journal *Den'*, which accused the Jesuits of supporting the Polish uprising. Aksakov wrote, "I confess that I find it absolutely absurd and scandalous to contemplate that the Jesuits might be permitted to return to Russia after their expulsion in 1821 by the Emperor Alexander I." "To allow the Jesuit order to reenter Russia—they are the same now as then—would be to admit willingly and knowingly a gang of cheats, thieves, and other con artists; no, that is an understatement, they are one hundred times worse."[37]

Martynov responded to Aksakov's editorial in a letter published in *Den'* on 2 May 1864. Martynov's response in turn led Iurii Samarin to publish a series of letters attacking the Jesuits which were also published in *Den'* and republished as *Iezuity i ikh otnoshenie k Rossii.*[38] Samarin's text relied heavily on French and other Western European anti-Jesuit writings. He referred to the Jesuits' alleged lack of trustworthiness, their subversiveness and support of regicide. He cited the anti-Roman Catholic and anti-Jesuit writings of Guettée, Dmitrii Tolstoi, and others. He also referred to the traditional sources of anti-Jesuitism such as Sanchez, the *Monita Secreta,* and Escobar. For example, he wrote that the word *Jesuitical* had assumed a meaning completely opposite to the meaning of *Jesus:* "A *Jesuitical* oath, a *Jesuitical* word, a *Jesuitical* welcome, does not mean a trustworthy vow, a truthful word, or an honorable welcome; escobarderie (from Escobar, the well-known Jesuit theologian) does not mean straightforwardness." He went on to argue that the Jesuit reputation for falsehood is prevalent throughout Europe.[39]

In 1867, the decision by Pius IX to canonize Josaphat Kuncevich led Russian Orthodox critics to complain about Catholic aggressiveness toward the Eastern church. Kuncevich, the first Byzantine rite Catholic priest to be canonized, had served as archbishop of Polotsk before his murder by Orthodox Cossacks in 1623. Catholic historiography portrayed Kuncevich as a martyr of the faith slain by infidels.[40] The Orthodox considered Kuncevich the "persecutor of Orthodoxy" and the "scourge of the Slavs," perhaps because the bishop had forbidden Orthodox peasants to bury their dead in consecrated ground.[41] The Russian press was filled with attacks on the Vatican decision to canonize Kuncevich, in the *Sankt-peterburgskie vedomosti,* the *Russkii invalid,* and the *Moscovskie vedomosti.*[42]

Kuncevich was called "one of the most ardent oppressors of the Russian people in the confines of ancient Poland." The Orthodox interpreted his canonization as a Vatican attack on Russia. Whether or not Kuncevich was indeed a "scourge of the Slavs" is a matter to be settled by historians of the seventeenth century. The issue here is the Russian Orthodox response to his canonization. The Orthodox saw the Vatican decision to canonize Kuncevich as evidence of Catholic hostility to Russia and to the Orthodox church, even if that was not the Vatican's intention.

Meanwhile, Pius IX's attempt to elicit Orthodox participation in the Vatican Council misfired. The pope sent a letter of invitation to "all the bishops of the Eastern rite," a form of address apparently meant to include Greeks, Russians, Ethiopians, and other Eastern Orthodox. This invitation asked the Orthodox to return to unity with Rome in order that they might participate in the ecumenical council. The Orthodox bishops were asked to make a profession of faith similar to that of the Second Council of Lyons and Ferrara-Florence. The letter also made a disparaging reference to the Orthodox church.[43] In September 1868, the papal letter "To all the bishops of the Eastern church not in communion with the Apostolic see" was delivered to the Orthodox bishops by missionaries, not via Vatican diplomatic channels. The contents of the letter had been made known beforehand in Roman newspapers. Ecumenical Patriarch Grigorios VI refused to accept the letter. He cited the pope's decision to call the council without consulting the other patriarchs, the prior publication of the letter in the press, and his own opposition to papal primacy and infallibility as grounds for the refusal. The Orthodox also probably resented Pius IX's decision to convene the council on the feast of the Immaculate Conception of the Virgin Mary. Since the Orthodox church rejected the Immaculate Conception as a Latinist innovation, the pope's decision to convoke the council on 8 December could only be regarded as a deliberate provocation of the Orthodox East.

Russian Orthodox opposition to Rome was asserted in various publications, including some by influential members of the Russian government. Dmitrii Tolstoi's work, *Romanism in Russia: An Historical Study,* claimed that friendly relations between St. Petersburg and the Vatican were impossible.[44] The Ober-Procurator of the Synod declared "it is impossible to satisfy Rome by any concessions in conformity with the interests and dignity of the state." He argued that the Catholic church will consider any concession a "weakness"; hence, "relations between this ecclesiastical authority and temporal governments find their sole expression in constant struggle."[45] Tolstoi argued that Rome places temporal power over service to God and acts out of a need for complete domination.[46] He concluded, perversely, that the Russian government should act to "protect" the Roman Catholic church in Russia from the corruption of Rome. He thought the imperial government should introduce measures to correct "the complete decadence" of Catholic monastic life, the want of civilization among their clergy, and their unchristian covetousness."[47]

Tolstoi's book showed how unlikely it was that Gagarin could attain his goals. Russian sensitivity to the Vatican's "outside" influence on imperial religious affairs would surely not diminish so long as Tolstoi remained in office, nor would it decrease during Pius IX's assertive papacy. This was further shown by the Russian censors' banning of *La Réforme du clergé russe* in 1867. A circular from the Ministry of the Interior in 1870 still proscribed the text from "public circulation."[48]

A second work, Mikhail Ia. Moroshkin's *Iezuity v Rossii s tsarstvovaniia Ekateriny II do nashego vremeni,* accused the Jesuits of using violence to achieve their objectives in Poland and the Western regions of Russia.[49] The book condemned the Jesuit influence over Russia's nobility; according to the author, the Jesuits had affected "the Buturlins, Golitsyns, Volkonskiis, Gagarins, Shuvalovs, Balabins, Rostopchins, Tolstois, Kologrivovs, and others. . . . Orthodox people from the highest Russian families [turned] into the most malicious enemies of the Russian church and the Russian people."[50] Moroshkin reserved much of his anger for the Russian Jesuits who

> upon converting to Latinism, not only became members of the Society of Loyola, but founded in Paris the *Kirilo-Mefodievskii* Society, made up mainly from Jesuits, Russian by extract, with the sole goal of catching Russians in their Latin nets. Propaganda . . . from the [Jesuit] Russians, which we hear is successful, is becoming ever more prominent among colonies of Russian exiles in Paris. But not satisfied with their successes in Paris, the Jesuits from Russia want to spread this false apostolic work into Russia, hoping to reestablish themselves in Petersburg. They have found for themselves several disciples in Petersburg and Moscow, write entire epistles to us, publish different brochures in which they argue with us, try to convince us to join the Latin rite and to leave the Greek schism. They mourn our darkness and ruin, they spread sedition among the Bulgarian Orthodox, they slander the Bulgarians in Greece, the Greeks in Bulgaria and the Turks in both.

> To whom among the Russians is unknown the deeds of the Jesuits Gagarin, Martynov, Golitsyn [sic], and others![51]

Having faced opposition from the Slavophiles in the late 1850s and early 1860s, Gagarin now had to face opposition from the growing Panslavist movement in Russia. For example, the Russophilic second Pan-Slav congress in Moscow in 1867 demanded the Russification of all Slavs. Like the Slavophiles, the Russian Panslavists envisioned a messianic role for Russia and equated Russianness with Orthodoxy. As one Panslavist, Nikolai Danilevskii, wrote, "From an objective, factual viewpoint, the Russian and the majority of Slav peoples became, along with the Greeks, the chief guardians of the living tradition of religious truth, Orthodoxy, and in this way they continued the high calling which was the destiny of Israel and Byzantium: to be the chosen people."[52] The Panslavist vision lay at the heart of Dostoevskii's famous speech at the Pushkin monument in 1880:

> the Russians of the future will comprehend that to become a genuine Russian means to seek finally to reconcile all European controversies, to show the solution of European anguish in our all-human and all-unifying Russian soul, to embrace in it with brotherly love all our brothers, and finally, perhaps to utter the ultimate word of great, universal harmony, of the fraternal accord of all nations abiding by the law of Christ's Gospel![53]

Like the Slavophiles, the Panslavists were deeply hostile toward Roman Catholicism and the Jesuits. In *The Idiot,* Dostoevskii's Prince Myshkin called Catholicism "an unchristian religion" which was "worse than atheism" because "it preaches a distorted Christ, a Christ calumniated and defamed by it, the opposite of Christ!"[54] Dostoevskii condemned Roman Catholicism for its lust for earthly authority, its fanaticism and deceit, and for its value system, which he thought prepared the way for socialism, the great modern error.[55] Dostoevskii saw the Jesuits as the chief propagandists of Roman Catholicism, and therefore as chiefly responsible for Catholicism's false path.[56]

Considering Dostoevskii's hatred for Roman Catholicism and the Jesuits, it is not surprising that he had a very low view of Gagarin. In his *Diary of a Writer,* Dostoevskii compared Gagarin with the radical Westerner Vissarion Grigor'evich Belinskii:

> And so there developed two types of civilized Russians: the European Belinskii, who, in those days, denied Europe, and proved a Russian in the strictest sense, notwithstanding all errors which he had uttered about Russia; whereas the full-blooded, noble Prince Gagarin, having become a European, deemed it necessary not only to embrace Catholicism but straightway to leap over to the Jesuits. Which, then, of the two—tell me now—is a greater friend of Russia? Which of the two remained more Russian?[57]

In his *Notebooks for the Possessed,* Dostoevskii described Gagarin as one who "overlooks the Russian people," who "hates—not conditions in Russia, but the Russian people," who was not concerned with the Russian people, religion, customs, history, or future, but only wished to obtain rent from landholdings and live in Paris.[58]

Dostoevskii appeared to portray Gagarin in the character of Nikolai Andreevich Pavlishchev in his novel *The Idiot.* Pavlishchev is described there as a Russian "of good birth and fortune, a Court chamberlain . . . who preferred to give up the service and everything else and go over to Roman Catholicism and become a Jesuit, and quite openly, too, almost with a sort of fanaticism."[59] Pavlishchev had been converted by an Abbé Goureau, a Jesuit, who, I believe, represents Ravignan. Pavlishchev's conversion and decision to enter the Jesuits are quite similar to Gagarin's own personal history, for Gagarin, too, was a government official "of good birth and fortune" who had been converted by the actions of a French Jesuit and who "preferred to give up the service and everything else to go over to Roman Catholicism and become a Jesuit." Apparently, by 1869 Dostoevskii had come to consider Gagarin an archetypical Russian convert to Catholicism: "If a Russian is converted to Catholicism, he is sure to become a Jesuit, and a rabid one at that."[60]

The Russian Orthodox press vituperatively attacked Gagarin's work, although the criticisms were generally of the ad hominem variety. Typical in this respect was the comment in *Russkii arkhiv,* which wrote of Gagarin, "Emigrant-apostates lack the means truly to understand their former country; Gagarin still presents himself as a renegade-fanatic of a new faith who wants to discredit his old faith and to show all its blemishes to the people who confess it."[61]

The anti-Jesuit polemics issued by the Russian government and church suggest that, by 1870, official Petersburg was seriously alarmed about the danger of Jesuit inroads into Russian high society. As Martynov told Beckx:

> To official Russia, we are already known under the name of the "Jesuit Fathers of Versailles." People believe we have opened there [in Petersburg], in great secret, a boarding school for Russian children. St. Petersburg has given us the honor of dreading us, probably because it imagines that the Jesuits have a million means of operating from a distance and a totally secret manner of action that can only be perceived after the effect is produced. Thanks to the most violent and unhealthy attacks against the Company, people assume we have a very great influence in Russia; one writer of talent has even dared to write in a Russian gazette that the presence of a single Russian Jesuit in St. Petersburg or Moscow would be the signal for a great number of conversions in high society.[62]

If the Russian Orthodox church and the Russian government feared the Russian Jesuits, the Jesuits themselves did not feel that their publications were having much of an effect in Russia. Martynov admitted that, up to 1869, "our Russian books have only barely penetrated into Russia." He hoped that the time would come when Jesuit books or piety could easily cross the Russian border, but he did not predict that would happen any time soon.[63] Gagarin attributed the Jesuits' lack of success to difficulties in publishing Russian texts outside of Russia and to the fact that the majority of the Russian presses outside Russia remained "entirely under the influence of the Russian government or clergy, or even under that of revolutionary refugees."[64] It is hard to escape the conclusion that the Jesuits' limited impact in Russia was due less to their own direct efforts than to the energy of their enemies. In spite of the ecclesiastical censorship and the problems of publishing in the emigration, Gagarin's ideas circulated in Russia mostly through the publications of his opponents. For example, Russian priests translated Guettée's letters to Gagarin for publication in the ecclesiastic reviews of many dioceses.[65]

Gagarin responded to his Orthodox opponents by defending the sincerity of his earlier decision to enter the Catholic church. He claimed he understood why Russian Orthodox authorities found his conversion so irritating: the Orthodox could not bring themselves to admit that a Russian might conscientiously embrace the Catholic church, because their own entrance into Orthodoxy had been based less on conviction than on "calculation."[66] Gagarin argued that his conversion and decision to enter the Jesuits was sincere and that his opponents' portrayal of the Jesuits was false. He dismissed as falsehood the allegation that the Jesuits follow the maxim, "the end justifies the means." He asserted flatly that "it is not permitted to do evil for a good result . . . and if the Jesuits were ever to adopt a maxim so perverse, I would not remain one day among them."[67]

Gagarin and Martynov responded to other Russian Orthodox attacks. Martynov wrote an apologetical article in *Études* supporting the canonization of Josaphat Kuncevich. He cited favorable testimonials from Orthodox and Byzantine Catholics who knew Kuncevich and who portrayed him as a man of kindness and peace, whose teaching and conduct were "exemplary and holy."[68] Gagarin answered the polemics of Samarin, Tolstoi, and Moroshkin. He decried their "blind prejudice" and "inveterate hatred of the Jesuits."[69] He accused Tolstoi of attributing certain statements to the Jesuits "without giving the slightest proof of their authenticity." He accused Moroshkin of falsifying documentation and purveying false statements from earlier anti-Jesuit writings.[70] Gagarin described Samarin's attack on the Jesuits as "violent" and "exaggerated."[71] He also decided to answer Samarin's personal attacks on him:[72]

> You do not love them [the Jesuits]. I am not surprised and you have a right to your opinion. They are forbidden to enter Russia. You, it seems, might have held your tongue, but you cannot deny that sooner or later this prohibition could be repealed, not because the Jesuits have some influence in Russia, but simply because Russia's self-interest demands it; if the roots of Catholicism in Russia are to be separated from the roots of Polonism, the return of the Jesuits is necessary. You do not agree with me and consider the presence of the Jesuits in Russia as dangerous and injurious. You have the right to that opinion. To what means do you resort in order to achieve your goals? You portray the Jesuits as a gang of robbers and scoundrels. But your readers are not that naive. If one tenth or one hundredth part of what you speak against the Jesuits were true, you would not take up the trouble to write against them, they could not have any influence and in your eyes they would be quite harmless. Assume for the moment that I am allowed to live in Moscow. I am sure that you would not be afraid that I would kill or poison you. Of what are you afraid? You fear me because I am an honorable man, with deep convictions, and have the ability to convey these convictions to others.[73]

Gagarin also responded to anti-Jesuit writings in a more general fashion. He argued that, although Western European anti-Jesuit writings had been refuted long ago, sooner or later they would enter Russia and would be believed because "there are no Jesuits in Russia to refute them and the [Jesuit] works which can be published abroad have no chance of penetrating that country."[74] In light of this problem, Gagarin called for a full-scale history of the Jesuits in Russia. He recommended reprinting materials written by Jesuits living in Russia during the suppression and reprinting a collection of his own historical investigations. He wanted to prepare for "that blessed day" of the Jesuits' return to Russia by "dissipating the prejudices and for destroying the false and calumnious assertions of ignorance and bad faith."[75] In a letter to Martynov, Gagarin wrote:

> No one is so fearful of the Jesuits as are people in our native country. The Russians depict us in bad faith and with unimaginable prejudice, yet the force of truth is so great that we can now take advantage of the short-sightedness of our adversaries. . . . We can very legitimately hope that the appearance of a serious history of the Jesuits in Russia will produce in public opinion a complete reversal in our favor and open Russia to us.

Gagarin offered to write a history of the Jesuits in Russia, while Martynov worked on the revision of liturgical texts; meanwhile, Balabin could also contribute to the work.[76]

In order to facilitate his history of the Jesuits in Russia, Gagarin proposed to move l'Oeuvre des SS. Cyrille et Méthode to Rome where he could work in the Jesuit archives.[77] However, Beckx refused Gagarin permission to come to Rome. He wrote, "It would be very unfortunate to let l'Oeuvre des SS. Cyrille et Méthode come to an end. I believe it will one day bear precious fruits. *Fructum feret in patientia*. . . . If you would encounter problems by staying in Versailles, and the Provincial believed it more useful for you to reside at Vaugirard, I would not oppose that. . . . However, when you want to move a great distance, it is not appropriate to abandon your work without grave motive. *Nolite transire de domo in domum.*"[78]

On 10 April 1869, Ponlevoy proposed to Beckx that the Russian Jesuit residence at Versailles be transformed into a residence for French Jesuits. He wrote, "The [Russian] mission at Versailles which was to last only three years, ends with the departure of Father Pierling. The small Russian community has had its day. . . . The residence could become French and the Russians could remain there, since their work is more nominal than real. Besides, Father Gagarin cannot live with Father Pierling any longer." Beckx approved of the transformation on 20 April 1869. A letter from Balabin indicated that he also approved of the transformation and did not want l'Oeuvre des SS. Cyrille et Méthode transferred to Rome.[79]

Gagarin's hope to move to Rome to participate in the Vatican Council was stated on 12 October 1869, in a letter from Bishop Félix Antoine Dupanloup of Orleans (1802–1878) to Beckx. The bishop asked that Gagarin accompany him to Rome. Beckx opposed Dupanloup's request and told Ponlevoy:

> There would certainly be some inconveniences should Father Gagarin go to Rome in the present conditions. Bishop Dupanloup has not truly requested him as his theologian; he has asked only to send him to Rome for the duration of the Council, in the interest of the Eastern churches. I have responded to the bishop, that at the beginning of the commission he requested an advisor; then I proposed Fathers Gagarin and Martynov and he chose Father Martynov. I added that if his [Gagarin's] presence is needed later, I would be obligated to summon him.

Beckx added that Dupanloup had asked for one Jesuit, not two, and that he was concerned that there were already a sufficient number of Jesuits on the Commission for Eastern Affairs with the participation of Johann Bollig (1821–1895) and Martynov.[80] On 20 November 1869, Beckx informed Gagarin of his decision not to permit him to go to Rome:

> I learn that you prepare to come to Rome as a theologian for the Monseigneur of Orleans. This is, without a doubt, a misunderstanding. Monseigneur Dupanloup never asked you to serve as *his theologian.* He simply thinks it advisable to summon you to Rome to give advice on Eastern affairs. I have responded that I cannot agree, for the moment at least. At the beginning I offered a choice between Fathers Gagarin and Martynov, and the Commission has chosen Father Martynov. We understand, dear Father, that in these conditions your position in Rome would be very false.[81]

Beckx's refusal to permit Gagarin to take part in the Vatican Council was very disappointing to Gagarin, who saw himself as the foremost Jesuit working on the affairs of the Eastern church. While Beckx wrote that he did not want Gagarin to participate in the projects of the Commission for

Eastern Affairs because of a fear that the commission would become dominated by the Jesuits, concern about Gagarin's working relationship with Martynov was certainly not far from his mind. For Beckx, the issue was Gagarin's ability to participate fruitfully as a member of the commission without seeking to impose his ideas unilaterally.

At the end of December 1869, the Russian Jesuits moved to rue des Bouronnais 40. Only Gagarin and Balabin remained. Pierling had ceased to serve as superior and Martynov was in Rome participating in the Vatican Council. Gagarin now proposed to move l'Oeuvre des SS. Cyrille et Méthode to Brussels in order to be with the Bollandists. Knowing the views of Beckx, he had to drop this idea. The Russian Jesuits decided to return to Paris. Gagarin wanted to move to a house on rue Lafayette, but in the end he and Balabin moved to rue de Sèvres 35. From Rome, Martynov joined them.[82] Problems between Gagarin and Martynov arose again. For example, Balabin received a sum of sixty thousand francs from his family which he wanted to use to pay the pension for Martynov. He wrote Beckx:

> By thus paying the pension of Martynov in a fixed manner, there would be the advantage of removing a sort of dependence with regard to Father Gagarin who is quite hard on him and which has entailed very great inconveniences. Thus, Father Gagarin can no longer refuse to pay the pension of Father Martynov when the latter finds fault with a work, which although approved by his superiors, does not please the former for some reason or another. Father Gagarin is the head of the work and at the same time the procurer. This fact puts Father Martynov always in a type of difficult dependence vis-à-vis Father Gagarin and removes a certain liberty of rapport necessary for the tranquility of his spirit.[83]

On 25 October 1871, Beckx approved Balabin's request.[84]

Gagarin continued his work for church union at rue de Sèvres where he established Oeuvre de Ste. Olga in 1873. Gagarin's association, under the protection of the Sacred Heart of Jesus and its patron, Saint Olga, was designed to defend Catholic interests in Russia through prayer and financial assistance. As Gagarin had previously stated, prayers for the assistance of Russian Catholics and the conversion of non-Catholics were most important. Several Russian women participated in the group, including Countess Elizaveta Buturlin, Princess Golitsyn, Princess Lazereva, and Princess Volkonskaia. The association had twenty-one members.[85]

In June 1875, Nikolai Leskov visited Gagarin in Paris. Leskov's visit was important for demonstrating that Gagarin's links to Russia remained strong despite the passage of time and despite the hostile Russian response to his writings. Leskov's visit was also important because the impetus for the visit came from Ivan Aksakov, who, just seven years earlier, had written a vitriolic attack on the Jesuits. Aksakov's view of Gagarin had improved as a result of Gagarin's assistance in providing Aksakov with copies of Tiutchev's poetry and letters. In a letter to Gagarin on 24 November/6 December 1872, Aksakov wrote, "I see that interest in Russian literature is still dear to you, that Russian feeling lives in you, that, [despite] the decrees of personal exile from the homeland, you have not broken spiritual union with it."[86] Thus, when Leskov informed Aksakov of his decision to visit Paris, "Aksakov told me that I would give him pleasure if I would visit the Jesuit Prince Gagarin in Paris and write of how I found him."[87]

Leskov arrived in Paris with an interest in religious problems, in the life of the Catholic church, and in Catholic schools. Gagarin offered to show Leskov several Catholic schools in Paris. Leskov found his meetings with Gagarin to be very useful. In a letter to A. P. Miliukov, he wrote, "Gagarin is a sweet old gentleman [*milii barin*], who still exudes the atmosphere of the Pushkin circle. What a difference from all that Russian scum [*svoloch'*] who form the present-day Russian reading room in Paris!"[88] Leskov also wrote that "He [Gagarin] was not a sly man and did not match the generally vulgar presentation of the Jesuits. In Gagarin, until the end of his life, was contained much Russian simpleheartedness and grandness, joined with a particular attachment to fantasy, which can often be noted in many Russian people of the upper class."[89] Gagarin was also favorably impressed with Leskov: "it is always very pleasant to have relations with Russians, when they are not infected by insurmountable preconceptions and nihilistic tendencies. And from you there is still much to receive."[90]

In addition to conducting a tour of different Catholic schools, Gagarin also provided Leskov with information relating to various Catholic devotions such as those to the Sacred Heart and Holy Name of Jesus. Gagarin also provided Leskov with copies of his work, including *La Réforme du clergé russe*, *Sokrovishche khristianina*, and *Liubopitnikh svidetelsv o neporochnom zachatii Sv. Devy.* Leskov wrote that he found *Liubopitnikh svidetelsv* "very amusing and unequivocal" although he had disagreements with Gagarin's other texts.[91] Leskov admitted that in *La Réforme du clergé russe*" was much justice." However, Leskov argued that Gagarin's discussion on Russian monastic life "forgot our amazing traveling monks, they are countless!"

> Why did you not give evidence about the lofty souls, now residing in the mountains, in the caves and valleys of the land? Without them there is no picture of Russian monasticism, but only a sketch of the homes of bishops and *stavropigii.* Or did you not know of Seraphim of Sarov, Parfenii Goloseevskii, Markarii of Optina and the divine hermits of Solovki and Valamo? Admitting this deficiency would please me.[92]

As for *Sokrovishche khristianina,* Leskov wrote that he had problems with Gagarin's low view of humanity, the doctrine of original sin, and his "Old Testament" presentation of God as "terrible and awful."[93]

In 1876, Gagarin published his last major work, *L'Église russe et l'Immaculée Conception.* This work, like his previous publications regarding the primacy of the pope, was an attempt to prove that the Russian church had historically believed in the doctrine of the Immaculate Conception, as shown through early theological writings and Russian liturgical texts.[94] In the first part of this text, Gagarin referred to the late seventeenth-century writings of Lazar Baranovich, Antonii Radivilovskii, and Ivan Galiatovskii.[95] According to Gagarin, each of these writers supported the Catholic doctrine of the Immaculate Conception. Galiatovskii wrote, for example,"The third great thing that God has done for the most pure Virgin, was to exempt her from original sin, because the most pure Virgin was conceived and born without original sin."[96] Gagarin argued that this support of Catholic doctrine could not have been the result of the Catholic influences at the Academy of Kiev because, "one must not forget, the Academy of Kiev was in open war with the Polish Jesuits," that Baranovich and Galiatovskii were selected by the Ukrainian bishops to defend the Orthodox church, and that their writings "attack with violence the Roman church, on the question of the procession of the Holy Spirit, on the use of leaven[ed bread] and communion under one species, on the primacy of the pope, and they would not have hesitated to attack the doctrine of the Immaculate Conception, if they had believed it an innovation of the Latins and a break in tradition."[97]

Further evidence, for Gagarin, came from the teachings of the Old Believers which also indicated a belief in the Immaculate Conception. For example, one profession of faith asserted, "This is why she [Mary] alone, predestined before the generations and announced by the Prophets, the Mother of the Creator of the universe, not only did not participate in the original stain, but she always remained pure as the heavens and entirely good.[98] In another document, the Old Believers listed among the reasons they did not accept the Russian church as the true church that "The Russian church does not believe in the Immaculate Conception."[99] Thirdly, Gagarin claimed to find support for a Russian belief in the Immaculate Conception from Russian liturgical texts which referred to Mary as "all beautiful and immaculate," "pure and ineffable," and "NO ONE IS IMMACULATE, EXCEPT YOU, MOTHER OF GOD."[100]

Gagarin suggested that the Orthodox had forgotten these earlier teachings under pressure from Protestantism. He pointed to Protestantization both in Constantinople and in Russia. As for Constantinople, Gagarin asserted that it was corrupted by Calvinist doctrines in the seventeenth century under Patriarch Cyril Lucaris. He said that the new Russian teaching denying the Immaculate Conception "has come to Moscow from Constantinople, but Constantinople borrowed it from the Protestant universities of England, Germany, and Holland."[101]

Gagarin linked Protestantization in Russia to the corrupting influences of Peter I and Feofan Prokopovich as well as the "semi-Protestant academies of the nineteenth century organized by Speranskii."[102] Gagarin concluded his text by decrying "anarchy" in the Russian church as well as the Orthodox commitment to respect external forms over internal piety.[103]

N. Subbotin, professor of the Ecclesiastical Academy of Moscow, contested Gagarin's claims in a text entitled *Pis'mo k. o. Gagarinu, "sviashchenniku Iezuitskago ordena v Parizhe."* Like earlier Orthodox writers critical of Gagarin's attempts to prove that traditional Russian theology was in agreement with Catholic doctrines, Subbotin accused Gagarin of taking texts out of context and of mistranslating passages.[104] Subbotin argued that the Slavonic word *neporochnaia* did not have the same meaning as *immaculate* and that it had also been used to describe others besides Mary.[105] As for the Old Believers, Subbotin argued that Gagarin was mistaken in his views of the Old Belief and that "As an observer, closely acquainted with the history and life of the schism, I have come to this conclusion; indeed, any thorough study of the schism will necessarily reach the conclusion, that there is no people who more boldly and arbitrarily distort and violate the teachings of the historical church [than the Old Believers]."[106] In any case, Subbotin argued, not all Old Believers supported the same teachings and those cited by Gagarin may have been influenced by Catholicism or at least sought Catholic support.[107] Subbotin also criticized Gagarin's observations concerning the Protestantization of the Russian church, noting that Feofan Prokopovich had studied at Kiev and that perhaps his Protestant ideas came from that academy. Furthermore, documents demonstrated that the Russian teaching on Mary arose before, as Gagarin claimed, Constantinople had been influenced by Calvinism.[108]

In conclusion, Subbotin claimed that "the Russian church, like her mother the Greek church, has never *believed* the teaching about the Immaculate Conception, that is, the Church has not taken it as a dogmatic teaching of faith. In the theological texts of the Greco-Russian churches it is impossible to find anywhere where *such a belief* was expounded with appropriate clarity and definitiveness."[109] As for the writings of the Ukrainian clergy at Kiev, Subbotin argued that they could not be taken as accurately presenting the teachings of the old Russian church.[110]

In an unpublished response to Subbotin, Gagarin admitted that no definitive and binding teaching on the Immaculate Conception could be found in Orthodoxy. Nevertheless, Gagarin said that his translations from Orthodox theologians were neither aberrations nor expressions of personal opinion, but were understood by the laity as reflecting Orthodox teaching. He also provided other texts from the Old Believers, showing a "traditional belief" in the Immaculate Conception. Gagarin argued that the teaching of the Immaculate Conception had not been condemned by the Russian church, and therefore one was free to believe in it.[111]

Subbotin's decision to publish his response to Gagarin's text further demonstrated how Orthodox responses to Gagarin helped to make Gagarin's views available to Russians despite official government censorship. Ivan Osipin wrote, "In refutation of the false evidence of the well-known apostate Jesuit Prince Ivan Gagarin, who in a particular brochure selected evidence from history and the ecclesiastical practice of the Russian Orthodox church in order to demonstrate that our church unconsciously confessed the Roman dogma about the Immaculate Conception of the Virgin Mary, our professor wrote an article which thoroughly refuted the entire false testimony of the apostate from Orthodoxy."[112] Again, by making Orthodox familiar with objections to Gagarin's views, these writers made the views themselves available to Orthodox audiences.

In 1877, Gagarin collaborated with a prayer society for the union of churches that had been established at a monastery of the order of Augustinian Recollects at the Sanctuary of the Merciful Heart of Jesus at Saint-

Nazaire-sur-Loire. This society, approved by the bishop of Nantes, had as a goal "to bring Our Savior Jesus Christ, present to us in the sacrament of the Eucharist, to the schismatic peoples of the East."[113] Its members were to arrive at this goal through the use of "the all powerful arm of prayer" and recite each day, especially after communion, one Our Father or the following prayer:

> My God, my God, why have you abandoned your beloved Son? Come deliver him. My good Jesus, may the mercy of your heart hasten the day when there will only be one flock and one Pastor! Holy Spirit, enlighten all men with your divine light! Immaculate Virgin, Saints of God, join your prayers to ours.[114]

The prayer society claimed to have witnessed a "surprising movement" of the "schismatic" churches returning to Rome. It included 40,000 members and also prescribed various devotions for the society which offered plenary and partial indulgences.[115]

The Countess de Pimodan asked Gagarin to help her spread the society to various churches, including Notre Dame des Victoires and Sacré-Coeur of Montmarte; she also related the decision to spread the society to the United States and the Austrian part of Poland. She listed eighty-six religious orders that wanted to pray for union.[116]

After Gagarin returned from Syria, his various publications and proposals demonstrated a growing desire to focus his work on the plight of Russian Catholics, whether to deliver them from religious persecution or prevent the establishment of a Roman Catholic ecclesiastical college under the control of the Russian government. His change in focus was to at least some degree caused by a desire to avoid angering the Poles and Russians as well as by the desire to make his objectives more realizable. If conversion could not be immediately achieved, then he would promote religious freedom.

His proposals, whether for union or for religious freedom, proved inherently problematic because he was unable to separate the religious and national questions from either the Polish or the Russian concepts of national identity. In fact, Gagarin's own belief that a Catholic Russia was destined to play a great role in European civilization demonstrated that the links between the two issues could not be separated in his own mind. Furthermore, Gagarin's identity as a Jesuit continued to limit his success, leading him to think that he must change Russia's perception of the Jesuits through a series of historical monographs.

Gagarin faced opposition from his fellow Jesuits as a result of his inability to work in partnership with others. His exaggerated self-image, his desire for complete control of the work of the Russian Jesuits, and his criticisms of his coworkers fostered poor relations among them and with those superiors whose support was needed for the enactment of many of his proposals. Gagarin's aristocratic heritage limited his ability to accept his coworkers as equals; his commitment to church unity as a personal mission stood in the way of accepting contributions from others. Part of the problem was that Gagarin labored for thirty-five years to foster church unity, with little to show for it.

Later in his life, while he continued his work of publishing the history of the Jesuits in Russia and continued to keep himself abreast of events in his homeland, increasing problems with gout limited his participation in the work of l'Oeuvre des SS. Cyrille et Méthode.[117] The rise in power of the Republicans in France further limited Gagarin's ability to work on church union in a stable atmosphere.[118]

Since the Jesuits had already faced expulsion from Italy in 1859, 1860, and 1870, from Spain in 1868, and from Germany in 1872, Gagarin grew concerned over French debates regarding the Jesuits and wanted to protect his library from dispersion. Learning that private goods would not be confiscated by the government, Gagarin and Father Pitot, superior at the residence on rue de Sèvres, hoped to use the will of William Palmer, who had left many of his texts to the Jesuits, as proof that the Bibliothèque Slave was the private property of the Russian Jesuits.[119] Gagarin also sought to move l'Oeuvre out of France: either to England, where a Russian married to an Englishman, Madame Bodenham, née Moravska, offered a place in Hereford; or to Rome, where Leo XIII had shown an interest in the unity of churches.[120] However, Pierling wanted to keep the work in Paris. He argued, "It is only in Paris that one can have a European center."[121]

Unfortunately for the Jesuits, the political situation in France grew worse. In 1876, the Chambre passed the Law of Freedom of Higher Education. Article 7 of that law stated that "No one is allowed to participate in public or private education, or to direct an educational establishment of any type, if he belongs to an unauthorized religious congregation." The proposed law, directly targeted against the Jesuits, was rejected in the French Senate, but passed as a decree on 29 March 1880. The decree accorded three months to the Jesuits to dissolve themselves and evacuate the establishments they occupied in France. On 29 June 1880, the Jesuit order was expelled from France; only three Jesuits were permitted to remain. On 31 August 1880, Jesuits were expelled from all French colleges.

The French authorities placed seals on the residence of the Russian Jesuits, and for some time the Bibliothèque was inaccessible. Martynov alone was present to assist in the transfer of the Jesuits' possessions; Balabin was at the college on the rue de Madrid, Pierling was at Rome, and Gagarin was sick and resting in Evian, Switzerland, at the residence of Princess Léonille Ivanovna Sayn-Wittgenstein, née Bariatinskaia (1818–1918). He later spent three months at Lausanne. Before the expulsion, Martynov put some of the collections of the Bibliothèque into cases which were stored at the residences of M. Riant and M. de Beaucourt, who were friends of the Jesuits. M. de Beaucourt was also president of the Société bibliothèque on the Boulevard Saint Germain.

Initially, Pierling, Balabin, and Gagarin wanted to move to Rome. However, on 28 July 1880, Gagarin wrote, "Rome had much seduced me, but I am returning there [to Paris]."[122] Thus, during the summer of 1880, Balabin worked to obtain passports for himself and the other Russian Jesuits which would serve as a means of returning to Paris and obtaining the property of the Bibliothèque from the Russian ambassador.[123]

Pierling, fearing destruction of the library, suggested selling everything to the duke of Norfolk who would leave the library to an English Jesuit. This would preserve everything. However, Father Pitot opposed this idea: "It seems to be inspired by fear. And fear of what?" Pitot did not want to give the property to strangers, and Pierling agreed.[124]

When Gagarin returned to Paris, he stayed with Balabin at an apartment provided by Count Vassart d'Hozier on rue de Rivoli 205. The Russian Jesuits lived there with Father Unzueta of the Spanish missions and worked in the libraries on rue de Sèvres and rue de Rivoli. In August 1880, the provincial of Paris asked Gagarin to depart for England to teach a course on ecclesiastical history in Latin. Gagarin saw this as an opportunity to move l'Oeuvre to England. However, Martynov argued, "Would it be a question by chance of burying l'Oeuvre de S. Cyrille in the family crypt which has already received the body of *Études?*" A few days later, Gagarin was told to remain in Paris.[125] In the summer of 1881, Pierling finished work at the Roman archives and returned to Paris. In 1882, Martynov went to the Bollandist college, Saint-Michel of Brussels.

On 19 June 1882, Ivan Sergeevich Gagarin, S.J., died. According to Father Charles Clair, S.J., Gagarin's last words were those of the exiled Pope Saint Gregory VII, "*Dilexi iustitiam et odi iniquitatem propterea in exilio moriar!*" [I sought justice and hated iniquity, as a result I die in exile!][126] On 20 June 1882, Father Balabin celebrated the funeral mass for Gagarin at the Church of the Madeleine. Several members of the French nobility and the Senate of the French Republic attended the funeral. Gagarin was buried in the Jesuit section of the Montparnasse cemetery. Balabin went to Cairo in 1888, where he died in 1895. Martynov died at Cannes in 1894.

In 1901, a French law on religious associations required the Jesuits to leave their houses. The Bollandist Fathers of Belgium accepted part of the Bibliothèque in July of that year, while the province of Paris preserved the property. In 1905, the Jesuits installed the Bibliothèque Slave at the Bibliothèque Bollandienne at Saint Michel. In 1908, Pierling left Paris with the remaining texts and moved to Brussels, where he received a donation from Nicholas II of the *Polnoe sobranie zakonov Rossiiskoi Imperii.* In 1922, after Pierling died, M. J. Rouët de Journel assumed responsibility for the Bibliothèque until the autumn of 1970. He returned the Bibliothèque Slave to Paris at rue de Sèvres 33 in the former Jesuit residence. In 1970, Father René Marichel was named director. In 1979, the journal *Simvol* was established. In 1983, the Bibliothèque Slave was moved to the Centre d'études russes Saint-Georges in Meudon. The combined holdings of the two libraries amounted to more than 100,000 volumes. The Bibliothèque's present director, Father François Rouleau, declared, "One can hope that the Bibliothèque Slave can still fulfill its role best not only by preserving Russian culture in the West, but also serving as a link between the Western world and Russia, between Catholicism and Orthodoxy."[127]

S. L. Frank has argued that the Russian *intelligent* always "avoided reality, fled from the world, and lived in a world of phantoms, of dreams, of a pious faith outside of day-to-day historical life."[128] This was certainly the view of Gagarin held by some of his associates. Pierling wrote, "He [Gagarin] had the essentially Russian character. He began many things, but he never achieved anything."[129] Vladimir Pecherin called Gagarin the "Don Quixote of Catholicism."[130] Joseph Burnichon argued that Gagarin launched many projects, but lacked perseverance.[131]

Pierling, Pecherin, and Burnichon were not incorrect in their assessments of Gagarin. Nor were these views significantly different from those of Gagarin's superiors. Gagarin did begin many projects which ended without achieving any real result. His polemical writings achieved a greater effect than his proposals for union.

Yet he did leave an important legacy. *Polybiblion* praised Gagarin:

> Father Gagarin wrote much about Russia and for Russia; reading the titles of his numerous publications demonstrates that his religious life did not diminish his patriotism: for everything he did was inspired by the desire to enlighten his compatriots, to procure for them the happiness of the Catholic faith that he did not wish to enjoy alone. He left a vast correspondence which also demonstrated the astonishing activity of his spirit. Those who met him knew that the austerity of the religious life did not remove the distinction of his manners, the charm of his conversation; at the same time [he was] knowledgeable and full of appeal, serious and enjoyable; loyalty of character and generosity of heart were within him.[132]

The *Istoricheskii viestnik* presented Gagarin as one who "becoming a Jesuit . . . did not stop being Russian," and who continued to be interested in the fate of his country.[133] Aleksandra Smirnova-Rosset asserted that Gagarin "preserved into his old age ardent feelings of love" for Russia.[134]

In fact, several prerevolutionary Russian journals expressed favorable views of Gagarin and his work. V. A. Bil'basov argued that Gagarin "was conscious of the abnormal development of the Russian system and was prepared to devote all his strength to the service of his country, burning with love for it."[135] The journal *Golos* published an extremely favorable article about the Bibliothèque Slave which described Gagarin as "a man of extensive education" who, along with Martynov, Pierling, and Balabin, "merited at least their names to be known to the Russian public."[136] As for the Bibliothèque, a contributor to *Golos* wrote, "In Russia, even, one would not find many libraries which could rival it." The writer sent the Russian Jesuits "a warm salute." It concluded: "We see in them intelligent men, well-educated men of talent."[137] Even the Russian Orthodox church found favorable words for "an apostate to his faith," calling Gagarin "a very outstanding man."[138]

Even if Gagarin failed to bring about the union of churches, the influence of his ideas continued after his death. Vladimir Solov'ev, considered to be Russia's first true philosopher, became acquainted with Gagarin's ideas as a result of his contacts with Martynov and Pierling. Solov'ev spent time at the Bibliothèque Slave and read Gagarin's 1866 response to Samarin. In a letter to Martynov, Solov'ev wrote:

> The Eastern Orthodox church *de jure* is not separate from the Catholic church, the virtual separation of the hierarchy and church does

> not have at the present time any decisive significance and no one is forced to accept it. Why I say "at the present time" I will explain now with the help of the deceased Gagarin. (I thank you for sending his beautiful letter, which of course should be affixed to my critique of Samarin.) He points out the unorthodox (in the narrow sense of the word) Slavophilic thought about the church. At the present time, our "separated church" obliges these unorthodox ideas, since it frequently accepts them without protest, it frequently approves them.[139]

Solov'ev's views, during his pro-Catholic period, were quite similar to those of Gagarin. Solov'ev believed that, while the Catholic church had made mistakes, it was an active historical force. Thus, by seceding from universal Christianity, Orthodoxy had become subservient to nationalism and the Russian ecclesiastical authorities had become subservient to the secular authorities. Solov'ev even argued that the true nature of Orthodoxy was better reflected among the Old Believers than in the state church.[140] Solov'ev believed unification of churches to be the best means of resolving Russia's problems. He called for a union between the pope and the Russian tsar akin to Gagarin's earlier proposal in *La Russie sera-t-elle catholique?* Solov'ev believed that such a union would permit Russia to end the sin of schism and to realize its vocation by reuniting the Slavic nations and establishing a new civilization. Union would also permit the papacy to realize its theocratic mission, "for the priesthood can only find the proper milieu for its ultimate incarnation in the Slavic element." Union would obtain for Rome a pious and enthusiastic people, a faithful and powerful defender.[141] Solov'ev believed church union would end the Polish problem, especially if Poland were to play the key role of mediator in the establishment of this union. Union would also end the problem of nihilism.[142] Despite the similarities between Gagarin's ideas and those of Solov'ev, Solov'ev did not follow Gagarin into Catholicism. He said, "I belong to the true Orthodox church. Only by professing true Orthodoxy, I, who am not Catholic, recognize Rome as the center of universal Christianity."[143]

While not due to the influence of Gagarin, there were other developments in Russia's relationship with Rome and Roman Catholicism which did coincide with Gagarin's goals. In 1905, the Russian government passed an edict of toleration which permitted anyone to leave the Orthodox church without loss of rights and without penalties.[144] In response, between 1905 and 1909, 233,000 Eastern rite Catholics returned to union with Rome. There were also Russian converts, such as Father Alexis Zerchaninov, who, along with several other Orthodox priests, became Catholic. In 1908, Zerchaninov opened a chapel in St. Petersburg where he established a Russian Catholic church.[145] Furthermore, in early 1914, Sergei Sazonov, the Russian foreign minister, suggested an alliance with the Catholic church in the government's struggle against socialist and revolutionary movements.[146] After the Russian revolution, a representative of Grand Duke Kiril Vladimirovich contacted Cardinal Gasparri, the papal secretary of state, in an attempt to enlist Vatican support for the restoration of the monarchy. In return for such support, the Grand Duke promised, upon his occupation of the Romanov throne, to grant official recognition to Russian Catholicism in the form of a Russian Exharchate and to approve an eventual Catholic-Orthodox union.[147]

Gagarin's ideas also continued to influence Jesuit and Roman Catholic views of the Orthodox church. Caesarius Tondini took up Gagarin's work for church union by attempting to prove that the Russian Orthodox accepted Roman Catholic dogma and by promoting prayer societies as a means of obtaining union. Tondini modified Gagarin's slogan *Catholicism or revolution.* Whereas Gagarin had spoken of a political revolution, Tondini wrote, "We venture to put [forward] the same dilemma with reference to a *religious* revolution, and extend it to the whole Oriental Orthodox church—*Catholicism or revolution!*"[148] J. G. A. M. Remmers noted that the 1887 *Kirchenlexikon oder Encyklopädie der Katholishen Theologie und ihrer Hilfswissenschaften* included an entry for *Byzantinisme* by Cardinal J. Hergenröther which cited Gagarin. Remmers noted that others also used Gagarin's term of Byzantisme.[149]

Gagarin also had some influence on Byzantine Catholic metropolitan Andrei Sheptyts'kyi's desire to work for church union.[150] Sheptyts'kyi opposed hostile polemics and wanted to create a Russian Catholic church free from Polish influence.[151]

Bishop Michel d'Herbigny, S. J., studied at the Bibliothèque Slave, where he became familiar with Gagarin's ideas. He referred to Gagarin and the other Russian Jesuits as "glorious ancestors."[152] Like Gagarin, Herbigny wanted to use indigenous clergy to proselytize the Orthodox, to separate the Catholic and Polish questions, and to maintain the Eastern rite. He saw Russia's alternatives as either Catholicism or Bolshevism. He opposed attempts to emphasize nationalism over Catholicism and believed that the Russians were not responsible for the schism. Herbigny also believed that a converted Russia would serve as the best means for the eventual conversion of China.[153] In 1922, Herbigny was appointed president of the Pontifical Oriental Institute. In 1925, he created a special Pontifical Commission for Russia. In 1926, he attempted to restore the Roman Catholic hierarchy in the Soviet Union. In 1929, Herbigny established a new Collegium Russicum which served as an important Russian emigré center and offered lectures by Dmitri Merezhkovskii and Zinaida Gippius.[154]

The Jesuit order as a whole also continued to work for church union. In 1880, the Jesuits reformed the Basilian order. In 1887, they trained Byzantine Catholic clergy at the Collegium Russicum. In 1917, the Pontifical Oriental Institute was founded under Jesuit direction to foster research and train missionaries. In 1922, Edmund Walsh, S. J., was appointed head of the Papal Relief Mission to Russia which fed 158,000 children a day during Russia's terrible famine. Several Jesuits, including Walter J. Ciszek, S. J., conducted clandestine work in the Soviet Union during World War II. In 1969, Metropolitan Nikim celebrated mass at the Collegium Russicum during a visit to Pope Paul VI. Jesuit cardinal Augustine Bea transmitted to the Russian Orthodox church an invitation to send observers to the Second Vatican Council.

Despite Gagarin's continuing influence on the Jesuits and other Catholics, the problem of Latinization continued. In the United States, many Ruthenian Catholics joined the Russian Orthodox church as a result of the disapproval of married Byzantine priests by Roman Catholic bishops. For example, Archbishop John Ireland of St. Paul refused to accept Father Alexis Tóth (1854–1909) as pastor of the Ruthenian Catholic parish in Minneapolis because he was a widower. Father Tóth and his parishioners responded by joining the Russian Orthodox church in 1891 and founded seventeen Orthodox parishes for other Ruthenian Catholics who had been angered by Latinization.[155] The Jesuit reforms of the Basilian order transformed it into a "kind of Ukrainian Jesuit order with a hybrid rite and Latin spirit and discipline."[156] At a congress in Velehrad in 1907, Polish Jesuit Jan Urban, citing Solov'ev, argued that the Russian Orthodox should be defined as a "church." Urban believed that the Orthodox church was also part of Christ's mystical body, and he argued that the Russian Orthodox church possessed a true hierarchy and valid sacraments. Urban also opposed Roman Catholic proselytism among the Orthodox. Urban's views were well received by most of the delegates, but shortly thereafter he received a reprimand from higher church authorities in Rome and subsequently dramatically changed his views.[157]

In recent history, there have been favorable signs of rapprochement between the Orthodox and the Catholic churches. In 1925, Dom Lambert Beauduin founded the Monastery of Union at Amay-sur-Meuse (moved to Chevetogne in 1939). This "double rite" community worships according to the Latin and Byzantine rites. The community also publishes *Irénikon.* In December 1965, Paul VI and Ecumenical Patriarch Athenagoras mutually revoked the anathemas of 1054. In December 1987, John Paul II and Ecumenical Patriarch Dmitrios jointly rejected all forms of proselytism.

John Paul II has issued several apostolic letters and encyclicals indicating a new spirit of ecumenism in the Roman Catholic church. Like Gagarin, the pope is a Slav who greatly desires unity and who sees Saints Cyril and Methodius as symbols of the earlier unity between East and West, a unity which existed despite differences in theological, disciplinary, and liturgical traditions.[158] As a Slav, John Paul II recognizes the importance of Slavic culture in the Christian church yet opposes any "nationalistic arrogance."[159] Like Gagarin, the pope puts forth the idea of Catholicism as the "decisive element for civil and human progress." However, the pope also believes that there are certain gifts that the East could offer the West as a result of union.[160] Among these gifts are the Orthodox emphasis on the monastic life and apophatic theology.[161] While apologizing for Catholic sins against unity, the pope asserts that any union requires a role for the pope.[162] However, the pope's role is to be a servant, the *servus servorum Dei.* There also must be a place in any union for the Catholic magisterium. Other issues that must be resolved include the role and place of scripture and tradition, the nature of the Eucharist, the nature of ordination, and teachings on the Virgin Mary.[163] The pope believes that union must come through dialogue, in which the Byzantine Catholic churches will have a full role.[164] Union requires that the West learn about the East and it must come through truth and love, not through absorption or fusion.[165] Like Gagarin, John Paul II believes that the most important tool for union is prayer.[166]

Despite Gagarin's failure to achieve church union, he left an important legacy. His *Études* continues to publish, his Bibliothèque Slave continues to attract scholars from around the world. Solov'ev and d'Herbigny continued to spread his ideas. Present papal ecumenical initiatives operate under many of the same principles which Gagarin put forward: recognition of the validity of the Eastern rites; the need for a papal role in any church union. Even if Gagarin did not achieve his primary objective of church union, his ideas helped to lay the foundation for modern Roman Catholic ecumenical initatives toward the East.

As for Russia, initial hopes of greater religious freedom and the birth of a Russian Catholic church were crushed by the Bolshevik revolution. Today there is still great mistrust between Orthodox and Catholics in Russia. Orthodox fear Catholic proselytization, Catholics remember Orthodox/Communist persecutions. Furthermore, the conflation of Orthodoxy and nationality remains.

Conclusion

Personal contact with the West and the influence of such thinkers as Schelling, Chaadaev, Ancillon, and Jouffroy led Gagarin to the conviction that Russia's social and political backwardness was directly attributable to its separation from Catholicism. By following the Byzantine Empire into schism from Rome, Russia had separated itself from the mainspring of Western social and intellectual progress; in turn, the subjugation of the Orthodox church to Russian secular authority became inevitable. Gagarin, therefore, reasoned that church union reattaching Russia to Catholicism would restore Russia to social and intellectual parity with the West.

Seeking the best means of personally fostering this union, he joined the Society of Jesus. Gagarin's choice was costly. He lost the right to visit Russia and his family; he lost his inheritance; and he suffered decades of calumny—all to save the homeland that rejected him.

Through a myriad of proposals, Gagarin suggested establishing missionary and prayer organizations. He published historical and polemical texts and journals in French and Russian as a means of convincing the Russian Orthodox to follow his own path to conversion. Gagarin sought to persuade his fellow Russians that Orthodoxy and Catholicism were in agreement on important issues of dogma, that union with Rome would not mean a change in rite. Rather, union would liberate the Russian church from secular control, put an end to the prospect of socialist revolution, and immeasurably enhance Russia's noble future. To carry out his ambitious plans, he needed to convince his fellow Jesuits to support his strategy for church union; he also needed to convince fellow Catholics to see that Latinization was detrimental to the cause of union. Roman Catholic authorities would have to learn to see union with the East as a historical imperative for Rome as well as for the Orthodox.

Despite decades of work on behalf of church union, Gagarin failed in his mission. His acerbity, his hostility toward coworkers and other Jesuits, and his pride surely contributed to this failure, but then, of course, church union could never have been achieved by the initiative of one man. In any case, Gagarin had hoped for backing from the Jesuit order but had never received it, largely due to the disunity which existed within the society. Furthermore, internal contradictions within his program also contributed to his failure. He claimed that Russians must choose either Catholicism or Revolution, but this slogan ignored the roots of revolutionary ideology in the West. His assertion that the Russian church was inferior to the West, that Byzantine Catholic churches needed the help of Latin rite churches to survive, made it tempting for his critics to argue that Latinization was the best means of resolving the ecclesiastical problems of the East. Gagarin said that the source of Western progress was "Catholicism," but Romanist conservatives identified that source more specifically as "Roman Catholicism."

Gagarin's ideas failed in the West, partly because many Roman Catholic theologians never accepted the Orthodox as equals. For Rome, union meant that the Orthodox would have to shoulder the historical blame for the events of 1054; that the Orthodox would now have to bring their doctrines into agreement with those of the Vatican; that in union the East would assume a lesser status. Moreover, the French Jesuits had little interest in Orthodoxy: they were more concerned to fight against liberalism within the Church and to support the proclamation of papal infallibility.

Since its 1960s church council, Vatican II, the Catholic church has expanded its understanding of the church of Christ to include those who may not "visibly" be part of it. The teachings of Pope John Paul II have also moved the Roman Catholic church further in the direction of Gagarin's desire that the Eastern church be recognized as equal in dignity to the church of the West. Certainly difficulties between the Orthodox and Catholic churches remain—for example, over proselytism, over the *filioque*, and over the nature of the papacy. However, even on these issues Rome has signaled a new willingness to enter discussion with the Orthodox on a basis of equality.

In the East, Gagarin's proposals had no real possibility for success. Historical fear of the Jesuits and antipathy toward Gagarin led the Orthodox to view his proposals for union with skepticism. His proposals were seen as attacks on both Russian Orthodoxy and Russian autocracy. After all, Gagarin called on the Russians to accept papal authority, that is, the authority of a foreigner. Accepting the authority of the pope could only diminish the autocrat's authority, since the tsar would no longer control the affairs of the Orthodox church. Orthodox conservatives thought that enacting Gagarin's proposals would betray Russia's national heritage. They predicted that church union would mean the abandonment of

Orthodoxy, the end of the autocracy, and the complete redefinition of Russian national identity.

Since Russian national identity was bound up with Russian Orthodoxy, a threat to one meant a threat to the other. Orthodox religious nationalists believed that to sacrifice the integrity of the Eastern church would expose Russia to the same disaster that had befallen Rome and Constantinople. In short, church union would mean the end of the Third Rome. The same impulse that led conservative nationalists to equate Russian identity with Orthodoxy also led to the persecution of the non-Orthodox, since members of other confessions were "non-Russians." In the eyes of religious nationalists, Orthodox Christians who converted to Catholicism should be ostracized by the Russian community as apostates and traitors; traditionally non-Orthodox peoples, such as the Poles, should be forcibly converted. As a result of their unwillingness to live in comity with "heretics" and "apostates," conservative Russian Orthodox found themselves committed to the oppression of Russian Catholics and to the persecution of the Poles and Byzantine rite Catholics. The Orthodox also discovered that this policy made ecclesiastic reform more difficult and the threat of revolution inside and outside the church harder to oppose. In the end, Orthodox persecution of the non-Orthodox served only to magnify the problems of multiconfessionalism the Orthodox authorities sought to solve. Persecuted religious minorities resisted even more strongly integration into Russian society.

Gagarin's ideas, had they been more broadly accepted in Russia, would have required an enormous change in the Russian conception of national identity. It is doubtful that a Catholic Russia would have been free from the problems of socialist revolution or of Polish uprisings. Accepting the ecclesiastical authority of the pope would have been insufficient to completely end the subjugation of the Russian church to the state, since much would have depended on the degree to which the tsar was willing to relinquish his authority. Nor would acknowledging papal authority have put an end to the ecclesiastical problems Gagarin described. Furthermore, Gagarin's plan for church union left open the problem of accommodating the church to non-Catholics within a Catholic Russia, and therefore his plan might not have eliminated religious persecution in the empire. In short, the problems in Russia and within the Russian church could not have been solved simply by redefining Russian religious identity: these problems required additional political and social adjustments.

Despite Gagarin's failure to achieve church union, however, his influence was not negligible. In Russia, Gagarin's attack on the catholicity of the Orthodox church helped motivate Alexei Khomiakov to develop his concept of *sobornost'*, one of the pivotal ecclesiological doctrines of modern Orthodoxy. Gagarin's ideas were studied and developed by many noteworthy figures of the nineteenth and twentieth centuries, including Haxthausen, Tondini, Lavigerie, Pius IX, d'Herbigny, and Solov'ev. Gagarin was regarded by his contemporaries as one of the century's most influential advocates of church union. Today, while *Études* no longer concerns itself with issues of church union, the Bibliothèque Slave which Gagarin founded remains one of the foremost repositories of information on nineteenth-century European religious history.

Gagarin's proposals and the reasons for their failure cast light onto contemporary events. After seventy-four years of communist rule, revitalized Orthodoxy has asserted itself as the one true source of Russian national identity. Recent calls by Orthodox authorities to restrict non-Orthodox confessions have demonstrated that the Russian Orthodox have not yet learned the lesson preached by Gagarin: any attempt to promote religious unity by political means will produce not religious unity but political instability. Let us hope, as Gagarin did, that the spirit of Orthodox self-assertion will yield to humility, that persecution will end and religious comity begin, that the Russian Orthodox and Roman Catholic alike will listen to the best angels of their natures.

Notes

Preface

1. For other historiographical views of Gagarin, see N. P. Antsiferov, "I. S. Gagarin-Gertsenu," *Literaturnoe nasledstovo* 62 (1955); A. S. Buturlin, "Imel li I. S. Gagarin otnoshenie k paskviliu na A. S. Pushkina?" *Izvestiia Akademii Nauk SSSR* 28, 3 (1969); and Mikhail Iashchin, "Khronika predduel'nikh dnei," *Zvezda* 8 (1963), which present Gagarin as a misguided oppositionist of the autocracy and/or a Vatican agent. Typically, Russian historiography has refused to consider that Catholicism might be a valid religious expression within Russian tradition. In the West, research has been done by Dennis Linehan, S. J., "Jean-Xavier Gagarin and the Foundation of Études," *Diakonia* 2 (1987); David M. Matual, "Ivan Gagarin: Russian Jesuit and Defender of the Faith," *Diakonia* 1 (1991); J. G. A. M. Remmers, *De Herenigingsgedachte van I.S. Gagarin, S.J. (1814-1882)*, Tilburg, 1951 (reprinted in part as "La réunion des Églises selon Ivan Serge Gagarin, S. J. [1814–1882]," *Plamia* 86); and Clotilde Giot, "Jean Serguéiévitch Gagarin: premier Jésuit russe et artisan de l'union des Églises" (diss., L'Université Jean Moulin Lyon III, 1993). However, Linehan and Matual fail to address Gagarin as a Russian Catholic; Remmers and Giot fail to examine Russian sources on Gagarin. See also the brief presentations by Gregory Freeze in "Gagarin: A Critical Perspective on the Russian Clergy and Church in the Nineteenth Century," Introduction, *The Russian Clergy* by Ivan Gagarin, S. J. (Newton: Oriental Research Partners, 1976), and W. Śliwowska, *W kregu proprzedników Hercena* (Wroclaw, 1971). For more information on Gagarin's life before his conversion, see Richard Tempest's works: "Ivan Gagarin: Diplomatist, Diarist, Apostate," *Symposion* 2 (1997): 98–134; "Ivan Sergeevich Gagarin (20 July 1814–20 July 1882)," *Russian Literature in the Age of Pushkin and Gogol: Prose—Dictionary of Literary Biography* 198 (1999): 126–131; and "Mezdu Reinom i Senoi (molodye gody Ivana Gagarina)," *Simvol* 32 (1994): 137–163.

2. For more information on issues involving the Russian question, see Georges Florovsky, *Ways of Russian Theology*, trans. Robert L. Nichols, Collected Works of Georges Florovsky, vols. 5–6 (Belmont: Nordland, 1979, 1987). For more information on the nature of the Russian Church in the nineteenth century, see Igor Smolitsch, *Geschichte der russischen Kirche, 1700-1917*, 2 vols. (Leiden, 1964, and Wiesbaden, 1991), and Gregory L. Freeze, *The Parish Clergy in Nineteenth-Century Russia: Crisis, Reform, Counter-Reform* (Princeton: Princeton University Press, 1983).

3. For more information on the history of the Jesuits in the nineteenth century, see William V. Bangert, S.J., *A History of the Society of Jesus* (St. Louis: Institute of Jesuit Sources, 1986); Thomas J. Campbell, *The Jesuits, 1534-1721: A History of the Society of Jesus from Its Foundation to the Present Time* (New York: Encyclopedia Press, 1921); and Donald Treadgold, *The West in Russia and China: Religious and Secular Thought in Modern Times* (Cambridge: Cambridge University Press, 1973).

4. Florovsky, *Ways of Russian Theology* I, 36.

5. Sergei Semenovich Uvarov, 1843, cited in W. Bruce Lincoln, *Nicholas I, Emperor and Autocrat of All the Russias* (De Kalb: Northern Illinois University Press, 1989), 241-242. Emphasis is in original.

6. By 1864, there were 2,847,000 Catholics in Russia and 4,855,000 in Poland. The Russian Catholics represented about 4 percent of the Russian [non-Polish] population—larger than Protestants and Jews, somewhat smaller than Muslims and significantly smaller than the Russian Orthodox, who numbered about 62,436,595. See "Russie," *Dictionnaire Des Missions Catholiques, Encyclopédie Théologique,* ed. J.P. Migne, 60 (Paris, 1864), 763-802.

7. Here I am using the terms "unionism" and "ecumenism" as defined by Ètienne Fouilloux in "L'oecumènisme d'avant-hier à aujord'hui," *L'oecuménisme unité chrétienne et identités confessionnelles* (Paris, 1984).

Chapter One. Moscow, Munich, and Petersburg

1. Isaiah Berlin, "A Remarkable Decade," in *Russian Thinkers,* ed. Henry Hardy and Aileen Kelly (New York: Penguin Books, 1979), 118.

2. "Gagarin" came from the surname "Gagava," borne by one of the early members of the family.

3. This background information comes from genealogical material contained in BS, Rouge 2, the article by Father Charles Clair, S.J., "Premières années et conversion du prince Jean Gagarin," *Revue du monde catholique* 74 (1883): 832-833, and Donald R. Mandich and Joseph A. Placek, *Russian Heraldry and Nobility* (Boynton Beach: Dramco Publishers, 1992), 260.

4. Clair, "Premières années," 25-27.

5. During the Soviet period, this house would become the Maksim Gor'kii museum.

6. The rotation was fallow, winter crop, clover, spring crop, with a few variants. See A.M. Anfimov, *Krupnoe pomeshchich'e khoziaistvo Evropeiskoi Rossii* (Moscow, 1969), 195; "Sergei Ivanovich Gagarin," *Russkii biograficheskii slovar'* (New York: Kraus Reprint Corporation, 1962), 92-93.

7. For additional detail on the Gagarin family land in Iasenevo, see N.M. Moleva, "Iasenevo," *Voprosy Istorii* 4 (April 1984): 184-188.

8. V. A. Bil'basov, "Samarin Gagarinu o Lermontove," *Istoricheskiia monografii* 2 (1901): 414.

9. Richard Tempest, "Ivan Gagarin: Diplomatist, Diarist, Apostate," *Symposion* 2 (1997): 102.

10. Ibid., 100–101.

11. J. G. A. M. Remmers, "La réunion des Églises selon Ivan Serge Gagarin, S. J. (1814–1882)," *Plamia* 86, 16. Clotilde Giot, "Jean Serguéiévitch Gagarin: premier Jésuite russe et artisan de l'union des Églises" (diss., L'Université Jean Moulin Lyon III, 1993), 24. Pavel Pierling, *Le prince Gagarin et ses amis* (Paris: Beauchesne, 1996), 11.

12. Clair, "Premières années," 835.

13. Vavara Gagarina cited in Giot, "Gagarin," 25.

14. BS, Verte 3.

15. Clair cited in Giot, "Gagarin," 27.

16. Peter K. Christoff, *Iu. F. Samarin, An Introduction to Nineteenth-Century Russian Slavophilism,* vol. 4 (San Francisco: Westview Press, 1991), 14.

17. Nol'de cited in Christoff, *Samarin,* 18.

18. James T. Flynn, *The University Reform of Tsar Alexander I: 1802–1835* (Washington D. C.: The Catholic University of America Press, 1988), 214.

19. Flynn, *University Reform,* 189.

20. Christoff, *Samarin,* 29.

21. Most of the information regarding Gagarin's place on the Table of Ranks and his history with the Ministry of Foreign Affairs comes from an *attestat* dated 26 August 1842 from the Department of Financial and Accounting Affairs of the Ministry of Foreign Affairs published by Leonid Shur in "K biografii I. S. Gagarina," *Simvol* 12 (1984): 200–203.

22. Tempest wrote that "Sergei Ivanovich and Vavara Mikhailovna cherished for their only son a fitting rank and position in a society of high ambitions, [and] decided to send him abroad so that he could complete his education and acquire the habits of a man of society." Richard Tempest, "Mezhdu Reinom i Senoi (molodye gody Ivana Gagarina)," *Simvol* 32 (1994): 139. Also found in Ivan Gagarin, *Dnevnik. Zapiski o moei zhizni. Perepiska,* trans. Richard Tempest (Moscow: Iazyki Russkoi Kul'tury, 1996), 15.

23. Gagarin, "Zapiski o moei zhizni," *Simvol* 32 (1994): 168–169. Also found in Gagarin, *Dnevnik,* 253–254.

24. Gagarin, "Zapiski," 169–170. Also found in Gagarin, *Dnevnik,* 255.

25. Gagarin, "Zapiski," 170. Also found in Gagarin, *Dnevnik,* 256.

26. Ivan Gagarin to A. N. Bakhmetev, 28 October 1874, GPB, f. 326, n. 305, E. P. Kazanovich.

27. Thomas F. O'Meara, O. P., *Romantic Idealism and Roman Catholicism: Schelling and the Theologians* (Notre Dame: University of Notre Dame Press, 1982), 10.

28. Ibid., 113.

29. Schelling argued, "History is at once a manifestation of freedom and the progressive revelation of God, 'For God never *is,* if by being one means that which is manifested in the objective world; if he *were,* we would not be; but he reveals himself progressively. By his history man provides a proof of God's existence, but a proof which can be completed only by history in its entirety.'" Émile Bréhier, *The Nineteenth Century: Period of Systems, 1800-1850,* vol. 6 of *The History of Philosophy,* trans. Wade Baskin (Chicago: University of Chicago Press, 1968), 143-144. Emphasis in original.

30. Cited in Giot, "Gagarin," 31. Giot asserted that these comments would have only been important for the Slavophiles. She is incorrect in not recognizing Gagarin's own messianic ideas. For example, Gagarin wrote "And if old Europe should die, it would be with us [Russia] that Thought would blossom with the most splendid color." E. Gershtein, *Sud'ba Lermontova* (Moscow: Khudozhestvennaia literatura, 1986), 146. Also note Gagarin's comments to Samarin, "the West was in decline," although both America and Russia were young. Gagarin to Samarin on 2 April 1838, cited in Christoff, *Samarin,* 42. As mentioned before, Nadezhdin, Davydov, Pavlov, and others at Moscow University would have exposed Gagarin to Schelling's ideas. See Georges Florovsky, *Ways of Russian Theology,* 2, trans. Robert L. Nichols, Collected Works of Georges Florovsky, 6 (Belmont, 1987), 10.

31. Richard Tempest, "Na chashke chaia u Shellinga," *Simvol* 27 (1992): 283-286. See also Gagarin, "Dnevnik (1834-1842)," *Simvol* 34 (1995): 230; or Gagarin, *Dnevnik* 54-55. Gagarin noted that he did not like Lerminier's views because they failed to answer the great questions of philosophy. In fact, he would later refer to him as a "former Saint-Simonian" and write, "If it is true that men should be divided into two classes: the philosophers who march ahead and fire the beacons that illumine our path, and the masses who follow them at a distance, if it is true that when philosophers release their ideas into the world, the masses gradually adopt these ideas and transform them into beliefs, then Lerminier could never hope to be included among those celebrated enlighteners of humanity." Gagarin, cited in Tempest, "Ivan Gagarin: Diplomatist," 105.

32. Victor Cousin was the founder of spiritualistic eclecticism. Cousin believed that reason belonged to everyone. Eclecticism proposed a reconciliation of all systems and retention of their valuable elements, a mixture of the best of society. He applied these views to political philosophy and argued in support of democracy; he thought that a government should also be composed of different parts of civil society. Theodore Simon Jouffroy was also a member of the eclectic school. He believed that Russia was destined to civilize Asia. Jouffroy also believed that philosophy would replace Christianity and that different philosophical systems represented different states of progress. The Scottish school was based on Thomas Reid's and Dougold Stewart's philosophy of "common

sense" which influenced the eclectics. Friedrich Ancillon saw the point of departure of philosophical thought in a dualism expressed in several pairs of correlative terms: subject-object, thought-nature, freedom-necessity, mind-matter, psychology-physics. This dualism is not a constructed notion, but a primitive fact, i.e., self-consciousness also brings awareness of what is not oneself. Ancillon believed there were two worlds separated by this dualistic reflection, and that a unity needed to be reestablished within duality. Interestingly, Moscow metropolitan Filaret's (Drozdov) ideas on Christian education resembled those of Ancillon, who argued that God and creation were coterminous, for both the universe and God were infinite. Ancillon further argued that the highest and best works of God could be contemplated and expressed in poetry and philosophy. God could be understood by a rational inquiry into God's creation. See Robert L. Nichols, "Metropolitan Filaret and the Slavophiles," *St. Vladimir's Theological Quarterly* 4 (1993): 323.

33. Tempest, "Ivan Gagarin: Diplomatist," 284.

34. Pierling, *Le prince*, 28.

35. Gagarin, "Dnevnik," 230, or Gagarin, *Dnevnik*, 56. Diary entry for 26 May 1834. Jouffroy greatly influenced Gagarin's views on the development of Christian civilization in Europe and the eventual primacy of Christian civilization in the world. Gagarin writes that "In *Mélanges philosophiques* of Jouffroy, there are many wonderful pages dedicated to civilization or, rather, different types of civilization, which [were involved in] dividing the world amongst themselves [Christian, Buddhist, Muslim, and pagan].... He beautifully demonstrates their diverse links, the future which belongs entirely to Christian civilization, and the progress which it should accomplish until that time when it subdues the rest." Diary entry of 17 August 1834, Gagarin "Dnevnik," 254–256, or Gagarin, *Dnevnik*, 100–101.

36. Gagarin, "Dnevnik," 229, or Gagarin, *Dnevnik*, 52.

37. Diary entry of 22 October 1834, cited in Pierling, *Le prince*, 37–38. Gagarin is speaking of Speranskii's *Obozrenie istoricheskikh svedenii o svode zakonov, sostavlennikh iz aktov, khraniashchikhsia vo II otdelenii sobstvenoi E.I.V. kantseliarii* (1833).

38. Diary entry of 23 June 1834, Gagarin, "Dnevnik," 250, or Gagarin, *Dnevnik*, 90.

39. Ivan Gagarin to A.N. Bakhmetev, 20–23 December 1874, GPB, f. 326, n. 305, E.P. Kazanovich. Gagarin wrote, "when I saw that the people with whom I sympathized; instead of rejecting the physical force [that was] so repulsive to me, [they] always called for it; when I saw the malicious reproaches of the revolution of 1830; when I more closely examined the mixture of dirt and blood, covered in the name of freedom—I found a depressing portrayal of my first and dearest illusion. There was a huge void in my soul, everything collapsed and that fantasy world, in which I had previously found protection, appeared before me in ruins." "Zapiski," 170, or Gagarin, *Dnevnik*, 256.

40. At this time, Gagarin considered Goethe, Napoleon, and Byron the "great triad of the epoch." Tempest, "Mezhdu," 143, or Gagarin, *Dnevnik*, 22.

41. Diary entry of 16 June 1834, Gagarin, "Dnevnik," 243, or Gagarin, *Dnevnik*, 78.

42. Tempest, "Ivan Sergeevich Gagarin (20 July 1814–20 July 1882)," *Russian Literature in the Age of Pushkin and Gogol: Prose. Dictionary of Literary Biography* 198 (1999): 127.

43. Cited in Pierling, *Le prince*, 30–31.

44. Diary entry of 1 July 1834, Gagarin, "Dnevnik," 252, or Gagarin, *Dnevnik*, 94.

45. Ivan Gagarin to A. N. Bakhmetev, 20–23 December 1874, GPB, f. 326, n. 305, E. P. Kazanovich. Tempest sees the source of this belief in the influence of Schelling and Goethe. Tempest, "Ivan Gagarin: Diarist," 110. Another source of Gagarin's religious thought at this time was the journal *The Globe*. Gagarin noted, "This journal was written by men of much talent, who under the Restoration were the chief opposition in the philosophic and literary sphere, and who, after the July Revolution, almost completely occupied the important positions and controlled the public spirit. It was in *The Globe* which appeared the famous article by Theodore Jouffroy entitled 'Comment les dogmas finissent.' The death of Christianity was announced there soon thereafter and in general the spirit of the journal was far from being Christian." Gagarin to A. N. Bakhmetev, 4 November 1874, GPB, f. 326, n. 305, E. P. Kazanovich.

46. Diary entry of 19/31 October, cited in Pierling, *Le prince*, 38.

47. Diary entry of 5/17 December 1834, cited in Pierling, *Le prince*, 41.

48. Gagarin, undated journal entry, cited in Giot, "Gagarin," 40. Emphasis in original. Gagarin became interested in the ideas of nationalism through the influence of Schelling and reading Ancillon's *Die Vermittelung der Extremen*, which "affirms the laws of nationalism [narodnosti] and history. This is a great service, which he provides for humanity." Diary entry of 23 June 1834, Gagarin, "Dnevnik," 250, or Gagarin, *Dnevnik*, 90.

49. Gagarin to Bakhmetev, 20–23 December 1874, GPB, f. 326, n. 305, E. P. Kazanovich.

50. Gagarin journal entry 26 September 1834, cited in Charles Clair, S. J., "Premières années et conversion du prince Jean Gagarin," *Revue du monde catholique* 75 (1883): 40.

51. Diary entry of 17 August 1834, Gagarin, "Dnevnik," 254–255, or Gagarin, *Dnevnik*, 100.

52. Berlin, "A Remarkable Decade," 123.

53. Apparently Gagarin was particularly attracted to the pretty Duchess de Berry (Marie-Caroline de Bourbon-Sicile), the mother of Count Chambord Ferdinand-Marie-Dieudonné d'Artois, the Bourbon pretender. According to Tempest, Gagarin had an eye "for beautiful women, especially highborn ones." Tempest, "Ivan Sergeevich Gagarin," 127.

54. Tempest, "Ivan Gagarin: Diplomatist," 117.

55. It is unknown whether Gagarin succumbed to temptation, but he would write three years later of meeting a woman outside London on a stagecoach, "who claimed to have a husband and children, professed herself to be in love with me, and invited me to an assignation in London." Gagarin found the whole thing "rather unremarkable." Gagarin, cited in Tempest, "Ivan Gagarin: Diplomatist," 121, 122.

56. Tempest, "Ivan Sergeevich Gagarin," 127. Tempest sees this as a possible reference to Pushkin's *The Queen of Spades.*

57. F. I. Tiutchev to Gagarin, 2/14 May 1836, cited in K. Pigarev, *Zhizn' i tvorchestvo Tiutcheva* (Moscow, 1962), 75.

58. Gagarin to F. I. Tiutchev, 12/24 June 1836, cited in Bil'basov, "Samarin Gagarin," 417.

59. Pigarev, *Zhizn,* 75.

60. F. I. Tiutchev to Gagarin, 3 May 1836, cited in F. I. Tiutchev, *Stikhotvoreniia* (Moscow, 1935), 294.

61. F. I. Tiutchev to Gagarin, 3 May 1836, GPB, f. 326, n. 305, E. P. Kazanovich.

62. Ivan Aksakov, "Stikhotvoreniia F. I. Tiutcheva," *Russkii arkhiv* 2, no. 5 (1879): 118.

63. BS, Rouge 2.

64. Gagarin wrote, "Prince Viazemskii gave me a love for the literary life." Gagarin, cited in Leonid Shur, "Spiski stikhotvorenii Pushkina v arkhive I. S. Gagarina," *Revue des études slaves* 1–2 (1987): 348.

65. D. Strémooukhoff, *La Poésie et l'idéologie de Tiouttchev* (Paris, 1937), 17.

66. Gagarin and Ivan Aksakov used the occasion provided by Gagarin's delivery of Tiutchev's unpublished poetry and letters to discuss the degree to which Tiutchev embraced the Slavophilic ideas that would later be apparent in his poetry. Gagarin argued that Tiutchev had no religious or Slavophilic tendencies during his period at Munich. Aksakov disagreed. The correspondence on this issue can be found in Shur, "I. S. Gagarin—izdatel' F. I. Tiutcheva i khranitel' ego literaturnogo nasledstva," *Simvol* 11 (1984): 197–229. An analysis of this argument can be found in R. Lane, "Tiutchev in the 1820s–40s: An Unpublished Correspondence of 1874–1875," *Irish Slavonic Studies* 3 (1982): 2–13.

67. In a 31 August 1874 letter to Pierling, Gagarin wrote that he was a friend of Tiutchev's before he "had become infatuated with panslavism." See Shur, "Neosushchestvlennoe izdanie stikhotvorenii F. I. Tiutcheva 1836–1837gg (po materialam arkhiva I. S. Gagarina)," *Oxford Slavonic Papers* 19 (1969): 112.

68. F. I. Tiutchev, "La Papauté et la question romaine au point de vue de Saint-Pétersbourg," *Revue des deux mondes* (1850): 117–133.

69. Mikhail Iashchin, "K portretu dukhovnogo litsa," *Neva* 3 (1966): 189.

70. Gagarin to F. I. Tiutchev, March 1836, cited in Shur, "Materialy o dueli i smerti A. S. Pushkina v arkhive I. S. Gagarina," *Simvol* 10 (1983): 250.

71. Tempest argued that the character of the main hero of this work, Ivan Vasilevich, was partly written for Ivan Gagarin. See Tempest, "Mezhdu," 152. A. Nemzer further argued that the visionary ideas attributed to Ivan Vasilevich, and ironically treated by Sollogub, correspond with those held at the time by Grigorii and Ivan Gagarin. Like Ivan Vasilevich, Grigorii and Ivan Gagarin had a Western upbringing. However, Nemzer rejected the idea that Ivan Vasilevich was in any sense a "portrait" of the Gagarins. Furthermore, Ivan Vasilevich exuded a desire to separate himself from the West and become acquainted with the Russian peasant; the latter desire was not Gagarin's. See William Edward Brown, Afterword, in *The Tarantas: Impressions of a Journey (Russia in the 1840s),* by Vladimir Sollogub, trans. William Edward Brown (Ann Arbor: Ardis, 1989), 146.

72. Letter of Pushkin to Benkendorf, cited in S. A. Tsipeniuk, "Issledovanie anonimnykh pisem, sviazannykh s duel'u Pushkina," *Kriminalistika i sudebnaia expertiza* 12 (1976): 81.

73. P. E. Shchegolev, *Duel' i smert' Pushkina* (1987), 398–399. Part of the reason for the suspicion of Gagarin was that he maintained contact with Heekeren for at least a decade after Pushkin's death. See letter of Heekeren to Gagarin, 17 September 1847, found in Ia. Polonskii, "Literaturnii arkhiv I. S. Gagarina II," *Vremennik obshchestva druzei knigi,* vol. 3 (1932): 139–158.

74. Dolgorukov, like Gagarin, came from a well-known family. He was a direct descendant of prince Mikhail Chernigovskii and participated in the aristocratic opposition to the autocracy. In 1860, he emigrated to the West and continued to write antigovernmental literature. N. Eidel'man, *Pushkin: iz biografii i tvorchestva 1826–1837* (Moscow, 1987), 383.

75. Eidel'man noted, "from the earliest years he was known as a violator of social mores and decorum. . . . From the beginning *le banacal* (bowlegged—as he was teased by aristocrats due to a limp) was evil and vindictive." See N. Ia., Eidel'man, *Gertsen protiv samoderzhaviia* (Moscow, 1984), 255.

76. Cited in Iashchin, "K portretu dukhovnogo litsa," *Neva* 2 (1966): 171.

77. Cited in Shchegolev, *Duel',* 398.

78. Iashchin, "K portretu," 170.

79. Ivan Gagarin, "Opravdanie iezuita Ivana Gagarina po povodu smerti Pushkina," *Russkii arkhiv* (1865): 1033.

80. Ibid., 1033.

81. N. M. Smirnov, diary entry of 1842, cited in "Iz 'Pamiatnikh zapisok,'" *A.S. Pushkin v vospominaniakh sovremennikov,* vol. 2 (Moscow, 1974), 239–240. P. A. Viazemskii in a letter to A. I. Turgenev on 30 October 1843 wrote of Gagarin, "He was always the instrument of some hand, always a hanger-on of strange ideas and well-known society, even the villainous Heekeren." Iashchin, "K portretu," 198.

82. K. K. Danzas, cited in "Poslednie dni zhizni i konchina Aleksandra Sergeevicha Pushkina v zapisi A. Ammosova," *A.S. Pushkin v vospominaniakh sovre-*

mennikov, vol. 2 (Moscow, 1974), 320. See also Mikhail Loniunov, "Neskol'ko zametok na stat'i *Russkago arkhiva,*" *Russkii arkhiv* (1865): 1409–1410. Loniunov refers to Danzas's claims that Gagarin had implicated Dolgorukov. Loniunov argued that this showed that Gagarin had some blame in the Pushkin tragedy.

83. Sobolevskii to Vorontsov, cited in Shchegolev, *Duel',* 406. Sobolevskii stated that Gagarin told him Dolgorukov was to blame. See also B. L. Modzalevskii, "Kto byl avtorom anonimnykh paskvilei na Pushkina?" *Novye materialy o dueli i smerti Pushkina,* ed. Modzalevskii, Oksman et al. (1924), 20–21.

84. S. Abramovich, *Pushkin v 1836 godu* (Leningrad: Nauka, 1989), 98.

85. Mentioned in an 1865 letter of Avgust Golitsyn to Gagarin, cited in Pierling, *Le prince,* 102.

86. Shchegolev, *Duel',* 399–400.

87. Shur, "Materialy," 252.

88. Dolgorukov to Gagarin, 29 July 1863, cited in Shur, "Perepiska I. S. Gagarina s P. V. Dolgorukovym (1860–1863)," *Simvol* 13 (1985): 243. Shur noted in a different article that the Russian government issued Ammosov's brochure because it was interested in discrediting dangerous émigrés. Dolgorukov was dangerous because of his antigovernment revolutionary periodicals. Gagarin was dangerous (as we shall see later) because of his pro-Catholic publications.

89. Petr Vladimirovich Dolgorukov, *Kolokol,* 1 August 1863, *Kolokol* 6 (1963): 1387.

90. Shur, 253.

91. Trubetskoi to Gagarin, 3 June 1865, cited in Iashchin, "K portretu," 187.

92. Gagarin, "Opravdanie," 1032.

93. Ibid., 1036.

94. Ibid.

95. Letter of Trubetskoi to Martynov, 30 May 1865, cited in Iashchin, "K portretu," 186–187.

96. Gagarin to N. I. Trubetskoi, 6 June 1865, cited in Shur, "Perepiska I. S. Gagarina s P. V. Dolgorukovim," 257–258.

97. Gagarin to Tiutchev, March 1836, cited in "Pis'mo Gagarina k Tiutchevu o Benediktove i Pushkine," *Knizhki nedeli* 1 (1899): 229.

98. S. L. Abramovich, *Pushkin, poslednii god—khronika* (Moscow, 1991), 362. Chaadaev gave Pushkin a copy of his letter since he hoped that Pushkin might be able to find a publisher.

99. Nikolai Leskov, "Iezuit Gagarin v dele Pushkina," *Istoricheskii vestnik* 25 (1886): 270, 272.

100. Leskov, 273. Gagarin's words to Leskov were also enough to convince Ivan Aksakov, who wrote, "You [Leskov] place him [Gagarin] before me alive in full stature and growth. I see and hear him as he is, and I share your sympathy for him, I feel sorry for him and I believe his words." Leskov, 272.

101. Shchegolev, *Duel',* 410.

102. L. Vyshnevskii, "Petr Dolgorukov i paskvil' na Pushkina," *Sibirskie ogni* 11 (1962): 157–170.

103. Iashchin, "Khronika predduel'nikh dnei," *Zvezda* 8 (1963), 176.

104. Ibid., 175, and Iashchin, "K portretu," *Neva* 3, 189.

105. Iashchin, "K portretu," 198.

106. Ia. L. Levkovich, "Novye materialy dlia biografii Pushkina, opublikovannye v 1963–1966 godakh," *Pushkin—issledovaniia i materialy* 5 (Leningrad, 1967), 379.

107. Ibid., 377–378.

108. Ibid., 377.

109. A. S. Buturlin, "Imel li I. S. Gagarin otnoshenie k paskviliu na A. S. Pushkina?" *Izvestia Academii Nauk SSSR* 28, 3 (1969): 278.

110. Ibid., 284–285.

111. L. Vyshnevskii, "Eshche raz o vinovnikakh pushkinskoi tragedii," *Oktiabr'* (March 1973): 215.

112. Tsipeniuk, "Issledovanie," 88.

113. Abramovich, *Pushkin, poslednii god,* 100. Also see Abramovich, *Pushkin v 1836 godu* (Leningrad, 1984), 85; N. Eidel'man, *Gertsen,* 384. Other articles about the anonymous letter are "Opravdanie iezuita Ivana Gagarina po povodu smerti Pushkina," *Golos* 197 (19/31 July 1865): 2, which is a summary and brief commentary of Gagarin's defense in *Russkii arkhiv;* Iurii Plashevskii, "O proiskhozhdenii paskvil'nogo 'diploma,'" *Prostor* 4 (1983): 177–184, in which the author argued that the letter was written by a Freemason; and I. Sidorov, "Eshche raz ob anonimnom 'diplome' i kn. P.V. Dolgorukove," *Voprosy literatury* 2 (1987): 177–180. Sidorov argued in support of Sal'kov's conclusion but did not mention Gagarin. There are some other articles about the event that could be useful for further information. A. Kozlov and Iu. Feofanov, "Istina bez prikras," *Izvestiia* 201 (28 August 1975): 6, discussed the investigations of Sal'kov and Tsipeniuk on the handwriting of Gagarin and Dolgorukov, but arrived at no new conclusions. I. Obodovskaia and M. Dement'ev, "Po sledam predvestnika gibeli," *Ogonek* 6 (February 1986): 20–23, concluded that neither Gagarin nor Dolgorukov wrote the anonymous letter. Ia. L. Levkovich, "Dve raboty o dueli Pushkina," *Russkaia literatura* 2 (1970): 211–219, examined Iashchin's work and Shchegolev's work but did not refer to Gagarin.

114. Gagarin to Viazemskii, 30 September 1839, cited in Gershtein, *Sud'ba,* 140–141.

115. Gagarin, preface, *Oeuvres choisies de Pierre Tchadaief—publiées pour la première fois par le Père Gagarin de la Compagnie de Jésus,* by Petr Chaadaev (Paris: A. Frank, 1862), 1–2.

116. Chaadaev to Turgenev, 1835, cited in Petr Chaadaev, *Philosophical Works of Peter Chaadaev,* ed. Raymond T. McNally and Richard Tempest, Sovietica, vol. 56 (Boston: Kluwer Academic Publishers, 1991), 162.

117. Ibid., 20.

118. Ibid., 15.

119. Ibid., 26, 31, 36.

120. Ibid., 17.

121. Ibid., 83, 226–227.

122. Chaadaev, *The Major Works of Peter Chaadaev*, trans. Raymond T. McNally (Notre Dame: University of Notre Dame Press, 1969), 159–160.

123. Chaadaev, *Philosophical*, 82.

124. Ibid., 219, 228–229. Regarding the *filioque*, at the First Council of Constantinople the Church's understanding of the relationship between God the Father and God the Holy Spirit was established in the creed of Nicea-Constantinople as follows: "The Holy Spirit proceeds from the Father." In the late eighth and early ninth century, the Church in France altered this phrase to say: "The Holy Spirit proceeds from the Father *and the Son* [*filioque*]." Pope St. Leo III condemned this addition in 808, but it gradually began to spread throughout the Western and Eastern churches, until by the time of Pope Nicholas I (800–867) and Patriarch Photius of Constantinople (820–891), many believed that the *filioque* had always been part of the Nicene Creed. Photius and others objected that the First Council of Constantinople had prohibited any changing of the creed, that no other ecumenical council had changed that prohibition, and that the *filioque* was theologically false. They argued that if the Father and the Son, outside of their divine essence, have something in common, i.e., that the Spirit proceeds from both the Father and the Son, the Spirit, which is no less a divine person, should also participate, and one arrives at the absurdity that the Holy Spirit proceeds from itself. The Western church accepted the *filioque* in the eleventh century.

125. Ibid., 179.

126. It is important to note that Pushkin clearly recognized Chaadaev's talents. He wrote:

In Rome he would have been Brutus,
In Athens, Pericles,
But here he is simply an officer of the Hussars.

Pushkin cited in Raymond T. McNally, *Chaadaev and His Friends* (Tallahassee: The Diplomatic Press, 1971): 11.

127. Gagarin to Ksavier Korczak-Branicki, no date (after 1879), BS, 70-3-B.

128. Gagarin wrote in his response to Samarin's attack on the Jesuits, "Pis'mo otsa Gagarina, sviashchennika obshchestva isusova, Iuriu Fedorovichu Samarinu v otvet na pis'ma, napechatannie v zhurnale 'Den',' *Simvol* 7: 182–189. "Take myself for example, the Jesuits did not convert me. Petr Iakovlevich Chaadaev set the foundation [for my conversion] on Basmannaia street in 1835 or 1836."

129. Gagarin, "Zapiski," 175, or Gagarin, *Dnevnik*, 268.

130. Gagarin, "Zapiski," 173, or Gagarin, *Dnevnik*, 263.

131. Gagarin, "Zapiski," 174, or Gagarin, *Dnevnik,* 264. Here is additional evidence of the influence of Ancillon and his views of the philosophical problem of dualism upon the ideas of Gagarin.

132. Gagarin, "Zapiski," 174, or Gagarin, *Dnevnik,* 266. Gagarin noted that he came to this conclusion in 1836 or 1837.

133. Gagarin, undated document, BS, Rouge 1.

134. Gagarin, undated document, BS, Rouge 1. In an appendix to *Conversion d'une dame russe à la foi catholique,* Gagarin pointed to the following marriages as evidence of a continuing union between Russia and the Vatican after the schism of 1054:

1. Iaroslav the Great and Ingigerd, daughter of Olaf, king of Sweden.
2. Maria Dobrogneva, Iaroslav's sister, with Casimir I, king of Poland.
3. Elizaveta and Anna, Iaroslav's daughters, with Harold, king of Norway, and Henry, king of France, respectively.
4. Anastasia with Andrew I, king of Hungary.
5. Inga, daughter of Vsevolod, with Henry IV, emperor of Germany, in 1089.
6. Ibislava, daughter of Grand Duke Sviatopolk-Mikhail, to Ladislas, son of Caloman, king of Hungary, in 1101.
7. Euphemie, daughter of Vladimir Monomakh, to Caloman, king of Hungary, in 1112.

Gagarin also noted marriages involving the granddaughters of Monomakh until 1147. For Gagarin, these marriages indicated that union between Russia and Rome existed for almost a hundred years after the schism. See Gagarin, appendix to *Conversion d'une dame russe à la foi catholique,* by Elizaveta Golitsyn (Paris: Douniol, 1862), 161–162.

135. Zhikarev approached Aleksandr Herzen about publishing the writings in a Russian translation. Herzen published a Russian translation of the "First Philosophical Letter" in *Poliarnaia zvezda* in 1861.

136. Gagarin, "Tendances catholiques dans la Société Russe," *Le Correspondant* 50 (1860): 289–305.

137. Letter of Zhikarev to Gagarin, 15 October 1860, cited in L. Shur, "I. S. Gagarin—izdatel' 'Filosoficheskikh pisem' P. Ia. Chaadaeva," *Simvol* 9 (1983): 226.

138. Michel Cadot, *La Russie dans la vie intellectuelle français (1839–1856)* (Paris: Fayard, 1967), 274.

139. Letter of Zhikarev to Gagarin, 12 May 1863, cited in Shur, "I. S. Gagarin—izdatel'" 232.

140. Gagarin, "Zapiski," 177, or Gagarin, *Dnevnik* 269.

141. Turgenev to P. A. Viazemskii, 9 April 1838, cited in Gershtein, *Sud'ba,* 144. Turgenev would meet with Gagarin in Moscow where they would discuss Chaadaev and Kireevskii. Ibid., 141. Turgenev also noted in a diary entry of 4 June

1841 that he, Gagarin, and Viktor Grigor'evich Tepliakov walked in the park and recited Lermontov's verses on Napoleon I. See Tempest, "Ivan Sergeevich Gagarin," 128.

142. A.V. Meshcherskii, "Iz moei starini, vospominaniia kniazia A.V. Meshcherskago," *Russkii arkhiv* 39 I (1901): 486.

143. Tempest, "Ivan Gagarin: Diplomatist," 126.

144. Membership in *Les Seize* included Gagarin, Boris Dmitrievich Golitsyn, Grigorii Gagarin, Aleksei Arkad'evich Stolypin, Ksavier Korczak-Branicki, Sergei Vasil'evich Dolgorukov, Aleksandr Nikolaevich Dolgorukov, Andrei Pavlovich Shuvalov, Aleksandr Vasil'chikov, Mikhail Lermontov, Petr Aleksandrovich Valuev, F. I. Paskevich, Nikolai Andreevich Gervais, Dmitrii Petrovich Fredriks, and Petr P. Shuvalov. These were all members of influential families and many would go on to important roles in Russian society. B. D. Golitsyn, A. P. Shuvalov, A. A. Stolypin, N. A. Gervais, Mikhail Lermontov, and S.V. Dolgorukov were military officers. B. D. Golitsyn was the son of the Moscow governor general. Grigorii Gagarin was an artist. Lermontov was a poet. Vasil'chikov would serve as a publicist. Gervais would serve as a secretary in the Russian mission at Dresden. Valuev would later serve as the tsarist minister of the interior. *Les Seize* met at the salon of Ekaterina Andreevna Karamzina and at the St. Petersburg homes of A. I. Turgenev and Petr Valuev. Gagarin was very close to Lermontov. See Tepliakov's letter to Gagarin in Leonid Chertikov, "Neopublikovannoe pis'mo V. G. Tepliakova k Kn. I. S. Gagarinu," *Revue des études slaves* 54 (1982): 480.

145. Christoff, *Iu F. Samarin,* 23–24.

146. Ksavier Korczak-Branicki, *Les nationalités slaves—lettres au révérend P. Gagarin, S.J.* (Paris: Dentu, 1879), 1–2. Emphasis in original.

147. Valuev, cited Gershtein, *Sud'ba,* 133.

148. Iu. F. Samarin to Gagarin, 19/31 July 1840, *Sochineniia Iu. F. Samarina* 12 (1911), 54.

149. Gagarin, "Dnevnik," 287, or Gagarin, *Dnevnik,* 170.

150. 11 January 1841 letter of Gagarin to S. P. Shevyrev, GPB, f. 850, n. 182, Shevyrev archives.

151. Gershtein, *Sud'ba,* 132–133.

152. Gershtein, "Kruzhok shestnadtsati," *Lermontovskaia entsiklopediia* (Moscow, 1981), 234–235. Eikhenbaum looks at similarities between the ideas of Chaadaev and the works of Lermontov for this conclusion.

153. Ibid., 234–235.

154. Christoff, *Iu F. Samarin,* 23–24. Note also Korczak-Branicki's words to Gagarin, "I ask you, in reading me, to have for one of *Les Seize,* the indulgence which you had close to forty years ago, when both of us, young and proud, would ruminate upon the questions which preoccupied us and which preoccupy us today." Korczak-Branicki, 16.

155. Valuev, cited in Gershtein, *Sud'ba,* 145–146.

156. Gagarin, "Zapiski," 172, or Gagarin, *Dnevnik,* 260. Gagarin said that he came to this conclusion in 1835.

157. Gagarin to Samarin, January 1836, cited in Giot, "Gagarin," 43.

158. Samarin to Gagarin, 1840, cited in Giot, "Gagarin," 43.

159. This document is found in BS, Bleu Clair 4.

160. This document is undated, possibly 1835, in any case it was written before Gagarin's conversion. The document is located in BS, Bleu Clair 3.

161. This document is also undated, possibly 1836. This document is found in BS, Bleu Clair 3.

162. Here Gagarin is relying on the ideas of Plutarch and Montesquieu.

163. Emphasis is Gagarin's.

164. Gagarin called this an aristocratic revolution.

165. Gagarin called this a democratic revolution.

166. This document, undated, can be found in BS, Jaune 2.

167. Bilbasov, cited in Gershtein, *Sud'ba,* 147.

Chapter Two. Paris: Conversion and Ordination

1. Gagarin, "Tendances," 317.

2. A. I. Turgenev to P. A. Viazemskii, 14/26 March 1838, cited in Shchegolev, *Duel'* 405. Note that the correspondence of Viazemskii and Turgenev also referred to a possible romantic relationship between Gagarin and Ol'ga Trubetskaia, the twenty-year-old sister of Sergei Trubetskoi—one of *Les Seize.* However, the information on this matter is scant. Gagarin does not mention it in his journal. See Gershtein, *Sud'ba,* 139, and Tempest, "Mezdu," 153, and "Ivan Gagarin: Diplomatist," 126.

3. Gagarin's letter to S. P. Shevyrev of 11 January 1841 asked him to inform Chaadaev, Khomiakov, Kireevskii, and M. P. Pogodin about his activities. GPB, f. 850, n. 182, Shevyrev.

4. Louis-Phillipe's prime minister in 1836–1839.

5. Parliamentary leader of the legitimists.

6. Gagarin described a young Saxon who wagered that within the space of three hours he could ride three different horses each three leagues, drink three bottles of wine, and sleep with three women. The Saxon won his bet and received great glory at the Jockey Club and at the foyer of the Opera. Gagarin called him a "strapping fool!" See Tempest, "Ivan Sergeevich Gagarin," 128.

7. See letter to Annenkov, 1 June 1842, BS, Rouge 1.

8. Gagarin, cited in Bil'basov, "Samarin Gagarinu," 419–420.

9. This document can be found in BS, Bleu Claire 3.

10. Gagarin, cited in M. J. Rouët de Journel, S. J., "Madame Swetchine et les conversions," *Études* 191 (1927): 188–189.

11. Gagarin, cited in Giot, "Gagarin," 62–63.

12. Gagarin told Stepan Dzhunkovskii, "In Paris, I read [Friedreich] Makeldey and [Ammon] Hurter: the history of Innocent III. In these writings, I found that the first ideas of the English constitution came from Rome." Gagarin, cited in Dzhunkovskii, "Russkii, sem let' iezuit," originally published in *Russkii invalid.* Copy found in BS, 70-6-A.

13. Svechina (22 November 1782–1857) was related to Gagarin through her sister, who was married to Grigorii Gagarin. Svechina converted to Roman Catholicism in 1815. Gagarin also participated in the salons of Madame de Bélissen and Duchess Claire de Rauzan.

14. Journal entry of 22 March 1838 cited in Pierling, *Le prince,* 42.

15. Journel, "Origines et premières années," *Études* 291 (1956): 171.

16. Gagarin, cited in Giot, "Gagarin," 69. Gagarin wrote, "Here I saw for the first time spirits completely free and completely diverse, voluntarily submitting their judgments and their opinions to one law, to one teaching which truly ruled over their souls."

17. Gagarin wrote about Lammenais, "There was in him much good. . . . In general, that which touched me the most about Lammenais was his towering intelligence, the finesse of his spirit, the sharpness of his language and his vivid interest in all the questions which now engage humanity." Cited in Giot, "Gagarin," 73–74.

18. Tempest, "Ivan Sergeevich Gagarin," 154.

19. Gagarin, cited in Journel, *Une Russe catholique—la vie de madame Swetchine (1782-1857)* (Paris: Desclée, 1953), 313. Svechina tried to serve as a matchmaker for Gagarin, but he had no intention of marrying. He felt that marriage would be an obstacle to his chosen career. Tempest, "Ivan Gagarin: Diplomatist," 126.

20. Letter of Svechina to Gagarin 22 June 1846, Sofiia Svechina, *Letters de madame Swetchine,* vol. 2, ed. Count de Falloux (Paris: Didier, 1862), 357.

21. Svechina, *The Writings of Madame Swetchine,* ed. Count de Falloux (New York: The Catholic Publication Society, 1869), 86.

22. Ravignan replaced Lacordaire.

23. Gustave-Xavier de Ravignan, S. J., *On the Life and Institute of the Jesuits* (Philadelphia: Cunningham, 1845), 134–135. Emphasis in original.

24. Ibid., 135.

25. Shuvalov converted 6 January 1843 and became a priest of the Barnabite order 18 September 1857. He founded l'Association de prières pour l'union à Rome des Églises d'Orient.

26. Grigorii Petrovich Shuvalov, C. R. S. P., *My Conversion and My Vocation* (London: R. Washbourne, 1877), 195–197.

27. Ibid., 197.

28. Gagarin, in a letter to A. I. Turgenev, described the Oxford movement, as "similar to our Moscow Orthodoxy, only wiser." See letter of 26 August/5 September 1841 published in "Neizdannye pis'ma I. S. Gagarina A. I. Turgenevu," *Simvol*

22 (1989): 22, or Gagarin, *Dnevnik*, 297. The Oxford movement (1833-1845) was an attempt by several Anglican clergy at Oxford University to restore Catholic doctrine and practices to an Anglican church which they believed had become too Protestantized. Such people as John Keble, John Henry Newman, William Palmer, Richard Hurrell Froude, and Edward B. Pusey spread their message of Anglicanism as a *via media* between Roman Catholicism and Protestantism through publication of religious tracts. The Oxford movement failed and many of its members converted to Roman Catholicism.

29. Letter of Gagarin to E. P. Gagarina dated 28 June 1845, cited in Tempest, "Mezhdu," 156. In a journal entry of 19 January 1841, Gagarin quoted with approval the words of de Maistre on the Jesuits, writing, "Look on those who attack them and on those who defend them and then you will decide for yourself." In Tempest, "Mezhdu," 158.

30. Letter of Gagarin to Samarin, February 1842, "Arkhiv slavianskoi biblioteki," *Simvol* 1 (1979): 168, 174. Additional letters from Gagarin to Samarin in which Gagarin defends papal primacy are found in "Pis'ma Iu. F. Samarinu," *Simvol* 35 (1996): 229-278.

31. Gagarin to Samarin, 26 February 1842, "Arkhiv slavianskoi biblioteki," *Simvol* 2 (1979): 167. Petrine primacy is the Roman Catholic doctrine asserting that Jesus gave Peter authority and jurisdiction over the entire church. Roman Catholics further believe that this authority is inherited by all popes. The Orthodox church believes that the pope merely has a primacy of honor and jurisdiction over his own specific region, Western Europe. The Orthodox believe that the pope has no authority to interfere in ecclesiastical affairs outside of this region.

32. Ibid., 170.

33. Gagarin to Samarin, 24 August/5 September 1842, "Pis'mo I. S. Gagarina Iu. F. Samarinu," *Simvol* 3 (1980): 166. Note the similarity of Gagarin's views regarding the progressive nature of Catholicism's involvement in Western civilization with his views on the progressive nature of Catholic doctrine. If Western civilization develops, so must its religion.

34. Gagarin to Samarin, February 1842, in ibid., 171. Samarin's responses to Gagarin made the traditional Orthodox objections: the pope desired secular power, the Roman Catholics have a false view of the procession of the Holy Spirit, the Byzantine Catholics formed a barrier to union. See letter of Samarin to Gagarin 13/25 August 1842, "Arkhiv slavianskoi biblioteki," *Simvol* 2 (1979): 172-181.

35. Gagarin and Kireevskii were on good terms with each other. Kireevskii said that he liked Gagarin, he only wished "that certain peculiarities [Gagarin's Roman Catholic views] did not interfere with our sympathy for each other." Letter of Ivan Kireevskii to Petr Vasilevich Kireevskii in 1842, cited in Peter Christoff, *I. V. Kireevskii, An Introduction to Nineteenth-Century Russian Slavophilism—A Study in Ideas*, vol. 2 (Paris: Mouton, 1972), 100. Gagarin wrote that Kireevskii was "de-

voted to Christianity from the bottom of his heart, but did not know how to recognize it in the West." Letter of Gagarin, no date, BS, Noire 1.

36. Letter of Gagarin to Kireevskii, 23 October/4 November 1842, "Pis'mo I. S. Gagarina I. V. Kireevskomu," *Simvol* 5 (1981): 152.

37. Gagarin to Kireevskii, 16 October 1842, cited in Kat'ia Dmitrieva, "Les conversions au catholicisme en Russie au XIXe siècle—ruptures historiques et culturelles," *Revue des études slaves,* vol. 73, 2–3 (1995): 323.

38. Letter of Gagarin to Kireevskii, 16/28 October 1842, "Pis'ma I. S. Gagarina I. V. Kireevskomu," *Simvol* 4 (1980): 179–180. Kireevskii's comments were published in his letter to Gagarin on 10/22 September 1842 published as "Pis'mo I. V. Kireevskogo I. S. Gagarinu," *Simvol* 3 (1980): 167–174. In this letter, Kireevskii accused the Western church of harboring an ambition for power and mistakenly joining spiritual and secular authority in the papacy. He further argued that the *filioque* was condemned by the Council of Jerusalem of 1447 and by the writings of John Damascene.

39. Gagarin, cited in Giot, "Gagarin," 85.

40. A Russian law of 21 March/2 April 1840 promised harsh punishments for Russians who converted from Orthodoxy to a different faith. Desiring to maintain "among my faithful subjects the integrity of the Orthodox faith," Nicholas issued the following punishments against anyone convicted of apostasy from Orthodoxy:

1. The convicted's property would be taken under guardianship in order to maintain in Orthodoxy those under the convicted's authority. The spouse of the apostate could not participate in the guardianship in any fashion.
2. Apostates from Orthodoxy could not employ the personal service of any Orthodox serf. Nor could the apostate live on a property on which Orthodox serfs lived.
3. Steps would be taken to insure that the children of apostates would remain in Orthodoxy.
4. Only by returning to Orthodoxy would these punishments be lifted.

See Russian Law #13280 of 21 March/2 April 1840, *Polnoe sobranie zakonov* 15 (Petersburg, 1841), 170–171. This law also showed how threatening to the social order the Russian government considered apostasy to be.

41. Journal entry of 1841, cited in Tempest, "Mezhdu," 158.

42. BS, Verte 1. Valerian Obolensky relates the curious information that Nicholas Ivanovich Turgenev had dinner with Ivan Turgenev, Avgust Petrovich Golitsyn, Nikolai Trubetskoi, Count Murav'ev-Amurskii (the Governor General of Eastern Siberia), and Ivan Gagarin in 1868. Nikolai didn't like the table manners of Gagarin at all, but Trubetskoi found them to be amusing. See Valerian Obolensky, "Russians in Exile—the History of a Diaspora," http://www.geocities.com:0080/soho/5254/dias4.html.

43. See Giot, "Gagarin," 88.

44. Gagarin, "Dnevnik," 317, or Gagarin, *Dnevnik*, 244–245. Note again Gagarin's appeal to the need to obey divine commands both spiritually and in the secular world.

45. Gagarin, "Pis'mo otsa," 188.

46. Gagarin had resigned from the Ministry of Foreign Affairs on 14 August 1842. He said later, "In my eyes were examples of other secretaries of our mission, who before me entered the Catholic church." Cited by Dzhunkovskii, BS, 70-6-A. In terms of the significance of the Roman Catholic population in Russia at this time, in 1846 there were six Catholic dioceses in Russia, exclusive of Poland—Mogila, Vilna, Minsk, Samogitia, Kamieniec Podolski, and Łuck-Żytomierz. In these dioceses there were 2,699,427 Catholics in 1,038 parishes and 94 deaneries. See James J. Zatko, "The Catholic Church and Russian Statistics," *The Polish Review* 5, #1 (Winter 1960): 45.

47. Gagarin's Testament 1842, BS, Violet. Many other Russians, like Gagarin, converted to Roman Catholicism. In his appendix to *Conversion d'une dame Russe à la foi catholique*, Gagarin listed several Russian converts from the Russian nobility including individuals from the Protasov, Golitsyn, Rostopchin, Tolstoi, Vorontsov, Buturlin, Shcherbatov, Shuvalov, and Ermolov families. This was important because it demonstrated that Gagarin's action, though unusual for a member of the Russian nobility, was certainly not unique. See Gagarin, appendix, *Conversion*, 183–190. I also wish to note the examples of Prince P. B. Kozlovskii (1783–1840) who converted in 1805 and agreed with many of Chaadaev's ideas, Princess Zinaida Aleksandrovna Volkonskaia neé Beloselskaia (1792–1862) who worked for church union, and the Decembrist M. S. Lunin (1787–1845). On the other hand, there were also several Parisians who converted from Roman Catholicism to Orthodoxy. In addition to Abbé Rene François [Vladimir] Guettée (1816–1892), who converted in 1862 and took Russian citizenship in 1875, the archives of the Russian Third Section list thirteen individuals who converted to Orthodoxy between 1845 and 1854. See the letter of Iosif Vasil'evich Vasil'ev (1821–1881) dated 9/21 March 1857, GARF, f. 109, 1 eksp., d. 100, 1857, op. 32, "O frantsuzkikh poddannykh, ispoveduiushchikh v Parizhe pravoslavnuiu veru." Vasil'ev worked in the Paris embassy church and worked to promote union between Orthodox, Anglicans, and Old Catholics. He converted both Guettée and J. Joseph Overbeck.

48. Gagarin to Samarin, 18/30 January 1866, "Pis'mo otsa," 182.

49. Samarin, *Iezuity i ikh otnoshenie k Rossii* (Moscow, 1866), 280. This was not the first time that Gagarin had become involved in discussions with Khomiakov regarding religion. A journal entry of 17/29 April 1840 mentioned a gathering at which Khomiakov criticized Roman Catholicism on the dogma of Purgatory, the *filioque*, and lack of adherence to the seven ecumenical councils. BS, Bleu Claire 3. Viktor Petrovich Balabin, the brother of Jesuit Evgenii Petrovich Balabin, concurred with Samarin regarding Gagarin's proselytism. He wrote that

Gagarin's "neo-Catholic zeal extends to such a degree, that at the slightest word of religion he begins to catechize." Letter of Viktor Balabin to Evgenii Balabin, January 1844, *Journal de Victor de Balabine, secrétaire de l'ambassade de Russie: 1842-1847* (Paris, 1914), vii–viii. I should also note a letter of Samarin to Gagarin from 23 April 1844 in which Samarin discussed the importance of Gagarin's participation in the discussions between the Slavophiles and the Westerners. Samarin wrote, "Yes, I was persuaded that you have forgotten neither Moscow nor the country of your birth. No, you have not forgotten anything, you remember everything, and it is sad to think how these memories should be overwhelming for you. But here equally, one has not quite forgotten you. I can tell you, in that familiar circle I have often observed how your name, mentioned by chance, provokes a disposition of sadness, how suddenly conversation is stopped and silence falls." Cited in Pierling, *Le prince,* 84–85.

50. Letter of Gagarin to Jesuit General Jean Phillipe de Roothaan, 9 February 1845, cited in Giot, "Gagarin," 95. Apparently, Gagarin also brought some miraculous medals with him to distribute in Moscow, but was unable to do so. See Samarin, *Iezuity,* 280. The miraculous medal was a Catholic religious medallion on one side of which was a representation of Mary standing on a globe and extending her arms. The medal was the inspiration of Catherine Labouré, who claimed to have received a vision of Mary. The medals were distributed as a sign of divine favor upon France and a sign of France's special role in world history. During the 1830s millions of the medals were distributed in France. A pamphlet describing the history and miracles attributed to the medal went through five editions between 1832 and 1836. See Thomas A. Kselman, *Miracles and Prophecies in Nineteenth-Century France* (Brunswick: Rutgers University Press, 1983), 78.

51. Gagarin cited in Giot, "Gagarin," 102. In his response to Dzhunkovskii's "Russkii, sem let' iezuit," Gagarin wrote, "And truly I was received in Moscow. Except for my parents, I did not reveal to anyone that I entered the Catholic church." He asserted that it was by his "conversations" and "type of thought" that people learned he was Catholic. Gagarin further stated that he told Iurii Samarin everything. Gagarin, Response to Dzhunkovskii, no date, BS, Verte 9.

52. Gagarin, cited in Giot, "Gagarin," 102

53. St. Ignatius of Loyola wrote, "the Society ought to labor more intensely in those places where the enemy of Christ our Lord has sown cockle [Matt 13:24–30], and especially where he has spread bad opinion about the Society or stirred up ill will against it so as to impede the fruit which the Society could produce. This is especially to be observed if the place is an important one of which account should be taken, by sending there, if possible, persons such that their life and learning may undo the evil opinion founded on false reports." St. Ignatius of Loyola, S. J., *Spiritual Exercises and Selected Works,* ed. George E. Ganss, S. J. (New York: Paulist Press, 1991), 308. William James wrote, "The apostolic thrust of Ignatius' spirituality was that a good Christian should be interested not only in

his own eternal salvation, but that of his fellow man." William A. James, "The Jesuits' Role in Founding Schools in Late Tsarist Russia," in *Religious and Secular Forces in Late Tsarist Russia,* ed. Charles E. Timberlake (Seattle: University of Washington Press, 1992), 48. Note that this desire has already been shown in Gagarin's testament of 1842, in which he prayed for the salvation of his family and friends, especially Iurii Samarin.

54. Roothaan had entered the Society of Jesus in Russia during the Suppression.

55. BS, 70-1-B.

56. Letter of Ravignan to Roothaan, 30 April 1842. BS, 70-1-B. Ravignan also mentioned to Roothaan Gagarin's desire to convert the Slavs, and that in the six and a half months that Gagarin spent in Russia, his conversion was known to his parents, but not to others.

57. Cited in Giot, "Gagarin," 111.

58. Letter of Varvara Gagarin to Ivan Gagarin, 24 November 1842, cited in ibid., 104.

59. Gagarin to Roothaan, BS, 70-1-B.

60. In one touching example of his parents' concern, his mother wrote on 5/7 July 1843, "We stopped near that tree, that young tree whose branches you pruned last year. We cried bitterly. You were with us then." BS, 70-3-A.

61. Sergei Gagarin to his son, 26 September 1843, cited by Giot, "Gagarin," 116.

62. He wrote, "I have too easily nourished the hope of pulling them from schism and of engendering them to Jesus Christ, as they have engendered my flesh." Gagarin to Roothaan, 20 April 1843, BS, 70-1-B.

63. Gagarin to Ravignan, 8 June 1843, cited in Giot "Gagarin," 111.

64. Gagarin to Roothaan, 13 August 1843, BS, 70-1-B.

65. Letter of Roothaan to Ravignan, 13 May 1843, ARSI, Reg. Epist. ad Prov. Franciae III (1843–1847), 29.

66. In a letter to Roothaan on 13 September 1843, Ravignan wrote that Gagarin was a fervent novice and "has a grace quite suited to the vocation." ARSI, Franciae 5–V, 19.

67. Ravignan, cited in Armand de Ponlevoy, S. J., *The Life of Father de Ravignan of the Society of Jesus* (New York: Catholic Publication Society, 1869), 184–186.

68. Cited in Giot, "Gagarin," 90.

69. These statistics come from the Catalogus Sociorum Provinciae Gallilae Societatis Iesu found in AFCJ.

70. Joseph Burnichon mentioned a Father Garebtzov [Zherbtsov] of Russian origin, but provided no information on him. Burnichon, *La Compagnie de Jésus en France: histoire d'un siècle* 4 (Paris: Beauchesne, 1922), 137. I was unable to find any information relating to him in the Russian archives or in ARSI. He was also briefly mentioned in Dzhunkovskii, BS, 70-6-A. Burnichon also men-

tioned a Father Ivan Fiorovich as a member of the Slavic group. Fiorovich was born in Dalmatia on 20 December 1819. He entered the novitiate on 3 May 1852. Gagarin had high hopes that "he would perform great services in the Missions. Unfortunately, his literary education has been completely neglected." Fiorovich lacked the ability to work for the Russian mission and instead spent a long and fruitful career in the French mission in Syria. Burnichon says that he was very popular among the workers in the port of Beirut. Burnichon, *La Compagnie,* 137.

71. Martynov was born in Kazan on 7 October 1821 into a family of Russian nobility. He studied philosophy at the University of St. Petersburg, where he received a gold medal. While serving as a tutor under Count Grigorii Shuvalov, he traveled to Germany, France, and Italy where he met Father Ravignan. He converted to Roman Catholicism in 1845 after having read writings of Rozaven, Ravignan, de Maistre, Theiner, and a letter of Gagarin on the truth of the Catholic church, which he said contributed principally to his conversion. Martynov would later work with Pius IX and Leo XIII on the Byzantine rite. He served as a pontifical theologian, worked at Vatican I, and became well known for his philological work and study of Slavic history. Author of *Les Manuscrits slaves de la Bibliothèque impérial de Paris* in 1858, Martynov died at Cannes on 26 April 1894.

72. Dzhunkovskii was born 12 February 1821 at St. Petersburg. He was a candidate in law at the University of St. Petersburg and upon graduation served abroad in the ministry of popular education. He converted to Roman Catholicism in 1845 and wrote more than 300 articles in *L'Univers, La Voix de la vérité, L'Ami de la religion,* and other publications, before leaving the Jesuits in 1853. From 1854 to 1861, he served in the missions for the north with the title of "apostolic prefect to the arctic countries." In January 1866 he returned to Russia and to the Orthodox church, where he wrote articles hostile to the Roman Catholic church and the Jesuits. He died in St. Petersburg on 25 February 1870. Angelo Tamoborra has written an extensive article on him entitled "Da Pietroburgo a Roma e ritorno Stepan S. Dzunkovskij (1821–1870)," *Rassegna Storica del Risorgimento* 76, #2 (1989): 179–216. See also I. Bazarov, "S. S. Dzhunkovskii i ego vozvrashchenie v pravoslavie," *Pravoslavnie obozrienie* (April 1866): 430–442.

73. Astromov (1824–?) would briefly work with Gagarin, but due to mental problems and disobedience to his superiors would later leave the society. Astromov was initially devoted to Orthodoxy and considered conversion as treachery. In 1846, he went to Italy with the family of a minister of state, Count Uvarov. This visit led to his conversion, partly due to the recently reported apparition of Mary in the church of Saint Andrei delle Fratte. On 9 September 1846, Father de Villefort wrote to the Jesuit Superior in Naples recommending Astromov, who "had that very day received Catholic communion for the first time." He was received into the Jesuits in October 1846. In 1847, he was ordained to the priesthood. Burnichon argued that Astromov was "seduced first by the ontologist mirage, then by the speculations of another Thomist, his teaching frankly turned

away from sound doctrine." He thought it was his mission to "restore to the philosophic truth its order and possibly the Catholic church itself." Burnichon, *La Compagnie,* 134–136. A letter from Jesuit General Beckx to Balabin on 20 August 1861 noted that Astromov had written a highly critical letter to the provincial of Tolouse in which he claimed to be under the direct inspiration of the Spirit of God. Astromov's letter was full of threats and reproaches. He would later be secularized, and he vanished from sight in 1864. ARSI, Reg. Epist. ad Prov. Franciae V (1857–1869), 221.

74. Balabin was born on 29 August 1815 in St. Petersburg. He was raised in the Orthodox church, although his mother was a French Catholic. A pure and pious youth, he was an artist and a mystic who liked devotional literature. He knew Zhukovskii and Nikolai Vasil'evich Gogol' and served as a page for the future Alexander II. Balabin was attached to the services of the Ministry of the Interior. He converted to Roman Catholicism in 1852 after reading the *Imitation of Christ* and the *Life of St. Theresa.* He died in Cairo on 20 January 1895.

75. Pavel Pierling was born on 1 June 1840 in St. Petersburg to a Roman Catholic family which had earlier come to Russia from Bavaria. He studied philosophy at the University of Posen. He left Russia in December of 1856 and began his novitiate in Austria. Pierling was an authority on the first false Dmitrii and the relations between Russia and the papacy. His major work was *La Russie et la Saint-Siège.* He died on 25 February 1922 at Brussels.

76. Letter dated 2 September 1843. ARSI, Francia 5–VII, 31.

77. Aksakov, cited in Samarin, *Iezuity,* 1. Emphasis in original.

78. Benkendorf was the head of the Russian Third Section. Note that Benkendorf did become a Catholic before his death. See Gagarin, *Dnevnik,* 325.

79. Turgenev diary entry of 28 September 1844, cited in Shchegolev, *Duel',* 405–406.

80. Letter dated 28 September 1844, cited in A. I. Turgenev, "Neizdannye pis'ma A. I. i N. I. Turgenevykh," *Simvol* 19 (1988): 236, or Gagarin, *Dnevnik,* 323. Also see letter of Turgenev to Gagarin 16/28 October 1844, Turgenev, "Neizdannye," 197, or Gagarin, *Dnevnik,* 326–327. Turgenev would also write to K. S. Serbinovich that Gagarin was not to blame for his conversion, but that responsibility was to be laid on himself, Serbinovich, Filaret, Murav'ev, and "all the lethargy of our Orthodoxy." Letter to Serbinovich, cited in Pierling, S. J., entry for Gagarin, *Russkii biographicheskii slovar'* (New York: Kraus Reprint Corp., 1962), 70. Turgenev thought that Gagarin would return to Russia with a Catholic priest, seek permission to build a Catholic chapel for his own use, and worship there in seclusion. See Richard Tempest, "Ivan Gagarin: Diplomatist," 99.

81. Letter of Turgenev to Gagarin, 16/28 October 1844, cited in Turgenev, "Neizdannye," 197, or Gagarin, *Dnevnik,* 326–327.

82. Herzen, cited in N. P. Antsiferov, "I. S. Gagarin—Gertsenu," *Literaturnoe nasledstvo* 62 (1955): 61.

83. Cited in M. P. Alekseev, "Po sledam rukopisei I. S. Turgeneva vo Frantsii," *Russkaia literatura* 1 (1963): 73–74. Herzen also had heard a rumor that Gagarin wanted to return to Russia as a Jesuit priest. He wrote, "However, all this is impossible: he will be seized at the border or prevented from entering Russia, or he might vanish without a trace. But why does he wish and strive for martyrdom. . . ." Herzen also blamed Gagarin's conversion on a "chance encounter with a Jesuit, a demented Catholic [de Ravignan]." Herzen, cited in Tempest, "Ivan Gagarin: Diplomatist," 99.

84. Diary entry for Herzen 8/20 January 1843, *A.I. Gertsen—Sochineniia v deviati tomakh,* IX (Moscow, 1958), 66–67.

85. Ibid.

86. Herzen, *My Past and Thoughts,* trans. Constance Garnett (New York: Vintage Books, 1974), 298. According to Korczak-Branicki, Herzen said that a non-Orthodox Slav shocked him as an anomaly and made the same effect on him as a bull without horns, cited in Korczak-Branicki, *Les nationalités,* 4. See also Andrzej Walicki, *Russia, Poland, and Universal Regeneration* (Notre Dame: University of Notre Dame Press, 1991), in which Walicki points out that Herzen made many anti-Catholic remarks.

87. Antsiferov makes this argument in his article "I. S. Gagarin—Gertsenu," 61–62.

88. Antsiferov believed the Polish Jesuit in Herzen's novel could be a reference to Korczak-Branicki, member of *Les Seize.*

89. See M. P. Alekseev, "Posledam," 75.

90. *A.I. Herzen—Sobranie sochinenii v tridtsati tomakh,* 14 (Moscow, 1958), 328.

91. Letter to Herzen, 11 June 1862, cited in Antsiferov, "I. S. Gagarin," 62.

92. Korczak-Branicki, *Les nationalites,* 3. Korczak-Branicki added, "Your reprovers, adding to the reproach of apostasy absurd calumnies, now come to accuse you of being controlled in your conversion to Catholicism, not by the lights of your judgment, but by some kind of ambition or by unrequited love! [a reference to Ol'ga Trubetskoi?]. . . . Among your relatives, there are even those who reject you as a black sheep. With a rare courage, you have known to persevere in a resolution generously taken and executed" (4–5).

93. Letter of Viktor Balabin to Evgenii Balabin, cited in Balabin, *Journal,* vii–viii. This citation is even more interesting considering Evgenii Balabin's later entry into that same novitiate. Viktor Balabin obviously had a high esteem for Gagarin; he wrote that Gagarin had said that after he ended his novitiate, he would be sent to preach the faith in distant countries before returning later to Paris. Viktor Balabin believed that, if Gagarin succeeded, he would "pale the star of Ravignan and Lacordaire, because he has if not more spirit and means than they, at least a vaster education, more encyclopedic than those gentleman."

94. Letter of Turgenev to A. Humbolt, 24 April 1849, cited in "Iz bumag V. A. Zhukovskago," *Russkii arkhiv* 11 (1873): 1523. Turgenev blamed Madame Svechina for encouraging Gagarin's conversion and called Gagarin "the most noble of converts."

95. Even Herzen, irreligious himself, considered a Russian Catholic to be an aberration.

96. Buturlin, "Imel," 281.

97. Letter of Sergei Gagarin to Ivan Gagarin, 1846, BS, 70-3-A

98. Archival documents in GARF stated that Ivan Gagarin had asked for capital of 300 million rubles, which Sergei Gagarin sent. See letter of the brother of Sergei Buturlin, 20 May 1845, and letter of Sergei Buturlin, 1845, in "Proisky si proizvodiatsia pod rukovodstvom sivshago nastavnikom molodogo kniazia Gagarina, frantsuzkago podannago, po imeni *Maren'-Darbel'*, kotoryi, kak kazhetsia, i sam ne chto inoe kak orudie Iezuitov," GARF, f. 109, 2 expd., 1845, d. 256, ll. 3–6, ll. 45–46.

99. Letter of Sergei Buturlin to Mariia Sergeevna Buturlina, 9 December 1854, GARF, f. 109, 1 eksp., 1852, d. 346, 174ob. A. S. Buturlin noted that Gagarin's sister continued to send money to her brother. Buturlin, "Imel," 281.

100. "Kratkaia zapiska," RGIA, f. 1151, op. 4, d. 26, 1854, Grazhdanskogo departmenta, o dvorianakh: kniaze Ivane Gagarine, Ivane Martynove i Stepane Dzhunkovskom. The "Kratkaia zapiska" regarding Balabin's sentence can be found in f. 1151, op. 4, 1853, d. 139. It should also be noted that the authors of the document included Vladimir Sergeevich Pecherin among the list of Russian nobility who entered the Jesuits. Pecherin was, in fact, a Redemptorist priest.

101. Letter of V. I. Shteingel' to I. I. Pushchin, dated 28 August/9 September 1854, in V. I. Shteingel', "Pis'ma V. I. Shteingelia k I. I. Pushchinu," *Letopisi gosudarstvennogo literaturnogo muzeia*, vol. 3: 378.

102. Gagarin, cited in Buturlin, "Imel," 280.

Chapter Three. The Beginnings of the Mission to the Slavs

1. Gagarin, cited in Giot, "Gagarin," 123.

2. St. Acheul was named for an early Christian martyr who died in 303 A.D. The novitiate is a period of two years of spiritual training undertaken after entrance into the Jesuit order. At the end of this period, vows of poverty, chastity, and obedience are taken.

3. Gagarin, 19 August 1843, cited in Giot, "Gagarin," 114–115. However, Gagarin still had not given up hope of converting his family. A letter from Father Rubillon to Gagarin on 22 August 1844 warned that Gagarin should "not proceed too quickly [with their conversion], and with the princes, your cousins, one must respect their independence for the good of their souls." BS, 64–5.

4. Letter dated 23 October 1843, ARSI, Franciae 6–XI, 44. Rubillon does not provide the location of this prison, though presumably it was either in St. Acheul or Paris.

5. Dzhunkovskii, BS, 70-6-A.

6. Letter of Gagarin to N. N. Sheremeteva, 7/19 July 1845, cited in "Ia sluzhu prostym riadovym soldatom v odnom iz mnogochislennykh polkov voiska dukhovnovo. . . ," *Simvol* 32 (1994): 182–183.

7. Pierling noted that Gagarin did contemplate passing over to the Eastern rite. Pierling, *Le prince*, 17.

8. Gagarin to Sheremeteva, 5 December 1846, Gagarin, "Ia sluzhu," 185. Gagarin also mentioned "The more and more that faith and love of God and Jesus the Redeemer penetrates my heart, the stronger and hotter in that heart is love for Russia"; he often prayed for his homeland.

9. See letters of Gagarin to Sheremeteva, 1846, 29 March 1849, Gagarin, "Ia sluzhu," 185–186, 188. Gagarin was not the only one to see his future in Russia. Pecherin wrote that two Jesuit missionaries informed him that Gagarin would be the head of the Russian Jesuits when God permitted them to return to Russia. See Vladimir S. Pecherin, "Zamogilnie zapiski," *Russkoe obshchestvo 30-kh godov XIX v. Liudi i idei. Memuari sovremennikov,* I. A. Fedosov, ed. (Moscow, 1989), 276.

10. Unfortunately, I was unable to find any archival information describing this proposal in either the Bibliothèque Slave or ARSI. However, it is probably quite similar to his proposals of 1845. Roothaan probably rejected Gagarin's initial proposal due to its construction so soon after Gagarin's arrival in the Jesuit order. Gagarin had yet to take final vows and as such had no permanent ties on which such a project could be established. Furthermore, it is possible that Roothaan wanted Gagarin to learn patience. See letter of Gagarin to Roothaan, 8 February 1845, BS, 70-1-C.

11. The tonsure is the cutting of hair in order to signify admission into a priestly order.

12. Albéric de Foresta (1818–1876) entered the Jesuits in 1837. In 1843, he began to work for the *Missions boréales.* This included Northern Europe, Northern Asia, North America, Greenland, Hudson Bay, Lapland, Finland, and Siberia. He wanted to collect geographic, ethnographic, and historic information in order to facilitate conversion of the peoples in these areas.

13. BS, 64–5.

14. BS, 64–5.

15. See letter of Ravignan to Roothaan, 8 September 1844, ARSI, Franciae 5–V, 30.

16. The citation does not list the three great evils. Gagarin probably is referring to problems of revolution, the schism between Orthodoxy and Catholicism, and the threat of an expansionistic Nikolaevan Russia which he addresses in many of his other proposals.

17. Gagarin is probably referring to the Russian Catholics living in Paris and Western Europe.

18. Gagarin, cited in Father Régis de Chazournes, *Albéric de Foresta de la Compagnie de Jésus, Fondateur des Écoles Apostoliques. Sa vie, ses vertus, et son oeuvre* (Paris, 1881), 95–96.

19. Ibid., 96.

20. Here are initial traces of Gagarin's later concept of *byzantinisme.*

21. Gagarin had in mind the works of Antonio Possevino, Petr Skarga, and other Jesuit activity before 1819.

22. Chazournes, *Alberic de Foresta,* 96–97.

23. Each of these proposals can be found in BS, 70-1-B.

24. Gagarin, cited by Dzhunkovskii in BS, 70-6-A. It is important to note that Dzhunkovskii included this citation in his text attacking the Russian Jesuits in Paris, so its veracity is in doubt. However, it is also important that Gagarin did see himself as the individual primarily responsible for the conversion of Russia and so certain megalomaniacal tendencies in him cannot be denied.

25. Note Gagarin's presentation of Nicholas I's Orthodoxy, Autocracy, and Nationality.

26. In another document in BS, Blue Claire 5, there is a proposal by Gagarin to establish departments of the Congregation of Propaganda, under a different name, in Italy; France; Spain; Portugal; Spanish and Portuguese America; Germany; Holland; Scandinavia; England; the United States; British America; the Slavic lands of Russia, Poland, Hungary, Moldova, Serbia, etc.; Turkey, Greece, Syria, Persia, Egypt, etc; India; China; Japan; Vietnam; Siam; and Africa. I mention this to show that Gagarin's interest in promoting missionary activity was not limited to the Slavs.

27. Roothaan to Gagarin, 1 May 1845, BS, 70-1-C.

28. Svechina to Gagarin, cited in Pierling, "Sofiia Petrovna Svechina," *Russkaia starina* (October 1900): 161.

29. See letters to Gagarin 11 May 1845 and 23 August 1845, cited in Svechina, *Lettres,* 344, 348–349.

30. Pierling said that it was possible that Gagarin and Pecherin first met at the home of Gagarin's aunt, princess Elizaveta Petrovna Gagarina. However, it can be firmly established that Pecherin visited Gagarin at St. Acheul in January of 1845. See Pierling, S. J., "Vladimir Sergeevich Pecherin v perepiske s Ivanom Sergeevichem Gagarinem," *Russkaia starina* 145 (1911): 60. Pecherin sarcastically described Gagarin as a "fresh and pious novice" with "a kind of sacred revulsion for money." Yet, "he receives annually from Russia 12,000 francs. *O, sainte pauvreté!! Pauvre homme!!*" Pecherin, "Zamogilnie," 250.

31. Pecherin to Gagarin, 13/25 January 1847, cited in Pierling, "Vladimir," 63.

32. Ibid.

33. Edward Bouverie Pusey (August 1800–16 September 1882) was an Anglican scholar at the University of Oxford and a key figure in the Oxford movement.

His struggle to defend traditional Catholic dogma and to base Anglican teaching on the writings of church fathers prior to the separation of East and West became known as Puseyism. Pusey did not convert to Catholicism.

34. Pecherin to Gagarin, 24 January/5 February, cited in ibid., 63.

35. Pecherin to Gagarin, 21 March 1850, cited in Pierling, *Le prince*, 150.

36. Pecherin, cited in Lucjan Suchanek, "Les catholiques russes et les pro-catholiques en Russie dans la première moitié du XIXe siècle," *Cahiers du monde russe et sovietique* 29 (July–December 1988): 365.

37. Bautain was a philosopher and a theologian. He had been appointed vicar-general of Paris in 1850 and taught at the Sorbonne from 1853 to 1862. A. N. Murav'ev (1806–1874) served as chamberlain to Alexander II and under-procurator in charge of foreign relations for the Russian church. He was a popular and prolific writer on Orthodox topics. It was his book on the Orthodox church which had influenced Gagarin's decision to convert to Catholicism.

38. Régis Ladous, "Catholiques libéraux et union des églises jusqu'en 1878," *Les catholiques libéraux XIXe siècle,* Collection du centre d'histoire du catholicisme (1974), 501.

39. Gagarin became acquainted with Terlecki's work through his correspondence with Pecherin. In his letter of August 1847, Pecherin wrote, "The Abbé Terlecki, whom you may know, hopes to establish a religious congregation for preaching the Gospel to the Slavs. This congregation would be entirely composed of subjects of Slavic origin. His two letters warmly invited me to engage in this work and to enroll me in the congregation. He imposed two quite extraordinary conditions: 1. to leave our order where I have made my religious vows, 2. to substitute the Greek rite for the Roman. Two things completely impossible, as you know well." Cited in Pierling, *Le prince,* 147.

40. This proposal can be found in the ASV, Archivio Particolare Pio IX, Oggetti Vari #450. Giot refers to a second proposal submitted on 26 January 1847, by a Russian or Ruthenian, and found in the archives of the Propagation of the Faith. This proposal was optimistic and encouraged by the conversions among the Russian aristocracy as well as the spread of liberal ideas in Russia. The author believed the time had arrived to work for the union of churches and exhorted the pope to preserve the Byzantine rite for those who wished to return to union. See Giot, "Gagarin," 171.

41. The statutes for this organization can be found in GARF, f. 109., 1 eksp., 1852, d. 346, ll. 88–94.

42. This proposal can be found in ARSI, Franciae 5–VII, 10.

43. A copy of this article can be found in RGIA, f. 706, n. 205, d. 148, Stat'i iz frantsuzkikh zhurnalov o katolichestve v Rossii ob ego missionerskoi deiatel'nosti, oba so'edinenii khristianskikh tserkvei, ll. 1–9.

44. Emphasis in original.

45. Here Dzhunkovskii is probably acting under the influence of Gagarin's argument about the revolutionary tendencies of the Slavophiles later expounded in *La Russie sera-t-elle catholique?*

46. RGIA, f. 706, n. 205, d. 148, ll. 10–16.

47. Niccolò Tommaseo was a poet and critic born in Sibenik, Dalmatia. He had asked the pope on 11 October 1847 to address "a word of peace" to the Orthodox and noted that it would be good at this time "when all people turn their regards toward Rome with respect and honor." Cited in Giot, "Gagarin," 172. On 11 August 1847 Luquet had also appealed for an encyclical on the union of Christians.

48. Pope Pius IX, "Aux chrétiens d'orient," *Lettre encyclique de S.S. le Pape Pie IX aux chrétiens d'orient et encyclique responsive des patriarchs et des synodes de l'Église d'orient,* trans. Demétrius Dallas (Paris, 1850), 13–14.

49. Ibid., 16.

50. Ibid., 18–19.

51. *Encyclical Epistle of the One Holy Catholic and Apostolic Church to the Faithful Everywhere, Being A Reply to the Epistle of Pius IX to the Easterns.* 6 January 1848. (New York: John F. Trow & Co., 1867), 13.

52. The Orthodox church considered the Roman Catholic use of unleavened bread in the Eucharist as a sign of an improper understanding of the nature of Christ. The Orthodox believed that leavened bread showed the full nature of Christ as both human and divine.

53. Ibid., 7.

54. Ibid., 12.

55. Gagarin became acquainted with de Buck as early as 1853 after de Buck sent Gagarin copies of his article on Father Bobola, S. J. Bobola had been murdered by the Cossacks after the Union of Brest. See James P. Jurich, "Ecumenical Journalism in 1853–1860: Victor de Buck and Russian Orthodoxy," *Revue d'histoire ecclésiastique* 87 (January–March 1992): 107.

56. Gagarin clearly had an influence on Dzhunkovskii's proposals. Dzhunkovskii's articles refer to the importance of Russian marriages with Western nobility and the role of Murav'ev's text in the conversion of the Russian Orthodox to Catholicism.

57. Gagarin to Father François Guilherny, cited in Giot, "Gagarin," 155–156. Specific texts mentioned by Gagarin were *Le Protestantisme comparé au catholicisme dans ses rapports avec la civilization européene* by Abbé Jacques Balmés; *Opuscules théologiques* by Alfonso Muzzarelli; *Lectures on the most important doctrines and practices of the Catholic Church* by Nicholas Wiseman; and *Lehrbuch der Dogmengeschichte* by Heinrich Klee.

58. A reference to Pusey of the Oxford movement.

59. Gagarin, "La Puséisme moscovite," *L'Univers* (12 April 1850): 1.

60. Ibid. (15 April 1850): 1.

61. The tertianship is a year of spiritual formation which completes a Jesuit's training.

62. Gagarin, *Union de prières pour la Conversion de la Russie et l'extinction du Schisme chez les peuples Slaves* (Brussels: Greuse, 1851), 5–6. Here Gagarin was referring to the prayer movement begun in England by Father George Spencer. The similarity to the goals of Société orientale pour l'union de tous les chrétiens d'Orient should also be noted in the desire to form prayer organizations for the reunion of churches.

63. Ibid., 10–12.

64. Ibid., 13–15.

65. Ibid., 16.

66. BS, 70-1-B.

67. Roothaan to Gagarin, 24 September 1851, BS, 70-1-C.

68. BS, 70-1-C.

69. Gagarin, cited in Giot, "Gagarin," 158–159.

70. Vaugirard was an ecclesiastical-theological institution.

71. Members included Henri Columbel, Raymond de Gassard, Charles de (Guiuaumont?), Paul Lauras, Charles de Maistre, Joseph du Ranquet, Emmanuel de la Rochethulon, Félix de Rocquefeuil, and Ernest de Toytot. Congregations were to express the spirit of the first Christians, being united in one spirit. They were to be attached to the celebration of the public feasts of Mary; to honor her divine motherhood; to follow her example in prayer and charity; to work under Mary's protection. Furthermore, members were to study their religion and to be attached to the precepts of God and church.

72. See Giot, "Gagarin," 161–166. See also Paul Baily, "Brugelette," *Les Établissements des Jésuites en France depuis quatre siècles,* ed. Pierre Delattre, S. J., vol. I (1949), 984.

73. BS, 70-3-B

74. Ibid. The reason for Gagarin's attitude toward the Italians was his view that the Italians were by nature revolutionary.

75. Palmer was an Anglican professor at Oxford who developed a great interest in the Russian church. He promoted intercommunion between Anglican and Orthodox churches and made journeys to Russia in 1840 and 1842. Palmer's projects failed and he later converted to Roman Catholicism. For further information see Ronald G. Lee, "The Theory and Practice of the Kingdom of God on Earth: the Anglo Catholic Conservative Utopia of William Palmer" (Diss., University of Notre Dame, 1996).

76. Notes of Clair, BS, 70-3-B. Gagarin's archives contain two responses to this issue in which he referred to the Father as the sole principal/primary cause and the Son as the "primordial" cause of the procession of the Spirit. The Father came first, then the Son, then the Holy Spirit. The Father was the source of all

divinity. Both Father and Son possessed the principle of divinity which was passed on to the Holy Spirit. The Holy Spirit received the principle from the Son, who received it from the Father. Therefore the Holy Spirit proceeded from the Father through the Son. See BS, Verte 1, and BS, Bleu Claire 1. Copies of Palmer's writings on the procession of the Holy Spirit can be found in BS, CD-20.

77. The letter was in response to an article by Gagarin (referred to as a "Jesuit friend of mine [a Russian by origin]") which claimed that Palmer had said that the church at Constantinople had nearly excommunicated the Russian church for accepting Protestants and Roman Catholics without rebaptism. Palmer wrote, "I scolded him [Gagarin], for his inaccuracy on my way through Paris and told him that there was no sign of any such zeal or warmth in the matter, on which he exclaimed to my amusement, 'Oh! that is the case, is it? So much the worse for them. That shows them in so much the worse light. I will write another article in *L'Univers* in that sense!' And in fact this is the worst sign about the Greeks, that they are careless and hypocritical, rather than over-warm in the matter." Cited in Alexei S. Khomiakov and William Palmer, *Russia and the English Church During the Last Fifty Years* I, ed. Birkbeck (London: Rivington, Percival, 1895), 148–149. Palmer's relationship with Gagarin continued until Palmer's death. Gagarin's archive contains correspondence between Palmer and Gagarin, a copy of Palmer's later work—*The Patriarch and the Tsar,* corrected by Gagarin—and correspondence between Palmer's brother, Edwin, and Gagarin. Palmer willed many of his Russian and Slavonic texts to Gagarin's Bibliothèque Slave upon his death.

78. Palmer, *Dissertations on Subjects Relating to the "Orthodox" or "Eastern-Catholic" Communion* (London, 1853), 321.

79. BS, Jaune 4.

80. It was this article to which Palmer referred in his letter to Khomiakov.

81. The branch theory held that there was only one catholic or universal church, but that it was divided into the Anglican, Roman Catholic, and Orthodox churches.

82. Gagarin, "Varietés," *L'Univers* (24 April 1853): 3. Gagarin added, "Reading certain passages of his book, one is tempted to ask if Palmer is not Catholic."

83. Gagarin, "M. Palmer et l'Église russe," *L'Univers* (10 May 1853): 1.

84. Letter of Gagarin to unknown, AFCJ, Gagarin fond.

85. Letter of Guilherny to Gagarin, 3 October 1855, BS, Bleu 14.

86. On the procession of the Holy Spirit, the authors wrote, "uzhe ot otsa i syna iskhodiaschavo." *Sokrovishche khristianina ili kratkoe izlozhenie glavnykh istin very i ob'iazannostei khristianina* (Paris, 1855), 10.

87. Other members were Marshal Bosquier, Vice Admiral Mathieu, Armand de Melun, Émmanuel de Rougé, Count Charles de Montelembert, Frédéric de Falloux, Broglie, Henri Alexandre Wallon, Louis Felicien Joseph Caignart de Saulcy, Baron Séguier, Natalis de Wailly, Louis René Tulasne, de Vitte, Garcin de Tassy, Jean Baptiste Flandrin, Melchior de Vogué et de Gabriac, Armand Prosper Faugère,

Count Charles de Bourmont, Felix Esquirou de Parieu, Le Serruier, Auguste Nicolas, Jacques Binet, Charles Hermite, Benoist d'Azy, Louis de Mas Latrie, Count Jules de Bertou, Count de Cotte, Count de Goyon, and Frédéric Ozanam. Members were generally soldiers, ambassadors, and nobles.

88. Xavier de Montclos, *Lavigerie: La Saint-Siège et l'Église de l'avènement de Pie IX à l'avènement de Léon XIII 1846–1878* (Paris: E. de Boccard, 1965), 143 note. Bruno Belhoste, biographer of Cauchy, argued that for L'Oeuvre "it was less a question of converting the Muslims than to restore the Orthodox of the [Turkish] Empire, over whom Russia believed it exercised a protectorate, to the Catholic faith." See Belhoste, *Cauchy [1789–1857]: Un mathméticien légitimiste au XIX siècle* (Paris: Belin, 1985), 210–211.

89. François Renault, *Le cardinal Lavigerie, 1825–1892: l'Église, l'Afrique et la France* (Paris: Fayard, 1992), 48–49.

90. Ibid., 51–52, 56–57.

91. This proposal is published in *Sacrum Poloniae Millennium* 2 (1955): 205–228. It should be noted that there is some disagreement as to whether Gagarin wrote this document or it was the work of another Jesuit. The similarities of this proposal with Gagarin's views at this time (1854–1856) lead me to believe that he did indeed write it.

92. "Notes du P. Gagarine sur l'histoire de Russie," BS, Gagarine X.

93. Gagarin referred to the following marriages:

1. Yaroslav and Ingigerd, daughter of Olaf Skotkonung of Sweden, in the early eleventh century.
2. Ingeborg (granddaughter of Yaroslav) and King Olaf I of Denmark, in the early eleventh century.
3. Vladimir Monomakh (grandson of Yaroslav) and Gytha, daughter of King Harold Godwinson of England.
4. Mstislav the Great (son of Monomakh) and Christine, daughter of King Inge Stenkillson of Sweden.

94. Gagarin, Questiones Scandinaves I and II, BS, Gagarine X.

95. Gagarin, "La Question Scandinave," *Plamia* 74: 24.

96. Gagarin, Questiones Scandinaves II, BS, Gagarine X

97. Gagarin, "Notice," 217.

98. Gagarin, Notes on History of the Russian church, BS, Jaune 4.

99. Gagarin, "Notice," 217. Gagarin noted that he wanted to write a history of the Slavs in general until the sixteenth century and later write a separate history of Poland and Russia. See Gagarin, Notes on History of the Russian church, BS, Jaune 4.

100. Gagarin, "Notice," 208.

101. Ibid., 207.

102. Ibid., 215.

103. Gagarin and others had previously argued for the need to maintain the Byzantine rite. In fact, in a letter to Roothaan on 25 August 1852, Gagarin suggested that Jesuit missionaries of the Byzantine rite could more easily enter the Turkish Empire and spread the Gospel than could those of the Latin rite. BS, 70-1-B. However, Gagarin's proposal here does indicate some weakening of a complete support for preservation of the Byzantine rite as practiced by the Slavs. He wrote, "but the Slavs have a certain inclination to follow the impulses of their heart, to attach themselves to the historic form of the exterior rite like a national monument, without contemplating and measuring the real value." Gagarin, "Notice," 208.

104. Ibid., 214, 225. In a later speech, Gagarin said, "I do not hesitate to say, the day when France wants this [the reunion of the Orthodox and Catholic churches], the day when it puts it in its thoughts and heart, this great cause will triumph over all obstacles." Gagarin, *De la réunion de l'Église orientale avec l'Église romaine—discours prononcé par le P. Gagarin, de la Compagnie de Jésus, le 27 Janvier 1860 dans L'Église de Notre-Dame des Victoires, à l'occasion de la fête de l'Oeuvre des Écoles d'Orient* (Paris: Peaucelle, 1860), 16.

105. Gagarin, "Notice," 211–214. Gagarin wrote, "When the Society has done this once, why can it not repeat it a second time?" Ibid., 209.

Chapter Four. Signs of Hope

1. Gagarin, *La Russie sera-t-elle catholique?* (Paris: Douniol, 1856), 81.

2. Letter of Gagarin to unknown, cited in Giot, "Gagarin," 178. Peter Johann Beckx (1795–1887) became general on 2 July 1853.

3. Letter of Gagarin to Studer, 1855, BS, 70-1-C.

4. Burnichon, *La Compagnie,* 137.

5. Beckx to Gagarin, 24 February 1855, BS, 70-1-C.

6. Giot, "Gagarin," 178.

7. Iakobos Georgios Pitzipios (1802–1876), author of *L'Église orientale* (1855) and *L'Orient-les reformes de l'Empire Byzantine* (1858).

8. Gagarin, cited in Angelo Tamborra, "Cattolicesimo e ortodossia russia nel secolo XIX," *Il battesimo delle terre russe* (Florence, 1991), 370. Emphasis in original.

9. Gagarin to de Buck, 14 March 1855, cited in Jurich, "Ecumenical," 110.

10. Gagarin, cited in Giot, "Gagarin," 178.

11. Gagarin to Carayon, 9 July 1855, cited in ibid., 178.

12. Gagarin to Guilherny, 21 November 1855, cited in ibid., 179. Note that Gagarin's comments demonstrate a desire to deceive the Russian reader as to the true nature of his activity.

13. Beckx to Studer, October 1855, cited in Journel, "Origines," 175.

14. Beckx to Studer, 12 October 1855, BS, 70-1-C.

15. "Voskresnie nabroski," *Golos* 185 (July 1880): 1. Rouët de Journel wrote, "The very clear idea of Father Gagarin and his Russian collaborators was the following: to prepare the reunion of the Eastern churches with the Holy See, and for that to address at the same time Catholics and schismatics: to make known to Catholics—the Orthodox churches, to schismatics—the Catholic church." Note here the similarity to Gagarin's proposal for *Nouvelles de Russie.* Journel, "L'Oeuvre des SS. Cyrille et Méthode et la Bibliothèque Slave," *Lettres de Jersey* (1922): 620.

16. In a letter to his aunt on 29 June 1846, Gagarin wrote, "Today is the feast of Saint Peter, prince of Apostles. I have always thought that it was very important to invoke the protection of this rock on which J[esus] C[hrist] had built his church for the end of the schism and the return to unity of all the schismatics." BS, 70-3-A.

17. Though stirred by Russia's "great and noble language," Gagarin chose to write in French.

18. Gagarin, *La Russie,* v–vi.

19. Aspects of the Orthodox rite that would be preserved were communion under two species, use of leavened bread, the Slavonic liturgy, and married clergy. Ibid., 18.

20. Ibid., 17.

21. Ibid., 2–4. Gagarin would continue to write about the "authenticity" of the Russian church and to note that in the Orthodox church there were "no errors properly called . . . only mistakes and gaps." Still, he argued, "that does not remove [the fact] that the Russian church and the Catholic church are two distinct churches, two different churches; and we say in the Creed that we believe in one sole church. It is certain there is only the true one of Jesus Christ; that it is that church to which one must belong to be saved [except in cases of good faith]." For Gagarin, if an Orthodox individual believed that he or she was a member of the true church of Christ, one committed that error in good faith and could be saved. However, once an Orthodox believer had doubts as to the Orthodox faith, he or she was obliged to identify the true church of Christ and belong to it. See letter of Gagarin to Countess Apponyi, no date, cited in Giot, "Gagarin," 354.

22. Gagarin, *La Russie,* 16–17.

23. Ibid., 20. Gagarin further defined his notion of Catholic in a speech on 27 January 1860, in which he stated, "At the equator, up to the poles, in the old world, in the new, among the peoples who march at the head of civilization, amongst the huts of the savages, everywhere you find the cross, the priest, the altar; everywhere the same faith, the same teachings, the same law, the same duties; everywhere you find the Catholic church." Gagarin, *De la réunion,* 12.

24. Gagarin, *La Russie,* 22–23.

25. Ibid., 23, 26.

26. Gagarin, *De la reunion,* 11.

27. Gagarin, *La Russie,* 19.

28. The earliest use of this term found was in a letter of Gagarin to Martynov, 9 July 1855, BS, 70-2-B.

29. Gagarin, *La Russie,* 29–33. Just as *byzantinisme* had led to the ruin of the Byzantine Empire, so would Nicholaevan ideology lead to the ruin of the Russian Empire. Gagarin would later attack what he called the "phantom" of the Nicholaevan tripartite formula of Orthodoxy, Autocracy, and Nationality which threatened the elimination of all national, ethnic, or religious differences in order to obtain complete uniformity. Ibid., 70–71. It thus violated Gagarin's definition of Catholicity, national diversity within the unity of belief. Russian historian, Pavel Miliukov, also claimed the connection between the relationship between church and state in Byzantium as "one of the most characteristic traits of Russian church history." Pavel Miliukov, *Outlines of Russian Culture—Part I: Religion and the Church* (New York: A. S. Barnes, 1960), 17.

30. Here Gagarin was referring to his earlier genealogical work and studies of marriages among the nobility of Rus' which demonstrated that until the fifteenth century Orthodox Russians and Roman Catholics married without a change in religion.

31. Gagarin, *La Russie,* 33–36.

32. The first signs of *byzantinisme* would have been schism between Rome and Moscow. As long as marriages between Orthodox and Roman Catholics occurred in Russia, Gagarin argued, Russia and Rome were in ecclesiastical union. Therefore, sometime in the fifteenth or sixteenth century schism arose in Russia, though Gagarin does not give a particular date. Schism itself did not mean ecclesiastical subjugation to the government. For Gagarin, the Russian church, though in schism, retained its ecclesiastical independence until the mid-seventeenth or early eighteenth century. Thus, Gagarin would argue that the seeds of *byzantinisme* were planted in the fifteenth century and produced the Holy Synod in the eighteenth century.

33. Gagarin, *La Russie,* 36–38.

34. Ibid., 19.

35. A letter of Evgenii Ivanovich Popov to A. I. Tolstoi of 18 December 1856 indicated that Gagarin was interested in Palmer's views on *La Russie.* See "K istorii snoshenii s inovertsami," *Russkii arkhiv* 32 (1894): 8.

36. Febronianism was created by Bishop Johann Nikolaus von Hontheim under the pseudonym Justinus Febronius. Febronianism was founded on the principles of Gallicanism and desired to facilitate reconciliation with Protestantism by diminishing the power of the Holy See. It argued that the power of the keys of Peter was entrusted to the entire church; that papal authority was unifying, rather than coercive; that the pope was subject to general councils. Febronianism was condemned by Pope Clement XIII on 27 February 1764.

37. Gagarin, *La Russie,* vii.

38. Ibid., 54.

39. Ibid., 50–51.

40. Ibid., 44–46.

41. Ibid., 75.

42. Ibid., 43.

43. Ibid., 63. Here Gagarin put forth ideas originally proposed by de Maistre and the Jesuits in Russia during the Suppression. He is also trying to refute the assertions of Tiutchev that Roman Catholicism was the source of revolution.

44. Ibid., 66–67.

45. Ibid., 69–70.

46. Gagarin had earlier made this link between violence and revolutionary activity while in Munich.

47. Several of the Slavophiles such as Ivan Kireevskii, Konstantin Sergeevich Aksakov, and Iu. F. Samarin had been influenced by Hegelianism early in their intellectual careers. However, all had come to reject the ideas of Hegel as evidence of the schism present in Western thought. Gagarin here is not calling the Slavophiles Hegelians, but rather is referring to the similarity between the Slavophiles and Herzen, who was also deeply influenced by Hegelian thought. Like the Slavophiles, Herzen believed that Orthodoxy was more faithful to the teachings of the early church than was Roman Catholicism and that, thanks to Orthodoxy, the Russian people had preserved the commune—the highest social-economic structure. Also, like the Panslavists, Herzen voiced desires to see Nicholas I wage war against Turkey in order to conquer Constantinople, which in turn would become the center of a great Greco-Slavic Empire. It is important to note, as Walicki does, that the similarity presented here did not exclude important differences between Herzen's views and those of the Slavophiles/Panslavists. Herzen would later reject the chauvinism of the Slavophiles, whereas the Slavophiles would reject Herzen's emphasis on a populist revolution by the peasants. See Walicki, *The Slavophile Controversy: History of a Conservative Utopia in Nineteenth-Century Russian Thought* (Notre Dame: University of Notre Dame Press, 1989), 587–588. Nicholas I also perceived an antigovernmental ideology among the Slavophiles/Panslavists, especially after Iurii Samarin's attacks on the Baltic Germans and his call for their russification.

48. In an earlier letter on 4 January 1848, Gagarin wrote to his provincial," There is one other observation that much affects me: this is the extraordinary resemblance between the doctrines of [Vincenzo] Gioberti on Italy, on its unity and political independence and the doctrines of the Panslavists on the unity and independence of the Slavs. Catholicism in the hands of Gioberti plays the same role for Italy that the schism in the hands of the Panslavists does for the Slavic nationality. In particular, there is the same tendency to exalt the personality of ethnicity, to

attribute to it, as it forms a national distinctiveness, the inviolable rights to unity and political independence; the same doctrine is found in all the movements which seek German unity, Scandinavian unity, and Swiss unity; but there is something particular to Italian unity and Slavic unity, this is the apotheosis of their nationalities within their religion." AFCJ, Gagarin Fond. In a letter to Haxthausen dated 7 January 1861, Gagarin wrote, "No one knows better than you the dangers which Panslavism presents to the world. The anti-Christian and antisocial doctrines which triumph today in Italy have begun to penetrate the Slavic peoples and among them this evil has only begun." Gagarin, cited in Raymond T. McNally, "Two Catholic Slavophiles? Ivan S. Gagarin and August von Haxthausen in search of church reconciliation (1857–1860)," *Canadian-American Slavic Studies*, 34, 3 (Fall 2000): 303.

49. Gagarin, *La Russie*, 72–75.

50. See McNally, "Two Catholic Slavophiles," 304.

51. Gagarin, *La Russie*, 78.

52. Ibid., 81, 84–85.

53. Gagarin to Balabin, 4 August 1856, cited in Giot, "Gagarin," 252. Note again here Gagarin's desire to conceal his own beliefs in the validity of Roman Catholicism as the one true church behind a greater openness to the Russian Orthodox.

54. With specific regards to Gagarin's use of the term *byzantinisme*, Tandonet has argued that his definition demeaned the competence of the Byzantine government and reflected Gagarin's sense of Russian national superiority over the Greeks. Congar argued that the term was intended by Gagarin to indicate the peculiar role of culture and politics in the development of Byzantine church-state relations. Roger Tandonet, "Le fondateur et l'union des églises," *Études* 291 (November 1956): 186–187. Congar, cited in Giot, "Gagarin," 230.

55. Fiorovich to Gagarin, 2 August 1856, BS, Bleu 4.

56. Ravignan to Gagarin, 13 July 1856, BS, 64–5.

57. Beckx to Gagarin, 14 October 1856, ARSI, Reg. Epist. ad. Prov. Franciae IV (1847–1857), 304.

58. Pecherin to Gagarin, 12 November 1858, cited in Pierling, *Le prince*, 152.

59. Svechina to Gagarin, 17 August 1856, cited in Journel, "Madame Swetchine," 322.

60. Shuvalov, *My Conversion*, 268. While Shuvalov thought that Gagarin's ideas were new and admirable, he did not see at that time any hope for their realization, though he hoped for such a possibility in the future. Like Ravignan he described the book as a tree "which shoots its roots into the heart of the Russian nation" and agreed that the book was too short. See letter of Shuvalov to Gagarin, 12 September 1856, cited in Pierling, *Le prince*, 204–206.

61. Letter of Newman to Gagarin dated 31 March 1857, cited in Tempest, "Ivan Gagarin: Diplomatist," 132–133.

62. The title of the Spanish translation was *Sera la Rusia Catholica?* The titles of the two German translations were *Wird Russlands Kirche das Papsthum anerkennen?* and *Wird Russland Katholisch Werden?*

63. Martynov to Brown, 27 July 1856. BS, 70-2-B. In a letter to Gagarin on the same day, Martynov also proposed distributing the text in Russia and Prague.

64. Martynov, Introduction, *O primirenii russkoi tserkvi s rimskoiu,* by Ivan Gagarin, S.J. (1859), i–ii.

65. Like Gagarin, Haxthausen believed that Russia had an important historical role to play and believed that the Slavs' missionary activity had "a greater chance of acceptance among the meditative and sensuous Asians than any other Christian rite." See August von Haxthausen, *Studies on the Interior of Russia, 1847–1852* (Chicago: University of Chicago Press, 1972), 301, 315–316.

66. From Haxthausen's introduction to *La Russie,* 39, copy found in BS, Bleu Clair 1. Haxthausen had received a copy of *La Russie* as a gift and saw his own ideas on the conversion of Russia expressed in Gagarin's book. See Martina Stoyanoff-Odoy, *Die Großfürstin Helene von Rußland und August Freiherr von Haxthausen—Zwei konservative Reformer im Zeitalter der russichen Bauernbefreiung* (Wiesbaden: Otto Harrassowitz, 1991), 88. Haxthausen had earlier contact with the daughter of Nicholas I, Olga von Württemburg. In 1852 and 1854, the two corresponded about the possibility of the reunion of churches. Haxthausen was extremely enthusiastic and believed that such a union was possible due to the general agreement on dogmas. Olga von Württemburg was much less enthusiastic and broke off correspondence, probably on the advice of her priest, I. Bazarov. Ibid., 89–90. The correspondence between Haxthausen and Bazarov on the union of churches can be found in I. Bazarov, "Po voprosy o soedinenii tserkvei vostochnoi i zapadnoi," *Chteniia v obshchestve liubiteli dukhovnago prosveshcheniia,* 9 (1887): 149–199.

67. Gagarin, cited in Giot, "Gagarin," 263.

68. Gagarin to Haxthausen, cited in ibid., 264–265. Martynov was not as enthusiastic as Gagarin regarding Haxthausen. He wrote, "he [Haxthausen] finds a little too easily concessions that he gives to the Russian church and the temporal power; and, pure Catholic that he is, seems inclined too much to the side of reconciliation and that is, possibly, not without detriment to theological and canonical principles." Martynov to Beckx, 1 November 1856, cited in ibid., 264.

69. Letter of Gagarin to Haxthausen, cited in ibid., "Two Catholic Slavophiles," 253.

70. Cited in ibid., 257, 259.

71. Haxthausen wanted to establish a journal like *Études* and wanted Gagarin to serve as editor, but Beckx forbade this, fearing that the journal would be too political. This, of course, was one of Beckx's concerns regarding *Études,* how to work toward the union of Russia and Rome without arousing the ire of the Russian government. See letter of Haxthausen to Gagarin, 22 August 1857,

and letter of Gagarin to Beckx, 18 April 1857, BS, 70-1-B. Also see Burnichon, *La Compagnie*, 139.

72. Haxthausen, cited in McNally, *Two Catholic Slavophiles*, 261.

73. Gagarin, cited in ibid., 264.

74. de Buck did not attend this meeting because he believed he would not contribute anything and had difficulty speaking German. See letter of de Buck to Gagarin, 13 May 1857, BS, 70-3-B.

75. Gagarin also wanted to connect the work of the *Petrusverein* with the indulgences granted for prayers to the Immaculate Conception. Gagarin to Beckx, 18 April 1857, BS, 70-1-B.

76. Antonelli was skeptical regarding the success of *Petrusverein.* Haxthausen told Gagarin that Antonelli had "a certain timidity in regard to the associate political questions. I believe, however, to have persuaded him that the Russian government, in its present position, should see as desirable the foundation of a German league of prayers for the union of the Russian church with Rome." Adrien Boudou, S. J., referred to Haxthausen's comment as a "good example of the blindness that an intelligent man can have who is possessed by a whim." Boudou asserted that Antonelli had good reasons for his skepticism due to the persecution of the Roman Catholic church in Russia. See Adrien Boudou, S. J., *Le Saint-Siège et la Russie—leurs relations diplomatiques au XIXe siècle: 1848-1883* (Editions Spes, 1923), 98-99.

77. Haxthausen had disapproved of the prayer in Gagarin's earlier work *Union de prières pour la Conversion de la Russie et l'extinction du Schisme chez les peuples Slaves.* He believed that one could no longer call for the "conversion" of Russia or the "extinction of the schism"—such talk was outmoded. See his letter to Gagarin dated 30 April 1857 in McNally, "Two Catholic Slavophiles," 265.

78. Earlier in 1854, in Bourges, the *Appel à tous les membres de l'Archconfrére de l'Immaculée Conception de Bourges* called for prayers for the conversion of Greek schismatics and Russians. It had 15,000 members.

79. Union of Prayers for the Reunion of the Orthodox church with the Catholic church, 1 September 1858, BS, 70-1-B. Gagarin deeply believed in the power of prayer to obtain union: "Without prayer all our efforts would be in vain; man plants, he waters, but it is God alone who gives growth; it is by prayer that the blessings of God will be on our work." See Gagarin, *De la réunion*, 6-7.

80. Gagarin to Beckx, 18 April 1857, BS, 70-1-B.

81. Haxthausen believed that, due to the favorable reception of his book *Studies on the Interior of Russia*, it would be easy for him to obtain the support of the Romanov royal family. See 13 December 1857 letter of Haxthausen to Ignaz Döllinger, cited in Stoyanoff-Odoy, *Die Großfürstin*, 90.

82. Grand Duchess Elena Pavlovna (1807-1873) was the wife of Grand Duke Mikhail, sister-in-law of Nicholas I, and aunt of Alexander II. She had become acquainted with Haxthausen through the efforts of Baroness Editha von

Rahden, friend and advisor to the grand duchess, who, like Elena, had an interest in peasant reform. In 1857, Elena Pavlovna persuaded Alexander II to invite the Sisters of Charity into Russia. Gagarin believed that this indicated a favorable opinion by the grand duchess with regard to Roman Catholicism. He wrote that the invitation demonstrated "extremely remarkable proof of the high sentiments of the grand duchess" and that she "had a quite rare grandeur of spirit. She loved the good and the true for the sake of the good and the true." However, the grand duchess had sought the aid of the nuns due to her interest in medicine, not religion. See letter of Gagarin to Haxthausen, 3 July 1857, cited in Stoyanoff-Odoy, *Die Großfürstin,* 92. Gagarin believed that the Romanovs were interested in union, he wrote to Beckx, "I do not believe I am exaggerating in saying that the question of reunion is seriously studied and that many influential members of the imperial family are favorable to that idea." Letter of Gagarin to Beckx, 3 October 1857, cited in Angelo Tamborra, "August von Haxthausen e la Russia: Il Momento Religioso," *Cristianitá ed Europa,* vol. 1 (Rome, 1994), 805.

83. Elena Pavlovna had invited Haxthausen to this meeting to discuss agricultural reform, not the union of churches. Haxthausen merely used the meeting as an opportunity to seek the grand duchess's assistance. There is no indication that Kavelin, Tarnovskii, or Kisselev had Roman Catholic sympathies.

84. de Buck wrote to Gagarin that "He [Haxthausen] is completely enthusiastic about the *Petrusverein.* He has prophesied a magical effect on the spirit and the life of his compatriots . . . though my eyes see only the negative, Haxthausen sees marvelous hopes." Letter of de Buck to Gagarin, 22 September 1857, BS, 70-3-B. A letter of Gagarin to Beckx on 3 October 1857 noted that the grand duchess enjoyed the materials she received from Haxthausen. BS, 70-1-B.

85. Adulf van de Wal, A. A., "Une correspondance entre le baron von Haxthausen et André Mouravieff," *Istina* 3–4 (1972): 471.

86. Pierling, *Le prince,* 160. Gagarin and Haxthausen were also encouraged at what they believed were the existence of a group of Russian nobility favoring union and conditions in Russia which were forcing Russia to seek union. See McNally, "Two Catholic Slavophiles," 273 and 276.

87. Emphasis in original. Filaret, from *Dialogues entre un chercheur et un convaincu* (1815), cited in P. Harang, P. S. S., "Une Correspondance entre le baron de Haxthausen et Mouravieff," *Istina* 3 (1969): 352. In 1833, Filaret had said, "Mark you, I do not presume to call false any church believing that Jesus is the Christ." Filaret, cited in Georges Florovsky, *Ecumenism I: A Doctrinal Approach,* Collected Works of Georges Florovsky, XIII (Belmont, 1989), 44.

88. Gagarin sent the letter in French because he thought it might be threatening to Filaret if the letter were in Russian. See McNally, "Two Catholic Slavophiles," 280.

89. Haxthausen wrote Gagarin on 22 August 1857 that "From now on, I will, it seems, be of influence in this matter, and it is important that I preserve their

[the Romanovs'] trust due to the important matters of union and because you have a bad name in Russia." Haxthausen to Gagarin, cited in Stoyanoff-Odoy, *Die Großfürstin,* 87.

90. Letter of Haxthausen/Gagarin to Filaret, 1859, cited in Pierling, *Le prince,* 160. The words of the prayer that Haxthausen/Gagarin wanted were, "Let us pray to the Savior for peace in the world, the prosperity of the holy churches of God, and the union of all. Grant that our lips and our hearts in one union may celebrate and glorify your glorious and magnificent name, Father, Son, and Holy Spirit, now and forever. Amen." This prayer taken from the Liturgy of St. John Chrysostom had also been the epigraph of an anonymous Russian work published in Berlin under the title *The possible reunion of the Russian Church with the Western Church without changing the rite of Orthodox custom.*

91. Pierling, *La prince,* 162.

92. In his response to Haxthausen, Murav'ev claimed that he had to respond because the laws of Russia did not permit a bishop to correspond with a foreigner who did not represent an ecclesiastical authority. Letter of Murav'ev to Haxthausen, 6 June 1859, cited in Harang, "Correspondance," 351.

93. Murav'ev, cited in Harang, *"Correspondance,"* 351–352.

94. See letter of Gagarin to Haxthausen, 16 August 1859, in McNally, "Two Catholic Slavophiles," 285.

95. Letter of Haxthausen/de Buck to Murav'ev, 1859, cited in Harang, "Correspondance," 355–356.

96. Haxthausen/de Buck, cited in ibid., 359.

97. Haxthausen/de Buck, cited in ibid., 367.

98. Letter of Murav'ev to Haxthausen, 15 April 1860, cited in Van de Wal, "Correspondance," 476.

99. Haxthausen to Murav'ev, 1860, cited in ibid., 478.

100. Ibid., 472. Apparently, Filaret had provided Tolstoi with copies of Murav'ev's and Haxthausen's letters along with a favorable letter of his own. Tolstoi had visited the grand duchess, who had been able to draw Tolstoi to her side.

101. Letter of Editha von Rahden to Haxthausen, 15 October 1858. Apparently, Elena Pavlovna was afraid that the Russian police were reading her correspondence. Stoyanoff-Odoy, *Die Großfürstin,* 95.

102. Ibid., 95.

103. de Buck to Gagarin, 20 July 1858, BS, 70-3-B.

104. Gagarin, *De la réunion,* 7.

105. A French edition of the brochure appeared in October 1862 in *La bulletin de l'Oeuvre des Écoles d'Orient* and in *Le Messager du Sacre Coeur de Jesus* in February 1863. A German edition appeared in April 1863.

106. A copy of this brief: *Brief of His Holiness Pius IX in Favor of the Association of Prayers through the Triumph of the Immaculate Blessed Virgin by the Con-*

version of the Eastern Schismatics and Especially the Russians to the Catholic Faith, dated 2 December 1862, can be found in BS, 70-2-C.

107. Vladimir P. (Untitled article on the Association of Prayers), *L'Union chrètienne* (19 July 1863): 302–303.

108. Gagarin and Daniel, Préface, *Études de théologie, de philosophie et d'histoire* 1 (1857): i–ii.

109. Publication of *Études* spanned from its foundation in 1857 to the present day with only three interruptions: between August 1870 and September 1871, following the capitulation of Sedan; an eight-year suppression from 1880 to 1888, following the promulgation of the decrees of Jules Ferry; and a period between 1940 and 1944 due to the Second World War.

110. The articles by Gagarin were "De l'enseignement de la théologie dans l'Église russe" and "Un document inédit sur l'expulsion des Jésuites de Moscou en 1689." Martynov also wrote some articles discussing the Slavs,"Le manuscrit de Rayrad " and "Fragments glagolitiques du IXe siècle."

111. Gagarin, "De l'enseignement de la théologie dans l'Église russe," *Études de théologie, de philosophie et d'histoire* 1 (1857): 2–3.

112. Ibid., 4–5.

113. Ibid., 1.

114. Ibid., 3.

115. Ibid., 10. St. Gregory Palamas (d. 1360) was a monk at the Orthodox monastery of Mount Athos and, from 1349, bishop of Thessalonica. He was a staunch defender of the doctrine of hesychasm practiced at Mount Athos and believed that the human body was sanctified through the sacraments and participated in prayer through the senses. St. Gregory was deeply hostile to Roman Catholicism and wrote over sixty works in defense of hesychasm. Hesychasm was a practice of monastic asceticism attained through earthly detachment and prayer designed to see the "uncreated light" of God, which was the same light which appeared at Christ's Transfiguration. Hesychasts believed that while no one could see God's essence, they could see the uncreated energy of God's action. It was uncreated in the sense that it was eternal. In contemplating the uncreated light, the monk would become united with God so completely as to become absorbed in him. The roots of hesychasm came from the platonic idea that God transcends all things, he is completely unknown. All one can know is his action. Hesychasts compared this idea to the sun and its rays. The rays were distinct from the sun, but there was only one sun. Opponents accused hesychasts of pantheism since they accepted nature's absorption into God. They also argued, usually borrowing from Aquinas, that there was no distinction in God between his essence and attributes. Roman Catholic Aristotelian philosophy argued that God was simple; he was pure act and, therefore, without distinctions. Any distinct uncreated light that was not the essence of God would be neither God nor a creature—or there

would be two Gods, an essence and an energy. Opponents also accused St. Gregory of blasphemy due to his assertion that he could see the light of God. Only a few in the West, such as Gilbertus Porretanus (d. 1154) and John of Verennes (c. 1396), had theological ideas similar to those of hesychasm.

116. Ibid., 14, 32.

117. Ibid., 38–40.

118. Ibid., 38. Gagarin said that Peter had an opportunity to authentically promote reunion between Rome and Russia, "but his Protestant entourage and especially his passions posed an unbreakable resistance to the accomplishment of this vast plan." See Gagarin, "Bibliographie—Monuments historiques relatifs aux règnes d'Alexis Michaelowitch, Feodor III et Pierre le Grand, czars de Russie," *Études de théologie, de philosophie et d'histoire* 4 (1860): 293.

119. Gagarin, "De l'enseignement," 41. Gagarin probably included this in deference to Polish hostility to *La Russie*. Although we do see elements of Adam Mickiewicz's views that Poland would achieve national greatness as a result of her subjugation, just as Christ achieved glory through his suffering and death.

120. Florovsky, *Ways*, 1, 126.

121. Gagarin, "Les Starovères, l'Église russe et le pape," *Études de théologie, de philosophie et d'histoire* 1 (1857): 4.

122. Ibid., 9.

123. Ibid., 9. Gagarin saw this as synonymous with his own arguments that the differences between Roman Catholicism and Russian Orthodox were equally "external" and the solution was the same—union entailing the preservation of Russian rites and the liturgy in exchange for recognition of the authority of the pope.

124. Makarii, cited in ibid., 18.

125. Ibid., 20.

126. Ibid., 21.

127. Ibid., 22. In 1847, a former Greek Orthodox bishop, Ambrosios of Sarajevo, embraced the Old Belief and consecrated two bishops for those Old Believers who remained loyal to the priesthood and the sacraments. These consecrations were not recognized as valid by the Orthodox Church.

128. Ibid., 23.

129. Ibid., 24–27.

130. Gagarin asserted, ". . . if it is not a divine institution, how to explain the existence of the papacy after eighteen centuries?" Ibid., 80.

131. Ibid., 30–31.

132. Here Gagarin cited Moghila's *Confession de la foi orthodoxe:* "The bishops, in the churches over which they preside, are well called the heads of these churches, but one must understand this reference in the sense that they are vicars of Jesus Christ each in his province and that they are private heads, whereas Jesus Christ himself is the prince of pastors." Ibid., 37.

133. Evidence that Gagarin used, for example, was the assertion of Saint John Damascene that "You [Peter] have received from the hands of Christ a church which has not been built by men, but by the Savior himself." Ibid., 48, and the letter of St. Theodore Studite to Saint Leo III, "O blessed Father, a public council has been held among us, with the participation of the magistrates—a council for condemning the Gospel of Christ of which you have the keys, having received them from Jesus Christ himself through the prince of the apostles and his successors, so that you have precedence, most saintly head." Ibid., 58.

134. Ibid., 66.

135. Ibid., 73. Gagarin later argued that if papal primacy had been a temporary concession, it would have best been discarded at the time of the Apostles, each of whom "received an abundance of light and grace." Their successors, the bishops, did not receive these gifts to such a degree. Thus, "if the Apostles had need of a guide, of a head, of a supreme pastor, this need should be yet even greater in this later time—the more the church expanded, the more it was necessary to attach all these members to the center of unity." Gagarin, *De la réunion,* 14.

136. Gagarin, "Les Starovères," 74. Gagarin argued that the existence of these phrases in Russian liturgical texts was further proof that the Russian church was joined to Rome when its liturgy was formed and, though Russia had separated from the Catholic church, it had preserved the texts previously used for prayer. Gagarin, "Bibliographie—Études sur la question religieuse de Russie," *Études religieuses, historiques et littéraires* 11 (1867): 602.

137. One Old Believer asserted that Peter the Great had borrowed the Russian imperial double eagle "from the impious satanic Roman pope." Another Old Believer argued that the Old Belief opposed the Russian government spiritually, not temporally. That is, the Old Believers did not support an insurrection, rather they wanted to maintain the official Russian Orthodox church in order to prevent freedom of religion for non-Orthodox. See Paul Call, *Vasily L. Kelsiev: An Encounter between the Russian Revolutionaries and the Old Believers* (Belmont: Nordland, 1979), 49, 99–100.

138. Father Bazarov was a Russian Orthodox priest and chaplain to the Russian consulate in Stüttgart. He and Haxthausen had exchanged letters on church unity in 1861.

139. The Russian church had set ages for marriages at nineteen for males and sixteen years for females, the Greek church at fourteen and twelve years.

140. Gagarin, "Publications russes sur le mariage," *Études de théologie, de philosophie et d'histoire* 2 (1858): 481.

141. Sebastian Laurentie, *L'Union* (7 January 1859): 1.

142. Beckx to Gagarin, 3 December 1858, cited in Giot, "Gagarin," 189.

143. Gagarin to Beckx, 15 November 1858, cited in ibid., 188–189. Gagarin's works would continue to have an important place in the goals of the Russian Jesuits. See letter of Balabin to Martynov, 17 April 1857, BS, 70-2-B.

Chapter Five. Signs of Failure: I

1. Gagarin, cited in, Giot, ibid., 120.

2. In this note I want to provide a list of hostile texts in various published or archival sources. I do not intend this list to be complete but to give some sign of the tremendous response generated by Gagarin's *La Russie sera-t-elle catholique?*

FRENCH SECULAR HOSTILITY

1. Article by Emile de la Bédolliere in *Siècle*. 23 July 1856.
2. Editorial by Eugene Izalguier in *Revue de Paris* (1856): 95–107.

POLISH NATIONALIST HOSTILITY

1. *Czaz* article in 1856.
2. *Przeglad Poznańskii* article in 1857.
3. Debate between Gagarin and *Przeglad Poznańskii* in pages of *l'Univers* in 1857.

GREEK ORTHODOX HOSTILITY

1. Stephanos Karatheodores, *Epikrisis ton peri enoseos Logon tou Ièsouitou Gagarin*. Published in French as *Orthodoxie et Papisme—Examen de l'ouvrage du Père Gagarin sur la réunion des Églises catholique grecque et catholique romaine par un grec membre de l'Église d'orient* (Paris, 1859).

RUSSIAN ORTHODOX HOSTILITY

1. Petr Artamov, *Iezuity krasnogo petukha nam pustili ili razvratitsia li Rossiia v latinskii katolitsizm? Sposviashchaetsia iezuitam Gagarinu i Martynovu Petrom Artamovym, viazemskim muzhchikom*, Nizhnii Novgorod, 23 September 1860. This document is found in GPB, f. 1000 sobr. otd. post. op. 2. n. 3. Note that one of Vasil'ev's letters indicates that this text was, in fact, written by Orthodox French Count de Laffite. See letter of Vasil'ev, 15/27 January 1859, *Parizhskiia pis'ma protoiereia Iosifa Vasil'evicha Vasil'eva k Ober-Prokuroram Sviateishago Sinoda i drugim litsam s 1846 po 1867 gg.* (Petrograd, 1915), 182–187. Gagarin also makes reference to "a threatening pamphlet" by a Laffite de Pelleporc. See letter of Gagarin to Beckx, 12 October 1860, BS, 70-1-C.
2. S. Baranovskii, *Otvet mirianina na knigu: "Stanet li Rossiia katolicheskoiu?"* (Berlin, 1859).
3. Ioann K. Iakhontov wrote ten "Letters to an Apostate of Orthodoxy" in *Dukhovnaia beseda* from 1858 to 1860. Published as *Pis'ma k otstupniku pravoslaviia* (1864).

4. *Kriticheskii razbor sochineniia g. Gagarina, chlena obshchestva Iezuitov—'La Russie sera-t-elle catholique,' to est' budet li tserkovnoe edinenie mezhdu russkoiu tserkoviu i rimskokatolicheskoiu?* 1859. This document is found in RGIA, f. 1161, op. 1, d. 410, archives of K. S. Serbinovich.
5. A. S. Khomiakov, "Encore quelques mots par un chrétien Orthodoxe sur les confessions occidentales a l'occasion de plusieurs publications religieuses, Latines et Protestantes," 1858. Republished in *L'Église latine et le Protestantisme au point de vue de l'Église d'Orient* (Hants, Gregg International, 1960).
6. *La Russie est-elle schismatique? Aux hommes de bonne foi.* Paris, 1859.
7. A. N. Murav'ev, letter to Balabin, 20 October 1856, published in *L'Union chrétienne.* Reprinted as "Letter to a Roman Neophyte" in *Voices from the East,* ed. Neale (London, 1859): 165–171.
8. Youssov, Response to *La Russie,* published in *L'Union chrétienne* (1859–1860): 93–96, 107–112.

See also the letter of Metropolitan Filaret to A. N. Murav'ev, 30 January 1857, published in *Pis'ma Mitropolita Moskovskago Filareta k A.N.M . . . 1832–1867* (Kiev, 1869), 503–504, and "O knigakh na kotorikh otstupniki ot pravoslavnoi tserkvi ostnovivaiut svoi nepravil'niia misli," *Pravoslavnyi sobesiednik* II (1855): 47–69.

3. Izalguier, editorial, 96.

4. Ibid., 100–102. Izalguier was a French socialist. The *Revue de Paris* was an eclectic and liberal paper. Its left-leaning sympathies led to its suppression from 1858 to 1864.

5. Gagarin, "Les partisans et les adversaires de l'union," *Études de théologie, de philosophie et d'histoire* 3 (1859): 58.

6. The hostility of Polish revolutionaries to Jesuits should also be mentioned. A letter of L. Oborskii signed by the Central Revolutionary Authority stated, "We know the republican principles, your sincere love of equality, of fraternity, your zeal and your good intentions for the liberation of Poland from the yoke of tyranny and that of the nobility and the Jesuits." Letter dated 3 June 1859 found in GARF, f. 109, 1 eksp., 1859, d. 87, op. 34 S zagranichnymi svedeniiami l. 104.

7. See Victor de Buck, S. J., "La Russie sera-t-elle catholique?" *Précis historiques* (1856): 544–545. See also letter from Gagarin, 22 August 1856, found in BS, 70-3-B and Pavel Pierling's article on Gagarin in *Russkii biograficheskii slovar',* 70–71.

8. *Czaz* cited by Martynov in a letter to Beckx in ARSI, Franciae 8–VII, 11.

9. de Buck wrote to Gagarin that "It [*Przeglad Poznański*] accuses you of too much politeness vis-à-vis the schismatic clergy and in particular of not calling them *schismatic.* They say that you do not have the courage to employ this epithet in a book which could fall under the eyes of your dear parents, of your childhood friends." Letter of de Buck to Gagarin, 9 January 1857, BS 70-3-B. Emphasis in original.

10. Response of *Revue de Posen* [*Przeglad Poznańskii*], in *L'Univers* (20 April 1857): 2.

11. *Przeglad Poznańskii* (29 May 1857): 1.

12. *Przeglad Poznańskii* (20 April 1857): 2. Some Poles denied that there had been any violence used to Latinize the Ruthenians. See letter of Martynov to Beckx, ARSI, Franciae 8-VII, 11.

13. *Przeglad Poznańskii* (29 May 1857): 1.

14. In a letter to Haxthausen dated 20 January 1857, Gagarin wrote that "I am not a partisan of polemic between Catholics, but I am determined to publish my response after many attacks." He noted that he had been attacked by at least four Polish journals. See McNally, "Two Catholic Slavophiles," 257.

15. Gagarin, in *L'Univers* (28 April 1857): 1.

16. Ibid. (20 January 1857): 2

17. Gagarin to Beckx, 18 April 1857, ARSI, Franciae 8-VII, 10

18. Gagarin, in *L'Univers* (20 January 1857): 2. In a letter to Haxthausen dated 26 February 1857, Gagarin noted that the editor of *Przeglad Poznańskii* had caused an uproar by asserting that the Jesuits had always been more favorable to the Latin rite and its superiority over the Greek rite. In Gagarin's view, it was the opinion of the pope and not certain Jesuits that mattered. He also asserted that the Poles wanted to turn a political question into a religious one in order to garner more support. McNally, "Two Catholic Slavophiles," 259.

19. Beckx to Gagarin, 30 April 1857, BS, 70-1-C.

20. Gagarin, "Les partisans," 56.

21. Giot, "Gagarin," 273.

22. Guettée to Gagarin, in *Lettres au Révérend Pére Gagarin de la Compagnie de Jésus touchant l'Église catholique orthodoxe & l'Église romaine ou défense de* La Papauté schismatique *contre les calomnies et les erreurs du parti jésuitique caché sous le pseudonyme de Boulgak* (Paris, 1867,) 88.

23. Khomiakov, "Encore quelques mots," 212. I wish to note that in the text of *Kriticheskii razbor sochineniii* every place where the author had written *Catholic* with respect to the Roman Catholic church, it had been crossed out and either completely removed or replaced with *Latin* or *Roman.*

24. Baranovskii, *Otvet,* 9.

25. Khomiakov, "Encore," 205.

26. Karatheodores, *Orthodoxie,* 77.

27. Baranovskii, *Otvet,* 5.

28. Karatheodores, *Orthodoxie,* 37-38, 56-57.

29. Murav'ev, "Letter," 169.

30. Khomiakov, "Encore," 206.

31. Murav'ev, "Letter," 166-167.

32. Samarin, *Iezuity,* 288.

33. Tolstoi, "Le Jésuites et la liberté est-ce la même chose?" *L'Union chrétienne* (12 January 1861): 87–88. Tolstoi erred by comparing a condemnation of liberalism in a text written by the Jesuit Father Brzorowski during the Suppression with Gagarin's call for liberty in Russia. The liberalism which Brzorowski condemned would be equally condemned by Gagarin due to its revolutionary links. Gagarin's call was for freedom of religion, not a weakening of the monarchic principle.

34. Baranovskii, *Otvet*, 16.

35. Youssov, "Response," 94.

36. Artamov, *Iezuity*, 3.

37. Youssov, "Response," 93. Note also the comment of Sergei Petrovich Suchkov: "When we speak of Father Gagarin, one understands that it is not his personality which we consider or debate. The Jesuit Father is only a *word*, it is the Company of Jesuits [with which] we have trouble, that is to say, those who personify most highly ultramontanism. Father Gagarin has offered his name to his superiors, he is only a passive instrument." Suchkov, "Les textes des Péres de l'Église tronqués ou dénaturés par le R. P. Gagarin," *L'Union chrétienne* (1859–1860): 268.

38. O., "Les Jésuites russes," *L'Union chrétienne* (1866): 373. Karatheodores called Gagarin "formerly Russian and Orthodox" and a "turncoat to his national religion." Karatheodores, 1. Guettée called Gagarin and the other Russian Jesuits, "a sect of pseudo-Russians who have left Orthodoxy for papism." See Jean Paul Besse, *Un précurseur Wladimir Guettée du Gallicanisme à l'Orthodoxie* (Lavardac, 1992), 126.

39. Youssov, "Response," 107. Emphasis in original.

40. Tolstoi, cited by Gagarin in "Tendances catholiques," 308. Even Abbé Guettée, the French convert, argued that Svechina left Orthodoxy because she did not understand the true meanings of "unity" and "universality" and that she had obviously read bad translations or texts about Orthodoxy. Guettée, "Réflexions à propos du sermon prononcé en faveur de l'asile de Madame Swetchine," *L'Union chrétienne* (1862): 218–219. Guettée blamed the conversion of Prince Avgust Golitsyn on the fact that "his mother entered at an age when he was not yet capable of understanding the importance of the act imposed on him." Guettée, *Lettres*, iii.

41. Khomiakov, "Encore," 221. Herzen wrote that Khomiakov could not truly understand Gagarin's motivations for conversion. Herzen's diary entry for 21 September 1844 stated, "Khomiakov came across as insolent and audacious as far as his [Gagarin's] incredible intention to return here to preach as a Catholic pastor, a naturalized Frenchman. 'Well, if he is convinced purely and nobly that Catholicism is the one door to salvation. . . .' 'How can he repudiate the fatherland?' Not [for repudiating] the fatherland, but for his salvation from hard labor, he took up the appearance of a Frenchman. This he [Khomiakov] could

not understand." A. I. Herzen, *A. I. Gertsen—sobranie sochinenii,* vol. 2, 389–390. Baranovskii wrote that Gagarin and Martynov converted because they did not know any Christian writings. Baranovskii, *Otvet,* 14. Peter A. Kropotkin (1842–1921) noted in his memoirs that Orthodox Russia considered Gagarin's entry into the Jesuits to be a "great embarrassment." Petr Kropotkin, *Zapiski revoliutionera* (Moscow, 1933), 25.

42. This idea also fit well with the Slavophile idea that the Russian gentry, with its passions for Western ideas, had separated itself from the truly Orthodox nature of Russia.

43. The Orthodox critics could point to the case of Dzhunkovskii as an example.

44. Youssov, "Response," 96.

45. Korol'ev, in a letter to *L'Union chrétienne* dated 18/30 December 1859, *L'Union chrétienne* (1859–1860): 87.

46. Anonymous, *La Russie est-elle schismatique? Aux hommes de bonne foi par un Russe orthodoxe* (Paris, 1859), 46, cited in J. G. A. M. Remmers, "La Reunion des Églises," 46.

47. Murav'ev, "Letter," 165–166.

48. Khomiakov, "Encore," 206.

49. Churchman, "Revue littéraires," *L'Union chrétienne* (1865): 288.

50. Karatheodores, *Orthodoxie,* 28.

51. Baranovskii saw an indication of this in the fact that while the title of the Russian translation of Gagarin's text included the word *primirenie* (union), the French text did not. For Baranovskii, this demonstrated that Gagarin only wanted Russia to be in agreement with the pope, not that he wanted a mutual reunion. Baranovskii, *Otvet,* 27.

52. Guettée, letter to Gagarin published in *L'Union chrétienne* (1859–1860): 245.

53. Khomiakov, "Encore," 217–218.

54. Karatheodores, *Orthodoxie,* 94–95.

55. Baranovskii, *Otvet,* 44. Remember Murav'ev's response to Haxthausen that the French clergy were equally oppressed by the French government.

56. Khomiakov, "Encore," 211–212.

57. Ibid., 213–214. The Orthodox believed this due to what they saw were previous attempts by Rome to Latinize the Byzantine Catholics. Karatheodores pointed to 1720 in Zamosh where "certain decrees altered or destroyed many rites established from high antiquity, with the approval of Benedict XIII. Youssov asserted that Latinization took place under John XIII in Bohemia, Poland, and Dalmatia. Karatheodores, *Orthodoxie,* 70. Youssov, "Response," 109.

58. Ibid., 111.

59. Actually, Napoleon crowned himself, but in the pope's presence.

60. Letter of Filaret to Murav'ev, 30 January 1857, *Pis'ma Mitropolita*, 503–504. Emphasis in original. In his text, Karatheodores also made reference to the revolutions in the Hapsburg Empire and noted that the Austrian emperor had to call for the aid of the Orthodox sovereign of Russia, Nicholas I, to suppress the forces of revolution. Baranovskii referred to revolutionary activity in Poland. Karatheodores, *Orthodoxie*, 3–5; Baranovskii; *Otvet*, 31.

61. Baranovskii, *Otvet*, 30, 36.

62. Note Khomiakov's 12 September 1856 letter to Hilferding, which says "I also want to mention the nasty book of Gagarin: *La Russie sera-t-elle catholique?* The entire goal of this rotten thing is to tell our government *that the Orthodox and Panslavist movement in Moscow is revolution disguised under an Eastern form, a form quite well conceived, much more powerful and elastic than all those which have been invented in the West.* The Jesuits are such scoundrels!" Found in "Pis'ma A.S. Khomiakova k Gilferdingu," *Russkii arkhiv* 16 (1878): 383–385. Emphasis in original.

63. Samarin, *Iezuity*, 281–282.

64. Christoff, *Iu. F. Samarin*, 337.

65. Karatheodores, *Orthodoxie*, 52.

66. Ibid., 78.

67. Youssov, "Response," 108.

68. Suchkov, "Encore quelques mots sur le sermon du P. Gagarin, Jésuite, sur l'union des Églises orientale et occidentale," *L'Union chrétienne* (1859–1860): 134. Guettée supported this position by arguing that the liturgical texts and prayers for administering the sacraments were of a doctrinal character, but hymns, prayers, or legends of the saints were not. Guettée, *Lettres*, 14.

69. See Suchkov, cited in Gagarin, "La Primauté de Saint Pierre et les livres liturgiques de l'Église russe," *Études religieuses, historiques et littéraires* 2 (1863): 526.

70. Suchkov, "Encore," 135.

71. Suchkov, "Les textes," 269–272,

72. Suchkov, "Observations préliminaires en réponse au R.P. Gagarin," *L'Union chrétienne* (1859–1860): 253, 255.

73. Suchkov, "Les textes," 267, 304.

74. Guettée, letter to Gagarin, 244.

75. Iosif Vasil'ev, "Vénération rendu à pétre Pierre dans les Églises orthodoxe et romain," *L'Union chrétienne* (17 July 1864): 292.

76. Vzgliad Russkikh raskolnikov na rimskuiu tserkov'," *Pravoslavnyi sobesednik* (1860): 297, 301, 303, 304.

77. Suchkov, "Examen de l'argument que les ultramontains prétendent trouver dans la liturgie russe en faveur de leur système papal," *L'Union chrétienne* (1861–1862): 172.

78. Guettée, "Réflexions," 217.

79. Gagarin, "Bibliographie—Histoire de la séparation des Églises d'orient et d'occident depuis ses premiers commencements jusqu'a nos jours; nouvelles études sur la séparation des Églises d'orient et d'occident; à mes critiques," *Études religieuses, historiques et littéraires* 7 (May 1865): 116.

80. Letter of Gagarin to Beckx dated 12 October 1860, BS, 70-1-C. See also Gagarin, "Bibliography—Histoire," 116. It is also important to remember that one of Murav'ev's texts had been partially responsible for Gagarin's conversion.

81. Gagarin, "Les partisans," 58–59. See also archival document entitled "Orthodox Texts," 1859?, BS, Bleu Claire 4.

82. Gagarin, *L'Église russe et l'Immaculée Conception* (Paris: Plon, 1876), 57–58.

83. Gagarin, "Bibliographie—Histoire," 115.

84. Ibid., 115. B. Shultze's views on this issue are in accord with those of Gagarin. Shultze argued that it was not the intention of the Eastern patriarchs to speak of the magisterium, but of the temptation of certain hierarchs to introduce new doctrines. See Shultze, cited in Giot, "Gagarin," 291.

85. Gagarin, *L'Église russe et l'Immaculée Conception,* 58–59. The Holy Synod, occupied by church leaders who, like Gagarin, were hostile to Khomiakov's destruction of the hierarchical principle of the church, prohibited publication of Khomiakov's texts until 1879 and even then prefaced the texts with the statement that the "vagueness and want of precision of certain expressions are due to their author's lack of specific theological training." This preface was repeated up to the 1900 edition of Khomiakov's works. As late as 1916, Russian Orthodox theologian Pavel Florenskii called Khomiakov's Orthodoxy "a perfected, improved Protestantism," questioned Khomiakov's political loyalty, and suggested that Khomiakov supported the idea of popular sovereignty. Andrzej Walicki asserted that Florenskii probably represented the opinion of a large section of Russia's higher clergy. See Walicki, *Slavophile,* 199–200. Russian thinker Konstantin Leontiev also argued that Khomiakov held Protestant ideas. Despite all of this, it should be noted that Khomiakov's ideas had a profound effect upon Orthodoxy and that Khomiakov's text *The Church Is One* is now considered by the Russian Orthodox church as one of the best expressions of Orthodoxy.

86. Gagarin, *L' Église russe,* 63.

87. Gagarin, *Réponse d'un Russe à un Russe* (Paris: Belin, 1860), 17, 63, 70.

88. See Gagarin, "La primauté," 528–542.

89. Ibid., 538.

90. Patriarch of Constantinople, cited in Gagarin, *Réponse,* 71. Emphasis in original.

91. Gagarin, "Les Partisans," 87–88.

92. Gagarin, "Tendances catholiques," 306.

Chapter Six. Signs of Failure: II

1. Karatheodores, *Orthodoxie,* 54–55.

2. See Ivan Kireevskii, cited in Christoff, *I. V. Kireevskij,* 375. Kireevskii believed that the presence of Roman Catholics, Protestants, Jews, Moslems, and pagans could not change the Orthodox character of Russia. It should be further noted that the Slavophiles and the Russian government had different conceptions of Orthodoxy. The Russian government saw Orthodoxy as manifested by the official state religion. The Slavophiles saw Orthodoxy as manifested by the peasantry and the ideas of communality.

3. Gagarin, "Pis'mo otsa," 185–186.

4. Perhaps that is why Aksakov affected peasant dress in the early 1850s.

5. It should be added, though, that the official government understanding of autocracy as unquestioned absolute authority was different from the Slavophile notion of autocracy as making the tsar the servant of the people.

6. Christoff argues that Slavophilism, in its most rudimentary form, rested upon Khomiakov's notion of *sobornost'.* Christoff, *K.S. Aksakov, An Introduction to Nineteenth-Century Slavophilism,* vol. 3 (Princeton: Princeton University Press, 1982), 426.

7. See *Russian Philosophy,* ed. Edie, Scanlan, Zeldin, Kline, vol. I (Knoxville: University of Tennessee, 1987), 216.

8. Gagarin, *De la réunion,* 11–12. Emphasis is mine.

9. Ibid., 11–12.

10. Khomiakov, "Lettre au rédacteur de *l'Union chrétienne* à l'occasion d'un discours du Pére Gagarine, Jésuite," 1860, published in *L'Église latine et le Protestantisme au point de vue de l'Église d'Orient* (Hants: Gregg International, 1960), 394–395. Emphasis in original.

11. Ibid., 394–395.

12. Ibid., 393, 397.

13. Ibid., 398. Emphasis in original.

14. Andrzej Walicki has noted that Khomiakov was probably influenced in this idea by the Roman Catholic romantic theologian J. A. Möhler, who contrasted the Protestants who represented "multiplicity without unity" with the Catholic principle of "unity in multiplicity," which permitted individuality in a communal society. Walicki, *Slavophile,* 192.

15. Letter of Ivan Aksakov to Gagarin dated 12/24 December 1874, published in Shur, "I. S. Gagarin—izdatel' F. I . Tiutcheva," 223–224.

16. Guettée, "Considérations générales sur le but que se reposent les fondateurs de *L'Union chrétienne,*" *L'Union chrétienne* (1859–1860): 2. Emphasis in original. See also Suchkov, "Encore" 134, and Baranovskii, *Otvet,* 3–4.

17. Suchkov, "Encore," 134.

18. Ibid.

19. Suchkov, "Observations," 252.

20. Ibid., 251. Note again the reference to the supposed ignorance of Gagarin.

21. Guettée, Letter to Gagarin, 245. Emphasis in original.

22. Gagarin, *Réponse,* 20.

23. Ibid., 17.

24. Ibid.

25. Letter of Pecherin to Gagarin, 9 June 1860, RGALI, f. 372, op. 1, d. 10 Pecherin Archive.

26. References to the need to keep from changing doctrines were less definitions of the term *catholic* than references to the ideas of *apostolic,* that is, how faithful the doctrines of the present-day church were to those espoused by the apostles. Furthermore, Gagarin had already addressed the error of this idea in his article "Les starovères, l'Église russe et le pape," in which he presented the problems of postulating immobility as an aspect of the church.

27. See Christoff, *K.S. Aksakov,* 143, 157.

28. Gagarin himself, in a February 1842 letter to Samarin, wrote, "Both churches equally believe and confess one holy, catholic [*sobornaia*] and apostolic church." See "Arkhiv slavianskoi biblioteki," *Simvol* 1: 171.

29. See Walicki, *Slavophile,* 249.

30. Letter of Sergei Aksakov on 10 August 1849, cited in Christoff, *K.S. Aksakov,* 143.

31. Letter of Khomiakov to Palmer, 1850, *Russia and the English,* 95–96.

32. Letter of Ivan Aksakov, 21 November 1859, cited in Christoff, *K.S. Aksakov,* 262.

33. It should be noted that Gagarin did not consider *La Russie* a denunciation of Samarin or the other Slavophiles. Rather, he considered the text an opportunity for Russia to embark on a new era under Alexander II. Gagarin called Samarin "very malicious, very unjust, very rash, but very conscientious." See Gagarin, "Pis'mo otsa," 183.

34. Ibid., 185.

35. Ibid.

36. Gagarin tended to rely on the writings of Bishop Makarii for support of his accusations that the Slavophiles did not represent the Orthodox church. For their part, the Slavophiles did not believe that Makarii's views were representative of Orthodoxy.

37. Letter of Father Nikolai to Gagarin, 10 December 1872, cited in Pierling, *Le prince,* 175. Father Nikolai converted on 20 June 1858 and was ordained on 21 March 1874.

38. Christoff, *Iu. F. Samarin,* 307.

39. Gagarin, "Les partisans," 59.

40. Letter of Khomiakov to Palmer, *Russia and the English Church,* 28.

41. Martynov to Beckx, 1 November 1856, ARSI, Franciae 8–VII, 8.

42. See letter of Beckx to Gagarin, 27 August 1860, BS, 70-1-C. *The Spiritual Exercises* were very important in the life of the Jesuits. They were directed toward the improvement of one's life and personal sanctification.

43. Gagarin to Beckx, 12 October 1860, BS, 70-1-C.

44. Beckx to Gagarin, 27 August 1860 and 27 October 1860, BS, 70-1-C.

45. Churchman, "Revue littéraires," 278.

46. "Nouvelle insinuation jésuitique," *L'Union chrétienne* (16 December 1860): 54–55.

47. See letter of Russian Ministry of Internal Affairs to the Third Section dated 23 June 1858, GARF, f. 109, 1 eksp., 1852, d. 346, ll. 247–248. See also V. I. Kel'siev, "'Ispoved' V. I. Kel'sieva," *Literaturnoe nasledstvo* 41–42 (1941): 292. It is probable that Dzhunkovskii and Gagarin believed that their calls for religious freedom and independence for the church would find support among the persecuted Old Believers.

48. Gagarin, Notes on first three years of Oeuvre de SS. Cyrille et Méthode, BS, 70-1-C.

49. Ibid.

50. Ibid.

51. Letter of Gagarin to Beckx, 4 November 1856, BS, 70-1-B.

52. Letter of Anne Apponyi to Gagarin, 26 February 1858, cited in Giot, "Gagarin," 351.

53. Beckx to Gagarin, 28 February 1857, BS, 70-1-C.

54. Letter from Ia. N. Tolstoi, 11/23 December 1852, GARF, f. 109, 1 eksp., 1852, d. 346, ll. 5–12, l. 70b. Emphasis is mine. Note that Tolstoi included Pecherin among the list of Russian Jesuits. Pecherin was, in fact, a Redemptorist priest. A letter of N. Sergievskii to Filaret also erroneously referred to Shuvalov and N. Trubetskoi as Jesuits. RGIA, f. 832, n. 1, d. 54, O katolicheskikh missionerskikh seminariiakh v Parizhe 1859–1860 gg., Letter 1, 1/13 April 1859.

55. Letter of Vasil'ev to Tolstoi, 16/28 June 1860, *Parizhskiia pis'ma,* 217–220.

56. Letters of Filaret to Murav'ev, 30 January 1857 and 13 February 1857, *Pis'ma Mitropolita,* 503–506. Emphasis in original.

57. Letter of Murav'ev to Filaret, January 1857, RGIA, f. 832, n. 1, d. 83, letter #23, O knigakh, broshurakh i stat'iakh, priznannykh vrednymi, l. 1. See also the text of P. N. Batiushkov, "O Latinskoi propagande na zapade Rossii," in which he voiced concern over Jesuit propaganda in Posen and Galicia. GPB, f. 52, n. 29. Archives of Pompei Nikolaevich Batiushkov.

58. V. F. Odoevskii, "O merakh protiv zagranichnoi russkoi pechati," *Russkii arhkiv* (1874): 34. In his diary entry for 27 July 1864, he commented on the prohibition of Martinov's work on Meletii Smotritskii and wondered if it would be thus impossible to answer that "sly and cunning filth." See Odoevskii, "Tekushchaia

khronika i osobie proishestviia. Dnevnik V. F. Odoevskogo 1859–1869gg.," *Literaturnoe nasledstvo,* 22–24 (1935): 182.

59. Gregory Freeze, "A Critical Perspective on the Russian Clergy and Church in the Nineteenth Century," Introduction, *The Russian Clergy,* by Ivan Gagarin, S. J. (Newton: Oriental Research Partners, 1976), 2.

60. Letter of Vasil'ev to Tolstoi, 15/27 January 1859, *Parizhskiia pis'ma,* 182–187.

61. See his letter to Haxthausen dated 24 October 1860, cited in McNally, "Two Catholic Slavophiles," 300.

62. See *Svobodnyi katalog Russkoi nelegal'noi i zapreshchennoi pechati XIX veka A-S,* Moscow, 1871, for reference to *O primirenii russkoi tserkvi s rimskoiu* and Gagarin's letter to Iurii Samarin. See *Alfavitnyi katalog socheniniiam na frantsuzkom, nemetskom, i angliiskom iazykakh zapreshchennym inostrannoiu tsenzuroiu ili dozvolennym k obrashcheniiu s iskliucheniem nekotorykh mest s 1856 po 1 iulia 1869 goda,* St. Petersburg, 1870, for reference to the banning of several other of Gagarin's texts including articles from *Études,* "Tendances catholiques dans la société russe" and *Réponse d'un Russe á un Russe.*

63. See for example the letter of Vasil'ev on 17/29 June 1859 which referred to Gagarin's travel to Jerusalem and the letters of 16/28 June 1860 and 21 September/3 October 1860 which referred to Orthodox criticism of Gagarin. *Parizhskiia pis'ma,* 217–220, 232–236, 251–252. Note that the activities of Gagarin and the other Russian Jesuits were also watched by the Russian Third Section. Vasil'ev himself fell under governmental suspicion when the secret police witnessed a meeting between him and Balabin. Vasil'ev said that he was trying to reconvert Balabin. See RGIA, f. 1151, op. 4, d. 139, 1853, l. 11ob, 14. Grazhdanskago departmenta o kollezhskom sovetnike Evgenie Balabine.

64. See letter of Murav'ev to Filaret, January 1857, RGIA, f. 832, n. 1, d. 83, letter #23. Also see letter of Filaret to Murav'ev, 13 February 1857, *Pis'ma Mitropolita.* Filaret was concerned that attacks on the Jesuits "might be a service to the Jesuits" by divulging their numbers and strength.

65. Odoevskii, "Tekushchaia," 37–38.

66. Letter of Vasil'ev, 15/27 January 1859, *Parizhskiia pis'ma.* Note, however, that Vasil'ev also said that "writings in Russian against Orthodoxy are more dangerous [than writings in French against Roman Catholicism]."

67. See letter of Ministry of Internal Affairs to the Ober-Procurator of the Holy Synod, 22 January 1858, and letter of Holy Synod to Karatheodores on 12 October 1859 in RGIA, f. 797, op. 28, d. 279, I otdeleniia II stola, Ob obiavlenii ot Sviateishago Sinoda blagoslovenii Grecheskomu professoru Marokorbato i sochiniteliu knigy soderzhashchei v sebe opravdanie frantsuzkoi broshury "La Russie sera-t-elle catholique?" 23 January 1858–12 October 1859. Vasil'ev was responsible for translating Karatheodores' text into French. See letter of Vasil'ev 25 September/6 October 1858, *Parizhskiia pis'ma,* 179–180.

68. Guettée, "Considérations générales," 1.

69. Letter of Gagarin to Alexander II, November 1856, ARSI, Franciae 8–VII, 8.

70. Gagarin, Franciae 8–VIII, 8.

71. Giot, "Gagarin," 274.

72. Letter of Vasilii Dolgorukov to Sergei Ivanovich Gagarin, 13 December 1856, GARF, f. 109, 1 eksp., 1852, d. 346, l. 218 ob.

73. Letter of Sergei Gagarin to Dolgorukov, 26 December 1856, GARF, f. 109, 1 exped., 1852, d. 346, l. 221 ob.

74. Letter of Ministry of Internal Affairs to Third Section, GARF, f. 109, 1 exped., 1852, d. 346, l. 226.

75. See letter of Gagarin to Beckx, 18 April 1857, ARSI, Franciae 8–VII, 10.

76. Letter of Filaret to Murav'ev, 30 January 1857, *Pis'ma Mitropolita*, 503–504. P. A. Viazemskii thought that Filaret's reaction was completely out of proportion to Gagarin's threat to Orthodoxy and wrote, "How important can one person be? What could Gagarin do in coming to Russia? Surely his coming could not threaten Orthodoxy and our steadfast church?" Cited in "Iz zametok kniaz'ia P. A. Viazemskago," *Russkii arkhiv* 39 (1901): 254.

77. See letter of Gagarin to Beckx, 18 April 1857, ARSI, Franciae 8–VII, 10. Note that public opinion was not entirely wrong on this matter. While Gagarin did truly wish to see his father, the prospect of conversion was never far from his mind.

78. Letter of S. I. Gagarin to V. A. Dolgorukov, 9 January 1857, GARF, f. 109, 1 eksp., 1852, d. 346, l. 228–229.

79. GARF, f. 109, 1 eksp., 1852, d. 346, l. 231.

80. Letter of Beckx to Gagarin, 28 February 1857, BS, 70-1-C.

81. Letter of Gagarin to Beckx, 18 April 1857, BS, 70-1-C.

82. Beckx to Gagarin, 12 August 1857, BS, 70-1-C.

Chapter Seven. Byzantine Catholics and the Middle East

1. Gagarin, "L'Avenir de l'Église grecque-unie," *Études religieuses, historiques et littéraires* 6 (1862): 195–196.

2. Journel, "L'Oeuvre," 621–622.

3. Fessard, cited in Giot, "Gagarin," 190.

4. Letter of Beckx to Gagarin, 7 January 1860, cited in ibid., 190–191.

5. Gagarin, cited in ibid., 193. Note again Gagarin's emphasis on his primary role in the conversion of Russia and the relegation of even other Russian Jesuits to a secondary responsibility.

6. Letter of Beckx to Gagarin, BS, 70-1-C.

7. Letter of Gagarin to Beckx, 12 October 1860, BS, 70-1-C.

8. Beckx, cited in Giot, "Gagarin," 193.

9. See letter of Beckx to Gagarin, 21 December 1860, BS, 70-1-C.

10. See letter of Mertian to Gagarin, 25 January 1861, BS, Bleu 14.

11. Ibid.

12. Gagarin was also concerned that his residence at Strasbourg would limit his ability to guide the direction of *Études*. Letter of Gagarin to Mertian, cited in Giot, "Gagarin," 192–193, and Journel, "L'Oeuvre," 622.

13. Ibid.

14. Gagarin, cited in Giot, "Gagarin," 310.

15. Ibid.

16. See Gagarin, "Trois mois en Orient," *Études de théologie, de philosophie et d'histoire* 3 (1859): 539. Furthermore, Gagarin also believed that one could not truly appreciate a pilgrimage to the Holy Land without having a copy of the Bible at hand. See Gagarin, "Bibliographie—Les saints lieux; Revue théologique de Tubingue," *Études de théologie, de philosophie et d'histoire* 3 (1859): 148.

17. Giot, "Gagarin," 310.

18. Gagarin wrote this article at the request of Father François Guilherny, who told him, "I hope also that your trip will not be without benefit for the religion of the Orient and to our [Jesuit] missions in Syria. Can you not gather some documents for a serious publication?" Guilherny also told Gagarin that he could have access to materials in the Jesuit archives on the subject of the Middle East. See letter of Guilherny to Gagarin, 3 October 1859, BS, Bleu 14.

19. Gagarin believed that without Catholic support of the Byzantine Catholic church in the Middle East, particularly in terms of promoting an indigenous clergy and indigenous schools, that Russia would support these things to the detriment of the Byzantine rite Catholics. Gagarin, "Les établissements russes in Terre-Sainte," *L'Ami de la religion* 10 (1862): 512.

20. Gagarin, "Trois mois," 563. In another article, Gagarin argued that to ignore the situation in the Middle East would be to leave the Byzantine Catholic church to the Protestants. See Gagarin, "Bibliographie—Les saints lieux," 150.

21. Gagarin, "Trois mois," 543–544. Here Gagarin pointed to the activity of the Latin patriarch Guiseppe Valerga (1831–1872), who advocated the creation of an indigenous Arabic clergy. It should be noted that Valerga also encouraged the Latinization of Byzantine Catholics.

22. Ibid., 546–547. Gagarin argued that although the Maronites possessed the greatest numbers, he did not believe they could attract non-Christians. He further argued that the Latin rite was foreign to the Middle East. The rite of the Melchite and Byzantine rite churches not in union with Rome, "the great rite of the Orient, the most authoritative by its origin, the most considerable by its extent and its antiquity," would serve as the unifying rite of the Arabic-speaking peoples.

23. Gagarin's participation in the formation of this organization with Baron Cauchy and Lavigerie has already been mentioned. It should be remem-

bered that the purpose of this organization was to create local educational institutions and collect aid for Catholic work in the Middle East.

24. Ibid., 556, and BS, Jaune 3. The school at Beirut, founded in 1840–1841, was open to all regardless of nationality or belief. Students were taught French and Arabic.

25. Gagarin, "Trois mois," 562.

26. The Jesuits established the college/seminary at Gaza on 2 February 1846. It was initially exclusively ecclesiastic, but later admitted laity. In 1859, it had one hundred students, more than forty of whom were destined for the priesthood. The school was divided into three parts: seminarists, students from the upper classes of the laity, and the youngest students of both types. Teaching was divided into classical and professional studies. Classical studies were preceded by a preparatory course in the elementary elements of French, and later Latin, according to the methods of the European colleges. Greek was taught during the final four years, and a special course was designed for students of the Melchite rite. After the classical studies were completed, the students took courses in philosophy and the physical sciences. Finally, students took three years of dogmatic and moral theology, hermeneutics, canon law, and ecclesiastical history. As for those who took professional studies, they began with the preparatory course in Greek and Latin, followed by three classes on French, history, math, and geography. This was followed by courses in languages based on the desires of the parents. These languages included Arabic, French, Turkish, or Italian. Syrian, Greek, and Chaldean were taught to those who needed to know them according to their rite. Hebrew was also taught. See ibid., 564–565. Mgr. Luquet also wanted to establish in Jerusalem a school to educate students in scriptural and theological issues of the Eastern church and to create a seminary similar to those in Europe. This was to be part of the Société orientale pour l'union de tous les chrétiens d'Orient, mentioned previously. Luquet did not obtain approval from Rome for this school.

27. Gagarin, "Bibliographie—Les saints lieux," 148–149.

28. Gagarin, "Trois mois," 562.

29. Ibid.

30. Ibid., 545–546.

31. Valerga to Gagarin, 15 July 1860, BS, Verte 1.

32. Gagarin to Beckx, 13 October 1860, BS, Verte 1. Gagarin told Beckx that the l'Oeuvre des Écoles d'Orient would support Gagarin's activity.

33. A brief history of the Bulgarian church until 1860:

343. A council of bishops meets in Sardica (Sofia).

865. King Boris I is baptized by a Byzantine bishop.

1054 (approximately). After a period of conflict between Rome and Constantinople, Bulgaria opts to align itself with Constantinople.

1204. Bulgarian church recognizes supremacy of pope.

1235. Bulgarian emperor makes an alliance with the Greeks against the Latin Empire in Constantinople; in return the Byzantine patriarch recognizes a Bulgarian patriarchate.
1393. Bulgarian church integrated into patriarchate of Constantinople.
1860, Easter. Bulgarian churches cease to commemorate the Ecumenical Patriarch in the liturgy.
1860. Bulgarian church seeking independence from Constantinople and fearing political hellenization, sees union with Rome as a means of retrieving national ecclesiastical traditions.

34. Letter of Gagarin to Bishop Jean Baptiste Malou, no date, cited in Giot, "Gagarin," 322.

35. Gagarin, cited in McNally, "Two Catholic Slavophiles," 303.

36. Gagarin was not the only Russian Jesuit deeply encouraged by the act of the Bulgarians. See letter of Pierling to Martynov, 8 February 1861, BS, 70-2-B.

37. Letter of Beckx to Gagarin, 26 January 1861, BS, 70-1-C. Barnabo was a Latinizer.

38. Letter of Lavigerie to Beckx, cited in Burnichon, *La Compagnie,* 133.

39. Letter of Fessard to Gagarin, February 1861, cited in Giot, "Gagarin," 324. Here we see another sign of the poor relations between Fessard and Gagarin as well as Fessard's view that Gagarin should separate from the French Jesuits.

40. Gagarin, cited in Journel, "L'Oeuvre," 635. It is important that even though Sokolski had been ordained an archbishop, the Bulgarians desired their own patriarchate as a sign of greater ecclesiastical honor. However, the pope did not believe that the small number of Bulgarian Catholics warranted the establishment of a Bulgarian patriarchate, thus he permitted only an archbishopric. It is also important that the establishment of a Bulgarian patriarchate in the Catholic church would only require papal recognition, not that of the other Byzantine Catholic patriarchates.

41. See letters of Gagarin to Beckx, 2 May 1861 and 3 May 1861, BS, Bleu Clair 4.

42. See letters of Gagarin to Beckx, 2 May 1861 and 4 May 1861, BS, 70-1-B.

43. Letter of Beckx to Gagarin, 25 May 1861, ARSI, Reg. epist. ad Prov. Franciae V (1857–1869): 210. Barnabo did not share Gagarin's views on the Bulgarians. See Burnichon, *La Compagnie,* 141.

44. Letter of Gagarin to Beckx, 15 June 1861, BS, 70-1-B. Gagarin was seeking to celebrate the Byzantine liturgy in order to demonstrate the continuing authority of *Allatae sunt,* which guaranteed the preservation of the Byzantine rite. Gagarin saw this as a means of combating the problems of Latinization.

45. Gagarin, cited in Giot, "Gagarin," 326–327. Gagarin hoped to obtain the support of Napoleon III for his projects. See letter of Gagarin to Beckx, 15 June 1861, BS, 70-1-B.

46. Gagarin to Beckx, 26 June 1861, cited in Giot, "Gagarin," 327.

47. Letter of Balabin to Beckx, 16 June 1861, ARSI, Franciae 8–VII, 23.

48. Letter of Beckx to Balabin, 6 July 1861, ARSI, Reg. epist. ad Prov. Franciae V (1857–1869): 212.

49. Gagarin to Beckx, 14 July 1861, cited in Giot, "Gagarin," 328.

50. Gagarin to Beckx, 25 August 1861, cited in ibid., 329.

51. Beckx to Gagarin, 29 August 1861, cited in ibid., 197.

52. Gagarin to Beckx, 20 November 1861, BS, 70-1-B.

53. Gagarin to Beckx, 30 November 1861, cited in Giot, "Gagarin," 330–331.

54. Beckx to Gagarin, 14 December 1861, BS, 70-1-C.

55. Gagarin to Beckx, 21 December 1861, BS, Bleu Clair 4.

56. Father Andrei/Agapius Honcharenko (Onufrievich Gumnitskii) studied at the Kiev Academy and became a monk in 1856. He had been attached to the chapel of the Russian embassy in Athens from 1857 to 1859. From 1860 to 1861 he served as a typesetter for Herzen and took part in the publication of Herzen's *Kolokol.* In April 1862, Honcharenko went to the Middle East where he met Gagarin at the Jesuit school in Syria. Gagarin sought Honcharenko's help in teaching the Bulgarians. Despite rumors that Honcharenko had joined the Byzantine Catholic church, he remained Orthodox. Gagarin refers to Honcharenko in his article "Mélanges—une nouvelle tentative de réunion entre l'Église anglicane et l'Église orientale," in *Études religieuses, historiques et littéraires* 9 (1865): 87, as working for the reunion of the Anglican church and the Russian Orthodox church. Apparently, he celebrated a liturgy in one of the Episcopalian churches of New York. *L'Union chrétienne* said that Honcharenko's ordination by a Greek bishop was "irregular" and that he had not received any proper papers from the Russian church authorizing his activities. *Den'* said it was possible that Honcharenko received papers from the metropolitan of Athens. Strangely, Gagarin does not indicate having any relationship with Honcharenko, perhaps because he and Honcharenko did not part favorably. In 1862, Honcharenko participated in the Greek revolution. In 1864, he emigrated to the United States where he published the journals *Alaska Herald* (1868–1873) and *Svoboda* (1873). See *Russkie pisateli 1800-1917*, Moscow: Sovetskaia entsiklopediia, 1 (1989): 624. Honcharenko's autobiography is *Spomniki* (Edmonton: Slavuta, 1965). See also Kel'siev, "Ispoved'," 284.

57. Letter of Beckx to Gagarin, 1 February 1862, BS, 70-1-C.

58. Gagarin's text, "Sur l'utilité de l'adoption du rite Grec par quelques pères de la Compagnie," was written late in 1861 under the encouragement of Lavigerie and was referred to in Gagarin's 30 November 1861 letter to Beckx. The text of this document can be found in BS, Bleu Claire 4. Beckx called this an "excellent document." See letter of Beckx to Gagarin, 7 January 1862, ARSI, Franciae 5–V.

59. These statistics were gathered by Isidore Silbernag and cited by Gagarin in "Constitutions et Situation présent de toutes les Églises de l'orient," *Études*

religieuses, historiques, et littéraires 9 (1865). Gagarin divides the Byzantine Catholic church into five sections:

1. Russia: the Ruthenian church, which was "violently destroyed" by Nicholas I in 1839 though some priests survived.
2. Poland: diocese of Chelm, Ruthenian.
3. Austria: Ruthenian, with episcopal see at Lemberg.
   In Hungary, Latin archbishop of Gran.
   In Croatia, Latin archbishop of Agram.
   In Transylvania, Romanian or Moldovan Catholic bishops under the metropolitan of Fogaracs.
4. Turkey: Melchite church of Syria, ten dioceses linked to Latin patriarch of Antioch at Beirut, Bulgarian church.
5. Two Sicilies: Albanian and Greek Catholics.

60. Gagarin, "Sur l'utilité," 1.

61. Ibid., 1–2.

62. Ibid.

63. Gagarin, "L'Avenir," 189–190.

64. Ibid., 192–193. See also "Sur l'utilité," 4–5, in which Gagarin argues that the three million plus Byzantine Catholics would survive if they were united.

65. Gagarin, "L'Avenir," 192–193.

66. Gagarin, "Bibliographie," *Bulletin de l'Oeuvre des Pèlerinages* (1862): 119. See also Lavigerie's letter to Dupanloup, 21 May 1862, in which he said, "The greatest, I would say almost the sole obstacle to the mass conversion of the East, is the fear of Latinism." Lavigerie, cited in Renault, *Le cardinal,* 67.

67. Gagarin, "L'Avenir," 194.

68. Ibid.

69. Ibid., 193.

70. Gagarin, "Les Églises orientales unies," *Études religieuses, historiques et littéraires* 11 (1867): 702.

71. Ibid., 699–700.

72. Gagarin, "L'Avenir," 196–198.

73. Thomas de Jésus, also known as Diego Sanchez of Avila, was the author of the texts *De unione orientalium procuranda* and *Cursus theologie completus.* Thomas de Jésus received most of his ideas on the reformation of the Byzantine rite from the Basilian Iosef Velamin Rutskii. See Cyril Korolevsky, *Metropolitan Andrew (1865–1944),* trans. Keleher (L'vov, 1993), 363–364.

74. In a letter to Beckx on 1 November 1856, Martynov also called for the introduction of Jesuits to the Slavic rite in order to deal with the problems of the Ruthenians and with hostility toward Latin rite Catholics. ARSI, Franciae 8–VII, 8.

75. Gagarin, "L'Avenir," 199.

76. Gagarin, "Les Églises orientales unies," 705–706.

77. Ibid., 704.

78. Gagarin, "Sur l'utilité," 12.

79. Benedict XIV, cited by Gagarin in "Mémoire sur l'utilité," 13.

80. Gagarin, "Les Églises orientales unies," 711. Gagarin would later express the need for a general revision of the Slavonic version of the Bible and a purging of "all the Bulgarisms, all the Serbisms and all the Russisms, and to reestablish as much as possible the text in its primitive purity, while introducing some necessary corrections." Gagarin argued that studies of the Paleoslovene language were advanced enough to undertake revisions and that such revisions would support Roman Catholic teachings. See Gagarin, *Le texte* Tu es Petrus et super hanc petram *dans la version slavonne de la Bible* (Versailles, 1871), 5.

81. Gagarin, "L'Avenir," 204.

82. Gagarin, "Sur l'utilité," 8.

83. See letter of Lavigerie to Gagarin, 12 April 1862, cited in Giot, "Gagarin," 333. Lavigerie probably did not want to mention Gagarin's involvement because of the previously mentioned concerns in the Vatican regarding Gagarin's overeagerness on the issues of the Byzantine Catholic churches and his acerbic character.

84. Pius IX, "Amantissimus: Encyclical of Pope Pius IX on the Care of the Churches," 8 April 1862, *The Papal Encyclicals 1740–1878*, ed. Claudia Carlen, I. H. M. (Wilmington: McGrath, 1981), 363.

85. Ibid., 364.

86. Ibid., 365–366.

87. Gagarin, "Les Établissements russes en Terre-Sainte," *Bulletin de l'Oeuvre des Pélerinages* (1861): 289–290.

88. Ibid., 292.

89. Ibid. (1862): 51–52.

90. Guettée, "Les Églises orientales unies," *L'Union chrétienne* (1867–1868): 37.

91. Ieromonakh Iuvenalii, *Neskolko slov po povody stat'i—"Russkiia ucherezhdeniia v sviatoi zemle"* (St. Petersburg, 1861), 7.

92. Ibid., 3–5.

93. See letter of Beckx to Balabin, 23 August 1862, ARSI, Reg. epist. ad Prov. Franciae V (1857–1869). In this letter Beckx says, "It is without a doubt that he [Gagarin] should be held faithfully current of all that concerns the work of *St. Méthode*."

94. Letter of Gagarin to Beckx, 2 October 1862, BS, 70-1-B. While Gagarin's transfer to Gaza helped him to escape the conflicts over *Études*, it caused some problems for the other Russian Jesuits. Martynov wrote Beckx, "The absence of Father Gagarin has made our work difficult; we need three [Russian speakers] to edit Russian publications. Since Father Astromov has proved entirely incapable of helping us, we will be obliged either to publish without following the

Institute's regulations or to renounce Russian publications; at least it will be easy to locate the required censor in Gaza. Would it not be simpler to address us to Father Brown, who knows Russian sufficiently and on whose judgment we can more surely rely?" See letter of Martynov to Beckx, 1 September 1862, ARSI, Franciae 8–VII, 30.

95. Gagarin to Beckx, 2 October 1862, ARSI, Franciae 8–VII, 30.

96. Letter of Gagarin to M. I. Zhikharev, 21 February 1863, cited in L. Shur, "I. S. Gagarin—izdatel' 'Filosoficheskikh pisem'," 231.

97. See list of texts in BS, Bleu 4.

98. See Beckx's letter to Martynov dated 10 August 1861: "The Holy Father has confided in you the mission to refute the errors propagated by *L'Union catholique* [sic] by articles written in Russian. You can count on the particular assistance of Our Savior in a work that his Vicar has directly confided to you." Angelo Tamborra, "La riscoperta di Cirillo e Metodio nel secolo XIX e il suo significato," *Christianity Among the Slavs: The Heritage of Saints Cyril and Methodius. Orientalia Christianina Analecta,* 231, ed. Edward G. Farrugia, S. J., Robert F. Taft, S. J, Gino K. Piovesana, S. J. (Rome: Pont. Institutem Studiorum Orientalium): 333.

99. Gagarin, Martynov, Balabin, Introduction, *Kirillo-Mefodievskii sbornik'* (1863): 1–3.

100. Letter of Beckx to Gagarin, 20 August 1864, BS, 70-1-C.

101. Giot, "Gagarin," 330.

102. In 1872, Constantinople declared the Bulgarian church schismatic. In 1945, the Ecumenical Patriarchate recognized the autocephalous nature of the Bulgarian church and the schism was ended.

103. Christoff, *K.S. Aksakov,* 241. The Slavophile K. S. Aksakov argued that "In language we find the first degree of nationality." Aksakov, cited in ibid., 205.

104. Elinor Murray Despalatović, *Ljudevit Gaj and the Illyrian Movement* (New York: Columbia University Press, 1975), 45–47, 54.

105. This undated document was probably written in 1862 and is found in BS, Bleu Claire 4.

106. The Latino-Slav rite existed primarily in Dalmatia and included 80,000 people. The Latino-Slav rite used the Latin missal and breviary; however, the words were Slavic with Latin characters.

107. Gagarin, "Mélanges—L'Alphabet de Saint Cyrille," *Études religieuses, historiques et littéraires* 6 (1862).

108. Ibid., 109.

109. Ibid., 109–110.

110. Ibid.

111. Ibid., 111–112.

112. Ibid., 113–114.

113. Gagarin referred to scholarship which indicated that St. Cyril invented Glagolitic and that Cyrillic was a later simplification. "In effect, the Cyrillic alpha-

bet is only the Greek alphabet, enriched by some letters special to the Slavonic languages." See Gagarin, *Le texte,* 2.

114. Gagarin, "Mélanges," 114.

115. Letter of Gagarin to Beckx, 22 April 1867, BS, 70-1-C. Gagarin stressed that he was only speaking of the Eastern Slavs, not the Poles, Czechs, or Bohemians; that is, he was speaking of the Ukrainians and Belorussians.

116. Gagarin, BS, 70-1-C.

117. John F.N. Bradley, *Czech Nationalism in the Nineteenth Century* (New York: Columbia University Press, 1984), 86.

118. Letter of Strossmayer to Franjo Racki dated 23 June 1868, cited in Racki, *Korespondencija Rački=Strossmayer,* vol. 3, ed. Ferdo Šišić (Zagreb, 1929), 67.

Chapter Eight. The Vatican and the Russian Church

1. Gagarin to Bakhmetev, 15/27 December 1874, GPB, f. 326, n. 305, F.P. Kazanovich.

2. Hassoun, cited in Franco de Wyels, "Le concile du Vatican et l'union," *Irenikon* 6 (1929): 375.

3. Giot, "Gagarin," 198.

4. Gagarin, cited in ibid., 198. In late 1860, Gagarin had proposed a similar college for Byzantine Catholics and Orthodox in Belgium, France, or Paris. He planned for the college to be open to Moldavians, Greeks, Serbs, Bulgarians, Russians, or others of the Eastern rite. He had hoped to present this idea to the German bishops. See McNally, "Two Catholic Slavophiles," 300–301.

5. Martynov to Beckx, 12 November 1864, ARSI, Franciae 10–XXIII, 2. Gagarin's ideas for a Russian college continued. See his letter to Pierling on 7 October 1871 in which he proposed the creation of a Russian Catholic college in Russia. BS, 70-2-A. Gagarin also worked with a young Russian, Prince Ivan Mikhailovich Tumanov, who wished to enter the Jesuits. See letter of Beckx to Gagarin, 28 November 1865, BS, 70-1-C. It was not until 1921 that a boarding school for Russians under the patronage of Saint George would be opened by the Jesuit Louis Baille at Constantinople. This school would later move to Meudon, France, where it assumed the name Centre d'études russes. At Rome, Pius XI established the Russian college (Russicum) in 1929 and placed it under the control of the Jesuits.

6. Gagarin, "Mélanges—une nouvelle," 84.

7. Ibid., 86.

8. Ibid., 90.

9. Ibid., 88–89.

10. Gagarin, "L'Anglicanisme et le schisme grec," *Études religieuses, historiques et littéraires* 10 (1866): 256.

11. Gagarin to Beckx, 30 January 1866, ARSI, Franciae 10–XXIII, 4.

12. Gagarin, "Les missionaries catholiques en Géorgie," *Études religieuses, historiques et littéraires* 10 (1866): 225.

13. Ibid., 232.

14. Ibid., 233, 316.

15. Ibid., 330.

16. Ibid., 221.

17. Gagarin, "Société de Marie," no date, BS, Jaune 2.

18. Gagarin, BS, Jaune 2. Gagarin said that Armenian and Polish Catholics could not receive aid from the society.

19. Letter of Gagarin to Beckx, 27 March 1866, BS, 70-1-C. Gagarin's fears as to the direction of his journal would only increase as the journal acquired a more liberal complexion. During the period between 1864 and 1867, Father Matignan wrote a series of articles in *Études* entitled "The Teaching of the Society of Jesus on Liberty." Because these articles were very sympathetic to individual liberty, Matignan received severe criticism. On 9 October 1866, Beckx cautioned the French provincial, Armand de Ponlevoy, that the journal was taking on a liberal tinge and that any other articles on liberty or ideas condemned by Pius IX's Syllabus of Errors would have to be reviewed in Rome before publication. Two years later Pius IX referred to Matignan, "If he were present we would ask him if he means to accommodate the doctrines of the church to those of modern society. Some people would wish to modify the Syllabus. This cannot be. Truth will ever be truth, and there cannot be a conciliation between truth and error." Disfavor also fell on the staff of *Études* due to its suggestion that a dogmatic definition of papal infallibility would be inopportune at Vatican I. See William V. Bangert, S. J., *A History of the Society of Jesus* (St. Louis: Institute of Jesuit Sources, 1986), 457–458.

20. Carayon to Gagarin, 3 May 1866, BS, Bleu 14.

21. Carayon to Gagarin, 14 May 1866, BS, Bleu 14.

22. Gagarin to Beckx, 27 March 1866, BS, Bleu 14.

23. This occurred on 23 April 1866.

24. Giot, "Gagarin," 199–200.

25. Ponlevoy to Beckx, 13 May 1866, cited in ibid., 200.

26. Ponlevoy, cited in ibid., 201.

27. Beckx, cited in ibid., 201–202. Father Carayon was also supportive of Gagarin's suggestion to establish a Russian-language journal. He said "this would be the best means of making certain ideas cross the borders [of Russia] . . . and if these ideas cross, the people will follow later. This journal—would it not one day be the passport for the Jesuits to Russia?" Carayon, cited in Giot, ibid., 201.

28. See Gagarin, "Nasha tsel'," trans. L. Shur, *Simvol* 8 (1982): 247–251.

29. Gagarin document, no date, after 29 October 1866, BS, Verte 1.

30. Gagarin, BS, Verte 1. Gagarin's archives contained a copy of Alexander II's letter dated 25 March 1864, the twenty-fifth anniversary of the suppression of the

Byzantine Catholics. Alexander wrote, "In the hope that God the omnipotent will bless your efforts which hold to the peace of the Orthodox church and which should procure for Him *again reunion through the establishment of one sole Universal Church, which, it is understood will be the tutelary of the emperor of Russia.*" Emphasis in original. BS, Jaune 1. Gagarin condemned the creation in St. Petersburg of a Roman Catholic ecclesiastical college under government control which was to examine issues relating to the Roman Catholic church in Russia. On each issue the college would determine whether the views of the pope needed to be obtained. The college would also determine whether papal decisions violated the laws of the empire. Gagarin believed that this college was an attempt to place the Roman Catholic church under a Synod-like control and would therefore cause a schism between the Russian Catholic church and the Vatican. See BS, Noire 1. This college was created by an ukaz on 10 May 1867. See also the encyclical letter of Pius IX, *Levate,* in which he also condemned Russian persecution of Roman Catholics and the attempts to establish the Roman Catholic ecclesiastical college in St. Petersburg. The pope said the college violated the constitution of the Catholic church and subverted ecclesiastical discipline. Pius IX, "Levate," 27 October 1867, *The Papal Encyclicals 1740-1878,* ed. Claudia Carlen, I. H. M. (Wilmington: McGrath, 1981): 369-391.

31. Gagarin, undated document in BS, Verte 1 .

32. Ibid.

33. Ibid. In Gagarin's speech at l'Église de R. R. P. P. Barnabites in Paris in December 1867 he called prayer the strongest and almost only recourse available for promoting union. Gagarin, *Discours prononcé dans l'Église de R.R.P.P. Barnabites à Paris, le decembre 1867,* BS, CS-2-A. Also, Pius IX called for a three-day period of prayer for the persecuted Catholics in Russia. Pius IX, "Levate," 391.

34. Pius IX, "Levate," 391.

35. Gagarin had already begun to look at the conflicts between the Black and White clergy in late 1860. See McNally, "Two Catholic Slavophiles," 300.

36. Gregory L. Freeze, Introduction, *Description of the Clergy in Rural Russia,* by I. S. Belliustin, trans. Gregory L. Freeze (Ithaca: Cornell University Press, 1985), 44.

37. Balabin to Beckx, 9 November 1859, ARSI, Franciae 8-VII, 34.

38. Freeze, Introduction, 46.

39. See Balabin's letter in which he wrote, "Emperor Alexander has sent a copy to all the bishops of the empire. The emperor has asked for ecclesiastical reforms. However, he can at best make appointments, but cannot provide the sacerdotal and apostolic spirit." Balabin to Beckx, 9 November 1859, ARSI, Franciae 8-VII, 34. Also note Gagarin's comment, "The fact is that Belliustin—the priest author of the memoir (his name is perfectly known in Russia), found in Bazhanov, confessor of the tsarina, a protector more powerful than a Moscow professor." Gagarin, "Bibliographie—Tableau d'une Église nationale d'après un pope russe," *Études religieuses, historiques et littéraires* 6 (1862): 687.

40. Belliustin to Pogodin, 8 July 1858, cited in Gregory L. Freeze, *The Parish Clergy in Nineteenth-Century Russia: Crisis, Reform, Counter-Reform* (Princeton: Princeton University Press, 1983), 212.

41. Gagarin, *The Russian Clergy,* trans., Makepeace (New York: AMS Press, 1970): 1.

42. Ibid., 6. Gagarin's *La Réforme du clergé russe* did not mention two of the key ideas contained within *La Russie sera-t-elle catholique?*—the historic ties between Russia and the Vatican and the problem of *byzantinisme.* Still, these notions continued to be important parts of Gagarin's view of the Russian church. In 1865, for example, he wrote:

> The Russian Church, as the Roman church, celebrated the ninth of May as the feast of the translation of the relics of Saint Nicholas of Bari, a feast that the church of Constantinople does not recognize. Generally one sees in this proof that at the end of the sixteenth century, forty or fifty years after Michael Cerulairius, the fatal rupture was not consummated between the Russian Church and the Holy See. One sees a confirmation of this fact in the numerous matrimonial alliances contracted by the Russian princes and princesses about the same time with the royal houses of Poland, Hungary, Denmark, Sweden, and France, without there being any trace of mixed marriages or the change of religion.

In the same article, Gagarin also reiterated his position on *byzantinisme* as opposed to schism: "one was before the other, but it pushed the other forward, it contained the seed. *Byzantinisme* was permanent, it was a way of development, but the ruptures which were the result of it and which have existed for a long time, are temporary." Gagarin, "Bibliographie—Histoire," 117–119.

43. Gagarin, *The Russian Clergy,* 8.

44. Ibid., 23.

45. Ibid., 16–19. As he wrote in a different article, "Hence, in these last years, the clergy formed in Russia a true tribe of Levi, an hereditary cast; the sons of priests were attached to the service of others, as serfs were attached to the soil; they had inherited hereditary and obligatory vocations." Gagarin, "L'Église othodoxe en Russie," *Études religieuses, philosophiques, historiques et littéraires* 22 (1878): 104.

46. Gagarin, *The Russian Clergy,* 20. This problem also concerned the Russian government. Freeze noted that several seminarians were arrested in Perm for participating in revolutionary circles and that, by the end of the 1870s, many White clergy voiced revolutionary ideas and opposition to the tsar. See Freeze, *The Parish Clergy,* 237, 396.

47. Gagarin, *The Russian Clergy,* 26.

48. Ibid., 31.

49. Ibid., 13, 34–35.

50. Ibid., 42. In another article, Gagarin wrote, "I am a very great partisan of the Slavic liturgy; but it is well to observe that if Russia had a Greek or Latin liturgy, the clergy would never have become so profoundly ignorant, and the flame of knowledge, in the hand of the clergy, would now shine over the entire nation." Gagarin, "Chronique religieuse de l'orient," *Études religieuses, historiques et littéraires* 10 (1866): 524.

51. Gagarin, *The Russian Clergy* 46.

52. Ibid., 49.

53. Ibid., 54–59.

54. Ibid., 80.

55. Ibid., 68.

56. Ibid., 86.

57. Ibid., 94, 99.

58. Ibid., 69–70.

59. Ibid., 97.

60. Ibid., 97.

61. Ibid., 101–102, 108.

62. Gagarin, "Bibliographie—Histoire de la séparation," 115.

63. Holy Synod, cited by Gagarin, *The Russian Clergy*, 125–126. Emphasis in original. Interestingly enough, Belliustin exhibited some of this Protestantism in his own correspondence which declared that Lutheran clergy were far superior to both Catholic and Orthodox priests since, "At least they do not conspire to suppress the intellectual development of their flock, nor hoodwink mankind with the miracles of the Madonna, relics, and similar nonsense." Belliustin, cited in Freeze, *The Parish Clergy*, 394.

64. Gagarin, *The Russian Clergy*, 113.

65. Ibid., 114–116.

66. Ibid., 153.

67. Ibid., 15. Emphasis in original.

68. Ibid., 169. Gagarin noted that this canon was the thirty-first in the collection of Dionysius Exiguus and the twenty-ninth in the collections of Hardouin and Mansi.

69. Ibid., 171.

70. Ibid., 171, 228–273.

71. Gagarin argued that two obstacles prevented Russia from recognizing the truth of the Catholic church: the hereditary caste of the clergy and its dependence on civil authority. See his article in *L'Apostolat* (10 May 1868): 290.

72. Gagarin, "L'Impératrice Anne et les Catholiques en Russie," *Études religieuses, philosophiques, historiques et littéraires* 22 (1878): 665.

73. Gagarin, *The Russian Clergy*, 278.

74. See Gagarin's article in *L'Apostolat* (29 June 1866): 465.

75. Freeze, *The Parish Clergy,* 199–200.

76. Ibid., 241.

77. Batiushkov, cited in ibid., 227.

78. Tolstoi, cited in ibid., 300.

79. Ibid., 253.

80. Ibid., 312–313, 318.

81. Ibid., 356–357, 370.

82. Bishop of Vladimir, cited in ibid., 359.

83. In regard to Gagarin's text, Freeze argues that it suffers from "serious deficiencies" since Gagarin did not use Russian Orthodox seminary journals or diocesan weeklies that discussed the problems of church reform. Furthermore, Freeze argues that Gagarin's polemics in defense of Catholicism do not enrich our understanding of the Russian clergy but merely repeat well-known historical facts. However, Freeze also writes, "Gagarin's book is still valuable for its sketch of the church, clergy and seminaries on the eve of reform." See Freeze, "A Critical Perspective," 3.

84. Freeze, *The Parish Clergy,* 459.

85. Obolenskii to Gagarin, 24 December 1876, cited in ibid., 388.

86. Gagarin, *The Russian Clergy,* iii–iv. Gagarin also pointed to the continuing problem of nihilism.

87. Gagarin, "Les Archives russes et la conversion d'Alexander Ier empereur de Russie," *Études religieuses, philosophiques, historiques et littéraires* 21 (1877): 49–50.

88. Letter of Father Nikolai to Gagarin, 28 May 1872, cited in Pierling, *Le prince,* 174. Like Gagarin, Nikolai condemned the poor state of clerical education. He wrote, "I myself have been for many years in a public establishment, and I have observed Russia long enough to know that religious instruction which is given there is nonexistent, despite the so-called course of *Zakon Bozhii.* No one knows his catechism. . . . But what is the source of this evil? It lies in the state of abasement to which the clergy has been reduced." Nikolai to Gagarin, 20 August 1878, ibid., 180–181.

89. Gagarin, "Les Églises orientales unies," 699.

90. Ibid.

91. Ibid., 700.

92. Ibid., 700, 705, 707–708. In his encyclical *Omnem Sollicitudinem,* on 13 May 1874, Pius IX again voiced his desire that the Eastern liturgies be kept in "pristine condition," and that their sacred canons be retained. See Pope Pius IX, "Omnem Sollicitudinem," 13 May 1874, *The Papal Encyclicals 1740–1878,* ed. Claudia Carlen, I. H. M. (Wilmington: McGrath, 1981), 439–440.

93. A. Lopukhin, "Tserkovno-religioznaia zhizn' v Rossii po vzgliadu anglichainina," *Tserkovnyi vestnik* 10 (1879): 4.

94. "Knizhnye zagranichnye vesti," *Russkii arkhiv* I (1873): 119.

95. Guettée, "Lettres au R. P. Gagarin sur la réforme du clergé russe," *L'Union chrétienne* (1866–1867): 295. Guettée's irrational hatred of the Jesuits can be best demonstrated in his accusation that the Jesuits were involved in an assassination attempt against Alexander II in 1866 and that Alexander II's enemies included "a well-known aristocratic-clerical party, which is as one with the Society of Jesus," known for its "tyrannicidal" doctrine. Geoffrey Cubit, *The Jesuit Myth: Conspiracy Theory and Politics in Nineteenth-Century France* (Oxford: Clarendon Press, 1993), 198.

96. Guettée, "Lettres," 36, 62. In another article Guettée referred to Gagarin, Martynov, Balabin, and Pierling as "Jésuites pseudo-russes." See Guettée, *L'Union chrétienne* (1866–1867): 69.

97. Guettée, "Lettres au R. P. Gagarin," (1865–1866) 411, (1866–1867) 26, 35. Note the irony here. Gagarin could not write about the Russian clergy because, although he lived in Russia for over twenty-five years, he had never studied with them. On the other hand, Guettée, a recent convert to Orthodoxy who spent most of his life as a Roman Catholic priest in France, presumed to have the intellectual authority to answer Gagarin.

98. Ibid., 238.

99. Ibid., 2–3.

100. Ibid., 150.

101. Ibid., 27, 35, 61.

102. Ibid., 22, 76–77.

103. Ibid., 101, 175.

104. Ibid., 160.

105. Ibid., 90.

106. Ibid., 150–151.

107. Ibid., 43–44.

108. Ibid., 240. Emphasis in original.

109. Ibid., 293.

110. Ibid., 411.

111. Ibid., 295.

Chapter Nine. Ends and Beginnings

1. Gagarin, "Bibliographie—Ma conversion et ma vocation," *Études de théologie de philosophie et d'histoire* 1 (1859): 455.

2. Ponlevoy, cited in Giot, "Gagarin," 202.

3. Ibid., 202–203.

4. Beckx, cited in ibid., 203.

5. Gagarin, 25 February 1865, cited in ibid., 204.

6. Anonymous letter to Ponlevoy, no date, BS, Lettres 11.

7. Gagarin to Ponlevoy, no date, BS, Verte 9. See also Gagarin's letter to Father Brown which mentioned Brown's accusations that Gagarin's proposals were injurious to the Polish nobility. Gagarin to Brown, no date, BS, Bleu Claire 4.

8. Korczak-Branicki, *Nationalités slaves,* 48–49.

9. Ibid., 83–84.

10. Ibid., 71.

11. Faustus Socinus was the founder of Socinianism, a movement which denied the divinity of Jesus and the existence of the Trinity, and attempted to explain religion rationalistically. Athanase Coquerel the Younger was a follower of Renan, who questioned the reality of miracles, the supernatural, and the divinity of Jesus. William Channing was a Unitarian interested in promoting rational faith.

12. Korczak-Branicki, *Nationalités slaves,* 397–399.

13. Gagarin and Korczak-Branicki also disagreed on the possibility of a Slavic union and the future development of Russia.

14. Gagarin to Ponlevoy, 8 October 1869, cited in Giot, "Gagarin," 260.

15. Gagarin to Korczak-Branicki, no date, cited in Pierling, *Le prince,* 112.

16. Gagarin, cited in ibid., 112.

17. Gagarin, cited in ibid., 112–113.

18. Gagarin, cited in ibid., 114.

19. Gagarin, second letter to Korczak-Branicki, BS, 70-3-B.

20. Gagarin, "Mgr. Lubienski—Évêque d'Augustowo," *Le Correspondant* XLIII (1869). Gagarin, Introduction, *La question religieuse en Pologne,* by August von Haxthausen (Berlin: Behr, 1877).

21. Gagarin, *La question religieuse,* 11. Much of Miliutin's inspiration for his anti-Polish policy came from Gagarin's cousin, Iurii Samarin. In 1863, Samarin published an article entitled "The Present-Day Scope of the Polish Question," in which he accused Poland of historic aggressiveness and claimed it had been corrupted by "Polonism"—a cultural force closely linked to Catholicism whose representatives were the Polish gentry and clergy. Samarin claimed that "Polonism" had transformed Poland into a "sharp wedge driven by Latinism into the very heart of the Slavonic world with the aim of splitting it into fragments." He concluded that the Russian government should declare "uncompromising war" on "Polonism" in the name of "Slavism," because Poland's future lay within the Slavonic world, not in the Latin world. Walicki has argued that Samarin's views were responsible for Miliutin's policy of creating antagonism between the Polish gentry and peasantry and attempting to undermine Polish Catholicism. Samarin's views were also responsible for Miliutin's successful attempts to persuade Alexander II to annul Russia's concordat with the pope and were the theoretical basis for Prince Cherkasskii's idea of replacing Latin with the Cyrillic alphabet. See Walicki, *Slavophile,* 492–493.

22. Gagarin, *La question religieuse,* 15. Gagarin, "Mgr. Lubienski," 508.

23. Gagarin, "Mgr. Lubienski," 509.

24. Ibid.

25. Note that Gagarin is not quite correct here. Catherine II, Paul, and Alexander I supported Jesuit activity in Poland precisely because they believed that, as Catholic clergy, the Jesuits would be better able to restrain the Polish independence movement. The three autocrats saw a link between Catholicism and Polonism, only not the same link which Miliutin and Samarin perceived.

26. Gagarin, "Mgr. Lubienski," 510.

27. Ibid.

28. Ibid., 506.

29. Ibid., 510.

30. Ibid., 519, 521.

31. Gagarin, *La question religieuse* 17–18.

32. Ibid., 11.

33. Ibid., 12, 20–21.

34. Ibid., 14.

35. Ibid., 19.

36. Ibid., 5–6, 23.

37. I. S. Aksakov, cited by L. Shur, "Iz istorii polemiki I. S. Gagarina so slavianofilami v 60-x gg. XIX v.," *Simvol* 7 (1982): 178–179.

38. For further information on the prevalence of anti-Jesuitism throughout Europe at this time, see Cubitt's *The Jesuit Myth.* Samarin's biographer, B. E. Nol'de, called *Iezuity* the "weakest of all his writings." Nol'de, *Iurii Samarin i ego vremia* (Paris: YMCA Press, 1978), 191.

39. Samarin, *Iezuity,* 24.

40. Both Martynov and Gagarin had expressed a desire to write favorably about Kuncevich in 1864 and 1865. See Martynov to Beckx, 12 November 1864, ARSI, Franciae 10-XXIII, 2, and Gagarin to Beckx, 25 February 1864, ARSI, Franciae 10-XXIII, 3. For a brief Catholic presentation of Kuncevich, see Herbert Thurston, S. J., and Donald Attwater, "St. Josaphat," *Butler's Lives of the Saints—Complete Edition,* 4 (New York: P. J. Kenedy & Sons, 1956), 337–340. For a fuller treatment, see Demetrius E. Wysochansky, O. S. B. M., *Saint Josaphat Kuntsevych: Apostle of Church Unity* (Detroit: Basilian Fathers Publications, 1987).

41. Iurii Samarin, *Iezuity,* 284–285. The Orthodox perspective of Kuncevich does have merit; Norman Davies wrote, "Archbishop Kuncewicz was no man of peace, and had been involved in all manner of oppressions, including that most offensive of petty persecutions—the refusal to allow the Orthodox peasants to bury their dead in consecrated ground. His death was the subject of outrage in Rome, but of some relief in his own diocese." See Davies, *God's Playground: A History of Poland,* vol. I (New York: Columbia University Press, 1982), 174–175. Wysochansky, of course, denies Davies' claim here. Wysochansky, 213.

42. See selections from Russian press in BS, 64 3.

43. Franco de Wyels, "Le concile," 380–381, 386.

44. Tolstoi wrote this work originally in French so that the West would know the "truth" about Roman Catholicism. Freeze, "A Critical Perspective," 4.

45. Dmitri Tolstoi, *Romanism in Russia: A Historical Study,* vol. 2 (London, 1874), 372–373.

46. Ibid., 373–374.

47. Ibid., 377–378.

48. Freeze, "A Critical Perspective," 2.

49. Mikhail Moroshkin, *Iezuity v Rossii s tsarstvovaniia Ekateriny II do nashego vremeni* I (St. Petersburg, 1867), vi.

50. Moroshkin, *Iezuity,* vii.

51. Ibid., viii.

52. N. Ia. Danilevskii, *Rossiia i Evropa* (St. Petersburg, 1995), 407. Originally published in 1869.

53. Dostoevskii, cited in Walicki, *The Slavophile,* 555. Also found in Fyodor Dostoevskii, *The Diary of a Writer,* trans. Brasol (London: Cassell, 1949), 980.

54. Dostoevskii, *The Idiot, Sobranie sochinenii,* vol. 6 (Moscow, 1957), 614–615. Originally written in 1869.

55. Ibid., 615.

56. Ibid., 515.

57. Dostoevskii, *The Diary of a Writer,* 357. This is the entry for 1876.

58. Dostoevskii, *The Notebooks for the Possessed,* ed. Wasiolek, trans. Terras (Chiago: University of Chicago Press, 1968), 113–114.

59. Dostoevskii, *The Idiot,* 613.

60. Ibid., 617.

61. "Politicheskie pamflety i smes'," *Russkii arkhiv* I (1880): 394.

62. Martynov to Beckx, 22 July 1869, ARSI, Francia 10–XXIII, 11. Note Odoevskii's comments on the issue of the boarding school in his journal, dated 25 March 1864, "Valuev and [V. A.] Dolgorukov say that permission will be given for a Jesuit boarding school in Petersburg—for preventing the spread of nihilism—but nihilism is the child of the Jesuits." Odoevskii, "Tekushchaia," 180.

63. Martynov to Beckx, ARSI, Franciae 10–XXIII, 11.

64. Gagarin document, no date, at Versailles, BS, Bleu Claire 4. Gagarin also attributed the Jesuits' limited success in Russia to the distance involved in reaching available presses and the high cost of publishing.

65. Guettée, "Lettres," 240.

66. Gagarin, "La mission catholique d'Astrakhan au XVIIIe siècle," *Études religieuses, historiques et littéraires* 9 (1866): 232.

67. Gagarin to Bakhmetev, 21 November 1874, cited in Pierling, *Le prince,* 72.

68. Ivan Martynov, "Saint Josaphat et ses détracteurs," *Études religieuses, philosophiques, historiques et littéraires* 19 (1875): 351–352.

69. Gagarin, "Mélanges—Missions des Jésuites en Russie (1804–1824)," *Études religieuses, historiques et littéraires* 13 (1869): 459.

70. Ibid., 461.

71. Gagarin to Beckx, 30 January 1866, ARSI, Franciae 10-XXIII, 4.

72. Gagarin showed this letter to Martynov, Balabin, Pierling, and some Russian Orthodox in France. He claimed that all viewed his response favorably. Gagarin to Beckx, 30 January 1866, ARSI, Franciae 10-XXIII, 4.

73. Gagarin, "Pis'mo otsa Gagarina," 187–188.

74. Gagarin, "Mélanges—Missions des Jésuits," 459–460.

75. Gagarin, *La Compagnie de Jésus conservée en Russie après la suppression de 1772* (Paris: Palmè, 1872), xviii.

76. Gagarin to Martynov, 11 March 1869, BS, 70-2-B. This was not the first time that Gagarin contemplated writing a history of the Jesuits. In 1855, he had the idea of publishing historic documents on the Jesuits. See the letter from Guilherny to Gagarin, 3 October 1855, BS, Bleu Claire 14. Gagarin published several articles and books relating to the history of the Jesuits in Russia which included:

"Anecdotes recueillies a Saint-Pétersbourg par le Comte de Maistre," *Études religieuses, historiques et littéraires* 12 (1868).

La Compagnie de Jésus conservée en Russie après la suppression de 1772 (Paris: Palmé, 1872). Part of the series "Les Jésuites de Russie (1772–1785)."

"L'Impératrice Anne et les Catholiques en Russie," *Études religieuses, philosophiques, historiques et littéraires* 22 (1878).

"Mélanges—Missions des Jésuites en Russie (1804–1824)," *Études religieuses, historiques et littéraires* 13 (1869).

Un nonce du pape a la cour de Catherine II (Paris: Palmé, 1872). Part of the series "Les Jésuites de Russie (1783–1785)."

Vie de P. Marc Falloppe de la Compagnie de Jésus (Paris: Plon, 1877). Part of the series "Les Jésuites de Russie (1805–1816)."

To these must be added Gagarin's reprint of Father Rozaven's *L'Église russe et l'Église catholique—lettres du R.P. Rozaven* (Paris: Plon, 1876). Gagarin called this "one of the best books that we can place in the hands of those who ask for justification for our faith and who accuse us of abandoning *the faith of our fathers.*" He said, "this book will find those souls, anxious to possess the truth, and contribute to dissipating their anxieties." Gagarin, 3–4. Emphasis in original.

77. Giot, "Gagarin," 207.

78. Beckx to Gagarin, 25 March 1869, cited in ibid., 207.

79. Ibid., 207–208.

80. Beckx to Ponlevoy, 2 November 1869, cited in ibid., 208.

81. Beckx to Gagarin, 20 November 1869, BS, 70-1-C. Emphasis in original.

82. Giot, "Gagarin," 209.

83. Balabin to Beckx, 29 September 1871, ARSI, Franciae 10–XXIII, 15.

84. Beckx to Balabin, 25 October 1871, BS, 70-1-C. Balabin later left for Rome to work as an editor for the Jesuit journal *Civiltà cattolica* and sent articles to *Dukhovnyi viestnik.* After September 1876, he served at the college of Saint Ignatius.

85. Gagarin, Oeuvre de Ste. Olga, 1873, BS, Jaune 4.

86. Aksakov to Gagarin, 24 November/6 December, cited in L. Shur, "Perepiska I. S. Gagarina s N. S. Leskovym," *Simvol* 17 (1987): 241.

87. Leskov, cited in ibid., 242.

88. Leskov to Miliukov, 12/24 June 1875, cited in Hugh McLean, *Nikolai Leskov: The Man and His Art* (Cambridge: Harvard University Press, 1977), 297. Leskov also related the curious information that the other Jesuits often "good-naturedly pat [Gagarin] on the tummy and sometimes make fun of him a bit." Leskov to Aksakov, 29 July/10 August 1875, cited in ibid., 297.

89. Leskov, "Iezuit Gagarin," 273. The journal *Russkaia starina* concurred with Leskov's perception of Gagarin: "In September 1878 we had the pleasure to visit I. S. Gagarin in Paris, on Rue de Sevres, in the Jesuit house. We met a very lively, wise man, keenly interested in everything that concerns Russia. Together with the honorable Russian scholar Martynov (also a member of the Jesuit order) he established the Cyril-Methodius museum—particularly devoted to Slavic-Russian books in the enormous library of the Jesuit fathers." Editor of *Russkaia starina,* in N. P. Varsukov, "Aleksandr Ivanovich Turgenev v ego pis'makh," *Russkaia starina,* vol. 34 (1882): 456.

90. Gagarin to Leskov, 6/18 June 1875, cited in L. Shur, "Perepiska I. S. Gagarina s N. S. Leskovym," 250.

91. Leskov to Gagarin, 10/22 June 1875, cited in "Leskov's Trip Abroad in 1875," ed. and trans. Edgerton, *Indiana Slavic Studies* 4 (1967): 94.

92. Leskov to Gagarin, cited in Shur, "Perepiska I. S. Gagarina s N. S. Leskovym," 245–246.

93. Ibid.

94. By "Immaculate Conception" Gagarin meant "that Mary did not contract the stain of original sin; that from the first moment of her existence she was in possession of the supernatural life, of the life of grace." Gagarin, *L'Église russe,* 8. This is important because what is presented here are two Catholic dogmas—the existence of original sin and the notion of Mary as completely sinless. While Orthodox universally deny the Immaculate Conception, many Orthodox believe that Mary was completely sinless. The area of disagreement is thus not over Mary's nature, but over the existence of original sin.

95. Baranovich spent six years as rector of the Academy of Kiev, later became archbishop of Chernigov and sat on the Moscow council of 1667. Antonii Radivilovskii was vicar of the Monastery of the Caves in Kiev. Ivan Galiatovskii served as rector of the Academy of Kiev.

96. Galiatovskii, cited by Gagarin in *L'Église russe,* 19.

97. Gagarin, *L'Église russe,* 22–23.

98. Old Believer profession of faith, in ibid., 30.

99. Ibid., 49–50.

100. Citations in ibid., 34–40. Emphasis in original.

101. Ibid., 54, 59–60.

102. Ibid., 12, 51.

103. Ibid., 51–52.

104. N. Subbotin, *Pis'mo k. o. Gagarinu, "sviashchenniku Iezuitskago ordena v Parizhe"* (Moscow, 1879), 17.

105. Ibid., 19, 22.

106. Ibid., 31–32, 37.

107. Ibid., 41.

108. Ibid., 48, 51.

109. Ibid., 66. Emphasis in original.

110. Ibid., 66.

111. Gagarin, Letter to Subbotin, BS, Noire 1. Subbotin agreed that the teaching of the Immaculate Conception was not a matter of dogma, but rather of opinion.

112. Ivan Terent'evich Osipin, "Ivan Terent'evich Osipin: Ocherk ego zhizni i deiatel'nosti," *Russkaia starina* (February 1888): 464. The journal for the St. Petersburg Ecclesiastical Academy made reference to and summaries of Gagarin's works *La primauté de saint Pierre et les livres liturgiques de l'Église russe, L'Église russe et l'Immaculée conception,* and "Les archives russes et la conversion d'Alexander Ier empereur de Russie," when it criticized them in "Zhurnal'noe obozrenie," *Tserkovnyi viestnik* 10 (1878): 13.

113. Brochure for *La Sainte union,* after 4 May 1880, BS, Bleu 6. It claimed that the sacrament of the Eucharist was being received by people not part of the true Church, i.e. the Orthodox.

114. Ibid.

115. Ibid.

116. See letters of the Countess de Pimodan to Gagarin, 30 May 1877, 4 March 1879, 2 September 1881, and 19 November 1881, BS, Bleu 6. The Countess de Pimodan related the curious prophecy that "Russia will be converted and the emperor, while working to extend his empire, will be stopped on the shores of the Danube by a sign similar to that which converted Constantine and which will have the same effect." See letter of 30 May 1877.

117. Gagarin published several articles in *Études* on the salon of Countess Golovin, on the relationship of Paul and Father Gruber, S. J., on anecdotes of Joseph de Maistre and Father Grivel, S. J., and on a discussion of the relations between the scholars of the Sorbonne and Peter I. Gagarin also provided others with material connected to the Jesuits in Russia in the hopes it would be published. See

his letter to M. I. Semevskii, 6/18 February 1879, cited in Shur, "Materiali o dueli," 263. Gagarin's continued interest in Russia can be shown by the hope he had in the ascension of Alexander III. See the letter of Carbonier to Gagarin, 24 March, 5 April 1881, BS, Bleu 3. As for Gagarin's illness, see the letter of Beckx to Gagarin from 20 April 1874 in which Beckx wrote, "I suppose your health is better, my good Father, and that the gout has left you liberty to follow the impulsions of your zeal. Endure, my Father, and work for the holy church, in particular for Russia." ARSI, Reg. Epist. Ad Prov. Franciae VI (1869–1882), 147. Also see Gagarin's letters to Olga Nikolaevna Smirnova from 28 March 1879 and 24 October 1879 in which he refers to suffering from the gout and being unable to undertake activity. RGALI, f. 485, op. 1, d. 228, Smirnova.

118. Led by Jules Grévy (1807–1891), president of France, the Republicans sought to suppress Catholic education and religious congregations, particularly the Jesuits. They believed that the Jesuits conspired against the French government, that Jesuit schools were designed to produce students holding reactionary views, and that the Jesuits were to blame for the French defeat in the Franco-Prussian War of 1870.

119. Giot, "Gagarin," 215.

120. Ibid., 214.

121. Pierling, cited in ibid., 213. Pierling wrote Gagarin that "I am intimately convinced that we end with something. The results already obtained are considerable; the Bibliothèque is known to all the Slavs, one must support its reputation. When the idea is grand and fecund, it suffices to put in its service energy and perseverance for arriving at an end. May God wish it so." Letter of Pierling to Gagarin, 14 December 1879, cited in ibid., 213.

122. Gagarin, cited in ibid., 216.

123. In January 1881, Gagarin, Martynov, and Balabin received Russian passports, but without the right to return to Russia. GARF, f. 109, 1 exped., 1852, d. 346, l. 299–300.

124. Pitot, cited in Giot, "Gagarin," 216

125. Martynov, cited in Giot, "Gagarin," 217.

126. Clair, "Premières annés," 831.

127. Rouleau, cited in Giot, "Gagarin," 219.

128. S. L. Frank, cited by Florovsky, *Ways*, vol. 2, 58.

129. Pierling, cited in Rouët de Journel, "L'Oeuvre," 625.

130. Pecherin, cited in Suchanek, "Les catholiques," 367.

131. Burnichon, *La Compagnie*, 132–133.

132. "Nécrologie," *Polybiblion* (XXXV): 166. Gagarin had written some articles for this journal.

133. "Nekrolog," *Istoricheskii viestnik* 11 (1882): 678. Compare this with Berdyaev's comments that "The Westernizing of Chaadaev, his Roman Catholic sym-

pathies, remain characteristically Russian phenomena." Nicholas Berdyaev, *The Russian Idea* (Boston: Beacon Press, 1962), 38.

134. Aleksandra Smirnova-Rosset, cited in Tempest, "Ivan," 130.

135. Bil'basov, "Samarin," 416.

136. "Voskresnie nabroski," 1.

137. Ibid.

138. *Polnyi pravoslavnyi bogoslovskii entsiklopedicheskii slovar'* I (1913), 603–604. This encyclopedia entry on Gagarin mentioned only his French publications.

139. Solov'ev to Martynov, 7/19 August 1887, cited in V.S. Solov'ev, *Sobranie sochinenii Vladimira Sergeevicha Soloveva,* Brussels, XI (1966), 395. See also P. Iosifova and N. Tsimbaev, "'Russkaia ideia' kak element natsional'nogo soznaniia," *Vestnik Moskovskogo universiteta,* seriia 8—istoriia, 2 (March–April 1993): 11. The authors argue that Solov'ev's ideas are quite similar to those of Gagarin in *La Russie.*

140. Walicki, *A History of Russian Thought: From the Enlightenment to Marxism* (Stanford: Stanford University Press, 1990), 383.

141. Florovsky, *Ways,* vol. 2, and letter of Solov'ev to Strossmayer, 29 September 1886, cited in Solov'ev, *La Sophia et les autres écrits français,* ed. Rouleau (1978) 314. Note that Solov'ev's ideas here regarding the benefits of church union for Rome were more in concord with the views of William Palmer than with Gagarin's. Considering the presence of many of Palmer's texts at the Bibliothèque Slave, it is certainly possible that Solov'ev was familiar with Palmer's ideas.

142. Walicki, *A History of Russian Thought,* 384.

143. Solov'ev, cited in Dmitrieva, "Les conversions," 336. I also wish to note the example of S.L. Frank, who although Orthodox, also made similar favorable remarks about Catholicism. In *God With Us,* Frank argued that Catholicism had done more for the Christian education of humanity than all other denominations. He described Catholicism as the "natural leader of Christendom." See Philip Boobbyer, *S.L. Frank: The Life and Work of a Russian Philosopher 1877-1950* (Athens: Ohio University Press, 1995), 193.

144. Children under fourteen years of age would also adopt the new faith, but if one of the parents remained Orthodox, so would the children. Children of fourteen years or older could not leave Orthodoxy until reaching the age of twenty-one.

145. James J. Zatko, *Descent into Darkness* (Toronto: Baxter Publishing, 1965), 26.

146. Sergei Sazonov, "Autocracy and the Vatican: On the Eve of the 'Imperialist War,'" *Journal of Church and State* 19 (Winter 1977): 80. Note also Peter Zaionchkovsky's comment that as early as the late 1870s the Russian government

observed that revolutionary agitation "had not found congenial company" among the Catholic populations. Zaionchkovsky, *The Russian Autocracy in Crisis, 1878–1882,* trans. Gary M. Hamburg (Gulf Breeze: Academic International Press, 1979), 61.

147. Léon Tretjakewitsch, *Bishop Michel d'Herbigny, S.J.: A Pre-Ecumenical Approach to Christian Unity* (1990), 123.

148. Caesarius Tondini, *The Popes of Rome and the Popes of the Oriental Orthodox Church: An Essay on Monarchy in the Church with Special Reference to Russia, from Original Documents, Russian and Greek* (London, 1871), 159.

149. Remmers, "La réunion," note 61.

150. Ivan Muzyczka, "Sheptyts'kyi in the Russian Empire," in *Morality and Reality: The Life and Times of Andrei Sheptyts'kyi,* ed. Paul Robert Magocsi (Edmonton: University of Alberta, 1989), 314.

151. Tretjakewitsch, *Bishop Michel d' Herbigny,* 46.

152. Ibid., 284.

153. Ibid., 27.

154. There would also be others of Russian and Slavic descent who would enter the Society of Jesus, such as Nikolai Bock (1880–1962); Ivan Kologrivov (1890–1954), author of *Essai sur la sainteté en Russie;* Stanislav Tyskiewicz (1887–1962); Grigorii Kovalenko (1900–1975); and Viktor Novikov (1905–1979).

155. Ronald G. Roberson, *The Eastern Christian Churches: A Brief Survey* (Rome, 1993), 61.

156. Tretjakewitsch, *Bishop Michel d'Herbigny,* 25.

157. Ibid., 42–43.

158. John Paul II, "Slavorum Apostoli," 2 June 1958, in *The Encyclicals of John Paul II,* ed. J. Michael Miller, C. S. B. (Huntington: Our Sunday Visitor, 1996), 229, 231. John Paul II, *Euntes in Mundum* (Washington, D. C.: United States Catholic Conference, 25 January 1988): 14.

159. John Paul II, "Slavorum," 239, 242.

160. John Paul II, *Euntes,* 18, 27.

161. John Paul II, *Orientale Lumen* (Washington, D. C.: United States Catholic Conference, 2 May 1995), 19, 32.

162. Ibid., 41.

163. John Paul II, "Ut Unum Sint," 2 May 1995, in *The Encyclicals of John Paul II,* ed. J. Michael Miller, C. S. B. (Huntington: Our Sunday Visitor, 1996), 916, 962, 967, 972.

164. John Paul II, *Orientale,* 53. John Paul II, "Ut Unum Sint," 951.

165. John Paul II, "Slavorum," 248.

166. John Paul II, "Ut Unum Sint," 927.

Bibliography

Archival Sources and Abbreviations

FRANCE

Meudon

BS: Bibliothèque Slave. An extensive description of the contents of Gagarin's papers can be found in E. N. Tsimbaeva, "Arkhiv slavianskoi biblioteki parizha," *Vestnik Moskovskogo Universiteta*, Seriia 8, Istoriia. 6 (1995): 86–94.

Vanves

AFCJ: Archives Françaises de la Compagnie de Jésus.
Catalogus Sociorum Provinciae Gallilae Societatis Iesu.
Gagarin fond.

ITALY

Rome

ARSI: Archivum Romanum Societatis Iesu.
Franciae 5–V.
Franciae 5–VII.
Franciae 6–XI.
Franciae 8–VII.
Franciae 10–XXIII.
Reg. Epist. ad Prov. Franciae, III (1843–1847).
Reg. Epist. ad Prov. Franciae, IV (1847–1857).
Reg. Epist. ad Prov. Franciae, V (1857–1869).
Reg. Epist. ad Prov. Franciae, VI (1869–1882).

VATICAN CITY

ASV: Archivio Segreto Vaticano.
Archivio Particolare Pio IX, Oggetti Vari #450.

RUSSIA

Moscow

GARF: Gosudarstvennyi Arkhiv Rossiiskoi Federatsii.
f. 109, 1 eksp., 1852, d. 346.

f. 109, 1 eksp., 1857, d. 100, op. 32 O frantsuzkikh poddannykh, ispoveduiushchikh v Parizhe pravoslavnuiu veru.

f. 109, 1 eksp., 1859, d. 87, op. 34 S zagranichnymi svedeniiami.

f. 109, 2 eksp., 1845, d. 256, Proisky si proizvodiatsia pod rukovodstvom sivshago nastavnikom molodogo kniazia Gagarina, frantsuzkago, po imeni *Maren'-Darbel'*, kotoryi, kak kazhetsia, i sam ne chto inoe kak orudie Iezuitov.

RGALI: Rossiiskii Gosudarstvennyi Arkhiv Literatury i Iskusstva.

f. 372, op. 1, d. 10, Pecherin.

f. 485, op. 1, d. 228, Smirnova.

St. Petersburg

GPB: Gosudarstvennaia Publichnaia Biblioteka im. M. E. Saltykova-Shchedrina.

f. 52, n. 29, Pompei Nikolaevich Batiushkov.

f. 326, n. 305, E. P. Kazanovich.

f. 850, n. 182, Shevyrev.

f. 1000, sobr. otd. post. op. 1, n. 3.

RGIA: Rossiiskii Gosudarstvennyi Istoricheskii Arkhiv.

f. 706, n. 205, d. 148, Stat'i iz frantsuzkikh zhurnalov o katolichestve v Rossii ob ego missionerskoi deiatel'nosti, oba so'edinenii khristianskikh tserkvei.

f. 776, op. 3, d. 836, Vypiska iz zhurnala zasedaniia S. Peterburgskago komiteta tsenzury inostrannoi, ot 15go sego noiabra za no 41, o sochineniiakh zapreshchenykh i pozvolennykh s iskliucheniiami.

f. 797, op. 28, d. 279, I otdeleniia II stola, Ob ob'iavlenii ot Sviateishago Sinoda blagoslovenii Grecheskomu professoru Marokorbato i sochiniteliu knigy soderzhashchei v sebe opravdanie frantsuzkoi broshury "La Russie sera-t-elle catholique?"

f. 832, n. 1, d. 54, O katholicheskikh missionerskikh seminariiakh v Parizhe 1859–1860 gg.

f. 832, n. 1, d. 83, O knighakh broshurakh i stat'iakh, priznannykh vrednymi.

f. 1151, op. 4, d. 139, 1853, Grazhdanskogo departmenta o kollezhskom sovetnike Evgenie Balabine.

f. 1151, op. 4, d. 26, 1854, Grazhdanskogo departmenta o dvorianakh: kniaze Ivane Gagarine, Ivane Martynove i Stepane Dzhunkovskom, Kratkaia zapiska.

f. 1161, op. 1, d. 410, K. S. Serbinovich.

Published Sources

Works by Ivan Sergeevich Gagarin, S. J.

———. "Anecdotes recueillies à Saint-Pétersbourg par le Comte de Maistre." *Études religieuses, historiques et littéraires* 12 (1868): 533–551, 777–798; 13 (1869): 84–99.

———. Appendix to Elizabeth Golitsyn, *Conversion d'une dame russe à la foi catholique.* Paris: Douniol, 1862.

———. "Arkhiv slavianskoi biblioteki." *Simvol* 1 (1979): 167–174; 2 (1979): 164–181.

———. "Bibliographie." *Bulletin de l'Oeuvre des Pèlerinages* (1862): 119–120.

———. "Bibliographie—Études sur la question religieuse de Russie." *Études religieuses, historiques et littéraires* 11 (1867): 602–603.

———. "Bibliographie—Histoire de la séparation des Églises d'orient et d'occident depuis ses premiers commencements jusqu'a nos jours; nouvelles études sur la séparation des Églises d'orient et d'occident; à mes critiques." *Études religieuses, historiques et littéraires* 9 (1865): 112–122.

———. "Bibliographie—Les saints lieux; Revue théologique de Tubingue." *Études de théologie, de philosophie et d'histoire* 3 (1859): 146–156.

———. "Bibliographie—Ma conversion et ma vocation." *Études de théologie de philosophie et d'histoire* 3 (1859): 455–456.

———. "Bibliographie—Monuments historiques relatifs aux règnes d'Alexis Michaelowitch, Feodor III et Pierre le Grand, czars de Russie." *Études de théologie, de philosophie et d'histoire* 4 (1860): 291–295.

———. "Bibliographie—Tableau d'une Église nationale d'après un pope russe." *Études religieuses, historiques et littéraires* 6 (1862): 685–689.

———. "Chronique religieuses de l'orient." *Études religieuses, historiques et littéraires* 10, no. 8 (1866): 381–388, 523–535; 10, no. 9 (1866): 113–125.

———. "Constitution et Situation présent de toutes les Églises de l'orient." *Études religieuses, historiques et littéraires* 9 (1865): 519–528.

———. "De l'enseignement de la théologie dans l'Église russe." *Études de théologie, de philosophie et d'histoire* 1 (1857): 1–61.

———. *De la réunion de l'Église orientale avec l'Église romaine—discours prononcé par le P. Gagarin, de la Compagnie de Jésus, le 27 Janvier 1860 dans L'Église de Notre-Dame des Victoires, à l'occasion de la fête de l'oeuvre des Écoles d'Orient.* Paris: Peaucelle, 1860.

———. "Dnevnik (1834–1842)." Trans. Richard Tempest. *Simvol* 34 (1995): 229–355.

———. *Dnevnik. Zapiski o moei zhizni. Perepiska.* Trans. Richard Tempest. Moscow: Iazyki Russkoi Kul'tury, 1996.

———. "Ia sluzhu prostym riadovym soldatom v odnom iz mnogochislennykh polkov voiska dukhovnovo . . ." *Simvol* 32 (1994): 181–188.

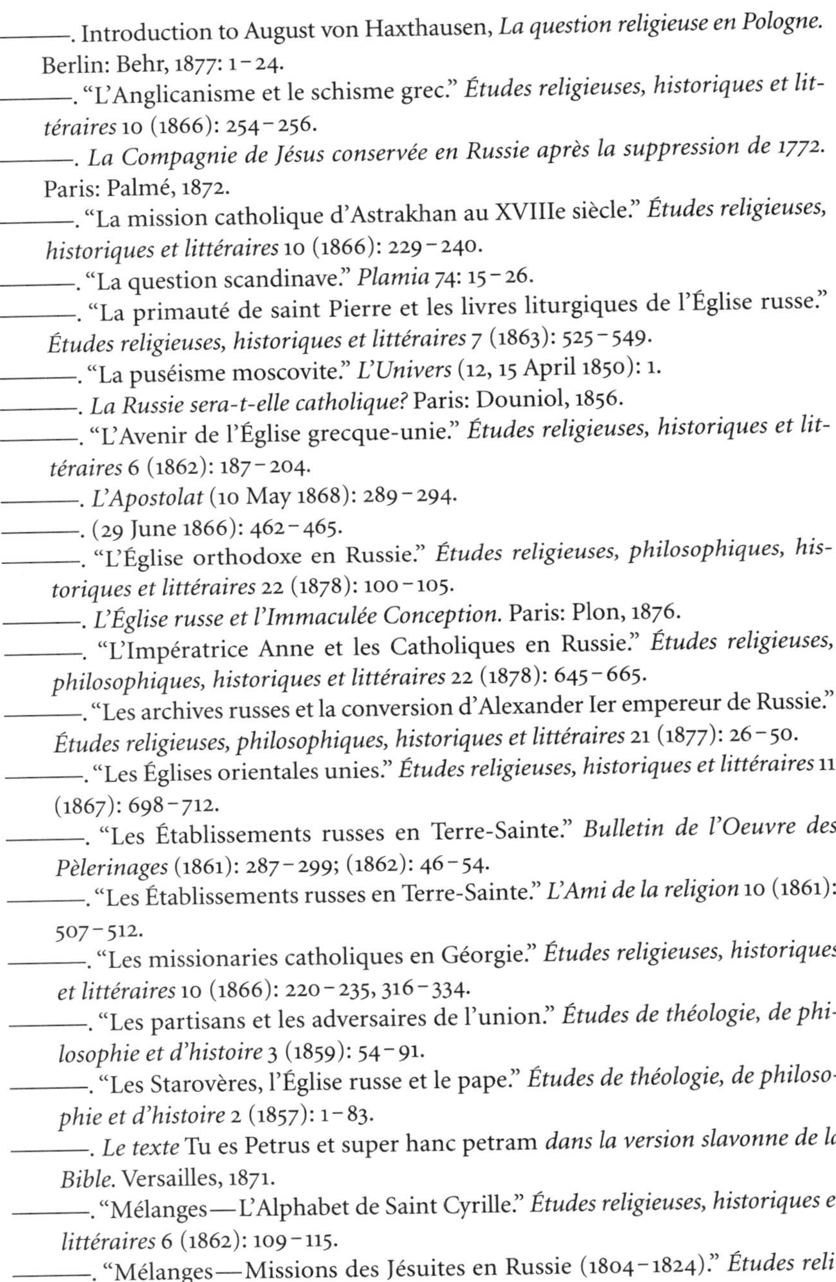

———. Introduction to August von Haxthausen, *La question religieuse en Pologne.* Berlin: Behr, 1877: 1–24.

———. "L'Anglicanisme et le schisme grec." *Études religieuses, historiques et littéraires* 10 (1866): 254–256.

———. *La Compagnie de Jésus conservée en Russie après la suppression de 1772.* Paris: Palmé, 1872.

———. "La mission catholique d'Astrakhan au XVIIIe siècle." *Études religieuses, historiques et littéraires* 10 (1866): 229–240.

———. "La question scandinave." *Plamia* 74: 15–26.

———. "La primauté de saint Pierre et les livres liturgiques de l'Église russe." *Études religieuses, historiques et littéraires* 7 (1863): 525–549.

———. "La puséisme moscovite." *L'Univers* (12, 15 April 1850): 1.

———. *La Russie sera-t-elle catholique?* Paris: Douniol, 1856.

———. "L'Avenir de l'Église grecque-unie." *Études religieuses, historiques et littéraires* 6 (1862): 187–204.

———. *L'Apostolat* (10 May 1868): 289–294.

———. (29 June 1866): 462–465.

———. "L'Église orthodoxe en Russie." *Études religieuses, philosophiques, historiques et littéraires* 22 (1878): 100–105.

———. *L'Église russe et l'Immaculée Conception.* Paris: Plon, 1876.

———. "L'Impératrice Anne et les Catholiques en Russie." *Études religieuses, philosophiques, historiques et littéraires* 22 (1878): 645–665.

———. "Les archives russes et la conversion d'Alexander Ier empereur de Russie." *Études religieuses, philosophiques, historiques et littéraires* 21 (1877): 26–50.

———. "Les Églises orientales unies." *Études religieuses, historiques et littéraires* 11 (1867): 698–712.

———. "Les Établissements russes en Terre-Sainte." *Bulletin de l'Oeuvre des Pèlerinages* (1861): 287–299; (1862): 46–54.

———. "Les Établissements russes en Terre-Sainte." *L'Ami de la religion* 10 (1861): 507–512.

———. "Les missionaries catholiques en Géorgie." *Études religieuses, historiques et littéraires* 10 (1866): 220–235, 316–334.

———. "Les partisans et les adversaires de l'union." *Études de théologie, de philosophie et d'histoire* 3 (1859): 54–91.

———. "Les Starovères, l'Église russe et le pape." *Études de théologie, de philosophie et d'histoire* 2 (1857): 1–83.

———. *Le texte* Tu es Petrus et super hanc petram *dans la version slavonne de la Bible.* Versailles, 1871.

———. "Mélanges—L'Alphabet de Saint Cyrille." *Études religieuses, historiques et littéraires* 6 (1862): 109–115.

———. "Mélanges—Missions des Jésuites en Russie (1804–1824)." *Études religieuses, historiques et littéraires* 13 (1869): 459–469.

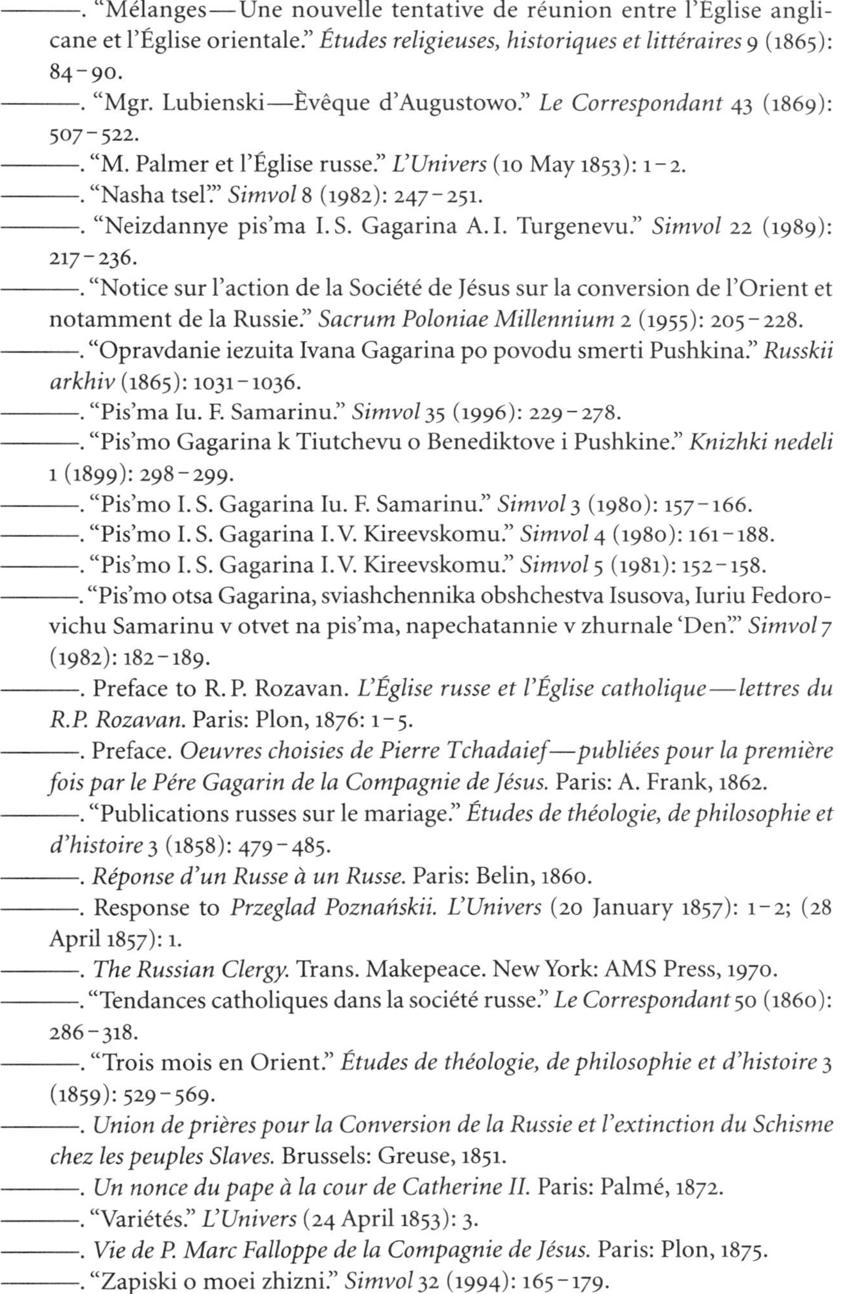

———. "Mélanges—Une nouvelle tentative de réunion entre l'Église anglicane et l'Église orientale." *Études religieuses, historiques et littéraires* 9 (1865): 84–90.

———. "Mgr. Lubienski—Èvêque d'Augustowo." *Le Correspondant* 43 (1869): 507–522.

———. "M. Palmer et l'Église russe." *L'Univers* (10 May 1853): 1–2.

———. "Nasha tsel'." *Simvol* 8 (1982): 247–251.

———. "Neizdannye pis'ma I. S. Gagarina A. I. Turgenevu." *Simvol* 22 (1989): 217–236.

———. "Notice sur l'action de la Société de Jésus sur la conversion de l'Orient et notamment de la Russie." *Sacrum Poloniae Millennium* 2 (1955): 205–228.

———. "Opravdanie iezuita Ivana Gagarina po povodu smerti Pushkina." *Russkii arkhiv* (1865): 1031–1036.

———. "Pis'ma Iu. F. Samarinu." *Simvol* 35 (1996): 229–278.

———. "Pis'mo Gagarina k Tiutchevu o Benediktove i Pushkine." *Knizhki nedeli* 1 (1899): 298–299.

———. "Pis'mo I. S. Gagarina Iu. F. Samarinu." *Simvol* 3 (1980): 157–166.

———. "Pis'mo I. S. Gagarina I. V. Kireevskomu." *Simvol* 4 (1980): 161–188.

———. "Pis'mo I. S. Gagarina I. V. Kireevskomu." *Simvol* 5 (1981): 152–158.

———. "Pis'mo otsa Gagarina, sviashchennika obshchestva Isusova, Iuriu Fedorovichu Samarinu v otvet na pis'ma, napechatannie v zhurnale 'Den'.'" *Simvol* 7 (1982): 182–189.

———. Preface to R. P. Rozavan. *L'Église russe et l'Église catholique—lettres du R.P. Rozavan.* Paris: Plon, 1876: 1–5.

———. Preface. *Oeuvres choisies de Pierre Tchadaief—publiées pour la première fois par le Pére Gagarin de la Compagnie de Jésus.* Paris: A. Frank, 1862.

———. "Publications russes sur le mariage." *Études de théologie, de philosophie et d'histoire* 3 (1858): 479–485.

———. *Réponse d'un Russe à un Russe.* Paris: Belin, 1860.

———. Response to *Przeglad Poznańskii. L'Univers* (20 January 1857): 1–2; (28 April 1857): 1.

———. *The Russian Clergy.* Trans. Makepeace. New York: AMS Press, 1970.

———. "Tendances catholiques dans la société russe." *Le Correspondant* 50 (1860): 286–318.

———. "Trois mois en Orient." *Études de théologie, de philosophie et d'histoire* 3 (1859): 529–569.

———. *Union de prières pour la Conversion de la Russie et l'extinction du Schisme chez les peuples Slaves.* Brussels: Greuse, 1851.

———. *Un nonce du pape à la cour de Catherine II.* Paris: Palmé, 1872.

———. "Variétés." *L'Univers* (24 April 1853): 3.

———. *Vie de P. Marc Falloppe de la Compagnie de Jésus.* Paris: Plon, 1875.

———. "Zapiski o moei zhizni." *Simvol* 32 (1994): 165–179.

Works co-authored by Gagarin

———, and Charles Daniel, S. J. Préface. *Études de théologie, de philosophie et d'histoire* 1 (1857): i–iv.

———, and Ivan Martynov, S. J. *Sokrovishche khristianina ili kratkoe izlozhenie glavnykh istin very i ob'iazannostei khristianina.* Paris, 1855.

———, and Ivan Martynov, S. J., and Evgenii Balabin, S. J. Introduction. *Kirillo-Mefodievskii sbornik* (1863): 1–3.

Other published works

Abramovich, Stella Lazarevna. *Pushkin, poslednii god—khronika.* Moscow, 1991.

———. *Pushkin v 1836 godu.* Leningrad: Nauka, 1984; reprinted 1989.

Aksakov, Ivan Sergeevich. "Stikhotvoreniia F. I. Tiutcheva." *Russkii arkhiv* II. 5 (1879): 118–138.

Alekseev, M. P. "Po sledam rukopisei I. S. Turgeneva vo Frantsii." *Russkaia literatura* 1 (1963): 53–85.

Alfavitnyi katalog socheniniiam na frantsuzkom, nemetskom, i angliiskom iazykakh zapreshchennym inostrannoiu tsenzuroiu ili dozvolennym k obrashcheniiu s iskliucheniem nekotorykh mest s 1856 po 1 iulia 1869 goda. St. Petersburg, 1870.

Anfimov, A. M. *Krupnoe pomeshchich'e khoziaistvo Evropeiskoi Rossii.* Moscow, 1969.

Antsiferov, N. P. "I. S. Gagarin—Gertsenu." *Literaturnoe nasledstvo* 62 (1955): 61–63.

Bailly, Paul. "Brugelette." *Les Établissements des Jésuites en France depuis quatre siècles.* Ed. Pierre Delattre, S. J. Vol. I (1949): 943–990.

Balabin, Viktor. *Journal de Victor de Balabine, secrétaire de l'ambassade de Russie: 1842-1847.* Paris, 1914.

Bangert, William V., S. J. *A History of the Society of Jesus.* St. Louis: Institute of Jesuit Sources, 1986.

Baranovskii, S. *Otvet mirianina na knigu: "Stanet li Rossiia katolicheskoiu?"* Berlin, 1859.

Bazarov, I. "Po voprosy o soedinenii tserkvei vostochnoi I zapadnoi." *Chteniia v obshchestve liubiteli dukhovnago prosveshcheniia,* 9 (1887): 149–199.

———. "S. S. Dzhunkovskii i ego vozvrashchenie v pravoslavie" (April 1866): 430–442.

Belhoste, Bruno. *Cauchy [1789-1857]: Un mathméticien légitimiste au XIXe siècle.* Paris: Belin, 1985.

Berdyaev, Nikolai. *The Russian Idea.* Boston: Beacon Press, 1962.

Berlin, Isaiah. "A Remarkable Decade." In *Russian Thinkers,* ed. Henry Hardy and Aileen Kelly. New York: Penguin Books, 1979: 114–209.

Beshoner, Jeffrey Bruce. "Father Ivan Sergeevich Gagarin, S. J.: The Responses of Granovskii, Kireevskii, and Chaadaev to the Russian Question." *Diakonia* (1996): 49–56.

Besse, Jean Paul. *Un précurseur Wladimir Guettée du Gallicanisme à l'Orthodoxie.* Lavardac, 1992.

Bil'basov, V. A. "Samarin Gagarinu o Lermontove." *Istoricheskiia monografii* 2 (1901): 413–424.

Boobbyer, Philip. *S.L. Frank: The Life and Work of a Russian Philosopher 1877-1950.* Athens: Ohio University Press, 1995.

Boudou, Adrien, S. J. *Le Saint-Siège et la Russie—leurs relations diplomatiques au XIXe siècle: 1848-1883.* Editions Spes, 1923.

Bradley, John F. N. *Czech Nationalism in the Nineteenth Century.* New York: Columbia University Press, 1984.

Bréhier, Emile. *The Nineteenth Century: Period of Systems, 1800-1850. The History of Philosophy.* Vol. 4. Trans. Wade Baskin. Chicago: University of Chicago Press, 1968.

Brown, William Edward. Afterword. *The Tarantas—Impressions of a Journey (Russia in the 1840s).* By Vladimir Sollogub. Trans. William Edward Brown. Ann Arbor: Ardis, 1989.

Buck, Victor de, S. J. "La Russie sera-t-elle catholique?" *Précis historiques* (1856): 544–549.

Burnichon, Joseph. *La Compagnie de Jésus en France: histoire d'un siècle.* Vols. 2, 4. Paris: Beauchesne, 1922.

Buturlin, A. S. "Imel li I. S. Gagarin otnoshenie k paskviliu na A. S. Pushkina?" *Izvestiia Akademii Nauk SSSR* 28, 3 (1969): 277–285.

Cadot, Michel. *La Russie dans la vie intellectuelle français (1839-1856).* Paris: Fayard, 1967.

Call, Paul. *Vasily L. Kelsiev: An Encounter between the Russian Revolutionaries and the Old Believers.* Belmont: Nordland, 1979.

Campbell, Thomas J. *The Jesuits, 1534-1921: A History of the Society of Jesus from Its Foundation to the Present Time.* New York: Encyclopedia Press, 1921.

Chaadaev, Petr Iakovlevich. *The Major Works of Peter Chaadaev.* Trans. Raymond T. McNally. Notre Dame: University of Notre Dame Press, 1969.

———. *Philosophical Works of Peter Chaadaev.* Ed. Raymond T. McNally and Richard Tempest. Sovietica 56. Boston: Kluwer, 1991.

Chazournes, Régis de. *Albéric de Foresta de la Compagnie de Jésus, Fondateur des Écoles Apostoliques. Sa vie, ses vertus, et son oeuvre.* Paris, 1881.

Chertikov, Leonid. "Neopublikovannoe pis'mo V. G. Tepliakova k Kn. I. S. Gagarinu." *Revue des études slaves.* 54 (1982): 477–480.

Christoff, Peter K. *A.S. Xomjakov. An Introduction to Nineteenth-Century Slavophilism.* Vol. 1. Mouton, 1961.

———. *Iu F. Samarin. An Introduction to Nineteenth-Century Russian Slavophilism.* Vol. 4. San Francisco: Westview Press, 1991.

———. *I.V. Kireevskii. An Introduction to Nineteenth-Century Russian Slavophilism.* Vol. 2. Paris: Mouton, 1972.

———. *K.S. Aksakov. An Introduction to Nineteenth-Century Russian Slavophilism.* Vol. 3. Princeton: Princeton University Press, 1982.

Churchman. "Revue littéraires." *L'Union chrétienne* (1865): 278–280.

Clair, Charles, S.J. "Premières années et conversion du prince Jean Gagarin." *Revue du monde catholique* 74 (1883): 831–842; 75 (1883): 27–41, 194–212, 525–537, 712–721.

Congregation for the Eastern Churches. "Instruction for Applying the Liturgical Prescriptions of the Code of Canons of the Eastern Churches." Online. EWTN. WWW. 6 January 1996.

Cubit, Geoffrey. *The Jesuit Myth: Conspiracy Theory and Politics in Nineteenth-Century France.* Oxford: Clarendon Press, 1993.

Danilevskii, Nikolai Iakovlevich. *Rossiia i Evropa.* Petersburg, 1995.

Danzas, Konstantine Karlovich. "Poslednie dni zhizni i konchina Aleksandra Sergeevicha Pushkina v zapisi A. Ammosova." *A.S. Pushkin v vospominaniakh sovremennikov.* Vol. 2. Moscow, 1974: 318–334.

Davies, Norman. *God's Playground: A History of Poland.* New York: Columbia University Press, 1982.

Despalatović, Elinor Murray. *Ljudevit Gaj and the Illyrian Movement.* New York: Columbia University Press, 1975.

Dmitrieva, Katia. "Les conversions au catholicisme en Russie au XIXe siècle: ruptures historiques et culturelles." *Revue des études slaves* 73, 2–3 (1995): 311–336.

Dolgorukov, Petr Vladimirovich. Letter. *Kolokol* (1 August 1863); reprinted in *Kolokol* 6 (1963): 1387.

Dostoevskii, Fyodor Mikhailovich. *The Diary of a Writer.* Trans. Brasol. London: Cassell, 1949.

———. *Idiot. Sobranie sochinenii.* Vol. 6. Moscow, 1957.

———. *The Notebooks for the Possessed.* Ed. Wasiolek. Trans. Terras. Chicago: University of Chicago Press, 1968.

Égron, A. *Le culte de la Sainte Vierge.* Paris, 1842.

Eidel'man, N. Ia. *Gertsen protiv samoderzhaviia.* Moscow, 1984.

———. *Pushkin: iz biografii i tvorchestva 1826-1837.* Moscow, 1987.

Encyclical Epistle of the One Holy Catholic and Apostolic Church to the Faithful Everywhere: Being a Reply to the Epistle of Pius IX to the Easterns. 6 January 1848. New York: John F. Trow, 1867.

Filaret [Drozdov]. *Pis'ma Mitropolita Moskovskago Filareta k A.N.M...: 1832-1867.* Kiev, 1869.

Florovsky, Georges. *Ecumenism I: A Doctrinal Approach.* Collected Works of Georges Florovsky. Vol. 13. Belmont: Nordland, 1989.

———. *Ways of Russian Theology.* Vol. 1. Trans. Robert L. Nichols. Collected Works of Georges Florovsky. Vol. 5. Belmont: Nordland, 1979.

———. *Ways of Russian Theology.* Vol. 2. Trans. Robert L. Nichols. Collected Works of Georges Florovsky. Vol. 6. Belmont: Büchervertriebsanstalt, 1987.

Flynn, James T. *The University Reform of Tsar Alexander I: 1802-1835*. Washington, D.C.: The Catholic University of America Press, 1988.

Fouilloux, Étienne. "L'oecuménisme d'avant-hier à aujourd'hui." *L'oecumènisme unitè chrètienne et identités confessionnelles.* Paris: Beauchesne, 1984.

Freeze, Gregory L. "A Critical Perspective on the Russian Clergy and Church in the Nineteenth Century." Introduction to *The Russian Clergy*, by Ivan Gagarin, S.J. Trans. Makepeace. Newtonville: Oriental Research Partners, 1976.

———. Introduction to *Description of the Clergy in Rural Russia*, by I. S. Belliustin. Trans. Gregory Freeze. Ithaca: Cornell University Press, 1985: 13–62.

———. *The Parish Clergy in Nineteenth-Century Russia: Crisis, Reform, Counter-Reform.* Princeton: Princeton University Press, 1983.

Gershtein, Emma. "Kruzhok shestnadtsati." *Lermontovskaia entsiklopediia.* Moscow, 1981: 234–235.

———. *Sud'ba Lermontova.* Moscow: Khudozhestvennaia literatura, 1986.

Gibson, Aleksey. "Towards a History of the Russian Catholics." *Symposion* 2 (1997): 79–97.

Giot, Clotilde. "Jean Serguéiévitch Gagarin: premier Jésuite russe et artisan de l'union des Églises." Diss., l'Universite Jean Moulin Lyon III, 1993.

Giusti, Wolf. "Slavofili e Cattolici in Russia: Annotazioni a proposito di I. S. Gagarin." *Annali—Sezione Slava.* Instituto Universitario Orientale 7 (1964): 71–116.

Guettée, Abbé René François [Vladimir]. "Considérations générals sur le but que se reposent les fondateurs de *L'Union chrétienne. L'Union chrétienne* (1859–1860): 1–5.

———. "Les Églises orientales unies." *L'Union chrétienne* (1867–1868): 35–37.

———. Letter to Gagarin. *L'Union chrétienne* (1859–1860): 243–246.

———. *Lettres au Révérend Pére Gagarin de la Compagnie de Jésus touchant l'Église catholique orthodoxe & l'Église romaine ou défense de* La Papauté schismatique *contre les calomnies et les erreurs du parti jésuitique caché sous le pseudonyme de Boulgak.* Paris, 1867.

———. "Lettres au R. P. Gagarin sur la réforme du clergé russe." *L'Union chrétienne* (1865–1866): 410–414; (1866–1867): 2–5, 11–13, 21–23, 25–27, 35–37, 43–44, 51–53, 61–63, 76–78, 91–93, 100–101, 149–152, 159–160, 174–176, 238–240, 253–255, 293–295, 302–304, 357–359.

———. *L'Union chrétienne* (1866–1867): 69.

———. "Réflexions à propos du sermon prononcé en faveur de l'asile de Madame Swetchine." *L'Union chrétienne* (1862): 217–219.

Harang, P. S. S., P. "Une correspondance entre le Baron de Haxthausen et André Mouravieff." *Istina* 3 (1969): 342–369.

Haxthausen, August Franz Ludwig Maria von. *Studies on the Interior of Russia: 1847-1852.* Chicago: University of Chicago Press, 1972.

Herzen, Aleksandr Ivanovich. *A.I. Gertsen—Sobranie sochinenii v tridtsati tomakh.* Moscow, 1954–1965.

———. *A.I. Gertsen—Sochineniia v deviati tomakh.* Moscow, 1955–1958.
———. *My Past and Thoughts.* Trans. Constance Garnett. New York: Vintage Books, 1974.
Honcharenko, Agapius. *Spomniki.* Edmonton: Slavuta, 1965.
Iakhontov, Ioann K. *Pis'ma k otstupniku pravoslaviia.* St. Petersburg, 1864.
Iashchin, Mikhail. "Khronika predduel'nikh dnei." *Zvezda* 8 (1963): 159–184.
———. "K portretu dukhovnogo litsa." *Neva* 2 (1966): 169–176; 3 (1966): 186–198.
Iosifova, P., and E. N. Tsimbaeva. "'Russkaia ideia' kak element national'nogo soznaniia." *Vestnik Moskovskogo Universiteta.* Seriia 8. Istoriia. 2 (March–April 1993): 3–15.
Iuvenalii. *Neskol'ko slov po povodu stat'i—"Russkiia uchrezhdeniia v sviatoi zemle.* St. Petersburg, 1861.
Izalguier, Eugene. Editorial. *Revue de Paris* (1856): 95–107.
"Iz bumag V. A. Zhukovskago." *Russkii arkhiv* 11 (1873): 1516–1529.
James, William A. "The Jesuits' Role in Founding Schools in Late Tsarist Russia." *Religious and Secular Forces in Late Tsarist Russia.* Ed. Charles E. Timberlake. Seattle: University of Washington Press, 1992: 48–64.
John Paul II. *Euntes in Mundum.* Washington, D. C.: United States Catholic Conference. 25 January 1988.
———. *Orientale Lumen.* Washington, D. C.: United States Catholic Conference. 2 May 1995.
———. "Slavorum Apostoli." 2 June 1985. *The Encyclicals of John Paul II.* Ed. J. Michael Miller, C. S. B. Huntington: Our Sunday Visitor, 1996: 228–253.
———. "Ut Unum Sint." 25 May 1995. *The Encyclicals of John Paul II.* Ed. J. Michael Miller, C. S. B. Huntington: Our Sunday Visitor, 1996: 914–976.
Journel, Marie Joseph Rouët de, S. J. "L'Oeuvre des SS. Cyrille et Méthode et la Bibliothéque Slave." *Lettres de Jersey* (1922): 613–648.
———. "Madame Swetchine et les conversions." *Études* 191 (1927): 183–204, 321–332.
———. "Origines et premières années." *Études* 291 (1956): 171–180.
———. *Une Russe catholique: la vie de madame Swetchine (1782-1857).* Paris: Desclée, 1953.
Jurich, James P. "Ecumenical Journalism in 1853–1860: Victor de Buck and Russian Orthodoxy." *Revue d'histoire ecclésiastique.* 87 (January-March 1992): 102–131.
Karatheodores, Stephanos. *Orthodoxie et Papisme: Examen de l'ouvrage du Pére Gagarin sur la réunion des Églises catholique grecque et catholique romaine par un grec membre de l'Église d'orient.* Trans. Vasil'ev. Paris, 1859.
Kel'siev, V. I. "'Ispoved' V. I. Kel'sieva." *Literaturnoe nasledstvo* 41–42 (1941): 253–470.
Khomiakov, Alexei Stepanovich. "Encore quelques mots par un chrétien Orthodoxe sur les confessions occidentales a l'occasion de plusieurs publica-

tions religieuses, Latines et Protestantes." 1858. In *L'Église latine et le Protestantisme au point du vue de l'Église d'Orient.* Hants: Gregg International, 1960: 191–308.

———. "Lettre au rédacteur de *L'Union chrétienne* à l'occasion d'un discours du Pére Gagarin, Jésuite." 1860. In *L'Église latine et le Protestantisme au point du vue de l'Église d'Orient.* Hants: Gregg International, 1960: 349–400.

———. "Pis'ma A.S. Khomiakova k Gil'ferdingu." *Russkii arkhiv* 16 (1878): 366–388.

Khomiakov, Alexei Stepanovich, and William Palmer. *Russia and the English Church During the Last Fifty Years.* Vol. 1. Ed. Birkbeck. London: Rivington, Percival, 1895.

Kireevskii, Ivan Vasilevich. "Pis'mo I.V. Kireevskogo I.S. Gagarinu." *Simvol* 3 (1980): 167–174.

"K istorii snoshenii s inovertsami." *Russkii arkhiv* 32 (1894): 5–24.

"Knizhnye zagranichnye vesti." *Russkii arkhiv* 1 (1873): 119.

Korczak-Branicki, Ksavier. *Les nationalités slaves: lettres au révérend P. Gagarin, S.J.* Paris: Dentu, 1879.

Korolevskij, Cyril. *Metropolitan Andrew.* Trans. Keleher. L'vov, 1993.

Korolov. Letter to *L'Union chrétienne. L'Union chrétienne* (1859–1860): 87.

Kozlov, A., and Iu. Feofanov. "Istina bez prikras." *Izvestiia* (28 August 1975): 6.

Kropotkin, Petr A. *Zapiski revoliutionera.* Moscow, 1933.

Kselman, Thomas A. *Miracles and Prophecies in Nineteenth-Century France.* New Brunswick: Rutgers University Press, 1983.

Ladous, Régis. "Catholiques libéraux et union des églises jusqu'en 1878." *Les catholiques libéraux XIXe siècle.* Collection du centre d'histoire du catholicisme. 1974: 485–525.

Lane, R. "Tiutchev in the 1820s–40s: An Unpublished Correspondence of 1874–1875." *Irish Slavonic Studies* 3 (1982): 2–13.

Laurentie, Sebastian. *L'Union* (7 January 1859): 1.

Lee, Ronald G. "The Theory and Practice of the Kingdom of God on Earth: The Anglo-Catholic Conservative Utopia of William Palmer." Diss., University of Notre Dame, 1996.

Leskov, Nikolai Semenovich. "Iezuit Gagarin v dele Pushkina." *Istoricheskii vestnik* 25 (1886): 269–273.

———. "Leskov's Trip Abroad in 1875." Ed. and Trans. Edgerton. *Indiana Slavic Studies* 4 (1967): 88–99.

Levkovich, Ia. L. "Dve raboty o dueli Pushkina." *Russkaia literatura* 2 (1970): 211–219.

———. "Novye materialy dlia biografii Pushkina, opublikovannye v 1963–1966 godakh." *Pushkin—issledovaniia i materialy.* 5. Leningrad, 1967: 365–381.

Lincoln, W. Bruce. *Nicholas I, Emperor and Autocrat of All the Russias.* DeKalb: Northern Illinois University Press, 1989.

Linehan, Dennis, S. J. "Jean-Xavier Gagarin and the Foundation of Études." *Diakonia* 2 (1987): 89–98.

Loniunov, Mikhail. "Neskol'ko zametok na stat'i *Russkago arkhiva.*" *Russkii arkhiv* (1865): 1404–1410.

Lopukhin, A. "Tserkovno-religioznaia zhizn' v Rossii po vzgliadu anglichanina." *Tserkovnyi vestnik* 10 (1879): 1–4.

Loyola, Ignatius, S. J. *Spiritual Exercises and Selected Works.* Ed. Ganss, S. J. New York: Paulist Press, 1991.

Mandich Donald R., and Joseph A. Placek. *Russian Heraldry and Nobility.* Boynton Beach: Dramco, 1992.

Martynov, Ivan Matveevich, S. J. Introduction to *O primirenii russkoi tserkvi s rimskoiu,* by Ivan Gagarin. 1859: i–ii.

———. "Saint Josaphat et ses détracteurs." *Études religieuses, philosophiques, historiques et littéraires* 19 (1875): 342–362.

Matual, David. "Ivan Gagarin: Russian Jesuit and Defender of the Faith." *Diakonia* 1 (1991): 5–18.

McLean, Hugh. *Nikolai Leskov: The Man and His Art.* Cambridge: Harvard University Press, 1977.

McNally, Raymond T. *Chaadaev and His Friends.* Tallahassee: The Diplomatic Press, 1971.

———. "Two Catholic Slavophiles? Ivan S. Gagarin and August von Haxthausen in search of Church Reconciliation (1857–1860)." *Canadian-American Slavic Studies* 34:3 (Fall 2000): 251–309.

Meshcherskii, A. V. "Iz moei starini, vospominaniia kniazia A. V. Meshcherskago." *Russkii arkhiv* 39 (1901): 470–504.

Mil'don, V. I., and A. L. Ospovat. "Gagarin." *Russkie pisateli 1800-1917. Biograficheskii slovar'.* 1. Moscow: 1989: 509–510.

Miliukov, Pavel. *Outlines of Russian Culture: Part I: Religion and the Church.* New York: A. S. Barnes, 1960.

Modzalevskii, B. L. "Kto byl avtorom anonimnykh paskvilei na Pushkina?" *Novye materialy o dueli i smerti Pushkina.* Ed. Modzalevskii et. al. 1924: 19–23.

Moleva, N. M. "Iasenevo." *Voprosy Istorii* 4 (April 1984): 184–188.

Montclos, Xavier de. *Lavigerie: La Saint-Siège et l'Église de l'avènement de Pie IX à l'avènement de Léon XIII 1846-1878.* Paris: E. de Boccard, 1965.

Moroshkin, Mikhail Ia. *Iezuity v Rossii s tsarstvovaniia Ekateriny II do nashego vremeni.* Vol. 1. Petersburg, 1867.

Müller, Peter. *Das Jesuitenbild des russischen Slavophilen Ju. F. Samarin (1819-1876).* New York: Peter Lang, 1996.

Muzyczka, Ivan. "Sheptyts'kyi in the Russian Empire." *Morality and Reality: The Life and Times of Andrei Sheptyts'kyi.* Ed. Paul Robert Magocsi. Edmonton: University of Alberta, 1989: 313–327.

Murav'ev, Andrei N. "Letter to a Roman Neophyte." In *Voices from the East.* Ed. Neale. London, 1859: 165–171.

"Nécrologie." *Polybiblion* XXXV: 166–168.

"Nekrolog." *Istoricheskii vestnik* 11 (1882): 679.

Nichols, Robert L. "Metropolitan Filaret and the Slavophiles." *St. Vladimir's Theological Quarterly* 4 (1993): 315–330.

Nol'de, B. E. *Iurii Samarin i ego vremia.* Paris: YMCA Press, 1978.

"Nouvelle insinuation jésuitique." *L'Union chrétienne* (16 December 1860): 54–55.

O. "Les Jésuites russes." *L'Union chrétienne* (1866): 372–373.

Obodovskaia, I., and M. Dement'ev. "Po sledam predvestnika gibeli." *Ogonek* 6 (February 1986): 20–23.

Obolensky, Valerian. "Russians in Exile: The History of a Diaspora," http://www.geocities.com:0080/soho/5254/dias4.html.

Odoevskii, V. F. "O merakh protiv zagranichnoi russkoi pechati." *Russkii arkhiv* (1874): 30–36.

———. "Tekushchaia khronika i osobie proishestviia. Dnevnik V. F. Odoevskogo 1859–1868 gg." *Literaturnoe nasledstvo.* 22–24 (1935): 79–308.

"O knigakh, na kotorikh otstupniki ot pravoslavnoi tserkvi osnovivaiut svoi nepravil'niia misli." *Pravoslavnyi sobesiednik.* 2 (1855): 47–69.

O'Meara, Thomas F., O. P. *Romantic Idealism and Roman Catholicism: Schelling and the Theologians.* Notre Dame: University of Notre Dame Press, 1982.

"Opravdanie iezuita Ivana Gagarina po povodu smerti Pushkina." *Golos* 197 (19/31 July 1865): 2.

Osipin, Ivan Teret'evich. "Ivan Terent'evich Osipin: Ocherk ego zhizni i deliatel'nosti." *Russkaia starina* (February 1888): 457–476.

P., Vladimir. [Untitled article on the Association of Prayers.] *L'Union chrètienne* (19 July 1863): 302–303.

Palmer, William. *Dissertations on Subjects Relating to the "Orthodox" or "Eastern-Catholic" Communion.* London, 1853.

Pecherin, Vladimir Sergeevich. "Zamogilnie zapiski." *Russkoe obshchestvo 30-kh godov XIX v Liudi i idei. Memuari sovremennikov.* Ed. I. A. Fedosov. Moscow, 1989: 148–312.

Pierling, Pavel Ospovich, S. J. "Kniaz' Ivan Sergeevich Gagarin." *Russkii biograficheskii slovar'.* New York: Kraus, 1962: 69–74.

———. "Sofia Petrovna Svechina." *Russkaia starina* 103 (1899): 541–557; 104 (1900): 147–165, 409–428, 621–642.

———. *La Russie et le Saint-Siège.* Vols. 1–5. Paris: Plon, 1906.

———. *Le prince Gagarin et ses amis.* Paris: Beauchesne, 1996.

———. "Vladimir Sergeevich Pecherin v perepiske s Ivanom Sergeevichem Gagarinem." *Russkaia starina* 145 (1911): 59–67.

Pigarev, K. *Zhizn' i tvorchestvo Tiutcheva.* Moscow, 1962.

Pius IX. "Amantissimus." 8 April 1862. *The Papal Encyclicals, 1740-1878.* Ed. Claudia Carlen, I. H. M. Wilmington: McGrath, 1981: 363–367.

———. "Aux chrétiens d'orient." *Lettre encyclique de S.S. le Pape Pie IX aux chrétiens d'orient et encyclique responsive des patriarchs et des synodes de l'Église d'orient.* Trans. Demétrius Dallas. Paris, 1850: 13–25.

———. "Levate." 27 October 1867. *The Papal Encyclicals, 1740-1878.* Ed. Claudia Carlen, I. H. M. Wilmington: McGrath, 1981: 369–391.

———. "Omnem Sollicitudinem." 13 May 1874. *The Papal Encyclicals 1740-1878.* Ed. Claudia Carlen, I. H. M. Wilmington: McGrath, 1981: 439–441.

Plashevskii, Iuri. "O proiskhozhdenii paskvil'nogo 'diploma'." *Prostor* 4 (1983): 177–184.

"Politicheskie pamflety i smes'." *Russkii arkhiv* 1 (1880): 394.

Polnyi pravoslavnyi bogoslovskii entsiklopedicheskii slovar'. Vol. 1. 1913.

Polnoe sobranie zakonov Rossiiskoi Imperii. Vol. 15. Petersburg, 1841.

Polonskii, Ia. "Knigokhranilishche russkikh iezuitov." *Vremennik obshchestva druzei russkoi knigi* 2 (1932): 65–72.

Ponlevoy, Armand de, S. J. *The Life of Father de Ravignan of the Society of Jesus.* New York: Catholic Publication Society, 1869.

Przeglad Poznańkii. Response to Gagarin. *L'Univers* (20 April 1857): 1–3; (29 May 1857): 1.

Racki, Franjo. *Korspondencija Raćki=Strossmayer.* Vol. 3. Ed. Ferdo Šišić. Zagreb, 1928.

Ravignan, Gustave-Xavier de, S. J. *On the Life and Institute of the Jesuits.* Philadelphia: Cunningham, 1845.

Remmers, J. G. A. M. "La réunion des Églises selon Ivan Serge Gagarin, S. J. (1814–1882)." *Plamia* 86: 15–26.

Renault, François. *Le cardinal Lavigerie, 1825-1892: l'Église, l'Afrique et la France.* Paris: Fayard, 1992.

Roberson, Ronald G. *The Eastern Christian Churches: A Brief Survey.* Rome, 1993.

Russian Philosophy. Ed. Edie, Scanlan, Zeldin, Kline. Vol. 1. Knoxville: University of Tennessee, 1987.

"Russie." *Dictionnaire des Missiones Catholiques. Encyclopédie Théologique.* Ed. J. P. Migne. Vol. 60 (1864): 763–802.

Russkie pisateli 1800-1917. Moscow: Sovetskaia entsiklopedia, 1989.

Russkii biograficheskii slovar'. New York: Kraus, 1962.

Samarin, Iurii Fedorovich "Arkhiv slavianskoi biblioteki." *Simvol* 2 (1979): 164–181.

———. *Iezuity i ikh otnosheniie k Rossii.* Moscow, 1866.

———. *Sochineniia Iu. F. Samarina.* 12. Moscow, 1911.

Sazonov, Sergei. "Autocracy and the Vatican: On the Eve of the 'Imperialist War'." *Journal of Church and State* 19 (Winter 1977): 75–82.

Shchegolev, P. E. *Duel' i smert' Pushkina.* Moscow, 1987.

Shteingel', V.I. "Pis'ma V.I. Shteingelia k I.I. Pushchinu." *Letopisi gosudarstvennogo literaturnogo muzeia.* Vol. 3: 367–379.

Shur, Leonid. "I. S. Gagarin—izdatel' 'Filosoficheskikh pisem' P. Ia. Chaadaeva." *Simvol* 9 (1983): 219–236.

———. "I. S. Gagarin—izdatel' F. I. Tiutcheva i khranitel' ego literaturnogo nasledstva." *Simvol* 11 (1984): 197–229.

———. "Iz istorii polemiki I. S. Gagarina so slavianofilami v 60-x gg. XIX v." *Simvol* 7 (1982): 178–181.

———. "K biografii I. S. Gagarina." *Simvol* 12 (1984): 200–203.

———. "Materialy o dueli i smerti A. S. Pushkina v arkhive I. S. Gagarina." *Simvol* 10 (1983): 249–267.

———. "Neosuschestvlennoe izdanie stikhotvorenii F. I. Tiutcheva 1836–1837gg (po materialam arkhiva I. S. Gagarina)." *Oxford Slavonic Papers* 19 (1969): 102–115.

———. "Perepiska I. S. Gagarina s N. S. Leskovym." *Simvol* 17 (1987): 241–260.

———. "Perepiska I. S. Gagarina s P. V. Dolgorukovim." *Simvol* 13 (1985): 210–253

———. "Spiski stikhotvorenii Pushkina v arkhive I. S. Gagarina." *Revue des études slaves* 1–2 (1987): 347–365.

Shuvalov, Grigorii Petrovich, C. R. S. P. *My Conversion and My Vocation.* London: R. Washbourne, 1877.

Sidorov, I. "Eshche raz ob anonimnom 'diplome' i kn. P. V. Dolgorukove." *Voprosy literatury* 2 (1987): 177–180.

Simon, Constantin, S. J. "I gesuiti e la russia." *La civiltà cattolica* 40 (18 November 1989): 355–367.

Śliwowska, W. *W kregu proprzedników Hercena.* Wroclaw, 1971.

Smirnov, N. M. "Iz 'Pamiatnikh zapisok'." *A. S. Pushkin v vospominaniakh sovremennikov.* Vol. 2. Moscow, 1974: 234–244.

Smolitsch, Igor. *Geshichte der russischen Kirche, 1700-1917.* Vols. 1, 2. Leiden, 1964, and Wiesbaden, 1991.

Solov'ev, Vladimir S. *La Sophia et les autres écrits français.* Ed. Rouleau. Lausanne, 1978.

———. *Sobranie sochinenii Vladimira Sergeevicha Solov'eva.* Vol. 11. Brussels, 1966.

Stoyanoff-Odoy, Martina. *Die Großfürstin Heline von Rußland und August Freiherr von Haxthausen: Zwei konservative Reformer im Zeitalter der russichen Bauernbefreiung.* Wiesbaden: Otto Harrassowitz, 1991.

Strémooukhoff, D. *La poésie et l'idéologie de Tiouttchev.* Paris, 1937.

Subbotin, N. *Pis'mo k. o. Gagarinu, "Sviashchenniku Iezuitskago ordena v Parizhe."* Moscow: 1879.

Suchanek, Lucjan. "Les catholiques russes et les procatholiques en Russie dans la première moitié du XIXe siècle." *Cahiers du monde russe et soviétique* 29 (July–December 1988): 361–374.

Suchkov, Sergei Petrovich. "Encore quelques mots sur le sermon P. Gagarin, Jésuite, sur l'union des Églises orientale et occidentale." *L'Union chrétienne* (1859–1860): 134–135.

———. "Examen de l'argument que les ultramontains prétendent trouver dans la liturgie russe en faveur de leur système papal." *L'Union chrétienne* (1861–1862): 187–191, 203–206, 211–213.

———. "Les textes des Péres de l'Église tronqués ou dénaturés par le R. P. Gagarin." *L'Union chrétienne* (1859–1860): 267–272, 283–285, 301–304, 364–367.

———. "Observations préliminaires en réponse au R. P. Gagarin." *L'Union chrétienne* (1859–1860): 251–256.

Svechina, Sofiia Petrovna Soymonova. *Lettres de madame Swetchine* Vol. 2. Ed. Comte de Falloux. Paris: Didier, 1862.

———. *The Writings of Madame Swetchine.* Ed. Comte de Falloux. New York: The Catholic Publication Society, 1869.

Svobodnyi katalog russkoi nelegal'noi i zapreshchennoi pechati XIX veka A-S. Moscow, 1871.

Tamborra, Angelo. "August von Haxthausen e la Russia: Il Momento Religioso." *Cristianità ed Europa.* Vol. 1. Rome, 1994: 797–815.

———. "Cattolicesimo e Ortodossia russa nel secolo XIX." *Il Battesimo delle terre russe.* Florence, 1991: 359–379.

———. "Da Pietroburgo a Roma e ritorno Stepan S. Dzunkovskij (1821–1870)." *Rassegna Storica del Risorgimento* 76 2 (1989): 179–216.

———. "La riscoperta di Cirillo e Metodio nel secolo XIX e il suo significato." *Christianity Among the Slavs: The Heritage of Saints Cyril and Methodius. Orientalia Christianina Analecta* 231. Ed. Edward G. Farrugia, S. J., Robert F. Taft, S. J., Gino K. Piovesana, S. J. Rome: Pont. Institutem Studiorum Orientalium, 1988: 315–341.

Tandonet, Roger. "Le fondateur et l'union des églises." *Études* 291 (November 1956): 181–195.

Tempest, Richard. "Ivan Gagarin: Diplomatist, Diarist, Apostate." *Symposion* 2 (1997): 98–134.

———. "Ivan Sergeevich Gagarin (20 July 1814–20 July 1882)." In *Russian Literature in the Age of Pushkin and Gogol: Prose,* 126–131. Detriot: Gale Research Co., 1999. Dictionary of Literary Biography 198.

———. "Mezhdu Reinom i Senoi (molodye gody Ivana Gagarina)." *Simvol* 32 (1994): 137–163.

———. "Na chashke chaia u Shellinga." *Simvol* 27 (1992): 283–286.

Thurston, Herbert, S. J., and Donald Attwater. "St. Josaphat." *Butler's Lives of the Saints.* Vol. 4. New York: P. J. Kenedy & Sons, 1956: 337–340.

Tiutchev, Fyodor Ivanovich. "La Papauté et la question romaine au point de vue de Saint-Pétersbourg." *Revue des deux mondes* (1850): 117–133.

———. *Stikhotvoreniia.* Moscow, 1935.

Tolstoi, Dmitrii A. "Les Jésuites et la liberté est-ce la même chose?" *L'Union chrétienne* (12 January 1861): 87–88.

———. *Romanism in Russia: A Historical Study* Vol. 2. London, 1874.

Tondini, Caesarius. *The Popes of Rome and the Popes of the Oriental Orthodox Church: An Essay on Monarchy in the Church with Special Reference to Russia, from Original Documents, Russian and Greek.* London, 1871.

Treadgold, Donald W. *The West in Russia and China: Religious and Secular Thought in Modern Times.* Cambridge: Cambridge University Press, 1973.

Tretjakewitsch, Léon. *Bishop Michel d'Herbigny, S.J.: A Pre-Ecumenical Approach to Christian Unity.* 1990.

Tsimbaeva. "Put'iskanii kniazia I. S. Gagarina—materialy russkikh katolikov iz frantsuzkikh arkhivov." *Voprosy filosofii* 7 (1996): 133–137.

———. *Russkii katolitsizm: zabitoe proshloe rossiiskogo liberalizma.* Moscow (1999).

Tsipeniuk, S. A. "Issledovanie anonimnykh pisem, sviazannykh s duel'u Pushkina." *Kriminalistika i sudebnaia expertiza* 12 (1976): 81–90.

Turgenev, Aleksandr Ivanovich, and Nikolai Ivanovich Turgenev. "Neizdannye pis'ma A. I. i N. I. Turgenevykh." *Simvol* 19 (1988): 185–252.

Van de Wal, A. A., Adulf. "Une correspondance entre le baron von Haxthausen et André Mouravieff." *Istina* 3–4 (1972): 468–480.

Varsukov, N. P. "Aleksandr Ivanovich Turgenev v ego pis'makh." *Russkaia starina* 34 (1882): 443–462.

Vasil'ev, Iosif Vasil'evich. *Parizhskiia pis'ma protoereia Iosifa Vasilevicha Vasil'eva k Ober-Prokuroram Sviateishago Sinoda i drugim litsam s 1846 po 1867 gg.* Petrograd, 1915.

———. "Vénération rendu à pétre Pierre dans les Églises orthodoxe et romain." *L'Union chrétienne* (17 July 1864): 292.

Viazemskii, Petr Andreevich. "Iz zametok kniaz'ia P. A. Viazemskago." *Russkii arkhiv* 39 (1901): 254–256.

"Voskresnie nabroski." *Golos* 185 (July 1880).

Vyshnevskii, L. "Eshche raz o vinovnikakh Pushkinskoi tragedii." *Oktiabr'* (March 1973): 206–215.

———. "Petr Dolgorukov i paskvil' na Pushkina." *Sibirskie ogni* 11 (1962): 157–170.

"Vzgliad Russkikh raskolnikov na rimskuiu tserkov'." *Pravoslavnyi sobesednik* (1860): 297–322.

Walicki, Andrzej. *A History of Russian Thought: From the Enlightenment to Marxism.* Stanford: Stanford University Press, 1990.

———. *Russia, Poland, and Universal Regeneration.* Notre Dame: University of Notre Dame Press, 1991.

———. *The Slavophile Controversy: History of a Conservative Utopia in Nineteenth-Century Russian Thought.* Notre Dame: University of Notre Dame Press, 1989.

Wyels, Franco de. "Le concile du Vatican et l'union." *Irenikon* 6 (1929): 366–396.

Wysochansky, Demetrius E., O.S.B.M. *Saint Josaphat Kuntsevych: Apostle of Church Unity.* Detroit: Basilian Fathers Publications, 1986.

Youssov. Response to *La Russie. L'Union chrétienne* (1859–1860): 93–96.

Zaionchkovsky, Peter A. *The Russian Autocracy in Crisis, 1878-1882.* Trans. Gary M. Hamburg. Gulf Breeze: Academic International Press, 1979.

Zatko, James J. "The Catholic Church and Russian Statistics." *The Polish Review* 1 (Winter 1960): 35–52.

———. *Descent into Darkness.* Toronto: Baxter Publishing, 1965.

"Zhurnal'noe obozrenie." *Tserkovnyi viestnik.* 10 (1878): 12–14.

Index

In this index, ISG is used as an abbreviation for Ivan Sergeevich Gagarin, S. J., and the use of *t* indicates a table found in the text.